Flamenco Music

Flamenco Music

History, Forms, Culture

PETER MANUEL

UNIVERSITY OF ILLINOIS PRESS
Urbana, Chicago, and Springfield

1 2 3 4 5 C P 5 4 3 2 1
♾ This book is printed on acid-free paper.

Library of Congress Cataloging-in-Publication Data
Names: Manuel, Peter, 1952– author.
Title: Flamenco music : history, forms, culture / Peter Manuel.
Description: Urbana : University of Illinois Press, 2023. | Includes bibliographical references and index.
Identifiers: LCCN 2023014983 (print) | LCCN 2023014984 (ebook) | ISBN 9780252045332 (cloth) | ISBN 9780252087455 (paperback) | ISBN 9780252054860 (ebook)
Subjects: LCSH: Flamenco music—History and criticism. | Flamenco music—Analysis, appreciation. | Flamenco music—Social aspects.
Classification: LCC ML3712 .M34 2023 (print) | LCC ML3712 (ebook) | DDC 781.62/610468—dc23/eng/20230405
LC record available at https://lccn.loc.gov/2023014983
LC ebook record available at https://lccn.loc.gov/2023014984

Contents

Preface

As a genre of "world music," flamenco is in several respects quite unique. On the one hand, it is a concert idiom with the sophistication, richness, and expressive power of jazz or an art music. Accordingly, it is "universal" not only in having the aesthetic appeal of an abstract music and dance genre that can stand on its own but also in its international popularity, being enjoyed and cultivated extensively in the Americas, greater Europe, Japan, and elsewhere. On the other hand, since its inception it has been nurtured and performed as a domestic tradition in Andalusian—and especially Gitano (Spanish Gypsy)—communities. As song lyrics, vocal inflections, and dance moves are passed from elderly aunties to children at parties and weddings, flamenco is for many people inextricably imbued with sentiments of family cohesion and ethnic identity in a manner that has little parallel in genres like jazz or classical music. Meanwhile, flamenco—with its remarkable dual status as both an "autonomous" art form and a socially embedded one—has long held a correspondingly diverse range of meanings for its artists and audiences, including many international listeners motivated by a naïve Romantic quest for the exotic and premodern.

Flamenco's complex socio-musical character and its inherent richness have also inspired a prodigious amount of intellectual interest, including generating, in recent decades, a veritable mountain of Spanish-language literature, from erudite books to online journals and other forms of digital discourse. Surprisingly, however, there has been no scholarly English-language book that covers flamenco in its historical, stylistic, and socio-musical dimensions. *Flamenco Music: History, Forms, Culture* attempts to fill this lacuna, aiming to provide a readable, concise, and rigorously scholarly study of this remarkable genre and incorporating the findings and insights of the best Spanish-language writing on the subject. In writing this book, my imaginary ideal reader has actually been myself, as of forty-some years ago when I began studying flamenco and had so many questions for which I was not finding easy answers.

As its title suggests, this book is divided into three large sections. The first covers history, attempting to reconstruct flamenco's evolution from antecedents in the Moorish period, through its consolidation from around the 1860s, and on to the present. The historical treatment addresses both the trajectories of specific musical forms as well as the social dynamics that conditioned and stimulated their evolution, especially the influence of Romanticism and a particular form of Spanish cultural nationalism in the nineteenth century. The second section analyzes flamenco style and describes all the major *cantes*, or song-types. The numerous staff notations in this section may naturally be intelligible only to the musically literate reader, but I have endeavored to present the material in a way that is broadly accessible. The third and final section of the book presents an overview of contemporary "flamenco culture" and addresses specific persistent themes, including globalization, gender dynamics, and perennial debates regarding "purity" versus innovation.

This volume discusses flamenco dance only insofar as it relates to music, and in some cases, whether regarding history or form, the two must indeed be considered jointly. However, for more than cursory coverage of dance the reader must consult other sources, though these are scanty, both in English and Spanish.

Flamenco Literature

The relative dearth of English-language literature on flamenco is striking, given the art's international renown, and much of the extant writing grows increasingly out of date as new developments arise and Spanish-language scholarship progresses. Among books aimed at the general reader, those of Donn Pohren, such as his *The Art of Flamenco* (1962), are engaging and informative (if dated), short on history and analysis, and unabashedly opinionated; they can be seen as supplemented by impressionistic surveys such as James Woodall's *In Search of the Firedance* (1992) and Robin Totton's *Song of the Outcasts* (2003). The scholarly literature is not extensive but includes some worthy studies. Timothy Mitchell's *Flamenco Deep Song* (1994) is an erudite and somewhat pugilistic critique of aspects of flamenco's social history and the ideologies animating it. Sandie Holguín's *Flamenco Nation* (2019) presents a different and in some ways more balanced portrayal of flamenco's changing relation to national identity since its emergence through the Franco era. Claus Schreiner's 1985 volume offers short essays on most relevant subjects, but these are uneven in quality and, again, dated. Loren Chuse's *The Cantaoras* (2003) provides a succinct summary of history and form along with a thorough and insightful coverage of the status of women in flamenco, past and present, buttressed by interviews with several leading singers. K. Meira Goldberg's *Sonidos Negros* (2019), applying ideas about African American culture to Spain, argues for a previously unrecognized conception of "blackness" at the heart of flamenco's historical image. Most recent is Ian Biddle's *The Flamenco Effect* (2021), exploring select aspects of flamenco music and culture. Other specific themes in flamenco studies have been addressed in books by Matthew Machin-Autenrieth (2016) and William Washabaugh (1996, 2012) and in focused articles by such scholars as John Moore and myself. Scholarly writing on flamenco dance, like dance studies in general, is woefully underdeveloped, as if congenitally stunted by the inability to notate dance accurately and intelligibly.

The world of literate flamenco experts has naturally included several Americans who have not been inclined to author books but who have contributed in other forms. Noteworthy in this respect have been internet forums, which have been especially active in the United States, where flamenco enthusiasts wishing to discuss the art cannot simply stroll over to the corner tavern as in Spain. From the 1990s Temple University Listserv to the present internet forum http://www.foroflamenco.com, much erudite and engaging discussion of the art has been engaged in, whether preserved or not, by Estela Zatania, Norman Kliman, John Moore, Richard (Ricardo) Marlow, the late Brook Zern, and others.

If English-language books on flamenco take up little more than half of a single narrow bookshelf, such as that in my office, the Spanish literature on flamenco is copious. The abundance of such writing is all the more remarkable considering that until the 1980s—that is, through the culturally stagnant Franco era—there were fewer than a dozen Spanish books of any substance on the art. Yet intellectuals have long had a prodigious interest and investment in flamenco, and Spain's post-Franco cultural awakening precipitated a veritable torrent of literature on the subject, much of it excellent and nearly all of it of some use and interest to the flamencologically inclined reader. Indeed, literature on Western pop or art music notwithstanding, I would opine that no other music genre worldwide has generated, per capita in relation to its audience, so much serious literature.

Most of this writing has been penned not by academics or even professional literati but, rather, by miscellaneous intellectuals steeped in the flamenco scene and fascinated by its history and culture. Literature would include biographies of musicians, histories of flamenco in particular cities, general surveys, anthologies of and commentary on lyrics, edited memoirs of elderly artists, compilations of snippets from nineteenth-century newspapers, and polemical tracts. Some authors, to be sure, are professional writers of sorts, such as veteran journalists and researchers José Luis Ortiz Nuevo, Manuel Bohórquez, Alfredo

Grimaldos, and the prolific José Manuel Gamboa. Only in the last decade have flamenco studies become recognized in and supported by the academic establishment, leading to a belated but felicitous abundance of genuinely scholarly writings. Particularly outstanding in reconstructing flamenco history from a musicological perspective has been the work of Guillermo Castro Buendía, including his *Génesis musical del cante flamenco* (2014), whose two volumes total more than twenty-six hundred pages. For reconstructing both dance as well as music history, the work of Miguel Ángel Berlanga Fernández is also remarkable. Among other scholars making significant contributions are such figures as Cristina Cruces Roldán, José Ortega, Faustino Núñez, Bernat Jiménez de Cisneros Puig, Manuel Martín Martín, and Norberto Torres. Meanwhile, each year sees the production of worthy doctoral dissertations that are felicitously available on the internet.

Non-Spaniards have also contributed to the Spanish literature on flamenco, starting perhaps with Argentine writer Anselmo González Climent, whose 1955 book, *Flamencología* (Flamencology), not only inaugurated but also named the field of flamenco studies. Austrian sociologist Gerhard Steingress has written insightfully on the sociocultural dynamics of flamenco's early history, and Anglophone Spanish resident Norman Kliman has contributed an erudite book and a widely consulted website. In a different medium is American-born Estela Zatania, who has authored a book and a steady stream of articles for online magazines. The internet, indeed, has fostered an exponential increase in the amount of public discourse on flamenco, whether in the form of blogs, dedicated websites, online magazines, or the often enlightening and engaging exchanges on Facebook and other social media. In writing this book, I have drawn heavily and unabashedly on this vast and impressive body of Spanish writing.

Acknowledgments

This book could not have been written without the input of all the flamenco teachers, friends, and casual acquaintances, in Spain and elsewhere, with whom I have interacted since the 1980s, when flamenco became a sort of intermittent interest of mine, often secondary to the North Indian or Caribbean musics that tended to preoccupy me. Aside from my productive trips to Spain, I have been fortunate to live in the New York area, whose numerous performers and "flamencologists" have been my best gurus. Basilio Georges and Dennis Koster did their patient best to teach me guitar, and while Alfonso Mogaburo Cid's attempts to teach me singing were on one level quite fruitless, I have learned greatly from his companionship and his generous comments on some of my writing, including a manuscript of this book. Much of my renewed engagement with flamenco was precipitated by the endlessly energetic and knowledgeable Meira Goldberg. Also rewarding have been interactions with Adrian Alvarado, my former CUNY colleagues María Luisa Martínez and Antoni Pizá, and local "flamencoholics" such as Brook Zern (d. 2019), who was an institution of sorts in the flamenco world. John Moore generously shared some of his valuable materials with me and, like Alfonso Cid, commented insightfully on the manuscript of this book. Special thanks are due to Estela Zatania, a supremely knowledgeable and astute journalist, author, and erstwhile performer, who subjected the manuscript to a close reading, catching various errors and contributing many more insights and bits of knowledge than are explicitly cited. Finally, I have always enjoyed and learned much from amicable and supportive correspondence with Spanish scholars, including Bernat Jiménez, Guillermo Castro Buendía, and Miguel Ángel Berlanga. However, I take full responsibility for the content of this book.

Map of Southern Spain

PART I

History

1

Pre-Flamenco Music

Reconstructing Flamenco Prehistory: Challenges and Conundrums

The reconstruction of flamenco prehistory—covering the period before the early 1800s, when the genre begins to coalesce and emerge into daylight—has constituted a formidable challenge for historians. The various music and dance forms that eventually evolved into flamenco were primarily cultivated as vernacular oral traditions, to a considerable extent among the lower classes, and thus were less likely to be documented in any form than were the genteel fine arts of the court and salon. Surviving music notations before the mid-nineteenth century, though of much interest, can provide only indirect and circumstantial indications about folk and vernacular musics, while notations of dance are even more scarce and imprecise. Historical enigmas, as we shall see, obtain even up to recent times, with, for example, the early twentieth-century coalescence of the basic cante of *bulerías* remaining inscrutable and the adoption of the very word "flamenco" remaining a mystery.

The distinctive challenges in speculating about flamenco prehistory are made even more difficult by a set of particular enigmas inhering to the genre. One of these involves flamenco's distinctive combination of archaic and, at the same time, quite recent features. It seems clear that many of flamenco's constitutive elements are many centuries old, certainly dating from the Moorish period, and possibly even embodying continuities with earlier Visigothic and Byzantine traditions. At the same time, as historians have well established, flamenco as a recognizable genre does not appear to have taken shape until around the 1860s, when various conditions inspired a creative coterie of Andalusian urban musicians and dancers to elaborate, enrich, professionalize, and standardize an extant set of forms—old and new, local and imported—into the coherent genre we now know as flamenco.

The heterogeneity of these source idioms itself constitutes another challenge to historical analysis, with Moorish-derived features syncretizing idiosyncratically with forms and stylistic traits of recent vintage or arrival in Andalusia. The particular combination of provincial isolation and transnationality is itself remarkable. In the 1960s flamenco chronicler Donn Pohren related visiting the hill hamlet of Coripe, some thirty miles south of the flamenco bastion of Morón, and encountering people who had never ventured to the latter town, not to mention further afield. And yet they were fond of flamenco, which comprised rearticulated elements not only from the Moors of seven centuries earlier but stylized versions of distant Latin American genres as well, like gold in a tooth filling derived from asteroids of collapsed stars.

What might seem to be self-evident historical connections can be further confounding in their own way. Does the percussive footwork found in both flamenco zapateado and *kathak* dance of North India (whence came the Roma) imply some historical connection between these dance traditions? (Probably not.) Does the *zambra* dance of the fifteenth-century Moors have any historical continuity with the dance, given the same name, performed by Granada Gitanos (Gypsies) from the mid-nineteenth century? (Possibly.) Is there any significant relation between the percussive hand-clapping of the Amazigh (Berber) *ahwash* of southern Morocco and the strikingly similar forms of flamenco *palmas*? (Who knows?)

Such enigmas, while remaining in many ways insoluble, have provided fertile ground for scholars, pseudo-scholars, and others to advance diverse theories in accordance with their various ideological agendas, which have themselves made the dispassionate study of flamenco prehistory all the more difficult and plagued with controversies. Particularly conspicuous was the early twentieth-century tendency, inspired by exoticizing Romanticism and Andalusian pride, to idealize Moorish Spain and attribute to it the roots of pre-flamenco music and dance. Countering this were various partisans who, to some extent motivated by Christian zeal, belittled these arguments in favor of theories foregrounding the influence of the pre-Moorish Visigoths or somewhat mythical "Tartessian" predecessors. Further complicating matters have been the ongoing fundamental uncertainty and disputation regarding the role of the Gitanos in creating flamenco and its ancestors. As various parties have advanced their agendas over the years, a number of spurious arguments have been made, but in recent decades a fresh generation of scholars—mostly but not exclusively Spanish—have made great progress in reconstructing flamenco history and prehistory, even if many aspects may ever remain speculative and enigmatic. In this section I provide an overview of flamenco history that incorporates the best of such recent scholarship and complements it with my own perspectives.

Flamenco Prehistory: The Moorish Legacy

Some of the most distinctive features of flamenco music and dance—such as melismatic and modal melodies and graceful hand and arm gestures—bear obvious similarities to Arab counterparts, and even in the nineteenth century it was common in the popular press to refer to early flamenco songs and dances, especially as performed by Gitanos, as "Moorish" or "oriental." Such references, despite their imprecision and exoticism, are not wholly inaccurate, although the Moorish contribution to flamenco, and to Spanish music in general, has in fact been the subject of much contestation and remains in many ways indicated by circumstantial rather than concrete evidence.

The founding of Islam in the early seventh century precipitated a dramatic explosion of Arab imperialist and proselytizing zeal, leading to rapid military conquests stretching from the Indus River in the east to the Pyrenees Mountains in the west. In the year 711 an army of Muslim Arabs and Amazigh (in Spain: Moors) landed near Gibraltar and in subsequent decades conquered the entire Iberian Peninsula, being halted in 732 by the Franks at Tours. Over the next seven centuries, Moorish Spain, its economy grounded in a productive agricultural base, became a center of learning and artistic creativity, nourishing a celebrated (if occasionally exaggerated) *convivencia* (coexistence) in which Muslim, Jewish, and Christian communities lived side by side and interacted in relative harmony. From the eleventh century, the cultural ambience stiffened somewhat under the rule of the more fundamentalist Amazigh Almoravids and then Almohads, and Christian princedoms began chipping away at Moorish provinces in the centuries-long process of the Reconquest (*Reconquista*). The Moorish kingdom of Granada, however, lasted until 1492, when it was conquered by Ferdinand and Isabella, who unified Spain under Castilian Catholic rule and in the same year expelled most of the Jews (and also granted three small sailing vessels to an importunate adventurer from Genoa). Continuing the project of ethnic cleansing, in 1609 King Philip III ordered the expulsion of all people of Moorish ancestry. With this elimination of the country's productive business and agricultural classes, Spain, despite its American conquests, lapsed into an internal recession from which it did not genuinely recover until the 1970s.

Music flourished in Moorish Spain, although the paucity of documentation—including the complete absence of musical notations—greatly limits our knowledge of how it may have sounded. The advent, in 822, of Baghdadi poet-musician Ziryab to the court at Córdoba at once reinforced certain links with eastern Arab and Persian traditions and, more importantly, enlivened the local Moorish music scene and stimulated its emergence as an autonomous entity rather than some provincial copy of music in Baghdad or Damascus. In courts and the homes of nobles, variants of an "Andalusian" or

Arab-Andalusian ensemble art music came to thrive, enriched by the input of Jewish and Christian musicians. The most characteristic idioms were song forms—especially the *muwashshah*, in classical Arabic; the *zajal* (*zadjal*) in vernacular Romance Latin; and the lighter, lyrical, thoroughly bilingual *jarcha* (*khardja*), written in Hebrew or Arabic script, concluding the muwashshah. As noted by Manuel Pedro Ferreira (2016, 7) and others, the absence of notations makes it impossible to determine the exact mixture of Moorish and European elements in such music, though musical syncretism is certainly implied by the bilingual lyrics and was commented on by al-Tifashi, a thirteenth-century chronicler. The common use of stock tunes—as in flamenco—though hardly unique to Moorish Spain, was noted by Ibn Sida (d. 1066) in his encyclopedia, *Al-Mukhassas* (Livermore 1972, 33). Through Ziryab's inspiration, formal performances came to be organized into a suite called *nuba* or *nawba*. As Christian conquests proceeded over the centuries, Moorish court establishments, including their art music traditions, migrated to North Africa—specifically, it is believed, that of Córdoba to Algiers, of Seville to Tunis, and of Granada to Fez and Tetuan. These ensemble traditions have flourished until the present day, and their conservative spirit, reflected in the persistence of actual song texts dating from thirteenth-century Moorish Spain, affords some understanding, however incomplete and qualified, of how art music in Moorish Spain may have sounded.

The fifteenth century saw the advent to Spain of another ethnic group—the Gypsies, or Roma (in Spain: Gitanos)—who were to play a central role in Andalusian music culture and eventually flamenco. (The word "gypsy" has fallen out of favor in some circles and hence is avoided in this book unless used deliberately to invoke its former association with stereotypes.) The Roma—evidently related to agricultural low castes (especially Doms) in North India—had migrated from Rajasthan and adjacent regions from the eighth to eleventh centuries, perhaps accompanying traveling armies as service personnel. Linguistic and other evidence indicates that many of them resided for a few centuries in Greek-speaking parts of the Byzantine Empire before scattering farther westward and northward as the Ottomans conquered the region. From the early 1400s, groups of Roma were formally requesting and being granted permission to enter Spain from France. The largest proportion of them eventually settled in Andalusia, perhaps partly because they were subject to less hostility and discrimination in that region's persistent multicultural and multiethnic ambience. They may have also come to live there to provide services for the Christian armies fighting the Moors in that period. Subsequently, many took up work as blacksmiths, horse traders, butchers, potters, basket weavers, and street vendors, while also being regarded as thieves, acquiring an ongoing degree of popular scorn that was exacerbated by their own proud social insularity and endogamy. To some extent offsetting this animosity, from the earliest period, was their renown as musicians and dancers, whether as street performers or—as portrayed in Miguel de Cervantes's 1613 novella "La gitanilla"—invited artists in the homes of nobles. While it is certainly conceivable that the Gitanos may have brought with them dance and modal song styles from Byzantine lands, or perhaps even India, Cervantes depicts them performing Spanish genres (*seguidillas*, *zarabandas*, *villancicos*, and *romances*), albeit in their own colorful manner. Of interest in the present discussion is the Gitanos' relation to Moorish culture and its music.

The India Connection—or Lack Thereof

The Indian ancestry of European Roma (including Gitanos), coupled with the striking similarities that can be found between flamenco cante and dance, on the one hand, and certain North Indian modes and dance styles, on the other, has generated much commentary and speculation. The Indian origins of Roma people are most obvious, and indisputable, in genetic evidence and in affinities between Romani dialects and the Sanskritic languages (rather than Sanskrit per se) that would have been spoken in northwest India around the end of the first millennium CE (and would be similar to modern Hindi and related Rajasthani languages such as Marwari). The Spanish Romani dialect, Caló, though no longer a living language, survived as a lexicon—with many words of Indic and Greek origin—until the nineteenth century. A handful of Sanskritic-derived Caló words remain common, including in flamenco lyrics, such as *duca* (or *duquela*), cognate with Hindi *dukh* (pain, sorrow). It is generally assumed that European Romani people are to some extent descended from the Dom (retroflex, flapped "d"), a low caste abundant throughout North India. Historically, the Dom have primarily been farmers but also folk drummers and performers. A North Indian proverb states, "If a Dom woman cries, she cries in song."

The musical and choreographic resemblances between flamenco and certain North Indian arts are intriguing. Much flamenco singing—especially in the Gitano-associated cantes such as *siguiriyas*—is eminently compatible with the North Indian *rāg* Bhairavi and, more significantly, with cognate modes used in Rajasthani and Punjabi folk music. In the realm of dance, the most conspicuous affinities lie in the elegant ("oriental") hand gestures of both flamenco and, for example, Rajasthani folk dance, and, of course, in the percussive footwork of both flamenco zapateado and kathak, the classical dance of North India.

These resemblances have been especially obvious to dancers who have studied both flamenco and kathak (see, e.g., Phillips 2013) and have facilitated various collaborative fusion projects involving the two traditions. They have also naturally provoked speculation that they represent historical continuities paralleling the genetic and linguistic ones. Aside from some clearly specious notions (e.g., that the guitar came from the sitar), the argument would be that some of the endogamous and proudly independent Roma preserved these music and dance features over the course of their centuries-long peregrinations (including an extended rest stop in Greek domains); for various historical reasons, these features largely died out among most European Roma communities but were able to take root and thrive, in rearticulated form, in Moorish Andalusia. More specifically, in reference to modal and melodic continuities, one could hypothesize that the Bhairavi-like Phrygian mode borne by the Roma died out in Persian, Turkish, and Levantine Arab dominions when modes with quarter tones came to predominate there, and in European lands where common-practice harmony came to prevail, but could survive in Moorish Andalusia—just as the "oriental" hand gestures characteristic of Romani dancing elsewhere in Europe could have been reinforced in Andalusia by Arab-derived dance styles. This scenario is not utterly implausible, though it is certainly speculative and, accordingly, might be entirely wrong; that is, it is equally possible that flamenco's modal features derive overwhelmingly from music prevalent in Moorish Andalusia.

As for the conspicuous prominence of percussive footwork in both flamenco and kathak, an attempt to posit historical continuity would again have to confront the relative absence of such footwork techniques in Roma dancing in other lands between India and Spain. Wherever the tradition originated, Gitanos were documented as performing dances with zapateo (wearing ankle bells) in Spain since the 1580s, and zapateo dances were common in the *canario* and *jácara* of sixteenth- to seventeenth-century Spanish theater, subsequently falling out of fashion until being revived in nineteenth-century flamenco, probably via Creole influence from Latin America, especially the Mexican *jarabe* (Castro Buendía 2014b, 23; F. Núñez 2021, 260–61, ch. 12).

While the Moorish influence on Andalusian music, and subsequently flamenco, is taken for granted in some quarters, it continues, as mentioned above, to be a subject of considerable academic contestation in some circles, enlivened by various social agendas and a general lack of documentation on which to ground solid evidence. Thus, for example, Gitano guitarist and flamencologist Pedro Peña Fernández (2013, 202–229), in an explicitly gitanocentric volume, argues that the Moriscos (former Muslims, or their descendants, living in Christian territories) had been driven out of Seville and Cádiz provinces—the subsequent cradle of flamenco—after the Christian reconquest of those areas (in 1236 and 1248) and well before the advent of the Gitanos, and that Moorish cultural influence was extirpated in the Inquisition. A complementary viewpoint asserted by Catalan musicologist Felipe Pedrell (1841–1922) was that the distinctive features of flamenco and Andalusian music were Byzantine in origin and were merely transmitted rather than shaped by the Moors (1900, 74–76).

However, the diverse sorts of evidence for significant Moorish influence on Spanish and especially Andalusian music culture are abundant, even if some of the arguments of early "Arabist" scholars such as Julián Ribera (1927) have been much disputed.[1] Firstly, large numbers of Moors—perhaps as many as 40 percent—avoided expulsion, and many thousands (including, as it were, another Cervantes character[2]) managed to return to Spain from North Africa, where they had been abused and even enslaved (e.g., Dadson 2011). DNA studies have shown that today as many as 10 percent of Spaniards have North African ancestry. Several post-Reconquest sources document the ongoing and substantial presence of Moors and Moriscos, and even today various persons and entire communities—such as that of the town of La Puebla de Cazalla—are commonly referred to, however impressionistically, as "*morisco*."

Particularly relevant are the evident links with Andalusian Gitanos. Many Moriscos joined the ranks of the similarly olive-complected Gitanos and other groups of beggars, bandits, and wanderers, leading, for example, the writer of a document of 1610 to aver, "Many of the abundant Gitanos are presumably Moriscos."[3] While the expulsion of Moriscos from Valencia appears to have been quite thorough (gutting that region's agricultural economy), evidence indicates that in provinces such as Murcia and Seville, tens of thousands of Moriscos remained (whether converting to Christianity or not) or returned as farmworkers and even slaves (see, e.g., Goodwin 2015, 306–318). In farm estates of Seville and Cádiz provinces—the subsequent crucibles of flamenco—many evidently worked alongside and eventually assimilated with settled Gitanos. Hence, perhaps, the abundance of Gitano farm laborers in Seville province, despite the fact that farming has not been a traditional occupation of Gitanos in other parts of Spain. In Granada and elsewhere, Gitanos took up many of the same professions, such as smithing, as were practiced by remaining Moriscos, alongside whom they would have worked. Further, as Pierre Lefranc (n.d. a, 1) has documented, many Gitanos were dragooned to work in galleons through the mid-1700s and, subsequently, through the early 1800s in arsenals and prisons, where they lived and toiled alongside captured North African Arab pirates.

Moreover, Gitanos may have felt a natural cultural affinity with the similarly persecuted Moriscos and, accordingly, adopted many Moorish customs, including music (see Lefranc 2000, 47–56). In many flamenco lyrics, Gitanos nostalgically invoke the Moors and refer to each other as such—for example, *mi mora* (my Moorish woman)—while often associating themselves with Moorish heritage in common discourse.[4]

Even more significant than the persistence of Moriscos themselves is the fact that post-Reconquest Andalusian culture had already evolved as such a deeply syncretic entity that the Moorish elements could by no means be purged by a simple expulsion of many or even most Moors themselves. Evidence of musical syncretism is in its way conclusive. Before the expulsion, Moorish instruments had come to be widely adopted, with the *'ud* (*al 'ud*) developing into the lute, the *rabāb* generating the bowed *rebec* and subsequent viols, and the *daf* and *bendir* becoming the *pandero* (tambourine, with or without jingles). Most importantly, the oval-shaped, round-backed *guitarra morisca* blended with the Greek-derived *kithara* by the ninth century to form the *guitarra latina*, direct ancestor to the somewhat larger Spanish guitar. Moorish ensembles of stringed instruments and percussion may well have been the forebears of the Málaga-province groups, called *pandas*, of guitars, violins, and tambourines, that still accompany *verdiales* songs; and the flamenco format of the guitar providing loose, flexible (though not precisely heterophonic) accompaniment to singing finds a precedent in Arab-Andalusian music (Cruces Roldán 2003, 73, 27–28). The similar formal structures of Moorish muwashshah and zajal, on the one hand, and medieval rondeaus and *virelais*, on the other, have often been noted, although scholars differ as to which of these inspired the other or whether they evolved together.[5] Explicitly syncretic are the Mozarabic (that is, of Christians in Islamic lands) jarchas that constituted seminal forerunners of Spanish *romance* ballads and lyric poetry in general. Such syncretism is overt in the thirteenth-century volume *Cantigas de Santa María* of King Alfonso X ("El Sabio," the Wise/Learned) of Seville, whose decorative miniatures show players of assorted Arab and European instruments (see fig. 1). Many of the *cantigas* themselves in this compilation are in zajal form, and composers seem to have freely adopted tunes from Moorish zajals and other vernacular sources. (A few cantigas are in Phrygian mode, though most are in G and F modes.) Further, many of their rhythms adhere to Arabic rather than the French mensural models that prevailed elsewhere in Europe.[6]

Figure. 1. An illustration from the *Cantigas de Santa María* showing Arab and Christian lutenists

Of course, what would be of most interest—and what is sadly lacking in such iconographic and textual evidence—is documentation that would enable us to trace to Moorish culture aspects of actual music, especially scales, modes, rhythms, and stylistic features. Extant Arab-Andalusian (in Spanish: *andalusí*) art music in North Africa may provide certain clues, but even in the Moorish period such a rarefied court idiom may have been quite distinct, in both form and social milieu, from the vernacular musics that would have been more likely ancestors of flamenco. Further, it is difficult to extrapolate backward to the Moorish period from andalusí music as practiced today, even if one is tempted to make connections between the abundant rhythmic sixes, twelves, and hemiolas of that music and of flamenco. Finally, it is possible that some of the andalusí establishments may have relocated to the Maghreb prior to certain significant musical developments in the Arab and Moorish worlds, such as, according to some, the spread of Hijāz-type modes discussed below.

As it is, the strongest—though often circumstantial—evidence for Moorish influence on flamenco comes from musical affinities themselves.

A particularly distinctive feature of flamenco singing is its melismatic style, which is not characteristic of most other forms of European song and, by contrast, is common in North African music, past and present. Muwashshahs rendered in Arab-Andalusian music today are markedly melismatic, and al-Tifashi also commented on the distinctively melismatic character of Moorish song. Melismas also pervade modern-day Arab singing, from Quranic chant (in Muslim thought, technically not "music") to commercial pop tunes, everywhere from Iraq to Morocco. Another distinctive feature shared by flamenco and Arab and North African music is its modal—rather than chordal harmonic—character. Traditional *cante jondo* (deep song) forms such as siguiriyas and *martinete* are largely modal in structure, and as discussed later, the chordal guitar accompaniments to common *cantes* (song-types) such as *soleares* and bulerías are dispensable and arguably nonstructural.

Modality would have been a feature not only of Arab music but also of medieval Spanish Visigothic and Mozarabic as well as contemporary Jewish music (of which even less is known), Byzantine plainsong, and whatever folk traditions the Roma would have brought with them. This compatibility would certainly have facilitated the sort of syncretic collaboration between Arab and Christian musicians suggested by the *Cantigas* illustrations (cf. Wright 1992, 567); as Guillermo Castro Buendía (2014a, I:68) and others suggest, medieval Spanish musicians and musical entities could travel easily between social milieus, and the same melody could serve both as a muwashshah and a cantiga. However, attributing modality and related characteristics of flamenco to Gregorian or Byzantine chant would require explaining why other European musics (including medieval virelais and rondeaus) lack these features. What is overwhelmingly probable is that flamenco's modal and melismatic character derives from Moorish Spain's Arab-inflected music culture, with which compatible Byzantine, Visigothic, Jewish, and Romani music forms were able to syncretize in ways that may never be reconstructed but generated a distinctive and rich Andalusian music tradition. Thus, it was this primarily but not exclusively Arab musical style, instilled over seven centuries of Moorish rule, that not only allowed modality and melismatic style to persist (unlike in the rest of Western Europe) but also imprinted a particular form of modality and modal harmony on the Andalusian musics that evolved into flamenco.

Modal Affinities between Flamenco and Arab Musics

For musically lettered readers interested in such matters, further observations can be made about the evident roots of flamenco modality and modal harmony. In general, the predominant and most characteristic scale in flamenco, as discussed later, is a form of what could be called the "altered Phrygian" (E) mode,[7] with much usage of the raised third degree (G♯). The latter coheres with the conventional tonic chord of E major (rather than E minor) and also affords an augmented second interval between the second and third scale degrees (i.e., F and G♯), which, in Arab and Turkish musics, is the distinguishing feature of the common Hijāz *maqām* (mode). Occasionally, as in flamenco's warm-up *temple* ("tem-play") phrase opening some cantes, the third degree is intoned in a neutral ("half sharp") manner, which resembles the neutral third degree common in much Arab music, especially the maqām Rāst (as well as Syrian intonations of this degree in Hijāz, or "Hijāz *gharib*").[8]

Other, more specific features of flamenco melodic and modal patterns reflect conspicuous affinities, and likely historical connections, with other musics, especially Arab. Quite a few centuries would have elapsed between the time the Dom/Roma left India and arrived in Iberia, but it is not entirely implausible to imagine that they may have brought with them a repertoire of folk songs, in common North Indian modes, that would find easy reinforcement in and compatibility with Moorish Andalusian music.

French flamenco scholar Pierre Lefranc (2000, 47–56) noted the remarkable similarity between common passages in flamenco *temple* phrases (and opening verse lines in *tonás*, soleares, siguiriyas, bulerías, and other cantes) and basic opening phrases in versions of Muslim *azān* (call to prayer) and *iqāma* (preceding call, inside the mosque itself). Though Lefranc did not specify, he was clearly referring to the azān in maqām Rāst, which is the single most common style of rendering azān in the Muslim world. These azān and flamenco *temple* passages share a basic structure of ascending syllabically to the fifth scalar degree (while skipping the second degree) and then descending, often to rest on the neutral third degree. However, it is not possible to establish a firm historical connection between these. Azān and iqāma are intoned in many melodies throughout the Muslim world, and nothing is known of how they were rendered in Moorish Spain (or anywhere else before the advent of recording). The most characteristic Moroccan style of azān, which is said to derive from Moorish tradition, does not resemble the Rāst azān, instead featuring a slowly rising monotone. However, the Rāst azān does exist in Morocco, alongside several other forms. It is entirely conceivable—if ultimately unverifiable—that a version of it was common in Moorish Spain and came to constitute a basic melodic model that was adopted in certain types of Andalusian song, especially as rendered and archaically perpetuated by Gitanos.

A similar ambiguity, it must be said, would pertain to the historical connection between the Hijāz-type configuration (e.g., E–F–G♯–A) in flamenco and in Arab music. In both flamenco and Hijāz, the fourth degree can serve as a relatively stable resting point, which in flamenco (from E) would be harmonized with an A minor chord. (In modern Arab music theory, this sort of secondary tonal center is called *ghammaz*, or "wink.") The distinctive Hijāz tetrachord, with its augmented second interval, is common in music of the Arab heartlands as well as in various Moroccan music genres; it also occurs in the Zidān maqām (rather than "Hijāz *mashriqi*") of North African Arab-Andalusian nuba music and was present, at least until the early 1900s, in the Hijāz of Tunisian *ṭubū'* (see Beyhom and Makhlouf 2021; d'Erlanger 1949). While as with the azān, it is not entirely possible to verify connections between these traditions and flamenco,[9] in Spain the Hijāz pattern occurs in various folk musics (Crivillé I Bargalló 1983, 312), and the inescapable conclusion is that its presence in flamenco derives from Arab music.

Special attention is due to a distinctive feature of flamenco Phrygian and Arab modality and its related form of modal harmony. As will be discussed in greater detail in chapter 4, alongside standard Western common-practice chordal harmony, flamenco uses a distinctive modal harmonic system sometimes referred to as "Andalusian" or "Phrygian." In this system, the chordal triadic vocabulary is drawn primarily from the pitch resources of the Phrygian and, to some extent, the Hijāz-type modal configurations. Thus, taking E as tonic, it would employ minor triads on the fourth and seventh degrees (Am, Dm), and major ones on the second, third, and sixth degrees (F, G, and C). The standard use of a major tonic triad (E major) rather than a minor one suggests affinities with the Hijāz mode insofar as it coheres with the use of the raised third degree in some contexts, affording the characteristic augmented second interval of Hijāz. Chords built on the fifth degree (B) are avoided.

Instead, the role of the "dominant" (i.e., the chord that most strongly demands resolution to the tonic) is played by the F (II♭) chord. The minor iv chord (Am) can constitute a relatively stable resting point, although remaining subsidiary to the E chord, which functions as a tonic and *finalis* (as in the fundamental progression Am–G–F–E; i.e., iv–III–II–I.) This secondary stability of the minor iv chord parallels the way that the fourth degree in Bayati and Hijāz functions as a relatively stable resting point.[10]

This modal harmonic system, rather than being unique to flamenco or Andalusian music, is widespread (with minor regional variations) in urban musics of the eastern Mediterranean, such as Greek rebetika and bouzouki music, Jewish klezmer, and much urban popular music of the Balkans and Turkey. (A particularly familiar instance of this tonality is in the Jewish folk song "Hava Nagila," which could be said to employ the Hijāz-type mode—in Yiddish terminology, *ahava raba*—as in the opening phrase E–E– –G♯ F E G♯–G♯ etc., with E major serving as the tonic chord and F as the dominant.)

The fact that essentially the same modal harmonic system is used in both flamenco and Eastern European and Turkish urban musics should not be attributed to some direct historical musical exchange between the two regions nor to some historical presence of church modes. Rather, the distinctive tonal system evolved as a syncretic entity precisely in regions (Andalusia, Greece, the Balkans) where an Arab or cognate Turkish modal system coexisted and interacted with Western common-practice harmony. In both flamenco and corresponding eastern Mediterranean musics, a compatible modal harmonic system developed as a logical, and indeed obvious, way of adapting triadic chordal harmony to a distinctive modal tradition. In Spain itself, this harmonic system evolved specifically in the region, Andalusia, where Moorish presence was most prolonged and its musical impact the strongest. The expulsion of most Moors in the seventeenth century did not signal the end of Arab influence on Andalusian music, not only because many Moriscos remained but also because by that time much Andalusian music was clearly heavily, if not overwhelmingly, Moorish in character, with "Moorish" denoting a syncretic entity incorporating Arab, Amazigh, Christian Spanish, and probably Jewish elements.

Moorish Music and Gitanos

The evidence reviewed here strongly suggests the survival, in syncretized form, of Moorish features—especially melismatic singing and a type of modality—in Andalusian music up to the 1860s, at which point they became central to the new genre of flamenco. What is less clear is how widespread and central these features were in Andalusian or Gitano music prior to that point. This question, indeed, remains controversial and becomes imbricated in various sociocultural issues and agendas, especially involving perennial debates about the role of Gitanos in the evolution of flamenco. One sort of gitanocentric argument is that presented by Peña Fernández, mentioned above, who would claim that Moorish survivals in Andalusian music were negligible and that flamenco's ostensibly Moorish elements (melismas, modality, etc.) in fact were brought by the Gitanos, as retained from their prior Indian and Greek backgrounds. As suggested, there are various problems with this hypothesis. A different sort of Roma-oriented argument would be that the Moorish elements were not only primarily preserved by Gitanos but also that over the centuries they pervaded Gitano music; this Moorish-informed Gitano music, it is implied, existed during this long era as a sort of parallel entity to mainstream Andalusian music, emerging from its obscure milieu in the mid-1800s to form the basis of cante jondo. This argument is basic to the "hermetic" theory discussed at greater length below. As suggested, the first part of this argument—that Gitanos did preserve, in some genres and to some extent, certain Moorish-derived musical features—does seem plausible. Several nineteenth-century references to Gitano dances and songs, such as the *caña* (possibly from Arabic *ghania* [song]), describe them as Moorish in character and in that sense clearly distinct from mainstream Andalusian music. Other parts of this argument, however, are problematic insofar as we are unable to generalize about Gitano repertoires and styles as a whole. We may recall, for example, Cervantes's (fictive) description, in "La Gitanilla," of Gitanos performing familiar Spanish genres (seguidillas, zarabandas, villancicos, and *romances*), in which he makes no reference to any Moorish elements, though these may have been present to some extent in such performances.

Perhaps the most plausible argument is that advanced most explicitly by Gerhard Steingress (esp. 1991, 75–81), who stresses the extent to which flamenco emerged in response to a nineteenth-century Romantic (including touristic) demand for a music and dance that was exotic, erotic, and "Moorish." The Gitanos—olive-complected, gifted in music and dance, and felicitously "exotic"—were able to rise to the occasion, in the process thoroughly orientalizing various extant dance and music idioms. In doing so, they could certainly draw on Moorish-derived features that they had retained, but they exaggerated and elaborated these features rather than simply making public some "hermetic" style of theirs. Gitano performers were thus absolutely central to the emergence and creation of flamenco, but the "oriental" style they cultivated and presented was to a considerable extent something elaborated and rearticulated in the early public flamenco period rather than being a central feature of mysterious hermetic genres that they simply transplanted to the stage. We shall return to these topics further below.

The Roots of Flamenco in Christian Spain to 1800

With the triumph over the Moors and the subsequent conquests in the Americas, Spain entered what is known as its "Golden Age," which extended roughly through the seventeenth century. Spanish energy and military dynamism seemed boundless, as Hernán Cortés and Francisco Pizarro, with incredible daring—and brutality—toppled the Aztec and Inca empires, and Vasco Núñez de Balboa slashed his way across Panama to the Pacific. Bullion from American mines funded the construction of glorious Spanish palaces, plazas, and cathedrals. As the seat of the Habsburg Empire, Spain governed the Netherlands and much of the Holy Roman Empire. Spanish culture also flourished, whether in the form of Cervantes's *Don Quixote*, the plays of Félix Lope de Vega, the paintings of Don Diego de Silva Velázquez and Bartolomé Estéban Murillo, or the polyphonic masses of Tomás Luis de Victoria.

Yet as students of Spanish history know, the gold of the "Golden Age" was in many ways a thin crust of gilt covering a fundamentally rotten and flimsy structure. Economically, Spain, having expelled its industrious Jews and Moors, was further bankrupted by endless European wars, a sparse and even declining population, outlandish court expenses, lack of coal and inland waterways, a popular disdain for any sort of productive labor, and a series of narrow-minded and dogmatic, if not outright imbecilic, monarchs. Since Spain failed to invest its mercantile profits in productive industry, most of the treasure from the mines of Potosí flowed straight through Cádiz and Seville to German and Italian creditors, while most Spaniards lived in a dismal poverty that seems hard to reconcile with the vastness of the empire and the glorious architecture in most Spanish cities. Meanwhile, the Renaissance values of education, intellectual freedom, and rationalism were stifled in Spain by a backward-looking counter-Reformation Catholicism, which offered the Inquisition in place of an inquisitive spirit.

Pre-Flamenco Musics in the Seventeenth to Eighteenth Centuries

As we have seen, the Christian conquest of Granada in 1492 and the expulsion of most Moors from 1610 did not erase the Moorish features in Andalusian music culture. A large percentage of Moors and Moriscos managed to remain or return, and while they or their descendants would have eventually converted to Christianity and ceased to speak Arabic, many aspects of their musical practices and forms would have persisted, including as adopted by the Gitanos with whom they mingled. Moreover, after seven centuries of Moorish presence, Andalusian music culture in general had become a thoroughly syncretic entity imbued with Arab- and Amazigh-derived features, including melismatic vocal style and particular forms of modality.

However, the decline of Moorish rule and demographic presence does occasion a shift in historical focus to the music and dance culture of Christian Spain, in which can be detected and reconstructed a continuous development of the forms that would evolve into flamenco in the mid-1800s. As mentioned above, these forms were primarily in the nature of vernacular, orally transmitted folk musics that were unlikely to be preserved in any notated form. Some song traditions that may have been significant sources of flamenco—such as farmers' recreational and work songs of Seville province—were absolutely undocumented until ethnographic recordings of the mid-twentieth century. Meanwhile, during this period, roughly spanning the sixteenth to eighteenth centuries, much of the documented Spanish and even Andalusian music—such as the Renaissance motets of Victoria—was thoroughly European in character, without any particular relationship to regional Spanish vernacular music.

Nevertheless, a variety of notated musics do allow the historian to reconstruct, in however circumstantial and incomplete a form, much of the contours of relevant pre-flamenco musics from the early 1600s onward. Some of these items constitute vernacular song and dance genres, such as the zarabanda, that were incorporated in stylized form into the repertoire of Western classical music. Others, such as the jácara, may not have been thusly "canonized" but came to be occasionally notated as items in the popular Spanish theater that served as a conduit between the realms of art music and folk song. Other genres, especially the fandango, flourished in a variety of forms, some of which—if only obliquely represented in surviving notated scores—came to constitute a basic and seminal core of flamenco forms. In recent years, Spanish musicologists—especially Castro Buendía (2014)—have made prodigious contributions to reconstructing the evolution of flamenco musical forms through assembling and analyzing such extant notations. Other scholars have supplemented these findings with astute perspectives on the sociohistorical circumstances conditioning flamenco's development (e.g., Steingress 1991; Campo and Cáceres 2013).

The African and Afro-Latin Input in Pre-Flamenco Music

While some of flamenco's most basic features must be attributed to Moorish legacy, and Gitanos came to constitute core performers and architects of flamenco itself, modern flamenco scholars have increasingly recognized the importance of the African or, more specifically, Afro-Latin contribution to pre-flamenco music and dance (Navarro García 1998; Martín-Casares and Barranco 2009; Martín 2000). This contribution would have come from two basic sources: firstly, the presence of Africans and their descendants in Spain itself, and, secondly and more seminally, the importation of creolized Afro-Latin music and dance genres from the Caribbean Basin in the sixteenth through nineteenth centuries.

Sub-Saharan Africans had been present in Spain since the Moorish period. From the 1400s, more substantial numbers were brought from West Africa, primarily as domestic slaves, to Christian dominions in the peninsula as Spanish and Portuguese ships worked their way down the coast of Africa. The numbers of Black people in the peninsula grew to the tens of thousands, with communities not only in the ports of Seville and Cádiz, where Black *cofradías* (associations) were established from the early 1400s, but also in inland towns throughout the south. In the 1570s, when Black people constituted around 6 percent of Seville's population, one chronicler wrote that the city looked "like a chessboard, with as many Blacks as whites."[11] Many Golden Age plays and *mojiganga* skits featured Black characters, and Spaniards seem to have been endlessly charmed and amused by Black pronunciation, which was highlighted in the works of playwrights such as Lope de Rueda, Quevedo, and Lope de Vega. Such *bozal* ("fresh off the boat") speech was also basic to the *guineos*, *cumbés*, *zarambeques*, *villancicos de negros*, and other *negrista* ("negro-esque") songs composed, in *costumbrista* spirit, by Golden Age musicians and poets, whether Black, white, Spanish, or Portuguese and whether based in either Iberia or the New World. Such *costumbrismo*—implying an active but often superficial interest in the regional Other—would in the nineteenth century come to animate much interest in Gitanos and their music and dance, as will be discussed later.

In Spain the musical activities and predilections of local Blacks were widely noted, whether appreciatively or not. In 1464, for example, the town council of Jerez was prevailed upon to formally restrict the rowdy musical gatherings of Black revelers. On the whole, however, Black musical and cultural activities—including the processions and pageants sponsored by the cofradías—were enjoyed by spectators and tolerated by authorities, especially since, unlike the Moors, Jews, or Blacks in the New World, Afro-Spaniards were not so numerous as to be seen as threatening. Their fondness for music was proverbial, as dramatized in many poems and stories, such as Cervantes's "El celoso extremeño." The latter story vividly depicts a social milieu of Black musicians who accompanied their *romances* about Moors with a three-string *guitarilla* (little guitar), which may have been a North African lute akin to the *guinibry*.

Unfortunately, little is known about the nature of the music performed by Afro-Spaniards during this period, though various references mention their lively processions featuring guitarists, percussionists, and controversially sensual dances. Much of their music clearly became creolized rather than traditionally West African in form, just as the ethnically diverse Africans in the peninsula spoke Spanish as a lingua franca and, over the generations, would have lost touch with the traditions of their ancestors. Indeed, Afro-Spaniards largely disappeared as an ethnic group, and modern Andalusians, like other Spaniards, do not display any particular negroid features, nor are they are darker in complexion than other Spaniards.[12] Accordingly, there are no specific features in flamenco music or dance that can be definitively traced to African presence in Spain, although such influence is not impossible. Probably the most significant music and dance legacy of the Afro-Spaniards involved laying a foundation for the popularity of the new wave of Afro-Latin songs and dances coming from the Caribbean in the early colonial era.

While in the nineteenth century Cuba, Brazil, and Haiti would come to be centers of neo-African and Afro-Latin music and dance in the New World, in the preceding centuries it was mineral-rich Mexico (New Spain), along with Peru, that hosted large numbers of African workers brought by Spanish colonists. From the early 1500s, sub-Saharan Africans were accompanying Spaniards to the Americas, whether as slaves, servants, or soldiers. A 1570s census of New Spain revealed that Black people outnumbered Spaniards 18,569 to 14,711 (Stevenson 1968, 476). By this period Afro-Latinos were creating their own syncretic song and dance forms that were also avidly cultivated, in further creolized styles, by resident Spanish composers (especially those attached to missions), in the form of the negrista songs mentioned above. Typical examples from the early 1600s would include the guineos of Portuguese-born but Mexico-based Gaspar Fernandes, which feature bozal dialect and constantly shifting, irregular 6/8–3/4, in that respect loosely reminiscent of familiar modern Mexican *son jarocho* and *son jalisciense* rhythms. (A still-popular guineo of Fernandes is "Eso rigor e repente," recordings of which can be found on YouTube.)

The syncretic Afro-Latin dance-music forms appear to have been the source for two crucial features of pre-flamenco genres—namely, compact chordal ostinatos (that is, repeated patterns) and, arguably, persistent 6/8–3/4 hemiola of the "I like to be in Ame-ri-ca" variety (*one*-two-three-*one*-two-three-*one*-two-*one*-two-*one*-two), which in Spanish would be called *hemiolia, sesquialtera* ("six that alters"), or "amalgamated" (*de amalgama*) rhythm. This form of hemiola appears to have existed in Spain well before the colonial era, as it appears prominently in the thirteenth-century Cantiga de Santa María no. 166 ("Como Poden"), and in some items in the *Cancionero Musical del Palacio* (such as the *folía* "Rodrigo Martínez," ca. 1490). In the sixteenth century it was fairly common in *romances*, villancicos, and Spanish-Italian *frottolas* (Binkley and Frenk 1995, 14). However, the pattern appears to have become more common in the seventeenth century, when it became primarily associated, in Spain, with Afro-Latin genres such as the cumbé and the zarabanda, and later in the Caribbean, with genres such as the *son huasteco* and Cuban *punto*. The latter genre went on to enjoy its own popularity, in stylized form, in Spain. The hemiola pattern could also be found in various Spanish vernacular musics predating the nineteenth century, such as jácaras, *canarios*, *jotas*, and the *paño moruno* melody (see, e.g., Castro Buendía 2014a, I:743). It is likely that the form, though long present in Spain, became popular first as a syncretic pattern in Afro-Latin Caribbean Basin music or as a product of the musical circuit between Andalusian ports and the Caribbean. From the Afro-Caribbean perspective, it could be seen as a creolized streamlining of the 12/8 polyrhythms pervading much West African music. Once established, this rhythm underwent further transformations and rearticulations in various genres on both sides of the Atlantic, in the process losing its original associations with Afro-Latin music and with Black Africans in general. Hence, for example, Lope de Vega, in an oft-quoted verse (in *El amante agradecio*, 1602), states that the syncopated *chacona* (a Latin American imported dance) arrived to Seville from the Caribbean "by post"—that is, presumably as orally transmitted by sailors and other travelers.[13] In the New World, the 6/8–3/4 hemiola became the basis of what Latin American musicologists call the *cancionero ternario* (ternary repertoire), and in Spain it would eventually be rearticulated, in specific forms, as a core flamenco rhythm.

The use of short chordal ostinatos in cantes like tangos and fandangos can also be traced to Afro-Latin origins, especially as imported from the Caribbean Basin. Ostinatos—encompassing melodies as well as rhythms—pervade sub-Saharan African music, from Zimbabwean *mbira* patterns to Ghanaian drum ensembles and Ugandan xylophone music. Ground bass or chordal patterns were popular in European music of the sixteenth and seventeenth centuries, including the *romanesca* (as in Luis de Narváez's popular guitar variations on "*Guárdame las vacas*" of 1538) and the indefatigable *passamezzo moderno* chord pattern, which persists even in modern pop songs such as the Rolling Stones' "Honky Tonk Women." However, as extended eight-bar entities, these had quite a different character from the compact, oscillating, one- or two-bar ostinatos that were particularly conspicuous in Afro-Latin (not "African") genres such as the zarambeque, cumbé, villancicos de negro, zarabanda, and fandango; these typically featured guitar variations, or *diferencias*, over a short chordal vamp, which could also accompany sung verses. Exemplary in this respect are the 1732 zarambeque, cumbé, and fandango of composer and guitarist Santiago de Murcia (1673–1739), who may have spent time in Mexico.

The zarabanda is particularly significant in the prehistory of flamenco. It was the first creole Caribbean genre to be documented, being mentioned as a dance form as early as 1539 in Panama (Castro Buendía 2014a, 160). Within a few decades it had become widely popular in Spain, where (like subsequent Caribbean Basin dances) it was ineffectively denounced and banned for its supposed lasciviousness. By the early 1600s, it was adopted by Italian composers (especially for guitar) and went on to become a standard item in Baroque suites, distinguished primarily by its halting ternary rhythm ♩ ♩ ♩ /♩. ♪ ♩

Our knowledge of the vernacular zarabanda's formal features is sketchy, as the only musical notations are of stylized versions of the genre as penned by lettered composers, and dance notations are nonexistent. Extant musical scores do not show vocal melodies, though they indicate that these comprised six verses, the last two serving as a refrain. The zarabanda chordal accompaniment evidently consisted of a repeated four-bar pattern in major key, consisting of Do–Fa–Do–Sol (e.g., C–F–C–G) chords rendered with the standard 6/8–3/4 hemiola. The Afro-Latin associations of the genre are suggested by these musical features, by the references to "zarabanda" in the lyrics of Afro-Latin pieces such as Fernandes's guineo, by the mentions of Black people dancing the genre (see F. Núñez 2021, 255), and, lastly, by the name itself, Zarabanda being a prominent deity in the Congolese-derived Afro-Cuban *palo mayombe* religion.[14]

The extant Spanish and Italian seventeenth-century zarabandas exhibit with particular clarity and regularity the pervasive hemiola and chordal ostinatos that would become hallmarks of Afro-Latin musics. These features are evident in the earliest sarabanda unearthed, a 1606 piece written for *chitarra spagniuola* (Spanish guitar) in Italy, where Spanish guitar music was the most popular type of vernacular music (in Hudson 1970; French sarabandes soon developed quite distinct forms). The best-known early zarabanda is that written for guitar by Spanish composer Gaspar Sanz (1640–1710), which consists primarily of variations on the pattern established in its first four bars (ex. 1.1).[15] The zarabanda, like the salon fandango that succeeded and to some extent derived from it, was quintessentially performed on guitar, and the practice of

Example 1.1. Zarabanda, Gaspar Sanz (1674)

playing (or composing) a string of diferencias on a short harmonic ostinato, as a ritornello between sung verses, constituted a clear precedent for the guitar *falsetas* of flamenco.

In the seventeenth century the Latin American–derived zarabanda and *chaconne/chacona/ciaccona*, and the Spanish *pasacalle/passacaglia*, were incorporated, in stylized and greatly decelerated forms, into the realm of Baroque art music (including renowned pieces by J. S. Bach). The Spanish zarabanda was particularly important as a choreographic ancestor to the nineteenth-century *jaleo* forms that fathered flamenco dance. As Berlanga (2021a) has outlined, the zarabanda, in its most characteristic (and then controversial) form, was typically danced by a solo woman with castanets; it was cultivated both as a vernacular "folk" dance and as a stage item in theater, with mutual stylistic interaction between these two contexts. By the early 1600s, Gitanos were already being appreciated for dancing it in their distinctive and colorful manner and were being hired by nobles and others to perform. The specific roots and form of their dance style remain conjectural, but it is entirely plausible that they constituted some syncretic synthesis of idioms that the Romani brought with them, together with Moorish and Afro-Latin-derived styles they encountered in Andalusia. Evidence suggests that over the centuries, many Afro-Spaniards, like clandestine Moriscos, mingled, interacted, and intermarried with the similarly socially marginal Gitanos. Accordingly, in the 1700s, for example, Gitanos were documented as performing otherwise extinct Black dances such as the *mandingoy* and cumbé (Martín 2000), and hemiola patterns, while persisting in certain non-Gitano musics (such as the paño moruno folk song), became central in pre-flamenco and flamenco musics.

The connections between Gitanos and Afro-Spaniards were significant and diverse in form (see, e.g., F. Núñez 2021, 128–35). *Tonadillas* and skits portrayed Afro-Gitano mulattos and showed Blacks and Gitanos performing each other's songs and dances. Under North American influence, blackface minstrelsy enjoyed its own popularity in the nineteenth century, and in stage shows, costumbrista depictions of Blacks and Gitanos tended to jumble together the two communities and their songs, as in this verse from an 1803 skit that, while making the first known reference to the merengue in connection with music, eulogizes Gitanos as quintessential exemplars of Spanish identity:

Ay que merengue tiene ese dengue
ay que jaleo tiene el meneo,
resuena el pandero resuena la gresca,
y viva y reviva nuestra gitanesca,
que es la sal de España y toda la tierra.

What *merengue* that *dengue* has!
What jaleo this wagging has!
Let the tambourine and fracas resound!
Long live our Gypsyness,
that is the salt of Spain and the world!

The Guitar

The guitar has always been the main instrument in flamenco, and it is not surprising that it played a similarly central role in the various genres that contributed to flamenco's prehistory. The guitar evolved over a period of centuries, but by the latter 1500s it had become a popular Spanish instrument, typically with five courses (doubled strings), in the tuning A–D–G–B–E—that is, like the modern guitar, but without the low E string. The Baroque-era guitar could be played in two basic styles: *punteado*, or plucking (to play melodies, counterpoint, arpeggios, and the like), or *rasgueado* (*rasgueo*), or chordal strumming. Punteado was more associated with academic art music and salon music, such as the classical compositions of Narváez (ca. 1500–1549); in the Baroque period it was also more typical of the similar *vihuela*, which was giving way in popularity to the guitar. Rasgueado, by contrast, was generally seen as cruder and more plebian (although it was modern in contributing to chordal rather than contrapuntal conceptions of music); its associated social milieu was correspondingly different. Because the guitar was portable, relatively inexpensive, and in its rasgueado form not formidably difficult, it became widely popular for accompanying dance, rowdy jácaras, church villancicos, street processions, theater songs, and various other vernacular genres. Although lettered composers such as Sanz did write for guitar, the instrument was more typically associated in the sixteenth to eighteenth centuries with lower-class barbers, casual strummers, and especially an urban subculture of Gitanos, Moriscos, Blacks, and other lumpen types. Wrote one oft-quoted chronicler in 1611:

> Ever since the guitar was invented, very few people have studied the vihuela. This is a sad loss, because a great variety of punteado music was played on that instrument, and now the guitar is little more than a cowbell, and is so easy to play, especially to strum, that there is scarcely a stable-boy who doesn't play it.[16]

In many barber salons, a guitar would be hanging on the wall, to be strummed by a waiting customer or by the barber himself if unoccupied.

By the latter 1600s, Spanish vernacular music, as imperfectly documented in notations of theater music and guitar compositions by Sanz and others, was illustrating elements that would eventually surface as core features of flamenco. Castro Buendía (2014a, ch. 3), surveying pasacalles, folías, romanescas, and jácaras from this period, finds several such pre-flamenco rhythms and harmonies, even if these may appear in passing rather than as pervasive features. He and other flamenco historians have taken special interest in the 1670s guitar music of Sanz,[17] several of whose ninety-some guitar pieces, which he nicely notated in tablature, represent his stylized settings of or diferencias on various popular dance-song genres. Particularly revealing are his versions of jácaras, which were light songs presented during the finales and *entre-acte/entreme* skits of theatrical comedies in the seventeenth century. While the form of the jácaras was not strictly standardized, certain tunes and chord progressions recur, revealing, among other things, occasional uses of the iv–III–II–I Andalusian cadence, in 6/8 meter. Sanz provides as a rasgueado exercise a reiterated chordal sequence that would become basic in flamenco; in the Dm/A tonality common in the music of the five-course Baroque guitar, it would be Dm–A–Dm–A–F–C–B♭–A–Dm. With A major serving, as it often did, as the altered Phrygian tonic, if one were to substitute a "dominant"-function B♭ for the Dm, the chordal sequence would become: B♭–A–B♭–A–F–C–B♭–A (Dm). Any flamenco guitarist would recognize the similarity of this sequence with the basic II♭–I oscillation of soleares, bulerías, and some forms of tangos (in *por medio* position of flamenco guitar), complete with the standard *cambio* (change) consisting of a passing move to the relative major (F), and thence via B♭ back to the altered Phrygian tonic. However, as Castro Buendía notes (2014a, 149–51), despite these affinities, the seventeenth-century jácara should not be seen as the direct progenitor of soleares and bulerías, but rather as an indicator of the presence of certain distinctive harmonic and rhythmic practices that would, in the mid-nineteenth century, become standardized and elaborated in soleares and, later, bulerías.

The predecessors of forms like siguiriyas—including modal, Moorish-influenced, perhaps especially Gitano versions of *romances*, work songs, and other genres—are precisely the sorts of idioms that would have been least likely to have been adapted, in however stylized a form, by an academic composer such as Sanz. Hence most aspects of their prehistory remain conjectural, including the extent to which they may have been accompanied by guitar. It seems clear that these song-types commonly would have been sung unaccompanied, as they are even today, whether on stage or in a family reunion. However, given that guitar was commonly used—including by Gitanos—to accompany such a wide range of genres, it would seem extremely likely that a guitarist present at a rendition of some altered Phrygian modal song form could easily, at the very least, use his instrument to percussively strum (in the aforementioned "cowbell" fashion) a tonic drone chord; and if he were to decorate his accompaniment with oscillations to a neighboring II♭ chord, then the effect could have been remarkably close to flamenco.

The Fandango

The fandango, as a family of musical forms, constitutes one of the basic cores of the flamenco repertoire—a veritable tree trunk with many fructiferous limbs. Tracing its history involves parallels with the older zarabanda. Both were song and dance genres, deriving in some form from the Caribbean Basin—quite probably with Afro-Latin input—that came to enjoy prodigious popularity in Spain. Both, as dance styles, were denounced and inconsistently banned for their alleged lasciviousness. As musical forms relevant to flamenco prehistory, both were primarily folk or vernacular genres, documented only in the form of light-classical versions penned by academic composers. Moreover, both featured reiterated, simple chordal ostinatos in ternary meter, which could also accompany or alternate with sung verse sections.

In other respects the genres differed. The zarabanda was, of course, a century earlier than the fandango, becoming faddish by the late 1500s and remaining in vogue through much of the seventeenth century. From its humble social origins it very quickly spun off, in stylized form, into the realm of Baroque art music while eventually dying out as a vernacular dance and song. In its notated form it featured a particular major-key ostinato, with persistent 6/8–3/4 hemiola, whereas the fandango ostinato, as will be discussed later, is in altered Phrygian tonality, with varying syncopation in place of a reiterated hemiola. Moreover, the fandango, far from expiring in the eighteenth century, continued vigorously long enough to become a basic family of cantes in flamenco. (Meanwhile, its career as a mainstream European art music idiom was limited to a handful of items, most notably one by Mozart and another by Boccherini.)

A preliminary task in reconstructing the fandango's evolution involves clarifying the quite distinct usages of the term, which can be seen as denoting three levels of specificity. In the most general sense, the word "fandango" has been used—especially in Latin America—to denote any kind of festive gathering with music and dance. Such a usage need not imply any specific kind of music or dance, and the researcher who gratuitously seeks or posits such links may reap and sow nothing but confusion.

In a somewhat more specific sense, the term "fandango," especially as used by flamenco specialists, denotes a family of Andalusian song-types—both flamenco cantes and folk forms—that share specific musical features. While these will be discussed further in chapter 5, at this point a crude schematic description will suffice. Specifically, the fandango forms (with a few exceptions) center on a *copla* or verse section, in major key, consisting of six *tercios* or musical phrases (usually five text lines, with the second line sung first and then repeated), in the basic progression I–IV–(V7)–I–V7–I–IV; the final IV serves as a pivot chord, becoming the dominant II in the relative altered Phrygian tonality of the subsequent *entrecopla* or *ritornelo* (*ritornello*) section, which features guitar falsetas and perhaps the Andalusian cadence. With the copla in C major and entrecopla in E Phrygian, the copla progression would be C–F–(G7)–C–G7–C–F, with the final F chord pivoting to E Phrygian. (In common parlance any verse may be referred to simply as a *letra*; "copla," aside from being a genre of Andalusian popular song, denotes a complete sung verse or stanza [e.g., of three, four, or five lines], while "tercio" means a single sung musical line.)

The specific flamenco cantes in the fandango family include fandango de Huelva and *abandolao* fandangos (in ternary meter, including verdiales, using a rhythm once associated with the *bandola* lute), and, in free rhythm, the *fandango natural*, *malagueñas*, *tarantas*, *granaínas*, and a few lesser-known forms. These are distinguished from each other primarily by their melodies along with their guitar tonalities and typical entrecopla falsetas.

Each of these fandango forms could be seen as consisting of two elements: the instrumental entrecopla/ritornello, in Phrygian tonality, and the sung copla, with its characteristic chord progression in the relative major key. As we shall note, these two elements have had differing degrees of relative importance in different forms of fandangos over the centuries. Moreover, this copla-ritornello format—including some of the specific chord progressions—was shared by various related genres, including such genres as the contemporary folía and the traditional Cuban punto (especially the *punto carvajal*, whose ritornello ostinato reiterates the Andalusian cadence). Finally, the most specific meaning of "fandango" involves the song forms that actually bear that designation, which would comprise the modern *fandango de Huelva* and *fandango natural*, and the eighteenth- and nineteenth-century fandango.

As with the zarabanda, early references to the fandango clearly indicate that its origin was the Caribbean Basin, especially Mexico, even if such references do not specify exactly what distinguished it as a genre. Early peninsular citations refer to it as a dance form, but fandangos—obviously with distinct musical features—were also being composed for strings and orchestra by chapel directors in Mexico in the late 1600s. By the mid-1700s the fandango, in somewhat diverse forms, was popular throughout much of Spain, as both an instrumental and a sung genre. Some of the variants were regional, while others were differentiated by social strata, performance context, and degree of musical literacy of the performer. In the eighteenth century, most relevant to flamenco history would be the sung and danced fandangos of informal fiestas, in which a guitarist would strum accompaniments to coplas and, in between these, play ritornello variations/falsetas or perhaps simply strum the iv–III–II–I or simply La–Re (A–D minor) ostinato; others present may have played castanets or *panderetas*. Not far removed from these in terms of style may have been fandangos as sung and danced on stage as light items in or between acts of tonadilla theater.

Most of the notated fandangos—like earlier zarabandas—that survive from the eighteenth and early nineteenth centuries consist, not surprisingly, of academic pieces for guitar or keyboard, which would have been marketed primarily to musically literate amateurs. Among the best-known eighteenth-century Spanish *fandangos de autor* are one, for guitar, of Santiago de Murcia (dated 1732) and the keyboard fandangos of Félix Máximo López (1742–1821), Domenico Scarlatti (1685–1757), and Antonio Soler (1729–1783), who said that his piece was inspired by some musicians from Veracruz that he heard.[18] These compositions consist mostly of decorated Dm–A ostinatos—standard in the five-course Baroque guitar—in triple meter, perhaps with an occasional digression to F, the relative major key, and concluding on A major, in accordance with the genre's dual, pendular tonicity. Murcia's fandango prominently features the iv–III–II–I (Dm–C–B♭–A) Andalusian cadence, indicating that this pattern was well in place by the early eighteenth century.

The relation of these academic instrumental fandangos to the vernacular Andalusian fandangos, with their sung verse sections, is unclear. The rarity of copla-like passages indicates that they represented to some extent a distinct instrumental tradition, with its own conventions. This might have related to a similarly instrumental fandango tradition of Valencia (Berlanga 2000) or might simply reflect that instrumentalists found more scope for elaboration in the ritornello than in the copla. Even in modern times, when flamenco guitarists play fandango de Huelva as solo items, they often emphasize falsetas on the ritornello rather than renderings of the copla.[19] Further, a few of the eighteenth-century notated fandangos, such as that of Máximo López, do contain copla-type passages. Collectively, these sources strongly suggest the presence, in the eighteenth century, of the basic musical features of the flamenco fandango—specifically, the alternation of a ritornello, in Phrygian tonality with some use of the Andalusian cadence, with a sung copla in the relative major (here, F), using a chord progression of F–B♭– (C7)–F–C7–F–B♭. These would be instrumentally rendered most typically by the five-course Baroque guitar, in the "por medio" Dm/A pendular tonality most suitable to that configuration.

The differences from some of the modern fandango forms documentable from the nineteenth century can also be noted. Firstly, the eighteenth-century fandango was in lively ternary rhythm, reflecting its association with dance, unlike the modern free-rhythmic fandango variants (*fandango natural*, granaínas, tarantas, and malagueñas), which have some of the character of "art songs." While the eighteenth-century fandango resembled, in this sense, the modern verdiales and fandango de Huelva, it lacked the latter's distinctive syncopation. Moreover, while the "por medio" tonality, with its Dm–A oscillation, can still be used for *fandango natural* and fandango de Huelva, more common are other guitar tonalities that exploit the use of the sixth string (low E), which was added to the guitar in the late 1700s and became standard a few decades later. Finally, as Castro Buendía's study reveals (2014, ch. 4), rather than adhering to the consistent distinctive rhythms of either the syncopated fandango de Huelva or the "abandolao" forms such as the verdiales—to be discussed below—the eighteenth-century fandangos exhibit a variety of rhythms, freely moving between typical seguidilla-, bolero-, and jota-type patterns and between 6/8 and 3/4, though with a preference for the latter.

Majos, Casticismo, Gitanos, and Music in the Late 1700s

In 1700 the Habsburgs were replaced by the French-descendant Bourbons, who ruled Spain for the next century. For the first half of this period, the inept monarchs proved no more effective than their predecessors, perpetuating ruinous European wars and failing to enact policies that might begin to lift Spain out of economic and sociocultural stagnation. From around 1750, however, the country's fortunes improved. With the definitive loss of its European dominions and ambitions, Spain enjoyed three unprecedented decades of relative peace, stability, and, in some sectors, actual prosperity. The Church's stranglehold on the economy and thought loosened somewhat, as Enlightenment ideas and French manners made new inroads and the Inquisition was relaxed.

The most significant progress was presided over by Carlos III (ruled 1759–1788), who constituted what in those dismal centuries of Spanish history would pass for an enlightened monarch. Avoiding costly wars, he promoted public works, education, and economic development and tried to persuade his subjects, via decree, that ordinary professions such as tanner, blacksmith, and tailor were honorable callings. Most Spaniards, however, remained mired in superstition, blind devotion to the Church, contempt for labor, and xenophobic hostility to Enlightenment thought.

A significant reform of Carlos involved the status of Gitanos. Since the early 1600s, after the novelty of their presence had worn off, Gitanos had come to be persecuted in various ways. Repeated official edicts had decreed their forced assimilation, banning their distinctive language, dress, and traditional occupations such as livestock trading, blacksmithing, and performing song and dance.

The reiteration of such edicts showed that they were not fully enforced, since Gitanos filled niches in the economy, and their performances were appreciated by many, including aristocrats. However, Gitanos enjoyed no legal rights and were often impounded to toil in galleys. Their persecution reached a climax in 1749, when around ten thousand were rounded up and sentenced to forced labor in galleys and arsenals, especially in Cádiz. The edict was revoked after a few months, but many hundreds remained enslaved for years (substantially enlarging the Gitano population of Cádiz). As debate about the "Gypsy problem" continued, in 1783 Carlos signed a decree that, like earlier ones, attempted to force them to assimilate, while at the same time granting them legal status and allowing them to settle down and pursue whatever occupations they liked. Many Andalusian towns soon came to host stable communities of Gitano blacksmiths, artisans, horse traders, and performers.

In terms of culture, until the latter decades of the century the elites of Spain, as encouraged by the Bourbons, tended to endorse French and Italian currents of thought and aesthetic tastes. If the seventeenth-century theater of Lope de Vega and Calderón, with their inserted jácaras and zarabandas, exhibited a seamless continuum and ongoing interaction between lettered and vernacular realms of culture, under the Bourbons a gulf between these milieus intensified. Leading literati such as Friar Feijóo (d. 1764) and Melchor de Jovellanos (d. 1811) promoted Enlightenment ideas that had little resonance among the lower classes. Foreign influence in the fine arts was equally pronounced. The most renowned and influential court musicians in the first half of the century were the Italians Scarlatti and Farinelli (1705–1782). Dance manuals, such as those of Pablo Minguet, were devoted primarily to French-style minuet and *contradanse* and, toward the end of the century, to the bolero, a dainty couple dance constituting a local elite counterpart to French court dances (not to be confused with its Latin American namesake; see Berlanga 2021a; Ivanova 1970, ch. 4). And yet a significant new tendency representing a particular sort of cultural nationalism was emerging from around the 1780s.

Approaching the Nineteenth Century

In the closing decades of the eighteenth century, the fine arts culture of Spain compared rather unfavorably with that of mainstream Europe. In German, French, British, and Dutch dominions, a capitalist revolution was taking place, in which a triumphant bourgeoisie was vigorously erecting gilded concert halls and opera houses as monuments to its own dynamism and creative energy. Beethoven, Schubert, and their cohorts were fashioning a new Romantic musical language to celebrate the unfettering of artistic genius from the traditional dependence on church and feudal patronage. In Spain, however, capitalist development and the growth of a middle class were spotty and limited to a few centers such as Barcelona and Bilbao, and there were no composers to rival those of Vienna or Paris. Such orchestras as existed were devoted to performing Italian operas that dominated concert halls.

And yet if Spain's classical music and dance culture was weak, what it did have was a thriving vernacular music and dance scene, ranging from rowdy song sessions in proletarian pubs to tonadilla and *sainete* music theater featuring *tiranas*, *polos*, and fandangos, often danced *a lo gitano* ("Gypsy-style," whether by actual Gitanos or not). Much Andalusian music, as we have seen, had a particular richness and flavor deriving from Moorish and Afro-Latin inputs centuries earlier—elements that were quite lacking in the ethnically more homogeneous mainstream European countries. And if Spain had fewer pianists and clarinetists per capita than French or German lands, it had a great abundance of guitarists, whether strumming "stable-boys," middle-class amateurs who learned fandangos and zarabandas of Sanz and Murcia, or semiprofessional—and, increasingly, Andalusian Gitano—virtuosos who enlivened taverns, roadside inns, and domestic *bailes de candil* (lamp-lit dances) with their colorful artistry.

From around the 1760s, this vernacular music and dance subculture came to be encouraged, appreciated, and even legitimized by a new spirit of cultural nationalism that took root in both aristocratic and plebian circles. One manifestation of this new sensibility was a costumbrista interest on the part of urban educated classes in regional folk and vernacular culture. A parallel development was the emergence of a colorful urban subculture in Madrid and Andalusian towns, centered on flamboyant lumpen ruffians called *majos*. The majos, imitating the fashions of Andalusian Gitanos, cultivated garish attire, a swaggering and aggressive demeanor, a street argot sprinkled with Caló, and, in their rowdy taverns, histrionic renderings of seguidillas and other popular songs. Their lifestyle and aesthetic were explicitly opposed to those of the genteel elite who aped Parisian fashions, whether in clothes or liberal ideas. As such, though regarded as threatening and uncouth by many, the majos were also celebrated as *castizo* (pure Spanish) by those who resented foreign influence and sought regeneration in a reactionary cultural nationalism.

While it would be inaccurate to speak of "majo music" per se, it is clear that the lumpen subculture of assorted majos, hustlers, vagabonds, and Gitanos was cultivating its own forms of fandangos, seguidillas, tiranas, and other genres, characterized by a flamboyant performance style that educated people regarded either with scorn, fascination, or some admixture of both. In the latter category was the 1799 description of such a song session by folklorist "Don Preciso" (Juan Antonio de la Iza Zamácola, 1756–1826), a nationalistic advocate of castizo music in opposition to Parisian and Italian imports. While praising the lower-class fondness for singing and composing seguidillas, he lamented "the grotesque habit of wrenching the voice off its hinges and the extravagant mania of spouting violent neighs and gurgles." He continued:

> Because who can possibly bear with patience one of these men who, drenched in sweat, tears off his shirt-collar buttons so that he can scream better? Who can tolerate that continuous clacking ("castanetting") of his lower jaw when singing? Who can hear without disgust that furious braying and wailing, in which they pass entire hours? What ears could possibly bear the continuous clanging on a bad guitar, and the atrocious weight of the right hand that slams down on the miserable strings like a mace? (In, e.g., Campo and Cáceres 2013, 257)

While one wishes that "Mr. Precise" had been more precise about what kind of musicians he was portraying, he was evidently describing the sort of flamboyant, hyper-expressive majo singing of seguidillas, tiranas, and the like that would evolve into flamenco. Indeed, his passage reads much like an uncharitable description of a flamenco siguiriyas or bulerías, complete with vigorously strumming guitar and a histrionic vocal delivery. It indicates that late eighteenth-century musicians were bequeathing to the next generation not only a set of distinctive modes, rhythms, harmonies, and song forms but also a colorful performance style, all of which were ripe for elaboration into what would come to be known as flamenco.

The Eve of Flamenco, 1800 to 1860

The years around 1800 may not constitute a dramatic watershed in flamenco prehistory, but in various ways the turn of the nineteenth century did lead to a new era, as the effective predawn glow of flamenco. One development was the steady increase in published and now-accessible historical documentation of all sorts, including musical scores, dance manuals, and assorted descriptions of performances and other related matters. As such, the historian has much more to work with than in earlier centuries, whether in terms of formal aspects of the arts or their sociocultural dimensions. Such documentation enables one to appreciate how several of the music and dance genres emerging and flourishing in the first half of the century are the direct parents, rather than remote ancestors, of the forms that would coalesce under the rubric of "flamenco" in the 1860s.

On the political level, the early decades of the century saw Spain traumatized by yet more chaos and violence. Particularly demoralizing were the British defeat of the navy in 1805, the revolt of South American colonies, and the 1807–1814 war against Napoleon, who ultimately installed yet another ignorant despot, Ferdinand VII, whose misrule (1814–1833) provoked civil war in 1833–1840. One result was a perpetuation of Andalusia's socioeconomic stagnation, in which the domination of reactionary landlords was further entrenched and any progressive thought was rejected as associated with French oppressors. The anti-French reaction intensified the backward-looking celebration of supposed castizo aspects of culture, especially as represented by Andalusian and Gitano arts. As such, while majos were essentially a late eighteenth-century phenomenon, Gitanos largely replaced them as objects of an exoticizing, Romantic interest, as perceived representatives of authentic Spanishness, and also as genuinely creative and dynamic musicians and dancers.

The contrast and, indeed, outright competition between castizo and *afrancesado* (French) cultural fashions was embodied most literally in contemporary dance styles.[20] Representing the Francophilic side of the spectrum were the bolero and other academic *bailes de palillos* (castanet dances) that, as social dances formalized for the stage, came to be retrospectively referred to in the twentieth century as the *escuela bolera* (bolero school). Though distinctively Spanish in some respects—including in features adopted in stylized form from Gitano dancing—these were seen as local answers to French ballet and contradanse, embodying the same spirit of restraint, classicism, and technical perfection. Taught by dance masters and performed as stage items and aristocratic social dances, they were typically dainty couple dances, with much leaping, leg extensions, and posturing on point, accompanied by seguidillas (or *seguidillas boleras*) with their typical ternary "bum-biddy-bum-biddy-bum-bum" rhythm.

Rivalling these genteel dances since the latter 1700s were the various castizo dances, including specific items such as the *cachucha*, *vito*, and *olé*, and others more loosely designated by the ambiguous term "jaleo" (lit., hubbub). These were primarily solo female dances, quintessentially performed as light interludes in popular theater (tonadillas, sainetes) and in other contexts. Unlike the formal bolero, they avoided leaps, on-point dancing, and castanets, instead highlighting the dancer's perceived natural and spontaneous grace and flair, especially as expressed through arm and hand movements (and, in the case of men, zapateo). The musical accompaniment, provided on guitar, voice, and palmas, consisted of popular songs such as tiranas, and *polos*, and other song forms again loosely referred to as jaleo, or *coplas de jaleo*, with a distinctively Andalusian flavor in their hemiola rhythms and "Moorish" modality. Both as music and dance forms, these forms of jaleo were direct forebears of what would coalesce as flamenco in the 1860s.

Andalusian Gitanos soon came to be regarded as the primary exponents of these pre-flamenco "jaleo" idioms, and even items performed by non-Gitanos were likely to be advertised as *jaleos gitanos*, indicating that their style was distinctive, colorful, and now perceived as castizo. As Berlanga (2021) highlights, these "Gypsy-style" jaleos were themselves descendants and perpetuations of the colorful zarabandas and chaconas that Gitana women had been performing for appreciative viewers—whether at outdoor festivals or the homes of nobles—since the sixteenth century. Ironically, while cultural nationalists celebrated these "castizo" arts in reaction against French fashions, these same Gypsy dances were sought out by French audiences and tourists inspired by a Romantic fascination with the exotic. Accordingly, Andalusian escuela bolera academies increasingly adopted more local forms of dance, such as seguidillas and fandangos, to entertain foreign visitors.

From the latter 1700s, Frenchmen, other Europeans, and even Americans such as Washington Irving had come to appreciate how they could visit Andalusia and savor a charming Moorish-inflected ambience, especially in the form of Gitano dance shows. Soon they were writing engaging, impressionistic accounts of their travels and of the colorful Gitano dancing they witnessed. By the early 1800s, such accounts in their turn were generating increasing numbers of tourists who visited Spain eager to see "Gypsy" songs and dances, whether in the caves of Granada or in roadside inns (*ventas*). While the ranks of these tourists may not have constituted a "flood," in a poor country like Spain even modest numbers of affluent visitors could provide a valuable stimulus to a local economy, especially its entertainment sector. And thus a feedback loop thrived, in which Europeans and even Americans avidly read travelers' accounts of Gypsy dance shows and flocked to Andalusian towns to see such presentations. These were dutifully arranged by innkeepers and café owners who booked Gitano troupes who knew how to cater to the tourists—who then went home and wrote more travelers' accounts of what they had seen. For their part, the Gitanos enacted their own feedback loop as they learned to exoticize their presentations and demeanor in response to public demand while internalizing and rearticulating these features in ways that were authentic to their own communities. Meanwhile, accounts also indicate that at many shows, audiences included knowledgeable local connoisseurs as well as naïve tourists, undoubtedly inspiring performers to present items that were at once colorful and artistically rich.

The fare presented at such shows was not called flamenco, and it foregrounded dance rather than singing, accompanied by an ensemble that could include violins, mandolin-like *bandurrias*, and panderetas along with guitar. However, the most popular and sought-out items were the jaleo styles, especially as performed by Gitanos. Many of the songs were popular tiranas, *polos*, or *canciones andaluzas* of contemporary tunesmiths, such as were also performed for purely Spanish audiences in sainetes, *zarzuelas*, and tonadillas. Collectively these genres constituted a fluid socio-musical continuum that linked the stage with the Gitano cave, and the classically trained guitarist with the proverbial strumming stable-boy. Flamenco, indeed, would emerge precisely as a product of such a mixed urban social milieu, resisting classification in any "folk-versus-classical" binary. Also reflective of the diversity of sources from which flamenco would draw is the way that many coplas from zarzuelas, canciones andaluzas, and other genres of this period would later go on to be sung, in different settings, in flamenco (Campo and Cáceres 2013, 395–97).

If tourist accounts of Gitano dance shows during this period tended to be impressionistic and superficial, a more detailed, reliable, and informative description of a Gitano performance was penned by one Serafín Estébanez Calderón ("El Solitario," 1799–1867), a costumbrista folklorist who was well familiar with Andalusian music and dance. In essays published in the 1830s,[21] Estébanez Calderón described his visit to a music and dance session in Triana, Seville's famed Gitano barrio across the Guadalquivir River. In a manner characteristic of future flamenco shows, the entertainment foregrounded cante (singing) as well as dance and featured some named professional singers of renown—especially El Planeta and El Fillo—who would subsequently become known as flamenco artists. The stylized jaleo (here meaning shouts of approval) that their singing elicited and other elements in Estébanez Calderón's account indicate that, as in subsequent flamenco, there was already a strong sense of connoisseurship surrounding the singing. He described the dancing as accompanied by small ensemble of two mandolin-like *bandolines*, bandurrias, and guitar. El Planeta commenced the fiesta by reciting (or singing?) an extended narrative *romance*—evidently unaccompanied[22]—in a style Estébanez Calderón characterized as clearly "morisco" and typical of certain Andalusian villages where Arab traditions had survived. Following the *romance* were various dance and cante items, including tonada, seguidilla, caña, *rondeña*, *polo*, "*pertenera*" (petenera?), and a malagueña rendered, in a distinctively new tune, by a young Gitana singer.

Guitar Music

Estébanez Calderón's account suggests that the guitar had not yet become the basic, sole accompanying instrument for pre-flamenco music and dance. However, a significant development in the early 1800s was the definitive spread and standardization of the six-string guitar configuration, with the low E being added in the 1750s but taking several decades to become standard. Its definitive addition enabled the use of an E Phrygian/A minor tonality in playing fandangos and other songs rather than being limited to the A Phrygian/D minor of the eighteenth century. Among the song-types characterized by this new sonority was the malagueña, as sung in Estébanez Calderón's fiesta. Meanwhile, the elimination of the doubled courses may have reduced the volume of the instrument slightly but greatly enhanced its ability to play punteado passages. With these developments, the guitar was now poised to become an instrument of considerable versatility.

Guitar music of this period exhibited in its own way the fluid continuum between folk and academic realms, such that much of it, like much pre-flamenco music in general, is best characterized by the felicitously ambiguous term "vernacular." Particularly outstanding in this regard was the music of Francisco Rodríguez Murciano, "El Murciano" (1795–1846), a guitarist of Granada who, though illiterate and a tavern keeper by profession, was a well-known musician, much imitated in guitar circles. Though El Murciano did not write or formally compose music, his musically literate son ("Malipieri") produced a few notations of his father's version of rondeñas/malagueñas, and Russian composer Mikhail Glinka, who befriended and studied with El Murciano, penned his own very similar notation of his teacher's rondeñas.[23] Murciano's rendering of this form is essentially cognate with a flamenco-style malagueña, with its lush arpeggios, interspersed *picado* and rasgueado passages, familiar flamenco-sounding falsetas, and even a passage in tremolo, a guitar technique that was until recently assumed not to have been adopted from classical guitar playing until several decades after El Murciano's heyday.[24] Murciano's soloistic music could be regarded, in one way, as a refinement of the customary interludes and ritornellos played in accompanying cante and baile; it could also be seen as perpetuating, on a vernacular level, the classical tradition, associated with Narváez and others, of composing short variations in a given chordal sequence, which would be called "diferencias" in the Baroque era, and "falsetas" in flamenco. Meanwhile, however, little is known of other vernacular guitarists during this pre-flamenco period, and the guitar had not yet assumed its role as the quintessential accompanying instrument, with a distinctive, sophisticated flamenco style.

A notable "lettered" guitarist of the generation after El Murciano was Julián Arcas (1832–1882), a professor, concert artist, and composer more on the classical end of the spectrum. Arcas composed numerous waltzes, preludes, variations, and the like and also wrote arrangements of orchestral works and items from operas and zarzuelas. Of greater interest here, he also composed items inspired by early flamenco, especially his "Soleá" of 1867. Notated in 3/4, it is a concert item rather than a mere stylization of flamenco, but parts of it are easily recognizable as based on contemporary playing. Arcas, in turn, was imitated by flamenco guitarists, illustrating the fluid, mutual exchanges between stage artists and their tavern counterparts (Rioja 2008).

Cantes in Evolution

During this period, the song-types mentioned by Estébanez Calderón and others, and documented in various notations, were a mixture of some, like malagueñas, that would go on to figure prominently in flamenco, and some, like the jaleo, that would evolve into differently named flamenco cantes, and others, such as the bolero, that would not. Still others bore flamenco-sounding names but were unrelated to flamenco namesakes; thus, the *granadinas*/granaínas of Estébanez Calderón's time was probably a 6/8 group dance song, similar to verdiales and unlike the free-rhythmic granaínas of flamenco, and the occasionally encountered "seguidillas gitanas" may have been more akin to the sevillanas couple dance rather than the flamenco siguiriyas. "Jaleo" seems to have denoted a variety of song-types—in various tonalities but most characteristically in a hemiola-laden meter—that would eventually coalesce into soleares, and later bulerías, with the popular caña and *polo* songs, or song-types, being absorbed essentially as soleares variants.

Various musical scores (especially as assembled by Castro Buendía 2014a, I:187–410) indicate that the fandango in this period had largely assumed its modern form, with a guitar ritornello (typically with iv–III–II–I/Am–G–F–E ostinato) punctuating a sung copla section of six lines in the relative major of C, modulating back to E altered Phrygian at the climactic end. Conforming to this format, but with distinctive melodies, guitar falsetas, and a particularly showy vocal style, was the malagueña, which became widely popular from the 1830s, as documented both in Estébanez Calderón's essays and in numerous advertisements, playbills, and other descriptions of concerts. Estébanez Calderón's account reveals, among other things, that the malagueña of his time was appreciated as a vocal item in its own right, rather than as a dance song, and that renowned singers were already popularizing their own distinctive "malagueñas"—that is, original stock tunes that, though newly composed, exhibited recognizable features of the cante.

2

The Café Cantante Period: 1860–1920s

It was in the 1850s–1870s that flamenco as a coherent genre definitively emerged. During this period, literally hundreds of venues presenting flamenco were founded throughout Andalusia and elsewhere. Through the collective creative efforts of dozens of artists—Gitano and non-Gitano—performance conventions and professional standards were established, formal structures of cantes and their accompanying bailes coalesced and became standardized, cante came to be appreciated on its own instead of merely accompaniment to dance, and the new genre came to enjoy a phenomenal level of popularity, among both Spanish connoisseurs and foreign tourists.

The emergence of flamenco at this moment was not a random event but a product of a particular confluence of sociohistorical developments. To some extent these comprised an intensification of early nineteenth-century trends, including a Spanish costumbrista celebration of Andalusian and especially Gitano music and dance, the steady stream of foreign visitors eager to see these performances, and a general spirit of Romanticism that idealized the exotic, the individual, and the "passionate" as antidotes to the alienation induced by modern industry, bureaucracy, and mass culture.

As we have seen, flamenco and its staged performance contexts did not emerge out of a vacuum. Precursors to particular flamenco cantes and dances had long existed and had been performed in professional and amateur contexts by Gitanos and others. Foreigners had been visiting Andalusia since the 1700s, and especially since the 1820s advertisements for dance shows often announced renowned Gitano singers, or *cantaores a lo gitano*—"Gypsy-style singers." From the 1850s, references to "música flamenca" were appearing, which, with other factors, led some flamencologists to argue that the inception of the genre should be dated to those years. Others opine that the proper coalescence of flamenco as an idiom should be dated to the 1860s–1870s, when it became professionalized in the context of the *café cantante*. This sort of venue was typically a medium-size urban club, open to the public, serving food and drinks, and presenting a vaudeville variety show that featured flamenco. Rough counterparts to British music halls and French cabarets, the cafés were attended both by foreign tourists as well as locals of diverse social classes who might be discerning connoisseurs; most allowed only male patrons. They typically offered a mixed fare of music ranging from Italian opera arias, saucy theater songs called *cuplés*, escuela bolera dancing, chamber arrangements of light-classical tunes, and, last but not least, flamenco. The cafés varied in size and character; some were modest venues, but a few could seat as many as a thousand patrons; some were more or less "respectable," but others hosted prostitutes and had back rooms to accommodate them. Meanwhile, flamenco continued to be performed informally in taverns and homes and, among Gitanos, at weddings and baptisms. Professional performers were also regularly hired for private parties, especially *juergas* (sprees) sponsored by *señoritos*—that being the term for an Andalusian landlord playboy, famously lazy, hedonistic, and exploitative, who might or might not be genuinely appreciative of flamenco and its performers. Collectively, these different contexts sufficed to sustain and nourish the emerging art. As Timothy Mitchell summarized, "As talented professionals perfect[ed] the flamenco guitar accompaniment and musical nationalism [did] away with the last vestiges of Italianate influences, flamenco found itself entering what came to be known commonly as its golden age" (1994, 125).

While the café cantante phenomenon and the general rise of flamenco were precipitated by the broad historical developments outlined above, a key role was played by a singular individual, one Silverio Franconetti (1831?–1889), born in Seville to an Italian immigrant father. From his youth, Silverio, though not a Gitano, immersed himself in the pre-flamenco, primarily Gitano milieu of taverns and fiestas in Morón, where he grew up, and then in Seville and Madrid, learning the incipient forms of siguiriyas and other cantes from legendary singers such as El Fillo, and earning some renown as a *cantaor* (flamenco singer, as opposed to a *cantante*—that is, a singer of other genres). At the age of twenty-five he relocated to South America, and upon returning in 1864, he immediately reestablished his reputation as a fine singer of siguiriyas and other early flamenco forms. Evidently inspired by both an entrepreneurial spirit and a wish to bring the "cante gitano" he loved to a broader audience, he became manager of a Seville café cantante in 1871 and established his own "Café de Silverio" in 1881. Meanwhile he continued to perform in these and other venues while energetically promoting other contemporary artists, including, in his later years, the young Antonio Chacón. His café became the model for the others that proliferated throughout much of the country.

In oral and subsequently written histories, Silverio is regarded as the founding father of flamenco per se. His acquaintance and chronicler Antonio Machado, discussed below, wrote, not unproblematically, "Silverio, in ennobling cante gitano . . . has created the genre of flamenco, mixing Gitano and Andalusian elements." Silverio was himself, by all accounts, a gifted singer and the creator of styles of siguiriyas—and their lyrics—that were transmitted to the next generations by his many followers. He was versatile and "complete," singing not only the Gitano-associated cantes but also broader Andalusian forms like malagueñas, all of which he integrated into a stylistically cohesive genre of "flamenco"—a term that he resisted as faddish.

"Flamenco," indeed, has continued to be a problematic term, denoting a genre whose boundaries are continually contested and whose etymology remains a perpetual enigma, despite the earnest investigations of scholars.[1] The original and primary meaning of "flamenco" is "Flemish," pertaining to the "Low Country" of Flanders, which was in fact ruled by the Spanish Habsburg dynasty for some two centuries until the late 1600s. Some writers have attempted to link flamenco to this connection, involving Flemish riffraff who mingled with Gitanos in Seville and Cádiz, or to Gitano families that served in Spanish armies and henceforth supposedly called themselves "flamencos" (Peña Fernández 2013, 51). The problem with these theories is that there is no documentation of the word being used in relation to Gitanos until the 1830s,[2] by which time the Flemish connection was ancient history.

What is documented is that from that decade "flamenco" had started to be used as a rough synonym for "Gitano" or, more properly, for the urban Andalusian subculture of Gitanos and other lumpen marginals. Various contemporary writers commented on the novelty of this usage. It might have derived from a Flemish jackknife called "flamenco" that was popular throughout much of Europe, including among Andalusian underworld ruffians. In other contexts the word could connote flaming, flamboyant, swaggering, or a "tough guy." Ultimately, however, the etymology of the word, like that of many slang terms, is uncertain and may ever remain so. Further, its precise origins may not be as important as the way it came to be used, for whatever reason, from the 1840s to the 1850s as denoting a "Gypsyesque" (*gitanesco*) subculture of performers, poets, and assorted bohemians centered on taverns, fiestas, and flamboyant, hyper-expressive forms of music and dance (like those of the eighteenth-century majos). Its usage in reference to the latter proceeded from adjectival to nominative—that is, for example, from 1840s references to "cante/canto flamenco," meaning "flamenco song" or "Gitano-style song," then, from around 1870, to merely "flamenco."[3]

The café cantante period also saw the first scholarly writings on flamenco, especially the 1881 anthology of flamenco lyrics titled *Colección de cantes fla-*

mencos, by Antonio Machado y Álvarez, or "Demófilo."[4] Machado was an academically trained folklorist who immersed himself in Seville's flamenco scene, befriending Silverio and a few other artists. His annotated compilation of around a thousand flamenco verses—many of which are still sung—is a landmark work, and the prologue (of about ten pages) would constitute the first attempt at a scholarly discussion of flamenco. Given the paucity of other contemporary writings, it is a basic resource for flamenco historians, and it also articulated certain interpretations that became paradigmatic in the thought of many intellectuals in subsequent generations. These ideas included dichotomies between Gitano and non-Gitano styles and forms, and between the "pure" and originary "cante gitano" of taverns and family reunions, as opposed to the mixed, "gacho-ized" (*gachó* meaning non-Gitano) fare called "flamenco" presented in the cafés cantantes. As we will discuss, modern flamencologists question the validity of these dualities and believe that Machado, despite his firsthand engagement with the flamenco scene, may not have known it intimately and was confused by the Romantic, racially essentialist ideas current in his time. Prominent among these in Spanish intellectual circles were the thoughts of the otherwise minor German philosopher Karl C. F. Krause (1781–1832).

A contemporary and somewhat contrasting study of flamenco lyrics was also undertaken by German linguist Hugo Schuchardt (1842–1927), who spent nine months in Spain, befriending Machado and conducting his own research on flamenco lyrics, primarily with an interest in assessing their linguistic relation to Spanish popular poetry in general. Although lacking Machado's deep engagement with flamenco and having little to say about flamenco as music (or dance), he brought a more dispassionate scholarly approach to bear. Most notably, he stressed that much of the poetry that Demófilo regarded as deeply Gitano in origin and character was better seen as a "gitanesco" category of Spanish poetry in general, often penned by non-Gitano poets. (Schuchardt published his study in German in 1881 and then evidently lost interest in the subject, such that it was not translated into Spanish until 1990.) Thus, if Demófilo saw cante jondo and flamenco poetry as emerging from hermetic Gitanos and then becoming "Andalusianized," Schuchardt regarded flamenco coplas essentially as Gitano-inflected Andalusian verse. Schuchardt's perspective may have been to some extent more accurate, but he linked it not only to a belief in the Gitanos' "lack of poetic talent" but also more broadly to a racist stereotype that Gypsies everywhere are incapable of creating anything but instead parasitically assimilate, borrow, or steal material from their host cultures (see Llano 2018, ch. 3).

By the decades around 1900, flamenco had become a sophisticated pan-regional genre, flourishing primarily in the towns of Andalusia and neighboring Extremadura and Murcia and in Madrid. One may generalize that it

Figure 2. Gitana dancing in tavern (Gustave Doré, 1874)

was performed in two interrelated contexts: professional and "domestic." The professional contexts comprised the public cafés cantantes along with private parties or other events sponsored by paying patrons. In certain towns, café cantante audiences would include handfuls of well-to-do tourists, but in most cases these would be outnumbered by local Spanish enthusiasts, who would also constitute patrons of private juergas. Meanwhile, flamenco was avidly performed as domestic fiesta music and dance in many communities, especially

Figure 3. Performers in a café cantante, 1880s

Gitano families. The two contexts could differ in character and, to some extent, in repertoire and personnel. The domestic fiesta, for example, might feature various "aunties" who were skilled singers and dancers but who would never perform professionally on a stage (often because their menfolk would not allow it). Conversely, stage shows might feature choreographed dance routines that would be unlikely to be reproduced at a party. Nevertheless, in other respects the two contexts were closely connected, nourishing each other. The domestic reunions were the cradles of professional performers, who then continued to enrich the family parties even while performing on stage. Songs, tunes, and dance moves would originate both among professionals competing for renown and among communities in a quintessential oral-tradition fashion and then circulate between milieus and regions.

In this same period, commercial recordings began to have an impact on the scene. Recording technology came early to Spain, and to flamenco, in the form of wax cylinders commercially marketed by Zonophone from 1896, featuring such vocalists as Juan Breva and Antonio Chacón. These were unique, non-reproducible recordings, such that a singer would typically perform facing four or five recording machines. Thousands of these cylinders were marketed, almost all of which are lost, but, fortunately, most of the singers featured on them also recorded on the shellac discs that entered the market in 1898, many of which survive. Some singers refused to record for fear of undercutting demand for their live performances, but others recognized how records would enhance rather than undermine their popularity and demand. The record business also both reflected and promoted a demand for novelty, in the form of new styles and items that sold reasonably well and were imitated by singers trying to keep up to date. Many performers clearly felt ill at ease in the makeshift recording studio setting, but a few adapted well, such as El Mochuelo (Antonio Pozo, 1868–1937), who exploited the new medium with much energy and flair (though later dying in poverty; see Gamboa 2004, 387–91).

Most recordings in the early decades featured the lighter cantes such as malagueñas, tangos, *tientos*, *farruca*, and *garrotín*. Many of these recordings sound a bit quaint and dated to the modern ear. The pacing is rather nervous and rushed, the guitar playing a bit repetitive, the *compás* (meter) sometimes irregular, and the guitarist and singer are occasionally out of sync, missing each other's cues. Meanwhile, the cante titles are often inconsistent with other contemporary as well as modern usages, especially regarding malagueñas, tarantas, and *cartageneras*.

The Yin and the Yang: Antonio Chacón and Manuel Torre

Flamenco history books covering the late nineteenth century abound with names of revered legendary singers, most of whom will remain legendary in the sense that they neither recorded nor gave interviews, nor were they otherwise properly documented. However, particularly outstanding in the generation after Silverio were two performers living until the 1920s whose lives and music were reasonably well documented and whose artistic personalities and contributions represent dramatically contrasting and complementary archetypes among flamenco personages—a veritable yin and yang, in the words of flamencologist José Manuel Gamboa (2004, 317).

Antonio Chacón is one of the three or four most important figures in the history of flamenco. Born in the flamenco crucible of Jerez, although a non-Gitano, from his youth he immersed himself in the town's flamenco scene and from his adolescence was singing semiprofessionally. At the age of fifteen he, guitarist Javier Molina, and a dancer undertook an extended trip through the length and breadth of Andalusia, during which they supported themselves by performing, and Chacón assiduously learned everything he could about regional song styles and repertoires. Through this trip, along with a subsequent contract of several months at Silverio's café and his own acquisitive efforts, Chacón developed an encyclopedic knowledge and command of contemporary cante forms. He spent the rest of his years singing—mostly at private events—throughout Andalusia and in Madrid, contributing much to the consolidation of flamenco in that city. He earned well and also lived well, such that he died in relative poverty, but without regrets or complaints. In 1898–1899 he recorded a few thousand non-reproducible cylinders, a few of which survive, along with sets of 78 rpm recordings made in 1909 and 1928. Although he was dismissive of the quality of these, they indicate the general nature of his singing, aside from being of historical interest.

In published interviews Chacón lamented the decline of what he called "cante gitano" (especially soleares and siguiriyas) in favor of the lighter fandango forms and especially the malagueñas (Martín Ballester et al. 2016, 76). Chacón was aware that he himself had contributed to this trend, favoring this repertoire in his own music, in accordance with market incentives and also perhaps an awareness that his sweet, high tenor voice and general style were more suited to these cantes than to the pathos-laden cante jondo styles. (Later purist detractors would accuse him of paving the way for the crooning style of Pepe Marchena that came to dominate in the 1930s.) Chacón's greatest legacy was his compositions and his transformations of regional wildflowers into refined cantes; aside from composing six *estilos* (stock tunes) of malagueñas, he appears to have effectively created the forms of granaínas (and media granaína), cartageneras, and several estilos of tarantas, all of which are basic entities in the flamenco repertoire.

The yang to Chacón's yin was represented by his contemporary, Gitano singer Manuel Torre (or Torres; Manuel Soto Leitón, 1878–1933). As a cantaor, Chacón could be said to represent a certain sort of non-Gitano archetype—urbane, literate, reliable as a singer, and responsible in his personal life. Torre, by contrast, personified a different stereotype—that of the impulsive, mercurial, bohemian Gypsy, illiterate and indifferent to wealth or fame but capable of singing with such expressivity that listeners were known to weep, tear their shirts, crush wine glasses in their hands, overturn tables, and even jump out of ground-floor windows (which, as related in various anecdotes, appears to have been one form of expressing aesthetic rapture). Torre was famously feckless with money, turning down lucrative invitations if he wasn't in the mood and squandering his earnings on pet hounds, fighting cocks, and pocket watches, spending so much that he died penniless with five children living in a shack. And yet he was celebrated for singing—when "duende" (ineffable inspiration) struck—with a power and pathos that surpassed even Chacón, who, ever the gentleman, praised and on occasion even supported him.[5]

Figure 4a. Silverio Franconetti

Figure 4b. Antonio Chacón

Figure 4c. Pepe Marchena (© alamy.com)

Figure 4d. Antonio Mairena (© alamy.com)

The Evolution of Cantes

It is during the café cantante period that most of the flamenco cantes assumed their modern forms. As we shall discuss, the cantes vary not only in form but also in the nature of their evolutions. Some, like certain forms of fandango, can be seen as roughly documentable products of a long, continuous development, culminating in the emergence of an *aflamencado* ("flamenco-ized") style. By contrast, characteristic melodies and guitar styles of other fandango variants—such as some tarantas—appear largely as original creations of particular musicians, such as Chacón and guitarist Ramón Montoya. Other cantes—especially *guajiras* and *peteneras*—constitute transformations of Latin American genres that, like the malagueñas, had become soloistic stage songs before being "flamenco-ized." Some, including the caña and *polo*, were broadly popular eighteenth- and nineteenth-century song and dance forms with stock tunes, performed in a continuum of styles and contexts that ranged from dainty salon pieces to *agitanado* ("Gypsy-style") solo renditions that were commonly perceived as "Moorish." And the evolution of still others—especially soleares and siguiriyas—remains enigmatic, inspiring a variety of theories, some more plausible than others. As discussed in greater depth below, one controversial approach has been the "hermetic theory," according to which these cantes—which do not have obvious counterparts in Spanish traditional music aside from flamenco—evolved in private Gitano contexts before surfacing in cafés cantantes. Opposing this would be the argument that these cantes did not exist as such until the processes of professionalization and elaboration precipitated by the café cantante phenomenon, however nourished by ongoing performance in Gitano milieus.

Fortunately, the café cantante period offers more sources to the historian than do earlier periods, allowing more extensive and rigorous studies, the most magisterial of which is Castro Buendía's two-volume set (2014a). The brief survey presented here draws heavily on this and other studies while offering its own perspectives and interpretations. The historical resources are of various kinds. One set comprises miscellaneous prose accounts, including those in newspapers, theatrical works, or the accounts of travelers or costumbrista writers. Another group consists of published notations of pieces, which, as in previous eras, are mostly "academic" compositions or settings of vernacular genres that may afford some indirect indications as to the form of the latter. A third set of sources comprises oral traditions, some of which may be quite unreliable but others reasonably credible, as in the case of early twentieth-century recordings of certain styles of cante that, according to their exponents, were created by elder acquaintances such as Silverio, Enrique el Mellizo (1848–1906), or Paquirri (Francisco Guanter Espinal, 1834–1862). For example, Antonio

Chacón and El Tenazas de Morón (1850–1933) are among the several singers who learned Silverio's cante directly from him and transmitted it, via recordings and performances, to subsequent generations. Antonio Mairena, in his grand "salvaging" project of the 1960s, gathered, renovated as needed, and recorded a great number of cante jondo estilos that he attributed, relying on oral traditions of varying degrees of reliability, to various Gitano singers dating back to the 1850s. And, finally, there are the abundant recordings themselves, starting from the years around 1900, which provide an incomparably richer historical resource but nevertheless fail to answer some basic questions about the early twentieth-century evolution of some forms, such as bulerías.

While specific cantes can be seen to have followed their particular historical trajectories, a few general features of flamenco evolution during this period can be noted. Among these are a consolidation of altered Phrygian tonality and its application or extension to certain extant song-types, such as jaleo and tangos. Guitar accompaniment in these cantes features a more-or-less static oscillation between I and II♭ chords, perhaps an ascent to iv, decorative iv–III–II–I Andalusian cadences, and a climactic "cambio" consisting of a brief III7–VI move to the relative major, and then a II♭–I return to the tonic. A related development is the dramatically enriched guitar playing and the close evolution of certain cantes, such as granaínas and tarantas, in tandem with specific guitar tonalities and repertoires of falsetas and accompaniment patterns.

A particularly important and basic development was the consolidation of the uniquely flamenco syncopated twelve-beat compás used in soleares, *alegrías*, and—in a distinctive form—bulerías. In a crudely schematic form, this compás (which is discussed in more depth in chapter 5) can be seen as a 3+3+2+2+2 hemiola pattern, with strong accents on beats three, six, eight, and ten and, in particular (when guitar is present), a typical pattern of moving to the dominant (whether Phrygian or major-key) on beat three and returning to the tonic on ten. As mentioned earlier, elements of this structure, and occasional passing similar passages, can be found in much older genres, such as the jácara. There is also a clear affinity to the Caribbean-derived "I like to be in Ame-ri-ca" hemiola, which, as noted earlier, had been manifested quite clearly in such Spanish genres as the seventeenth-century zarabanda. However, the particular structure of the flamenco compás, with its strong three-ten axis, does not appear to have taken shape as a basic chordal and rhythmic ostinato until the years around 1900. Furthermore, throughout the next several decades, many otherwise competent professional singers, especially in towns where guitar accompaniment was not customary, did not follow compás closely, or did so in an intuitive and approximate manner, and were even unaware of its beat counts. The presence of a guitarist and the format of performing on stage with dancers were crucial in standardizing the compás in these cantes.[6]

The basic melodic structures of the core of serious cante jondo forms—soleares, siguiriyas, and the a capella cantes of toná, martinete, *carcelera*, and *debla*—may have derived from a body of modal folk songs, including work songs (e.g., of threshing and sowing), lullabies (*nanas*), folk renderings of coplas (short verse stanzas), and recitative-like renderings of *romances*, or fragments thereof, in stock tunes. While the relation to rural folk song is unclear, some circumstantial evidence supports it. As Castro Buendía (2010) has shown, some rural Andalusian work songs and *romances* bear remarkable similarities to martinetes and other cantes in their use of melismas, Phrygian mode, and melodic contours. Gerald Brenan (1957, 108–109), writing of his years in the 1920s spent in a town in the Alpujarras Mountains south of Granada, describes the tremendous popularity of singing coplas, often in a flamenco-tinged style. This folk copla singing tradition largely died out with the advent of the mass media, but in flamenco contexts it was elaborated, standardized, and professionalized. Lefranc (2000, 42–47) notes how Gitano mothers sang fragments of *romances* as nanas, using modal melodic forms quite similar to those of soleares and siguiriyas, especially with an initial phrase, with a large range, repeated and then followed by another with smaller range. In professional contexts, Gitanos were known for their colorful rendering of *romances*, as documented in sources from Cervantes's "La gitanilla" (1611) to Estébanez Calderón's "A Night in Triana" (1830s). The link to soleares is explicit in the tradition of commencing a soleá with a *romance* fragment, as did seminal cantaora La Serneta (d. 1912; see Lefranc 2000, 44); alternately, *romance* passages could be rendered independently as flamenco items, in which case they would be called *corridas*. (It is particularly common to insert *romance* passages in Lebrija bulerías, which could accordingly be called *bulerías romanceadas*.) In the café cantante period, such tunes may have been extensively adapted to professional performance contexts, providing melodic models for flamenco cantes with the addition of plaintive lyrics, a melismatic, dramatic, "orientalized" vocal style, regular twelve-beat compás, and in the case of siguiriyas, a strongly modal (rather than harmonic) guitar accompaniment style. Similar processes presumably informed the "flamencoization" of the *saeta*, a traditional, unaccompanied solo song form associated with Holy Week processions.

However, the roles that Gitano, "morisco" versions of these recitative-like songs played in the evolution of siguiriyas and soleares remain ambiguous and raise perennial and unresolved questions about whether the process is best seen as one of "Andalusianization" or "Gypsification." That is, are soleares and siguiriyas best seen as fundamentally Andalusian genres (jaleos, *playeras*, *romances*) that were "orientalized" by Gitanos in the café cantante context in response to audience tastes? Or is it more accurate to regard them as evolving from distinctively Gitano ("morisco") versions of these ancestors (whether in public or private), that were then "Andalusianized" (adding guitar and chordal harmonies) for presentation in the cafes? We shall return to this question later but will not resolve it definitively. What can be plausibly asserted, on a general level, is that flamenco in its formal aspects can be seen as emerging from the confluence of three elements: modal, melismatic, recitative-like folk-song styles; distinctive twelve-beat hemiola meters informed by Caribbean music; and altered Phrygian chordal harmonies played on the guitar, featuring especially the iv–III–II–I Andalusian cadence (see Torres 2004, 29).

All of these processes are manifest in the evolution of soleares, insofar as it can be plausibly reconstructed. Soleares is perhaps the single most basic flamenco cante and is spoken of as the "mother" of all cantes, although it does not appear to have taken shape until the café cantante period and after such genres as the fandango and even the imported guajiras. As Castro Buendía, Berlanga (2020b), and others have noted, there is a clear evolutionary link to the earlier nineteenth-century, ternary-metered song and dance forms loosely called jaleo. It appears that a lachrymose and serious version of jaleo came to be called soleares, while incorporating some elements of the *polo* and petenera song forms, as well as Gitano versions of *romance* fragments. References to a dance form "soleá" appear from 1850 and as a song form ("*soledad*") from the following year, and by the 1860s soleares was being routinely performed as a flamenco item by professionals such as La Andonda and El Planeta (1789–1857), a singer regarded as the first flamenco cantaor per se and whose performance was described in Estébanez Calderón's 1830s essays. Oral traditions trace several specific soleá melodies to these singers, in a situation where professional vocalists needed to amplify the repertoire beyond whatever simple tunes were sung in the taverns and Gitano homes (Lefranc 2000, 143). In 1874 Eduardo Ocón published a "Soledad" using what we recognize as a very typical soleá estilo (p. 89). Notations of stylized instrumental versions of soleares also exist in the form of a few salon guitar pieces, such as Arcas's aforementioned 1867 "Soleá." Some actual soleares falsetas from the café cantante period—especially by "Maestro" Patiño (José González, 1829–1902, see ex. 4.7)—were transmitted and became basic items in the flamenco guitar repertoire (especially as taught to beginning students). Then, from the late 1890s with recordings by El Mochuelo, Chacón, and others, soleares at last emerged into historical daylight.

The inability to trace the particular melodic structures of soleares to earlier nineteenth-century forms has led some to argue for its "hermetic" evolution among private Gitano contexts, whence it was adapted (bowdlerized?) in the cafés cantantes. This argument will be discussed below, but at this point it may be relevant to note that the distinctive soleares compás does not appear to have become standardized until the early 1900s. Earlier versions—whether the falsetas of Patiño or the 1908 recordings of Manuel Torre—suggest a more standard 6/4 meter than the syncopated compás that would become intrinsic to the form. Most of the early recordings are also faster than modern counterparts, suggesting a cante that had not fully liberated itself from accompanying dance; finally, they often oscillate, in por medio tonality, between Dm and A (Re and La) in a manner reminiscent of the eighteenth-century fandango (Torres 2018, 204). That is, some aspects of the form clearly evolved during the early twentieth-century decades—in the later café cantante period.

The other main cante associated with Gitano origins and cultivation is siguiriya. Like soleares, its evolution is poorly documented, as it lacks clear counterparts in any form of music outside of flamenco, including theatrical or salon genres that might have been notated by composers or folklorists. The term would be an Andalusian variant of "seguidillas," which denotes a venerable verse form (typically four lines, of seven, five, seven, and five syllables, with *abcb* rhyme, often followed by a three-line *estribillo*, or refrain) and, historically, a great variety of styles in which it could be rendered, often with dance.

The most significant predecessors, and possible forebears, of the siguiriya were the *endecha*, a plaintive song form dating as far back as the fifteenth century, and, more directly, the playera. Like the jaleo, the playera seems to have existed in various forms, including a festive danced form, with guitar, which Charles Dembowski saw performed by some Gitanos in Cádiz and Málaga in the 1830s (1841, 249–52); "playera," indeed, could imply any merry song sung at the beach. However, tragic playeras may have become more characteristic, especially the weepy *plañidera* songs intoned by hired mourners at funerals (*plañir*, to wail). The term "playera," denoting stylized versions of these, especially as sung by Gitanos, became essentially synonymous with "siguiriya" by the 1870s, after which the latter term became more common. However, much remains unclear about the musical form of the earlier playera, or its relation to siguiriya, and the latter should not simply be regarded as a flamenco version of some Andalusian folk-song genre. Melancholy playeras were being accompanied by guitar from as early as 1816 (Castro Buendía 2014a, II:896), and an 1852 description (by Belgian visitor François Gevaert in 1852, in Castro Buendía 2014a, II:902) of Gitanos performing them in "Arab" or "arabesque" style, "in a tonality unrelated to our major and minor," strongly suggests flamenco Phrygian modality. Indeed, altered Phrygian tonality was well established in these genres, as exhibited in an endecha of 1552 and a "*plañera*" of 1820. An academic "seguidilla gitana" by Ramón Sezac, penned for piano and voice in 1882, reveals a formal structure that is essentially cognate with the modern siguiriyas (Castro Buendía 2014a, II:943–45, 1020–1021, 958–59). Steingress (1991, 105–107) argues for the importance of the Franciscan saeta as a vehicle for the transmission of archaic modal features, especially into the evolution of the siguiriyas; however, this revived version of the "Byzantine thesis," though not implausible, must remain hypothetical.

Early recordings of siguiriyas, for example, by Manuel Torre, are considerably faster and more rhythmic than the mature style, which is rendered in a languid, highly rubato manner. The fact that Silverio Franconetti often sang this cante accompanied by two guitarists (rather than one) also suggests a more rhythmic approach in his era (Torres 2018, 200). Meanwhile, much of the definitive coalescence of the cante can be attributed to known or legendary individuals, especially late nineteenth-century Gitanos Loco Mateo, Diego El Marrurro, Curro (Manuel) Molina, and El Nitri (Tomás de Vargas Suárez). Gitano oral traditions claim to trace some siguiriya forms back to the 1840s, as sung by El Planeta, El Fillo, and others. In subsequent decades, Silverio adapted the styles he learned from El Fillo and other Gitano elders into standardized melodies, which were perpetuated by his followers. Almost all of the estilos were created in Cádiz, the neighboring towns (collectively called "Los Puertos"), Jerez, or Triana in the latter nineteenth or early twentieth centuries.

Alegrías, another basic flamenco cante, evolved in a more transparent fashion than siguiriyas or soleares. From the 1850s, advertisements and other publications were mentioning the *cantiña* (a related form) and *canto alegre*, and by the late 1870s the term "alegrías" had become standardized. As Castro Buendía (2014a, II:1209–1330) and others have documented, its main forebear was the jota, a lively, ternary-metered folk dance and song genre that was popular in varied forms throughout much of Spain but especially in Aragón. The port town of Cádiz had long hosted a uniquely diverse population of migrants, sailors, merchants, and others from all regions of the peninsula (as well as a substantial Gitano community), such that the jota found fertile soil in the city's proverbially festive and merry ambience. Musically, the main development in the consolidation of alegrías was the setting of simple, singsongy tunes borrowed from the jota and other genres (such as the jaleo) to the distinctive twelve-beat compás of the soleares, with its typical axial move to the dominant on beat three and return to the tonic on or before beat ten. Enrique el Mellizo of Cádiz is believed to have been the most important figure in the creation and coalescence of the cante. Set in major-key tonality, the cante has no particular "Moorish" flavor.

Given the popularity of bulerías and its centrality in the flamenco repertoire since the 1970s, it is surprising that this cante did not definitively evolve until the 1920s–1930s. Variants of the word (e.g., "*burlería*"—joking, mocking, frivolity, etc.) date back to the seventeenth century, and in the late 1800s references appear to a festive form of "*baile de bulerías*." (A rival etymology traces the word to "bolero," from *voler* [to fly].) Recordings of bulerías, designated thusly, or by the vague term "*chuflas*" (meaning anything frivolous or humorous), were made from 1908 to 1909 (especially by the young Niña de los Peines [Pastora Pavón] with guitarist Ramón Montoya), but these reveal a genre still in formation, lacking the strong axis of beats three (II♭ chord) and ten (tonic I) and an uncertain shifting between Phrygian and major tonalities. Accounts from elders indicate that the cante and its rhythm were in fact little known until the late 1920s (Rossy 1966, 186), when it started to be recorded in recognizably modern form by cantaores such as Pavón and Niño Gloria (Rafael Ramos Antúnez, 1893–1954). Even during that period, singers like Manuel Vallejo regarded it as a light cante suitable only for dance or for aflamencado adaptations of popular songs such as "María de la O."

Flamencologists opine that bulerías emerged from at least two sources. The bulerías de Cádiz—usually in a major key—probably developed from the tangos (*tanguillos*) of Cádiz Carnaval (Moore 2012), with much input from the jota and the hemiola-based guajira. The more common Phrygian-key bulerías probably emerged from the closing, accelerated *remate* (finishing off) of soleares, though its guitar rasgueado, especially in early versions, shows affinities with the abandolao-style fandango (discussed below). The bulerías compás can be seen as a variant of that of soleares, and many bulerías estilos are simply accelerated soleares ones, retaining even the climactic chordal cambio in the penultimate verse line. However, bulerías as a cante is not simply an accelerated soleá. As discussed in chapter 5, it has acquired its own rich repertoire of estilos and guitar falsetas, its rhythms are more varied, and its compás—with its distinctive "kick" on beat twelve—has quite a different flavor from that of soleares, even while sharing the three-ten dominant-tonic axis. Meanwhile, its syncopated fast twelve-beat meter bears striking resemblance to some versions of Amazigh Moroccan vernacular music, and a historical connection between these two rhythms, dating to the Moorish period, cannot be ruled out.

The café cantante period also saw the coalescence of a diverse set of cantes that evolved as adaptations of song-types imported from Latin America. These were variously brought to the peninsula by music theater groups traversing the Atlantic, or returning Spanish soldiers, or by miscellaneous individuals who spent time in the Americas and returned to Spain. These song-types are designated cantes of *ida y vuelta*—that is, the "round-trip" of originally Hispanic entities that were creolized with some Afro-Latin flavor in the Americas and then returned to Spain, where they were flamencoized. In the process of being adapted to Andalusian music and flamenco—especially in its florid vocal style and general refinement—they underwent considerable modification, becoming quite distinct from their Latin American ancestors. As Estébanez Calderón wrote in 1831, "It's pointless to say that new songs and dances, however originally delightful and lascivious, arrive at Cádiz from the Indies; for they never take root unless, in passing through Seville, they leave as foul sediment all that is too crude" (1984, 15). Faustino Núñez, in his book *América en el flamenco* (2021), persuasively argues that almost all flamenco belongs in the ida y vuelta category in the pervasiveness of features, especially hemiola, chordal ostinatos, and rasgueado patterns, that came from Latin America or at least evolved in connection with it. Nevertheless, some cantes certainly exhibit more overt Latin American flavor than others.

The tango is a festive, Gitano-associated cante that, though customarily placed in the "ida y vuelta" category, became so thoroughly flamenco in form and style that it retains little Latin American character. Its evolution is both recent and obscure. The etymology itself of the word is less than certain and could conceivably be traced to the Latinate Spanish *tangir* (to play, touch; first-person present indicative: *tango*), and various similar words. However, the term as denoting a musical genre is more plausibly traced to the Afro-Cuban word "tango," which was used in nineteenth-century Cuba to denote various rowdy Afro-Cuban processions or music festivities. Esteban Pichardo's 1836 dictionary of Cuban Spanish defined it as "a gathering of bozal [as opposed to creolized] negros to dance to drums and other instruments." Cuban musicologists have traditionally referred to the rhythmic cell of the *habanera* and *contradanza* (*one*-and-two-*and-three*-and-*four*-and) as the *ritmo de tango*, although the term "tango" does not appear to have denoted any specific traditional music genre in Cuba (as it would come to do in Argentina and Spain).

From 1779, references to songs called "tango," "tango americano," or "tango negro" started appearing in Spain, especially in the context of light music theater (tonadilla, sainete, and zarzuela). The true popularity of the Spanish tango dates from the 1850s, when it became common in such theater shows. Most of these that were notated were stage songs modeled loosely on the Cuban contradanza or habanera, with its characteristic "ritmo de tango," which became, for theater-song purposes, a sort of quaint icon of Afro-Cuban music. The custom of calling these songs "tangos" may have derived from any number of sources; Molina and Espín (1992, 66) note that Cádiz Carnival troupes routinely adopted costumbrista themes, including fanciful versions of Afro-Cuban processional songs, such as might have given birth not only to the "tangos" still pervading that town's Carnival but also to other festive, Cuban-tinged songs and dances in duple meter. Rafael Marín wrote in 1902, "Madrid has tango fever; day and night, at all hours, one hears nothing else sung, and not twenty-four hours will pass before there is some alteration" (178). Various such popular songs, as well as other miscellaneous songs from other regions (such as the cantes of El Piyayo) became established estilos—that is, stock tunes to which new or old verses could be set. Early recordings of tangos often used a halting, triplet-laden rhythm of the Cádiz *tanguillo* rather than the loping, foot-tapping modern tango beat,[7] and the cante did not really assume its modern form until the 1940s–1950s, perhaps with some enrichment from the Granada zambra songs that were easily adapted to tango rhythm. Both tango and tanguillo rhythms are quite different from that of the zarzuela tango, as well as its direct ancestor, the Cuban contradanza. The tientos that emerged around the turn of the century, especially as popularized by El Mochuelo, exhibited a decelerated form of this tanguillos rhythm while sharing its core melodies with the flamenco tangos of Cádiz.

The flamenco-style tango that evidently emerged during this period—possibly through the innovations of El Mellizo—was quite different in form from any precedent in Cuba or the Spanish zarzuela. First, the tango adopted flamenco's characteristic altered Phrygian tonality (typically in A, "por medio"), with a soleares-like oscillation between tonic A and Phrygian dominant B♭ chords, leading to subsequent verse lines sung over an ascent to iv (Dm) and a descent to the tonic via an Andalusian cadence (and/or C7–F "cambio"). This development might have constituted an instance of the "orientalizing" process mentioned earlier, in which performers (especially Gitanos) responded to a contemporary Romantic fondness for a music that was exotic and "Moorish"-sounding. Second, the flamenco tango acquired a typical rhythm—comprising both a rasgueado pattern and palmas—that is, again, quite distinct from any Cuban or zarzuela-style precedent. And, finally, it came to feature some stock melodies that have nothing in common with any Cuban counterparts.[8] Accordingly, Antonio Mairena and Ricardo Molina (1979, 228) claim a distinctly Gitano origin for the tangos (along with soleares, siguiriyas, and other cante jondo), arguing, in effect, that the flamenco tango is an adaptation of a deep Gitano genre rather than a Gypsified version of an existing Spanish/Cuban form. However, they offer no particular supporting evidence for their argument. Given such ambiguities, tangos are only problematically grouped within the category of *cantes de ida y vuelta*.[9]

One cante that fits into this "round-trip" family far more clearly than tangos is guajiras. The primary source for this cante is the Cuban genre known as punto (or *punto cubano*). Although the term "punto" (from *puntear* [to pluck]) originally referred to lute technique, in nineteenth-century Cuba it came to denote the styles of rendering precomposed or improvised verses, accompanied primarily by stringed instruments such as *laúd* or bandurria. The primarily Hispanic origins of the punto are overt in the use of these instruments, the genre's association primarily with white or mulatto farmers—called *guajiros* in Cuba—and the predominance of the *décima* verse form. The latter, in its characteristic *espinela* form, consists of ten octosyllabic lines in the form *abbaaccddc*. Although created in Spain (by poet Vicente Espinel, 1550–1624) and popular in the sixteenth and seventeenth centuries there, the form subsequently all but died out in the peninsula but went on to be widely cultivated in Latin America, especially Cuba and Puerto Rico, where it became a vehicle for both lettered poets as well as rustic guajiros. In western Cuba, its sung versions became the main genre of *música guajira*, quintessentially in the *punto libre* form, in which a poet-singer intones verse sections (whether precomposed or improvised) to a simple stock tune, in free rhythm, that are punctuated by ritornellos in which the instruments render a chordal Do-Fa-Sol ostinato in creole hemiola ("I like to be . . .") meter, reflecting a degree of Afro-Latin influence.

By the late 1700s, a form of the Cuban punto had already returned to Spain, and in subsequent decades street vendors and blind musicians were selling inexpensive chapbooks of décimas to sing to the "Havana punto tune."[10] This imported song form thus took root in Spain and evolved in its own direction under the name "guajira." By the 1880s, guajira was a popular genre in zarzuelas and other contexts and was also an established flamenco cante, with its own characteristic stock tune (not corresponding to any known Cuban counterpart) and florid guitar accompaniment patterns, featuring the distinctive 6/8–3/4 hemiola rhythm. The flamenco guajira typically used décima lyrics, but since that verse form was no longer cultivated in peninsular Spain, the same handful of texts (often naïvely idealizing Cuban country life or sexy mulatto women) were recycled repeatedly. The guajira thus retains a strong "tropical" Cuban aroma, both in musical form and idealized lyric content—as well as its dance form, done by a woman gracefully wielding a shawl and fan.

A related minor form was the *tango del Piyayo*, whose creator, Rafael Flores Nieto (1864–1940) had resided in Cuba for several years. Often referred to in plural as *tangos de Málaga* or *cantes del Piyayo*, the Piyayo cante has a melody and *aire* (spirit) resembling that of the guajira, though it is set to a bouncy tango rhythm, with the guitar capriciously alternating between major and Phrygian tonalities. Traditionally, the tango del Piyayo, in accordance with its Cuban guajiro origins, often used a ten-line décima as text, though in the 1970s Camarón de la Isla and Paco de Lucía standardized the more accessible four-line *cuarteta* form, also popularized for dance by Antonio Gades. Yet another Cuban-derived ida y vuelta cante emerging in the early 1900s was the flamenco rumba, derived from Cuban light theater and cabaret songs—not from the traditional Afro-Cuban voice-and-percussion rumba.

A more important cante de ida y vuelta taking shape during this period was the *peteneras*. Despite various folk etymologies of the word,[11] or the supposed Jewish origins of the cante, flamenco researchers have established fairly conclusively that it derived from an early nineteenth-century song of the Petén region of Guatemala, which has since ramified into better-known Mexican forms (Castro Buendía 2014a, I:741–46; Molina and Espín 1992, ch. 4; Gamboa 2004, 242–43; Hernández Jaramillo 2009). By the 1820s, versions of this *nueva petenera americana* were being sung as stage items and theater tunes in Cádiz, the main port of entry of Caribbean songs and dances. By the 1840s, it was rivaling the *sevillanas* as a popular Andalusian dance item and was even being re-exported to the Americas, as in the *petenera gaditana* (Cádiz-style petenera) performed in Cuba in 1844 by some visiting Spaniards.[12] From the 1860s, Silverio and other early flamenco cantaores were adapting it into their repertoire, and in the 1880s, other singers—especially Medina el Viejo and Antonio Chacón—were shaping it into its modern form, especially as further popularized by Pastora Pavón and others. The flamenco petenera resembles the Mexican son huasteco (or *huapango*) "La Petenera"—like flamenco cantes, a stock tune to which different lyrics are set—both in its chord progression and its 6/8–3/4 hemiola rhythm. However, the flamenco petenera is languid and essentially free-rhythmic, such that the hemiola appears more as a subtle vestige in certain guitar passages rather than as a persistent isorhythm.

The café cantante period also saw the definitive elaboration and canonization of the fandango group of cantes, which constitute one of the most basic and important categories of flamenco song. As we have seen, forms of the fandango, as dance and music, had been popular since the early 1700s. Extant notations comprised primarily academic instrumental compositions that consisted mostly of variations over Dm–A ostinatos, perhaps with copla-like passages in the relative major, presumably imitating the sung sections of certain vernacular fandangos. It was Andalusian forms of these vernacular idioms that would form the bases of the flamenco fandango variants from the mid-1800s. (Elsewhere in Spain, other forms of dance-oriented fandangos, some related to the jota, have existed that are distinct from what Berlanga [2000, 179–81] calls the "*fandangos del sur*"—fandangos of the south—distinguished especially by their typical chord progression.) As mentioned, from the early decades of that century, these could assume their modern form of a copla section, with a standardized chord progression in major key, punctuated by guitar ritornellos, typically in E altered Phrygian, with prominent iv–III–II–I (Am–G–F–E) cadences. The main developments involved in becoming flamenco cantes were the enrichment of the repertoire of stock melodies, the cultivation of an expressive, melismatic vocal style, and, in some forms, a leisurely free-rhythmic rendering, all of which enabled the new styles to become serious art songs rather than mere dance accompaniment.

Since the nineteenth century (if not earlier), there have been two categories of vernacular Andalusian "fandangos del sur." One of these is the family of fandangos de Huelva, which, though completely undocumented until the early twentieth century, has comprised a set of traditional regional tunes, performed by amateurs in taverns, *peñas*, family fiestas, annual religious festivals and pilgrimages, and, traditionally, in nocturnal "bailes de candil" in towns of the Andévalo plateau and in the district capital of Huelva. These have had no particular association with Gitanos.

The other—and better documented—group of fandangos del sur consisted of the verdiales, malagueñas, and rondeñas associated primarily with Málaga province but also popular, in regional variants, in Granada province, southern Córdoba province (especially Lucena), and "the Levant"—that is, the area to the east, stretching between Linares, Almería, and Murcia. The most archaic form of these is the folk verdiales, traditionally performed in rural settings and now cultivated by groups of amateur enthusiasts, folkloric ensembles, and others both in the hills north of Málaga and in that city itself, as brought by rural migrants or visitors. The traditional verdiales has been performed by a *panda* group incorporating laúd and/or bandurria, violin, pandero (tambourine), and, in modern times, guitar, accompanying singers who take turns singing coplas, often in different tunes, perhaps while couples or trios dance. Traditionally these verses could be improvised in a spirit of friendly competition. The rhythm is typically an unsyncopated ternary beat, strummed in eighth notes; alternately, it is what from the 1960s came to be called the "abandolao" (or *abandolá*) bolero-style rhythm—roughly, bum biddy-bum biddy-bum bum (or "*-rón-gorrión panzón gorri-*")—supposedly after the mandolin-like bandola that was a precursor to the bandurria. A distinctive feature of some of the Málaga verdiales stock tunes (discussed below) is the ending of the third and fifth sung lines on a dissonant Fa (in C: F), which the accompanying instruments themselves resolve, as it were, to the tonic Do (C) chord. While this feature is distinctive of the verdiales of Málaga, most fandango types of other regions, including Huelva, also employ the abandolao rhythm. Verdiales could also be rendered by a singer with solo guitar, including as a light flamenco item, especially concluding a malagueña.

While the verdiales—perhaps under different names—was presumably common in the nineteenth century, the related urban fandango forms that became significant as flamenco cantes were the malagueña and the rondeña. The malagueña—mentioned as early as the 1770s—was flourishing by the 1830s, though it did not assume its modern, free-rhythmic style until around 1900. As noted above, Estébanez Calderón's description of the 1830s Triana fiesta he attended indicates its popularity as an expressive solo song, liberated from dance, in variants created by known vocalists. Meanwhile, El Murciano's rondeñas/malagueñas of the 1840s illustrate how it was also cultivated as a serious, sophisticated guitar form. (The rondeñas and malagueñas of this period differed only in their associated vocal melodies, such that the two terms were often used interchangeably. However, while the malagueña became increasingly popular and eventually came to be performed in free rhythm, the rondeña persisted as a minor cante in ternary meter, with "abandolao" strum, and its associated guitar idiom would come to be designated simply as "malagueña.") Meanwhile, with Estébanez Calderón's account of Seville and Murciano's activities in Granada, it is clear that the cante's popularity had spread well beyond Málaga and the verdiales zone.

There are clear affinities and presumed historical links between verdiales and malagueñas. Both are associated with Málaga province and share the same tonality; in flamenco performance, a malagueña can segue to a verdiales (or a *jabera*), and most of the core malagueña melodies exhibit the distinctive melodic dissonance mentioned above, which can be seen as a key aspect of malagueña's special flavor. However, as noted, by the 1830s semiprofessional artists were creating original malagueñas to be performed as solo songs for connoisseurs who appreciated novelty; by this time the "stage" malagueña was already flourishing as an entity parallel to the folk verdiales (Moore 2019).

The popularity of the malagueña surged even more in the second half of the century, in both the cafés cantantes and various other stage presentations. Malagueña singers competed and even shared the stage with singers of Italian opera arias, epitomizing the rivalry between Andalusian castizo music and foreign forms. Indeed, it is quite likely that the flamenco cantaores of malagueñas and other early flamenco cantes cultivated their showy, exhibitionistic style of singing partly in imitation—albeit in a different style—of the bel canto virtuosos who were their twin rivals of sorts. However, the malagueña of this period, though sung in a free-rhythmic style, was still accompanied by guitar (or other instruments) in a steady ternary beat, unlike the fully free-rhythmic form that became standard after 1900.

Particularly renowned and influential from the 1880s was Juan Breva (Antonio Ortega Escalona, 1844–1918), a cantaor from Málaga who sang while accompanying himself on guitar. Breva sang various cantes but was particularly renowned for his malagueñas, including two variants he created. He is sometimes spoken of as having been the first to cultivate the cante as a serious solo song, in flamenco style, but there were clearly others before him who did the same.[13] As was the practice in his time, his vocal phrasing was free-rhythmic, though he strummed in abandolao-style ternary meter. Breva achieved great popularity, performing extensively at prestigious venues in Madrid and even for King Alfonso XII (see, e.g., Rojo Guerrero 2015). Some of his fame may have resulted from his prominence at the dawn of the modern period. Unlike El Mellizo and El Canario, who were also important creators and performers of malagueñas and other cantes, Breva recorded several 78 rpm discs that circulated widely.

After Breva, the most important figure in the modern malagueña was Antonio Chacón (see, e.g., Martín Ballester et al. 2016). Chacón performed and recorded extensively and was particularly popular for his malagueñas, including the five or six that he composed and that are basic items in the flamenco repertoire today. Ironically, Chacón stated that he far preferred cante jondo to the malagueñas that audiences demanded of him and to which, he lamented, he had become a "prisoner." Chacón, with El Mellizo, is regarded as the primary figure in definitively freeing the malagueña from its metered, danceable ancestors, making it a veritable Andalusian counterpart to the Italian aria. This style came to be applied to the full repertoire of malagueñas, including those of Breva and others who originally sang them in meter (Moore 2019). Curiously, despite the well-established nineteenth-century tradition of rendering malagueñas in E Phrygian/C major, Ramón Montoya accompanied most of Chacón's malagueña recordings in the guitar tonality of tarantas (F♯ Phrygian/D major).

Chacón is also credited with composing and popularizing the modern forms of caña and of granaínas (and similar *media granaínas*), sung, like malagueñas, in free rhythm and quite distant from the traditional, verdiales-like granadinas fandango forms.[14] For his part, Ramón Montoya standardized the accompaniment of this cante with the B Phrygian/G major guitar tonality that was already popular in Granada and eastern Spain during this period. (The B7 chord popular during this period [B–D♯–A–B–E] eventually gave way to the modern coloristic voicings, more often arpeggiated than strummed, of B–F♯–G–D♯–E or B–F♯–B–D♯–E.)

A significant development during this period was the emergence of a rich set of fandango variants—especially the tarantas—associated with the hilly "Levant" inland from Linares, Cartagena, and La Unión. Although distant from the core flamenco "triangle" of Seville, Málaga, and Cádiz provinces, these areas had their own musical traditions, including a form, called *trovo* (cf., *trovador, troubador*), of improvising verses to guitar accompaniment. The cultural and demographic ambience of the region changed from the 1860s with the dramatic expansion of lead and zinc mining as the government sought to replace the minerals no longer available from former colonies in the Americas. The industry attracted tens of thousands of migrant workers, especially from Almería and other parts of Andalusia. As might be expected during this period, working and living conditions in Linares and other mining towns were dismal, but the communities soon developed their own lively music scenes. English chronicler Hugh James Rose in 1875 offered a vivid description of workers gathering in cramped barrack rooms every evening for song sessions (in Chaves Arcos and Kliman 2012, 228). Cafés cantantes flourished there from the 1860s. By 1900 the thriving town of La Unión boasted sixteen such venues on a single street (Álvarez Caballero 1981, 131). The new mining towns, populated by proletarian migrant workers, were quite distinct in sociocultural character from the triangle's ancient towns—some settled continuously since

Roman times—with their communities of stable Gitano clans and now visiting tourists (García Gómez 1993, 206–207). What came to link them musically to the flamenco hinterland was the stratum of verdiales-style fandangos (*cante abandolao*) and the cafés cantantes, which featured troupes touring from the western parts of Andalusia.

Reconstructing the evolution of the Levant cantes has been the subject of several studies, including works of Ortega (2011), Sánchez Garrido (2015), Castro Buendía (2011, 2015), García Gómez (1993), and especially Chaves Arcos and Kliman (2012). Such flamencologists have argued over whether these cantes should be traced to traditional folkloric songs of Almería, Cartagena, or Murcia; whether they were simply regional variants of abandolao-type verdiales; or whether they were essentially inventions of Chacón and Montoya or of Rojo el Alpargatero (Antonio Grau Mora, 1847–1907), a café-owning patriarch of the local music scene (see, e.g., Grande 1979, II:380–84). In crude terms, the predecessors of these cantes were mostly abandolao songs that either were brought to the region by migrant workers from the mid-nineteenth century or had previously existed there. Particularly distinctive were the *canciones de madrugá* (early morning songs) sung by miners on their way to work, often with lyrics about the mining life. Another source, argues Génesis García Gómez (1993, 232–45), comprised the songs of the legions of muleteers and wagon drivers (*tartaneros*), who sang constantly and even competitively as they transported goods to and from the mines.[15] In the cafés cantantes, more polished, elaborated, and soloistic versions of these and other songs were performed as *cante de alante* (or *cante adelante*, foregrounding the singer rather than accompanying dance) by professional vocalists. Accompanying them were guitarists who seemed to have a predilection for tonic seventh chords, especially the B7 chord eventually associated with granaínas and, from around 1908, the guitar tonality of F♯ Phrygian (and D major), whose tonic chord contained non-chordal tones on open strings (from low to high: F♯–C♯–F♯–G–B–E; see Chaves Arcos and Kliman 2012, 479–80). From around those years, these song styles were flamencoized and ramified as estilos, especially by the aforementioned Rojo and, subsequently, the visiting Antonio Chacón. Chacón then introduced them to other parts of Andalusia, so by the 1920s they were well-established constituents of the flamenco repertoire even as the mining industry itself collapsed.

These fandango variants came to be called *mineras*, cartageneras, *levanticas*, *murcianas*, and especially tarantas, with the etymology of the latter remaining obscure but probably either deriving from the custom of calling migrants from Almería *tarantos* or having something to do with spider bites and a superstitious musical treatment of them (Chaves Arcos and Kliman 2012, 150–51). However, nomenclature was inconsistent until the 1950s, with, for example, recordings designated by Chacón as "tarantas" later being called "cartageneras," and, conversely, "zambra" and "rondeña" items by Manuel Torre later being classified as "tarantos." In Chacón's versions of these cantes, the fandango chordal structure is audible, although flavored by the prominent flat seventh degree (C natural, in the copla key of D major) and secondary dominant E7 chords. In Chacón's wake the songs further decelerated, the melodic dissonances and tonal ambiguity were intensified, and the cantes acquired their own unique sort of haunting depth. The entire repertoire was revitalized by the founding of the Festival del Cante de la Minas in La Unión in 1961, which also helped inspire recordings, research, and other performances of the cantes.

The southern part of Córdoba province, especially in and around Lucena, hosted a form of abandolao-type fandango with a similarly distinctive use of flat seventh degree and, accordingly, tonic seventh chordal accompaniment. Under the inspiration of Niño de Cabra (Cayetano Muriel, 1870–1947) and other local singers, the *fandango de Lucena* was elaborated as a flamenco cante while retaining its abandolao rhythm.

The early twentieth century also saw the flamencoization of some other minor song-types, some of which were popular songs adapted from zarzuela. One was the farruca, derived, according to some, from Galician migrants to Andalusia; another was the garrotín, a light song—closer to a ditty than a cante—that came from Asturia and/or Catalonia to Andalusia via zarzuela troupes and was adapted to flamenco by singers like Manuel Escacena and dancers, especially Faíco (Francisco Mendoza Ríos, ca. 1850–1938).

The Guitar in Early Flamenco

If the primary function of the guitar in flamenco has always been to accompany cante and dance, the elaboration of guitar playing in the café cantante period must nevertheless be seen as a fundamental, rather than incidental, aspect of flamenco's evolution. The advent of a conventional format of vocalist plus guitarist precipitated a standardization of song forms and their particular compás patterns. Over the course of the café cantante period, specific guitar tonalities and falsetas became defining features of most of the cantes, together with vocal melodies. The dramatic enrichment of guitar playing itself became one of the most attractive and dynamic features of flamenco as a whole.

Some flamencologists—especially Antonio Mairena and Ricardo Molina, in their influential *Mundo y formas del cante flamenco* (1963, 143–44)—have asserted that the core Gitano pre-flamenco forms, such as toná and siguiriyas—were originally sung without guitar accompaniment, which was added only from the 1850s in the café cantante context. Supporters of this notion point out that there have always been some song forms, such as work songs, lullabies, muleteers' songs, and narrative *romances*, that would most typically be intoned in simple stock tunes without guitar. In addition, some flamenco cantes—especially tonás, martinetes, and saetas—are still sung without guitar, and indeed *all* flamenco cantes are quite often sung unaccompanied, especially in informal contexts but also sometimes on stage as well (achieving a somewhat austere but not undesirable effect). Guitars were relatively rare in many pre-flamenco circles and have remained so in towns such as Utrera and Lebrija, where many amateur singers, especially elders, prefer to sing unaccompanied because they are accustomed to singing that way and have no concept of how to match their singing to a guitar (see, e.g., Lefranc 2000, 26).[16]

Others, however, point out that the guitar, being relatively inexpensive and in simple forms not excessively difficult to play, was commonly used to accompany a great variety of vernacular song and dance forms, including by Gitanos, from around 1600 if not earlier (e.g., Campo and Cáceres 2013; Álvarez Caballero 2003, 13–22). Many references document the common use of the guitar among Gitanos in the eighteenth century, as did George Borrow in writing of 1830s Gitano culture (2015, 80). Castro Buendía (2014a, II:896) documents a lachrymose playera—a direct ancestor of siguiriyas—being sung with guitar in 1816, and an 1862 source describes a guitarist accompanying a "toná"—a term that in modern times denotes a cante that is only sung unaccompanied. What is perhaps most important is that cantes such as soleá and siguiriyas *did not become flamenco* until the 1850s–1860s, when they were professionalized, standardized, and elaborated precisely in conjunction with guitar accompaniment (see Rioja 2008). Thus, it would be incorrect to say that soleá and siguiriyas were "originally" sung unaccompanied before the café cantante period, when in fact it appears that soleá and siguiriyas, in recognizable forms, *did not exist* until that period.

Aside from the basic presence or absence of the guitar, another consideration is the way it was played in accompanying pre-flamenco singing, which could presumably range from minimal to elaborate. It is entirely likely that in many cases before the modern era, its role may have been primarily to strum the basic rhythm, the compás, while also providing a chordal drone of sorts. Such, indeed, can be to a large extent the guitar's function even today in renderings of siguiriyas and bulerías, especially in amateur contexts. It would be in the café cantante period that guitarists would have cultivated a more elaborate and virtuoso style, drawing from the playing of El Murciano and others.

Accordingly, Spanish guitar playing in the nineteenth century comprised a continuum between classical concert artists like Julián Arcas and unlettered vernacular musicians who mostly accompanied dances and songs such as fandangos and jotas, primarily using rasgueado and thumb strokes. Between these antipodes, however, was considerable interaction and flow, as artists such as

Arcas performed their versions of "national airs" and were imitated in turn by eclectic flamenco and pre-flamenco guitarists such as Paco el Barbero (1840–1910), whose concerts could include a potpourri of flamenco and items by Arcas, Verdi, and others. From the 1860s, when cafés cantantes proliferated around the country, demand for guitarists skyrocketed, especially as the custom of accompanying oneself while singing declined. As these emerging artists competed with one another, flamenco guitar playing as an art form grew rapidly in sophistication (see, e.g., Torres 2004, 2010; Álvarez Caballero 2003). As performers from diverse regions and backgrounds performed together on stage, the presence of guitarists contributed to the need for standardization of compás patterns and other features, and the music became at once richer and more regularized.

Oral traditions argue for the importance of certain key individuals, including the aforementioned Maestro Patiño, some of whose falsetas survive and who was a seminal figure in the emergence of a distinctive flamenco accompaniment style. Patiño is credited with the popularization in flamenco of the *cejilla*, or capo, the handy device (invented much earlier) barring the strings at a desired fret, which enabled vocalists to sing in whatever range was comfortable for them, with the guitarist adjusting accordingly. Patiño, based in Cádiz, also occasionally performed solos as early as 1865, as did his disciples Paco el Barbero and Paco de Lucena (Francisco Díaz Fernández, 1859–1898). Lucena, based in Sevilla and Córdoba, had acquired some classical guitar techniques with which he was able to enrich flamenco playing. His contemporary Javier Molina (1868–1956) is regarded as establishing the Jerez style of playing, perpetuated in the next generations by Perico el del Lunar (Pedro del Valle Pichardo, 1894–1964) and, subsequently, Parrilla de Jerez (Manuel Fernández Molina, 1945–2009), the brothers Manuel and Juan Morao, and their descendants. Meanwhile, Miguel Borrull Castello (1866–1926), who had studied concert music with Francisco Tárrega (1852–1909), established a Madrid "school" of playing, incorporating more classical touches than did the Andalusian styles.

In the formative decades of flamenco, there were quite a few female guitarists, but as the genre professionalized, they all but disappeared from the scene. In the cafés cantantes and other professional contexts, it became customary for the guitarist to also serve as the manager, who handled bookings, personnel, finances, and even musical arrangements; such roles were seen as inappropriate or infeasible for women. Further, respectable women would have been out of place in the *señorito juergas*, where prostitutes were often hired. As such, it is only in recent decades that a few women have come to acquit themselves well on the instrument (see, e.g., Cruces Roldán 2015; Cattaneo 2021).

A crucial development during this period was the standardization of the modern guitar itself by Antonio de Torres Jurado (1817–1892), who enlarged the instrument's body, fixed the string length, added modern braces, and introduced the use of lighter woods. He also standardized the distinction between the flamenco guitar and the classical guitar. Torres's flamenco guitar, as subsequently adopted by Manuel Ramírez and other makers, used light cypress instead of rosewood on the back and sides, along with old-style rear tuning pegs as opposed to mechanical horizontal ones. While these innovations made the instrument more accessible to impecunious players, the light wood also provided a louder, brighter sound suitable for accompanying song and dance and facilitated the traditional practice of holding the instrument in a near-vertical position. The flamenco guitar also retained slightly smaller dimensions and came to incorporate a plastic tap plate on the face to protect it from rhythmic *golpes* (fingernail strokes). The bridge and saddle were also set slightly lower than on the classical guitar, facilitating left-hand techniques like hammering-on and pulling-off while occasionally generating a light buzz, which is not regarded as objectionable.

In the 1860s, composer, scholar, and guitarist Eduardo Ocón undertook a study of regional guitar styles (published as *Cantos españoles* in 1874), noting, among other things, that there were three basic positions in which guitarists played the altered Phrygian tonality, with its iv–III–II–I Andalusian cadence. One was the A Phrygian por medio (in the middle) position (basic cadence: Dm–C–B♭–A), used to accompany fandangos, as dating from the eighteenth century. The second was the E Phrygian *por arriba* (on top) position (cadence: Am–G–F–E), used for malagueñas and rondeñas, taking advantage of the low E string standardized in the previous generations. The third was the B Phrygian position (Em–D–C–B) associated with granaínas, which was popular around Granada but little encountered to the west. Only from around 1910, as mentioned above, would the F♯ Phrygian *toque de Levant* appear, and from the 1920s it became standard in accompanying tarantas and its variants.

A landmark in flamenco history was the publication of a flamenco guitar method book in 1902 by Rafael Marín, a classical guitarist, who directed his book toward other musically literate, formally trained players who sought to learn flamenco. Marín's *Método de guitarra* (nicely reprinted in 1995), with its detailed notations and prose commentary, constitutes a rich source of information for the historian, both in what it includes (e.g., granaínas) and what it excludes (e.g., tarantas and bulerías, which had yet to take shape).

Far richer sources of information, of course, are the recordings of flamenco that appeared from the turn of the century. Several comments can be made about the guitar playing during this period (excluding, one might say, the revolution led by Ramón Montoya). On the one hand, it is effective and competent, with guitarists such as Lucena, Juan Gandulla (known as "Habichuela"), and Miguel Borrull displaying a strong thumb, picado, and rasgueado technique, and a lively, spirited style. On the other hand, as Norberto Torres (2004, 54–55) has noted, different guitarists tend to repeat the same finite stock of falsetas; the playing is generally rather rushed by modern standards, with no use of rests or pauses; the guitarist and singer sometimes seem to be out of sync; and the rendering of compás is often irregular, showing that the metrical patterns had yet to assume their more regularized, metronomic modern forms. In general, despite this period being nostalgically celebrated as the "Golden Age," the guitar playing is quite limited compared to that of later periods. Accompaniment tonalities also often differed from those of other decades, with, for example, the F♯ tarantas and B granaínas tonalities often being used to accompany malagueñas rather than E "por arriba" tonality standard both in the nineteenth century and since the 1920s. The same guitarist would accompany the same cante in different tonalities for different recordings, suggesting a kind of experimentation and freedom that did not persist.

Guitar playing of this period culminated in the towering figure of Ramón Montoya (1879–1949), who is regarded as the single most seminal figure in the evolution of flamenco guitar, elevating it from an "urban folk" accompaniment style to a sophisticated art form. Montoya, born in Madrid to itinerant Gitano parents, was largely self-taught but assimilated classical techniques of Tárrega and others from Miguel Llobet and traveled widely throughout Andalusia to gather regional styles. Hence, especially from around 1910, he enriched the traditional *toque* (playing) with more extensive use of arpeggio, five-stroke tremolo, and patterns played over the range of the neck rather than merely in first position. He invented (or popularized) the guitar forms of rondeña, with its C♯ Phrygian tonality and D–A–D–F♯–B–E tuning, and of mineras, in G♯ Phrygian. Several cantes, such as granaínas and tarantas, took their definitive shape through his decade-long close collaboration with Antonio Chacón. His ample commercial recordings, both as an accompanist and soloist, further spread his renown and influence. Hence it was largely he who, after some initial decades of experimentation, standardized accompaniment tonalities for most cantes, including F♯ Phrygian for tarantas. Perhaps most important was his brilliance as a composer of falsetas, which came to be basic components of the flamenco guitar repertoire and defining features of cantes like tarantas.

Gitanos and Non-Gitanos in the Creation of Flamenco: The Endless Polemic

For more than a century, flamenco has been argued about and fought over as intensely as it has been beloved, whether by intellectuals, journalists, performers, or ordinary enthusiasts. And of all the ongoing points of contention, none have been more persistent and fundamental than those pertaining to the relative roles of Gitanos and non-Gitanos in the art's history and essential character. (A common word for non-Gitano is *payo*, but in some contexts, especially in Jerez, that term can have derogatory connotations and hence is avoided in this book unless such connotations are deliberate.) To what extent, and in what sense, should flamenco be seen as a Gitano—rather than Andalusian, or Spanish, or even universal—art form (as jazz is said to be an "Afro-American" art)? And what are the criteria involved in addressing this question? Its early history and creation? The ethnicity of its leading performers, past and present? Some aspect of its ineffable essence?

This debate, in its various dimensions, has been waged for over a century in flamencological literature, journalism, and popular discourse. Involving sensitive ethnic issues, it has often taken a bitter and personal tone, generating accusations of racism from both sides. At this point we will confine ourselves to those dimensions of the polemic that pertain to flamenco's early history. The entire controversy is exacerbated by the lack of adequate historical documentation, which impedes any definitive resolution, however convincingly some analysts may continue to scour and interpret the finite set of historical references that exist. The various aspects of the polemic have been argued at times with insight and erudition and on other occasions with considerable confusion, imprecision, and insensitivity. In the present discussion, I will seek to clarify and assess the major arguments that have been presented, while offering some general interpretations.

The historical polemic comprises several issues that are in some respects interrelated and in other ways discrete, as treated here. Have Gitanos been significant creators of flamenco, or "mere interpreters"? Did they cultivate the core cante jondo forms in hermetic isolation before the café cantante period? Is it accurate to regard flamenco as comprising two distinct categories—of "cante gitano" and "cante andaluz"? To what extent did flamenco evolve in the café cantante period as a response to a naïvely Romantic, and often touristic, demand for exotic entertainment as opposed to emerging as an elaboration of an authentic Gitano art form rooted in family traditions?

Before looking at these questions individually, an initial point can be made to the effect that they do not necessarily relate to a broader question about the greater or lesser importance and role of Gitanos in the creation of flamenco. To be sure, various authors who have attempted to either celebrate or minimize the Gitano contribution have taken stances on these questions in order to buttress their general argument. An example is Pedro Peña, who, in his intriguing book *Los gitanos flamencos* (2013), argues in favor of the hermetic theory and the existence of the distinct "cante gitano" category in order to establish the fundamental importance of the Gitano contribution to flamenco. However, it could well be argued, as I would, that the preeminence of Gitanos as both creators and performers of flamenco is by itself abundantly clear and undeniable and does not in any way rest or depend on the hermetic theory or the viability of a "cante gitano" category.

Gitanos as Creators or "Mere Interpreters"?

One of the oldest controversies, and among the easiest to resolve, involves the notion that Roma musicians, whether in Spain or elsewhere, have never created anything per se but, rather, have merely been colorful, flamboyant, and generally gifted interpreters of extant material, from Hungarian *verbunkos* to the Andalusian fandango. This idea was first advanced in relation to Eastern European Romani, as in some writings by Franz Liszt and the young Béla Bartók. As noted above, German linguist Hugo Schuchardt applied this notion to flamenco in his own way in his 1881 study. Various Spanish flamencologists, such as Manuel García Matos, and other pseudo-flamencologists seem to have obsequiously perpetuated this notion, and it has continued to be occasionally voiced, whether in online forums or some publication that purports to be scholarly (e.g., Barrios 1989, 97–98). On the level of traditional stereotypes, it can imply that Gitanos would steal tunes the same way they stole chickens (see Leblon 2003, 64).

In assessing this argument, it should first be noted that flamenco is primarily a performative art. In that sense it differs from, for example, Western classical music, in which performance is certainly important and essential, but "greatness"—especially in historical retrospect—is primarily measured by skill in composition. To some extent, flamenco is in this sense more akin to jazz, some of whose most outstanding figures—such as Louis Armstrong or even Miles Davis—were not prominent composers per se, that is, of songs. However, to belittle these artists as "mere interpreters of other people's material" would be to misconstrue the nature of creation and excellence in jazz.

More important, however, is the easily demonstrable fact that to the extent that "creation"—that is, composition—is actually significant in flamenco, Gitanos have clearly been outstanding in this regard. First of all, the majority of estilos (stock tunes) in core cantes of soleá and siguiriya, and many estilos of fandangos, malagueñas, and other forms, have been composed by Gitano singers. As previously noted, doubts have been raised about the accuracy of many of the attributions of estilos to nineteenth-century cantaores, and the alleged creation of many estilos by this or that singer may have constituted little more than alterations of extant melodies. However, many familiar attributions—especially involving early twentieth-century singers—are perfectly reliable, leaving no doubt that a great bulk of the flamenco melodic repertoire was in fact composed by Gitano singers.

Perhaps an even more obvious form of composition and creation has been that of Gitano guitarists such as Ramón Montoya or Sabicas. Indeed, to call these figures "guitarists" is a bit like calling Liszt or Chopin "pianists." Virtuoso guitarists they certainly were, but most of what they performed was their own material—that is, falsetas composed by themselves. These falsetas went on to be ardently studied and mastered by thousands of guitarists in their wake, whether in Toledo or Tokyo. The remarkably fecund and original Montoya also created (or popularized) two guitar palos—rondeña and mineras—consisting of original tunings and tonalities, as well as a body of characteristic falsetas, and his falsetas in tarantas, together with the melodies of Chacón, have essentially constituted that entire cante. Even today, of course, prominent Gitano guitarists, like their non-Gitano counterparts, perform mostly their own material, and mention should also be made of the several Gitanos, like Diego Carrasco, who have been leading composers of *nuevo flamenco* songs. Collectively, these considerations should put to rest the conceit—dubious from its very first articulation—that Gitanos have been deficient as creators, and, indeed, it may be difficult to absolve from accusations of racism those who have advanced this idea.

The Hermetic Theory, "Cante Gitano," and Romanticism

A somewhat more tenacious debate has centered on the so-called hermetic theory, which has as its precondition the impossibility of documenting the early evolution of cantes such as soleá, siguiriyas, tangos, and the unaccompanied *palos* (an alternate term for cantes) such as tonás and martinete. Briefly, the hermetic theory argues that these cantes, or early versions of them, were created and cultivated in the first half of the nineteenth century or even earlier in insular Gitano contexts—weddings, baptisms, and other reunions—and then in the café cantante period they were presented to the public, being at once elaborated, Andalusianized, sweetened, and diluted in the process. The opposing viewpoint would be that soleá, siguiriyas, and tangos simply did not exist in any recognizable flamenco form until the café cantante period, when they took shape at the hands of professional Gitano and non-Gitano musicians as sophisticated, stylized reworkings of extant song forms.

The hermetic theory was first propounded by Antonio Mairena and Ricardo Molina and subsequently became accepted in some circles. Mairena and Molina, while reiterating the theory, never advanced extensive argumentation for it. However, they took as evidence "Demófilo" Machado's 1881 description of flamenco as emerging primarily from a distinct, obscure category of "cante gitano" that was then made public in hybrid form by Silverio and the entire café cantante phenomenon. Machado wrote:

> The cafés will soon completely wipe out cante gitano, in spite of the prodigious efforts of the cantaor of Seville [Silverio] to take it out of its obscure milieu, whence it never should have left if it wanted to remain pure and genuine. Upon leaving the tavern for the café, the Gitano genre "Andalusianized," becoming what today everyone calls flamenco. Silverio, in ennobling cante gitano, . . . created the genre of flamenco, a mixture of the Gitano element and the Andalusian.

And:

> These cantes, originating in taverns, when they were at their peak, were converted into public spectacles. The cafés . . . will soon finish off these cantes gitanos, by Andalusianizing them or, if you will, *gacho*-izing ["payo-izing" them], as the professional singers say, and they will go on gradually losing their primitive character and originality and transforming into a mixed genre, which will be called flamenco, as a synonym of "Gitano," but will actually be a confused mixture of diverse elements—the burlesque, the obscene, the profoundly sad, the boundlessly merry, the ruffianesque[,] etc.

A cornerstone of the Mairenista hermetic theory is the existence, asserted by Machado and many others, of a distinct category of "cante gitano" within flamenco as a whole. This notion continues to be hotly disputed, with some arguing that soleares, siguiriyas, bulerías, and the unaccompanied cantes are distinctively Gitano in evolution and ongoing character, and others insisting that this categorization is artificial and misleading. While we will return to this debate, at present we will address only the historical aspects of it.

Machado's interpretation of events cannot be casually dismissed. As noted above, he was a friend of Silverio and other musicians, had a degree of direct familiarity with the contemporary flamenco scene, and of course produced a masterly, landmark compilation of flamenco lyrics that single-handedly initiated the field of flamenco studies. At the same time, he was influenced by contemporary Krausist notions of discrete races and peoples with their distinctive, pure cultures; further, his knowledge of the flamenco scene may not have been deep. He has also been misrepresented; in contrast to Mairena's hermetic theory, he described this primordial cante gitano as based primarily in taverns, and occasional paid private fiestas, rather than Gitano homes. Unfortunately, Machado did not clarify what he meant by "pure cante gitano." Plain, repetitive, monotonous lullabies and tonás? Or recognizable forms of soleares and siguiriyas that needed only a modicum of refinement and standardization to be presented as "flamenco"?

Pierre Lefranc, in an original and thoughtful volume (2000), presented his own articulation of the hermetic theory based on the experiences of his informants, especially in reference to the 1940s and 1950s, which were a particularly dismal period for flamenco. In these culturally stagnant decades, the cafés cantantes were long gone, the Mairenista revival had not yet begun, and the only flamenco presented on stage consisted of trivial frippery for tourists, such that traditional (Lefranc: "authentic") flamenco performance—and estilo creation, by people such as Juan Talega (or Talegas, 1891–1971)—was largely confined to domestic (especially Gitano) reunions and private juergas.

A particularly sustained, extensive, and engaging argument for the hermetic theory is Pedro Peña's aforementioned *Los gitanos flamencos*. Peña offers a rather problematic vision of prehistory, dismissing the notion of Moorish input and arguing that Gitanos developed their own music culture based largely on traditions they brought from their centuries in Greece and, earlier, India. More compelling is his ethnographic portrait of the hereditary flamenco families, such as his own, in Lebrija and Jerez, where flamenco was constantly performed, whether at lively reunions or, for example, by an auntie singing a soleá learned from her grandmother as she did housework. Peña vividly portrays a vibrant, multigenerational community of professional and amateur singers and dancers who lovingly pass down songs, dance moves, and lyrics (including many found in Machado's 1881 compilation) from generation to generation and whose constant fiestas featuring soleá, siguiriyas, and bulerías had no counterpart in non-Gitano families. For Peña, the strength and uniqueness of this exclusively Gitano tradition constitute clear evidence for regarding these cantes as distinctively Gitano and for recognizing the homes of Gitano families as flamenco's real crucibles prior to the café cantante period. As such, he argues, the cante jondo forms are best seen as pure Gitano idioms that were Andalusianized in the cafés cantantes rather than being essentially Andalusian folk forms that were "Gypsified" in those contexts.

However, in recent decades the hermetic theory has fallen out of favor among flamencologists, and it does indeed have clearly problematic aspects. Some of these aspects can be dismissed fairly readily,[17] although others may remain persistent. The primary problem is the lack of evidence, which renders its core beliefs inherently hypothetical. Accordingly, as congenial flamencologist Brook Zern used to wryly assert, the proof of the hermetic theory is the fact that there is no evidence to support it.[18] (If there were documentation supporting hermetic creation, then it wouldn't be hermetic!) While one must take the account of Demófilo seriously, his failure to describe what constituted "pure Gitano cante" is problematic, as is the fact that the alleged hermetic period (ca. 1800–1850s) would have been decades before his own actual engagement with the scene. Even during that period, some form of siguiriyas—supposedly in "hermetic" gestation—was being sung in public by El Planeta, a professional and renowned cantaor (see Gamboa 2018, 391). Further, historical references, such as those of Cervantes, describe Gitanos singing familiar Andalusian genres, including villancicos, seguidillas, and *romances*, rather than some unique Gitano idioms. Moreover, we know that Gitanos were performing professionally from the early 1600s, and by the 1700s there was clear interest—including by foreign visitors—in seeing precisely their distinctive, colorful, and "exotic" song and dance styles. Given the abject poverty of most Gitanos, why would they have hidden such styles rather than avidly marketing them as best they could? Finally, while some veteran singers (such as Anica la Periñaca) attested that non-Gitanos were not allowed into Gitano weddings and certain other festivities, there is no reason to believe that the songs sung at these events differed significantly from those that were sung professionally. That is, there have always been "hermetic" performance occasions, but there is no reason to attribute creation solely or even primarily to those contexts.

Most importantly, as we have seen, some of the core aspects of the allegedly "pure Gitano" cantes, such as soleá—especially its distinctive compás—had not even taken their modern form by 1900, not to mention the early café cantante period. Bulerías does not seem to have emerged in its modern, recognizable form until the 1920s, when recordings, professional performance, and competition among Gitanos in the commercial scene had all been going strong for decades. One must thus acknowledge that the bulerías sung by Peña's aunties, or even the basic soleá compás that some elder informant of Lefranc rapped with his knuckles on a table, *did not evolve* until after 1900, far from deriving from some pre-1850 Gitano hearth (not to mention medieval Greece). That is, they were entities that clearly took shape in an active dialectic between public commercial contexts, semiprivate but still professional juergas, and, to be sure, domestic reunions among musician families. And as for the lyrics lovingly passed down among Gitano families from Machado's time to Pedro Peña's, it is known that many of these were penned by non-Gitanos, often in a costumbrista, Gypsyesque spirit, as is still commonplace today.

It may be useful to regard the hermetic and cante gitano theories as existing in either "extreme" or "moderate" versions. The "extreme" version, as I have suggested, is at best conjectural and at worst totally unsustainable. However, a "moderate" version, if unverifiable, is not implausible and is even acknowledged as such by some writers who take pains to discredit the standard version.[19] First of all, it is entirely likely that Gitanos preserved in their music some archaic Moorish features, such as melismatic style and distinctive modal and melodic forms—hence the several contemporary descriptions, however naïve and impressionistic, of their pre-flamenco music as "Moorish" in character. From the early 1800s, these features would have distinguished both idioms that they performed mostly among themselves (such as wedding songs) and their versions of other Andalusian genres, including festive dance songs and jaleos, that they, together with other lumpen bohemians, performed in various contexts, especially informal tavern sessions and paid performances for patrons, which were not strictly "hermetic." The Gitanos, as Timothy Mitchell (1994, 95) opines, were simply the most professionally oriented among the various marginal characters singing and dancing in taverns and fiestas. Similarly, some of the genres in question may have been broadly Andalusian, but the colorful, Moorish-tinged manner in which Gitanos performed them (whether in public or private) was idiosyncratic enough that one might, with some equivocation, see them as constituting a distinctive "cante gitano" category. Hence, for example, both Silverio and Chacón preferred the term "cante gitano" to "flamenco," and the former was clearly a common, emic term used by musicians and others from Demófilo's time.

And then came the cafés cantantes, driven by a particular conjuncture of sociocultural forces that included a market demand animated by the spirit of European Romanticism, which, partly as a reaction against the Industrial Revolution and the beginnings of mass culture, promoted art forms that celebrated individualism, intense emotional expression, and the archaic. The foreign (especially French and British) tourists who came in increasing numbers to Spain from the early 1800s (and who were later a major market for early flamenco recordings) thronged to the cafés cantantes to see "exotic" Gypsy performances, with their "passionate," "Moorish"-sounding songs and fiery dances. Thus, rather than obliging Gitanos to dilute and "Andalusianize" their traditional music, the new, exoticizing demand encouraged them to do just the opposite—that is, to exaggerate the Moorish elements such as melismatic singing and modality. Meanwhile, many nationalistic Spaniards, in a period of ongoing French and Italian cultural influence, came to see flamenco and Gitanos as embodiments of pure castizo Spanishness, which was ironic in view of the traditional disparagement of Andalusia, especially Gitanos, as contaminated with Moorish, Black, and other foreign strains.

German sociologist Gerhard Steingress (1991) has written insightfully on the Romanticism underlying the emergence of flamenco:[20]

> The cante "was born" as an artistic antithesis confronting the leveling and repressive mass culture. The anguished "cry" of the cantaor and the lyrics, interpreted in an individualistic manner were seen as a protest against a saturated and hypocritical society. The personage of the Gypsy served as symbol of this cultural resistance. . . . That is, the cante was created as an artistic product of the urban subcultures and the artistic proletariat, a typical phenomenon of Romanticism.[21] (135)

No doubt a Pedro Peña would find offensive the notion that the flamenco performed at his family reunions, so cherished as a core embodiment of pure Gitano culture, had evolved in part in order to satisfy the naïve, exoticizing tastes of foreign tourists. But perhaps the way that Gitanos and their non-Gitano cohorts so adeptly responded to such market demands could itself be taken as an indication of their artistic brilliance. Like all art forms, flamenco emerged as a product of its sociohistoric conditions, and yet its protagonists—the Gitanos and the broader artistic, lumpen subculture of Seville and other towns—were able to rise to the occasion and produce a genre that could be rich and universal rather than fake and shallow. The Gitanos in particular were the right people, at the right time, with the right traditions, values, and talents, to provide such an art form; it is as if after so many centuries of persecution and marginalization, their moment had come. The rapidly evolving genre—at once modern and drawing on archaic features preserved especially by Gitanos—was able to appeal both to ignorant tourists as well as a growing local audience of sophisticated connoisseurs. More remarkably, the first generations of flamencos—Gitanos and non-Gitanos—were able to forge the art form in such a way that it could both respond to these audience demands and legitimately serve as an authentic vehicle of their own community identity, aesthetics, and values. In this achievement, perhaps, lies the true brilliance of Gitano creation.

3

From Stagnation to Revival

The 1920s–1940s: Flamenco in a Holding Pattern

By 1920 the café cantante scene had declined. Several cafés persisted over the next few decades, but both in quantity of venues and quality of their offerings, the scene attenuated to the extent that flamencologists routinely came to refer to the previous decades as a "Golden Age" and the subsequent ones as a period of stagnation or, at best, stasis. The reasons for the decline are to some extent intangible but involved a number of developments. Competition from cinema and new commercial pop genres—especially the cuplé—played a certain role, but the more crucial factor was a concerted anti-flamenco campaign. This *antiflamenquismo* movement was, on a general level, an expression of a broad sentiment of crisis and soul-searching in the wake of Spain's disastrous loss of its remaining colonies in 1898, the social tensions accompanying industrialization and urbanization, and the awareness that Spain was failing to modernize in tandem with other European countries. As documented by Sandie Holguín (2019, chs. 1–2) and Samuel Llano (2017, 2018), the campaign was waged by various interest groups that could have quite distinct agendas and motivations but shared a belief that flamenco—along with its twin scourge, bullfighting—was backward, decadent, and linked to vice and immorality. (Bullfighting and flamenco have always been linked; *toreros* have traditionally been flamenco fans, several dance poses and moves imitate toreros, and some Gitano family dynasties, such as the Ortegas, have specialized in both professions.) One interest group was the Catholic Church, which felt itself on the defensive against growing secularism, socialism, and irreverent mass entertainment. The Church saw the cafés cantantes as anathema, with their saucy dancers, rowdy, wine-bibbing patrons, unhealthy mixing of social classes, and frequent links to prostitution. Catholic priests, writers, and assorted moralists hurled invective at the cafés, pressuring many municipalities to ban or strictly regulate them.

Although at the opposite end of the sociopolitical spectrum, socialists and anarchists—or at least their spokespersons—shared with the Catholics a disdain for the cafés cantantes. In forums such as the newspaper *El socialista*, they inveighed against flamenco, bullfights, drinking, and prostitution as bread-and-circus vices that distracted the working classes from righteous political struggle. Meanwhile, between the ideologies of the reactionary Church and the progressive leftists were assorted modernizers who saw flamenco and bullfights as epitomizing everything that was backward about Spain. Flamenco was especially objectionable, with its hysterical "oriental" vocal style, its fatalistic and morbid lyrics, and its scurrilous social alliance of lumpen Gitano performers and dissolute señorito patrons.[1] (Such sentiments cohered with parallels in other modernizing countries, like Turkey, where, under the influence of Mustafa Kemal Ataturk and republican ideologue Ziya Gökalp, traditional Turkish music was disparaged as backward and fatalistic.) While prominent "Generation of 1898" literati such as Miguel de Unamuno and Pío Baroja disparaged flamenco, its most tireless critic was one Eugenio Noel, who devoted the period from 1910 to 1920 entirely to attacking flamenco through penning six books of essays, founding six anti-flamenco societies, and giving countless lectures (see Holguín 2019, 75–79; Llano 2018, ch. 4).[2]

Opposition to flamenco derived particular bitterness from the awareness that many Europeans—especially French and British—saw Spain, whether favorably or unfavorably, as the land of Gypsies, bullfighting, and flamenco. In some cases, of course, foreign appreciation of a local music can inspire its legitimization, as happened when the Parisian vogue of the tango in the 1920s led Argentines to belatedly endorse their formerly disreputable dance form. However, for reform-minded Spaniards like Noel, the foreign perception of Spain as the land of Gypsies and castanets—rather than Velázquez and Cervantes—was a source of acute embarrassment. Indeed, the embarrassment of being seen as *España de la pandereta* (Spain of the tambourine) recalled the resentment that Spanish royalty, centuries earlier, felt about their country being regarded as a mongrel land of Blacks, Moors, and Jews—a sensitivity that helped provoke the expulsion of the latter two groups.

Yet another factor was the fear and loathing with which Madrileños regarded the Andalusian immigrants who had been pouring into the city since the 1840s. Such scorn applied both to impoverished labor migrants as well as the señoritos, each of whom were associated with *flamenquismo* and its supposed links to crime, drunkenness, prostitution, and the dissolute side of the unprecedentedly thriving nightlife scene (itself stimulated by the advent of electric lighting). Offsetting the costumbrista interest in Gitanos was a racist scapegoating that associated them and their music with all manner of social disfunction (Llano 2018, chs. 1, 2).

Flamenco's fans may have outnumbered its detractors, but facing such concerted opposition, the art suffered from a lack of support from institutions, elites, or literati, and the despised señoritos could hardly mount a coherent campaign in its favor. The only prominent intellectual to defend the art was Blas Infante, an energetic essayist and activist regarded as the founder of modern Andalusian cultural nationalism. In the years around 1930, Infante penned several essays on flamenco, which represented some of the earliest attempts at serious writing on the subject, though these were not published until after he had been murdered by the Fascists in 1936. Thus, despite its popularity in some circles, flamenco enjoyed no particular legitimacy or recognition as an art form and hence was particularly vulnerable to attack.

The Concurso de Cante Jondo of 1922

The more significant attempt by members of the cultural elite to support flamenco was a grand competition organized primarily by poet and playwright Federico García Lorca (1898–1936) and classical composer Manuel de Falla (1876–1946). Lorca, one of the most dynamic, colorful, and tragic figures in modern Spanish culture, was raised near Granada and had cultivated an interest in flamenco and Gitanos. For his part, Falla had become fond of flamenco during his years in Madrid and in 1921 settled in Granada, where he befriended the young Lorca. Both shared the nostalgic belief—voiced forty years earlier by Demófilo—that authentic cante jondo was in a state of decline and that it was properly performed only by little-known amateurs, while the cafés cantantes proffered only cheap fare—under the faddish name "flamenco"—for tourists and boors. (It was Lorca and Falla who promoted the distinction, however criticized, between cante jondo—such as soleá and siguiriyas—and the supposedly lighter *cante chico* forms, such as the fandango variants.) Lorca and Falla also saw a need to promote cante jondo—representing deep Spanish culture—as a bulwark against jazz and cheap European mass entertainment (Llano 2018, ch. 5). To address this crisis, with great energy and inspiration Lorca and Falla undertook the organization of a cante jondo competition, securing funds, generating publicity, making local arrangements, and inviting dignitaries. The event, known as the Concurso de Cante Jondo, took place, with considerable fanfare and some three thousand attendees, in Granada in July 1922 and featured guest performers and judges Antonio Chacón, Manuel Torre, and Pastora Pavón, as well as an extraordinary roster of distinguished observers, including Igor Stravinsky, Maurice Ravel, Joaquín Turina, Andres

Segovia, musicologist Felipe Pedrell, and leading Spanish literati. Conspicuously lacking, however, were worthy competitors, such that the event itself was widely regarded as something of a flop.

As chroniclers have noted, Lorca and Falla made two fundamental errors of judgment in conceiving and executing their competition. The first was to exclude professional performers from competing. Lorca and Falla had clearly been misled by a Romantic notion that has pervaded flamenco culture from its inception to the present: that "authentic" flamenco could only be found in intimate, amateur (especially Gitano) gatherings, and that the flamenco presented by professionals to the general public could constitute only a diluted facsimile of the real art. Despite having some familiarity with the flamenco scene, both men failed to see that the genre was then, as it is now, primarily an art form of professionals, developed and performed by talented specialists in professional contexts, albeit nourished by and existing alongside private, often family-based festivities. Though they scoured Granada's nooks and crannies hoping to find "authentic" cantaores, the only distinguished competitors (and prizewinners) were the septuagenarian Diego "Tenazas" Bermúdez—actually a retired professional—and a twelve-year-old prodigy named Manolo Ortega (1909–1973), who by the name Manolo Caracol would go on to an illustrious career as a cantaor. Another "discovery" was an ancient, blind beggar crone, "La Golondrina," who astounded listeners with her spirited singing and dancing, but, alas, she too turned out to be a former café cantante professional.

The second fatal error was to hold the event in Granada. Granada was, of course, hometown to Lorca and Falla, affording them the best resources for logistical support, and it did host a flamenco scene of sorts, primarily in the caves of Sacromonte, where Gitanos danced lively tangos for tourists and others. However, at that point in Spanish history, cante jondo—including the core cantes of siguiriyas and soleares—was to some extent a regional art, flourishing primarily in the towns of Seville and Cádiz provinces and, by extension, in Madrid. While Gerald Brenan (1957, 108), writing during this period, attested that amateur renditions of cante jondo were fairly common in the town south of Granada where he lived, professional-level cante jondo does not seem to have had much presence in Granada; that city, indeed, is a good hundred miles to the east of the flamenco epicenter and was not easily accessible by contemporary means of transport. Indeed, if Lorca and Falla had held their event in Seville or Jerez, they might even have attracted quite a few spirited amateur singers from local barrios. As it was, their choices doomed the event to a certain sort of failure, after which neither of them actively pursued an interest in flamenco. However, the concurso was not without positive effect, especially as it inspired subsequent similar events in Córdoba, Madrid, Huelva, and elsewhere and also persuaded a few of the cultural intelligentsia that flamenco was worth taking seriously as an art form.

The 1920s–1940s: The *Ópera Flamenca* Decades

With the decline of the cafés cantantes, public performances of flamenco did not end but in the 1920s came to be packaged in a new vaudeville-type form called *ópera flamenca*. These were commercial variety shows, presenting a mixed bag of popular songs and dances, operatic arias, perhaps even a comedian or juggler, along with a few flamenco items, generally foregrounding dance. They were staged in diverse venues that could accommodate large audiences, such as theaters and bullrings, even if the guitars, in the days before amplification, could scarcely be heard. The shows were certainly not operas but were labeled "*ópera flamenca*" by promoters as a means of avoiding stiff entertainment taxes that were levied on light commercial shows but not on opera and instrumental music.

The *ópera flamenca* shows, and the entire period they encompassed, are regarded as a relatively stagnant period in flamenco history. Flamenco had to share the "*ópera*" stage with various other entertainment genres, and to the extent that it was presented at all, it consisted mostly of lighter items, especially fandangos, sentimental Latin American–derived guajiras and *milongas*, flamenco-tinged commercial popular songs, and dance pieces. The prevailing style itself was often maudlin and trite, given to such mannerisms as decorative trills and showy melismas. Often the quasi-flamenco items were accompanied by an orchestra playing what soon became conventional patterns, such that spontaneous interaction between singer and guitarist was limited to one or two "traditional" items, which were seldom the jondo forms of siguiriyas or soleares. (As Fernando el de Triana asked in his 1935 memoir, "What crime has the guitar committed, that it should be replaced by little orchestras that are completely inappropriate for Andalusian song?" [294–95].) Lyrics were often mawkish laments, such as those in the song "Juan Simón," relating how the village gravedigger had to bury his own daughter. (This *romancillo* enjoyed phenomenal popularity in the early 1900s, in a manner that Molina and Espín [1992, ch. 5] relate to the mood of national self-pity indulged in by Spaniards in the wake of the disastrous Spanish-American War.) While flamenco came to be actively recorded and marketed by record labels including HMV and Odeon, these enterprises discouraged cantaores from singing cante jondo in favor of fandangos, Andalusian copla songs, and other accessible fare, much to the indignation of purists like Antonio Mairena, who sought to record only traditional cantes.

Some flamencologists have argued for a more charitable assessment of the *ópera* phenomenon (e.g., Camacho Galindo 1977, 138–43; Gelardo Navarro 2014). Most leading artists, including Pastora Pavón and Chacón, performed regularly in the shows, although they generally did so for lack of other venues. These spectacles certainly brought flamenco, in however marginal or bowdlerized a form, to a wide, even mass audience in a format free of associations with drinking, prostitution, or misbehavior that could be attacked by moralists. The art's popularity spread well beyond Andalusia, with Barcelona becoming a lively center. Advertisements reveal a healthy public interest in novelty and originality. Meanwhile, the expansion of the record industry from around 1927 did accommodate a considerable breadth of styles and cantes; Pastora Pavón herself recorded some 258 items (see Gamboa 2004, 408; Blas Vega 1995).

While the *ópera flamenca* shows lasted well beyond the 1920s, flamenco—along with many other aspects of Spanish life—struggled merely to survive from the Spanish Civil War (1936–1939) through the first decades of the Franco regime. Andalusia, the site of most of the fighting, was particularly ravaged during the war. Most professional performers were based in the cities—especially Madrid and Seville—where flamenco continued to be presented, in reduced amounts, in cafés cantantes, private parties, and other events. The three postwar decades, however, were a dismal era for flamenco and the arts in general. Culturally the nation was in a sort of coma for some thirty years. Part of the problem was sheer poverty, as the Franco regime persecuted its opponents, repressed labor unions, and embarked on an autarkic withdrawal from the world economy under which thousands died of starvation and millions more struggled merely to subsist. The state of formal music education reached a nadir in the 1940s and 1950s, and Spain's classical music tradition, in decline since the Baroque era, finally hit rock bottom. Meanwhile, in open alliance with the reactionary Catholic Church, the regime did its best to restrict, if not eliminate, all forms of modern culture, including urban flamenco (see Holguín 2019, part 3).

At the same time, through folkloric-tinged commercial cinema (*cine folklórico*), the state promoted an *españolada* image of a quaint, fun-loving, and conflict-free "Spain of the tambourine" in which Andalusian song and dance and a sanitized version of flamenco featured prominently (see, e.g., Pardo Ballester 2017, 261–87). While flamenco artists such as Manolo Caracol and Lola Flores were widely popular, some politically conscious critics saw the merry dance productions as window-dressing for Fascism. Meanwhile, public performances declined, and even taverns—long bastions of informal song sessions—were pressured to ban singing; many displayed signs saying "*Se prohíbe el cante*" (Singing flamenco is forbidden). Censors banned traditional cante, aside from fandangos, from Andalusian radio until 1962, and any cantaor who dared sing lyrics that could be remotely considered social-realist could be fined or imprisoned (Gamboa 2004, 33–34). In such unfavorable circumstances, it is not surprising that some of the best flamenco artists emigrated to seek their fortune in the Americas (or, like dancer Carmen Amaya and guitarist Sabicas, fled when Spain's Civil War broke out and simply stayed abroad).

While traditional cante received no institutional support from any quarter, the regime, via the female cohort (Sección Feminina) of the fascist Falange, supported a Coros y Danzas de España program that presented stage versions of various regional group dances, including Andalusian ones, by modestly attired women, both locally and abroad. The program studiously eschewed flamenco but did promote a degree of popular appreciation of regional folk music and dance (see Holguín 2019, ch. 6).

Private parties in which flamenco artists would be hired by patrons had been important performance venues since the earliest days of the genre and even in the pre-flamenco period. In the grim decades of the Franco regime, such parties—typically called juergas or fiestas—became the primary source of livelihood for most performers who still sought to earn a living through their art. Many bars in Madrid and in Andalusian cities and towns had rooms that patrons could rent, whether for a few hours or a few days, to host parties with flamenco. Performers might hang out in such venues every evening, hoping to be hired for juergas. Patrons might spirit performers off to their homes for fiestas, or even hire a horse-and-carriage or two, to spend the night carousing ostentatiously through the streets and serenading friends on their balconies above. A juerga could be sponsored by any person of means, but the quintessential patron in Andalusia was the aforementioned personage of the "señorito"—stereotypically, a despotic, dissolute landlord or his spoiled son. The Franco regime, in its reactionary socioeconomic policies, perpetuated the dominance of the Andalusian señoritos.

As private events rather than parts of public culture, juergas are documented primarily from reminiscences of performers, such as the garrulous Pepe el de la Matrona (José Núñez Meléndez, 1887–1980), Anica la Periñaca (1899–1987), or Pericón de Cádiz (1901–1980). From such accounts, it is clear that the juergas and their patrons varied greatly in nature. Some señoritos were ardent and sophisticated flamenco enthusiasts who appreciated the art of the cantaores and encouraged them to sing their best. As aristocrats, they were in fact the only Andalusians who could afford to patronize the better artists. A juerga might last all night or longer, during which a group of festive señoritos would drink, perhaps consort with prostitutes in a side room, doze off occasionally, and intermittently call on the flamencos to perform. Many such events were rewarding and enjoyable performance occasions for artists, with appreciative, knowledgeable listeners in a convivial, friendly setting. Guitarist Paco del Gastor (b. 1944) spoke fondly of the 1960s juergas in Morón:

> The señoritos would say, "Bring Mairena, bring Juan Talega, bring Diego [del Gastor]," and they'd occupy a room in the González bodega, and bring some rice and tapas that were out of this world, and they'd stay there for two days,

and people would tear their shirts listening to Mairena, Talega, and Diego. (qtd. in Curao 2011, 145)

Some patrons paid their musicians well, and a top performer like Chacón would of course demand an appropriate remuneration and not hesitate to request respectful attention and silence when he sang.

However, many juergas were exhausting, unremunerative, and even demeaning experiences for performers. Often, patrons simply wanted light, festive background music for their drunken and boisterous partying. Some of them treated the flamencos—typically Gitanos—as lowly menials to be rudely bossed about, mocked, and insulted.[3] Fees were generally not negotiated in advance, so the performers' payments were dependent on the mood of the patron at the end of the juerga—by which time he might be hungover, sullen, and regretting having spent so much on cases of wine; often he might avoid paying the performers at all.[4] Paco de Lucía described the juerga scene: "Some drunken señorito comes wanting to party, he picks a woman, a singer, a dancer, and a guitarist, and takes them somewhere to pass the night; my father never wanted me to be stuck in that scene" (qtd. in Téllez 2003, 73). As British flamenco Gerald Howson wrote, the system "forced the flamencos into a position of sycophantic dependency on their patrons and kept most of them in a state of near destitution" (1993, 259). In general, the juergas were simply unable to sustain many flamencos, however respected, beyond the most meager subsistence level of existence.

Meanwhile, through the 1960s—still in the pre-television era—flamenco continued to be performed as a standard opening item in traveling variety shows that also might feature jugglers, magicians, and perhaps a sexy "vedette" who sang and danced in sequins and feathers. Former singer and dancer Estela Zatania (2022) recalls touring with one such entourage:

> Upon arriving in a town, a loudspeaker was mounted on the roof of the lead vehicle, and we drove slowly around announcing the show in typically hyperbolic language, "internationally famous" and all that. After touring the area northwest of Madrid, . . . we headed for Extremadura, towns so small, not one street was paved. In one such town the municipal authorities had set up a makeshift "theater" in a large barn. A couple of confused pigs were escorted to another area, but someone had to remove the straw that covered the floor. Everyone in the company was given a pitchfork to clear space for "seating"—everyone but the guitarists[,] that is, who refused to help[,] alleging the need to protect their hands. People would be bringing their own folding chairs and crates to sit on.

Flamenco in the 1920s through the 1940s did not lack for talented artists, most of whom are fairly well documented on commercial recordings, despite commercial pressures to favor fandangos and light songs. Several singers, such as Niño Gloria or Tomás Pavón, were versatile, well-rounded cantaores. Some, such as Pepe Pinto (1903–1969) and Manuel Vallejo (Manuel Jiménez Martínez, 1891–1960), were well-rounded singers but were better known for the lighter fare they sang in order to pay their bills. Some, such as Pepe el de la Matrona, sang primarily at private parties, in which, depending on the tastes of their patrons, there might be demand for cante jondo. The long-lived and loquacious Matrona was, among other things, a protégé of Chacón, a direct link to nineteenth-century styles, and a celebrated raconteur, whose reminiscences were documented in interviews and a memoir. The flamenco scene in these decades was inhospitable for women singers, but perhaps the most revered, renowned, and complete vocalist of the era was the aforementioned Pastora Pavón, "La Niña de los Peines" (The Girl of the Combs, 1890–1969). Pavón excelled in all the cantes but played a particularly seminal role in popularizing peteneras and tangos. Despite being prohibited from singing, in different periods, by her mother and husband, she performed traditional cantes throughout the *ópera* period, struggling to maintain the art and her career. After a failed high-profile theater concert in 1949, she largely abandoned the stage.

Aside from Pepe Marchena, discussed below, the other most respected singer active during this period was Manolo Caracol, who, as mentioned, had achieved early fame as an award-winning prodigy at the 1922 Granada Concurso. In the lean years of the 1930s and 1940s, Caracol survived, and indeed prospered, by singing sentimental Andalusian copla songs, often accompanied by orchestra or organ and often in duet with his collaborator and consort, singer-dancer Lola Flores (1923–1995). Flores was a colorful and charismatic performer who, though not a Gitana, became a popular icon of Andalusian Gypsyness (partly through her stardom in cine folklórico). Flamenco purists scorned Caracol's commercial pop excursions, but he earned their devotion through his superbly expressive traditional flamenco, excelling both in the soulful siguiriyas and soleares as well as the festive bulerías and lending a particularly magisterial depth to fandangos.

Performing alongside these singers were the guitarists of the era, who collectively transformed flamenco guitar from being a serviceable accompanying style into a refined and sophisticated art form in its own right. The towering figure of Ramón Montoya, who remained active in their period, was joined by Manolo de Huelva (1892–1976), whose thumb-based style might be regarded as conservative (and "Gypsyesque"), and the younger Niño Ricardo (Manuel Serrapí Sánchez, 1904–1972), discussed below.

Special attention is due to Pepe Marchena (José Tejada Martín, 1903–1976), who was easily the most popular and influential singer of the era and, with his controversial style, managed to divide the flamenco audience—which by now included many passionately involved intellectuals—into two hostile camps, of worshippers and "haters." Tejada, a non-Gitano from Marchena, near Seville, sang from his adolescence in taverns in his hometown (whose name he adopted as a sobriquet) and around 1920 became popular in venues of Seville and Madrid. Within that decade he attained a fandom unprecedented for any flamenco artist and brought the art form as a whole—or his own version of it—to mass audiences; his style became the dominant idiom of the *ópera flamenca* phenomenon in general. He also provoked, among many in the flamenco world, an unprecedented outburst of vituperation and a sense that he was effectively destroying flamenco from within.

For the newcomer to flamenco, it may be initially hard to see what was so controversial about Marchena. Viewing a YouTube clip, one sees a nicely dressed gentleman of pleasant countenance singing melodiously in a bland, innocuous manner. Why all the fuss? Flamencologists—especially but not only Anselmo González Climent (1975)—have written erudite, flowery, quasi-philosophical essays ruminating on the aesthetics, spirit, and nature of "marchenismo" and its relation to flamenco history. For the present purposes, it may be more useful to focus on more objective aspects of his music. Easiest to note are some of his mannerisms, including his prefacing many songs, even on recordings, with spoken introductions in which he might announce himself in the third person—for example, as "Pepe Marchena, the King of Cante"—and then accord the subsequent song some spurious origin, such as "a sixteenth-century prayer from Marchena." With some items he would commence a verse by reciting rather than singing and then segue into song. Often he might start singing a given cante, such as a soleá, but instead of pursuing it to a conventional climax and conclusion, he would segue into another, such as a fandango, or a popular cuplé of the period, or a children's ditty set to bulerías. In general, he sang mostly fandangos and light guajiras, milongas, and his own invention, *colombianas*, which he adapted in 1931 from a popular Mexican song. In Donn Pohren's view, "his creations became wilder and further out, until he finally created himself right out of the limits of good flamenco" (1988, 137).

These departures would have sufficed to alienate purists, but it was Marchena's general style that was seen as most abominable to them, while endearing him to his many devotees (whose ranks certainly included top artists such as Pastora Pavón). Marchena made no attempt to sing in a passionate, anguished style, instead crooning softly, typically smiling pleasantly, with a conspicuous absence of histrionics, conveying the persona of an urbane, polished, unruffled nightclub entertainer (if not sommelier) attired in a "smoking jacket." Meanwhile, in contrast to traditional flamenco's rigorous avoidance of purely decorative melismas, he presented an ongoing rococo filigree of ornamentation, his agile voice fluttering about like a tweety-bird, up and down the gamut—especially, for example, at the concluding phrase of a fandango verse.

Marchena's style—often called *cante bonito* (pretty cante)—was cultivated, with some variation, by legions of followers, of whom the best known was Juanito Valderrama (Juan Valderrama Blanca, 1916–2004). While widely popular in the *ópera* era, by the 1960s Marchena and his imitators were coming to be vilified by flamenco purists, who saw them as redolent of Franco-style frippery and antithetical to the neo-traditionalism promoted by Antonio Mairena, discussed below. At present, however, Marchena and Valderrama are generally respected—perhaps partly because they are deceased, and the cante bonito style is no longer in vogue and hence is not a threat to mainstream flamenco.

Musical Developments: The Fandango

By the 1920s most of the repertoire of basic flamenco cantes was in place, and the most important new addition to the canon in that decade was the fandango. As outlined earlier in this chapter, in the first decades of the century Andalusia hosted a set of fandango variants, the best known of which were the folk verdiales, the well-established flamenco malagueñas, and the granaínas and tarantas that were being reworked into flamenco cantes by Chacón and others. The only fandango-family entities known by the name "fandango" were the variants flourishing as folk genres, often accompanying social dance, in towns in Huelva province. It was not until the mid-1920s that these started to be commonly performed and recorded as flamenco items, often with dramatic vocal delivery and sophisticated guitar accompaniment. The category of "fandangos de Huelva" soon came to comprise not only the rich store of many dozens of traditional melodies (typically associated with particular towns, such as Cabezas Rubias) but also a host of new tunes created by singers like Niño Gloria. In contrast to the elitist exclusion of fandangos from the 1922 Granada Concurso, fandango enthusiasts in Huelva held their own competitions in 1923 and 1924 that welcomed both fandangos and professional singers and were in some ways more successful than the Granada event (Canterla González 2014, 159–84).

A significant feature of these professional fandangos was the syncopated entrecopla style, with key chord changes (to Am and E, or La and Mi) falling mostly on the unaccented beat three of the 6/4 bar (see ex. 5.8 in ch. 5). This syncopation is present in the "Fandango (rasgueado)" in Eduardo Ocón's 1874 *Cantos Españoles*, and as a flamenco practice it may have been further standardized and elaborated from the mid-1920s by guitarists such as Manolo de Huelva, Manolo de Badajoz, and especially Niño Ricardo (see, e.g., Soler Díaz 2016, 61). In the same years, it also became common to sing the *fandango natural* in free rhythm, like the malagueña, granaína, and tarantas. These tuneful fandangos, whether metered or unmetered, quickly became the rage, supplanting the malagueña in popularity (Moore 2019) and coming to dominate the repertoire of the *ópera flamenca*, of Marchena, and of the dozens of "Niños" (roughly,

"The Kid from . . .") and other cantaores of the era. Particularly favored were singers with high tenor voices, like Manuel Vallejo, who typically reached up to D in the second octave above middle C in his fandangos. Cantaores such as El Sevillano (Antonio Pérez Guerrero, 1909–1989) and Niño Gloria managed to repeat the same small repertoire of fandango tunes with prodigious expressivity. At the same time, the idiom lent itself to cheap effects—such as interminable melismas at the conclusion of the stanza—and were accordingly disdained by singers like Chacón. In 1935 Fernando el de Triana lamented that with the exception of the *fandango de Alosno*, the rich repertoire of variants associated with particular towns in Huelva had been largely forsaken for what he regarded as trendy "adulterations" (279).

The 1950s–1960s: Revival and Mairenista Orthodoxy

In the mid-1950s, a dramatic revival of flamenco began to take place, inaugurating the genre's modern period and the dynamism that continues today.[5] On one level, the renovation was part of a general tentative revival of Spanish economy and culture. Because of its harsh dictatorship and its informal alliance with the Axis countries in World War II, Spain was left out of the Marshall Plan aiding Western Europe and had been essentially shunned as a pariah by the United States and other European countries. However, with the advent of the Cold War, its strategic location became an asset to the West, such that in 1953 the United States established military bases in the country, paying rent that injected a fair amount of capital into the economy. At the same time, there began an incremental but palpable revival of Spanish popular culture in the form of cinema, theater, concerts, and the popular press, however still circumscribed by an intolerant and xenophobic regime. Most directly relevant to flamenco was a series of four events that collectively marked and helped precipitate a renaissance of interest in the genre, legitimizing it as something more than seedy tavern music for Gitanos, prostitutes, and drunken señoritos. First, with microgroove technology having launched the era of the long-playing record, or LP, in 1954, a Swiss-Spanish enthusiast engaged guitarist Perico el del Lunar to produce a three-LP *Antología del cante flamenco,* with an accompanying booklet in Spanish, French, and English. Released a few years later in Spain, the set documented a wide range of veteran flamenco singers and their traditional repertoire and spawned a vogue of subsequent worthy anthologies, some produced by singers such as Antonio Mairena, Manolo Caracol, and Pepe Marchena. Meanwhile, as the local record industry itself took off, commercial recordings of flamenco in general proliferated, popularizing and legitimizing the art, providing models for aspiring performers, and garnering at least pocket money for those who recorded (and were fortunate enough to be paid at all).

Another seminal production was the publication in 1955 of the book *Flamencología (*Flamencology), by Argentine-Spaniard Anselmo González Climent. This was the first book to treat flamenco as a subject worthy of genuine study, and its title provided the term that has subsequently been adopted (not without reservations) for the field of flamenco studies in general. As did the 1954 *Antología* in the field of recording, *Flamencología* inaugurated a series of publications about flamenco, which commenced as a trickle and has since become a veritable and felicitous torrent, only further intensified in the internet era. (As with some other music genres, many performers and fans regard "flamencological" publications and their intellectual authors with disdain.)

González Climent's book inspired poet and flamencologist Ricardo Molina to collaborate with him in organizing the third landmark, in the form of an ambitious festival in 1956 in Córdoba, the Concurso Nacional de Cante Jondo, intended to revive the tradition that Lorca and Falla had hoped to begin twenty-four years earlier in their Granada competition. The annual Córdoba festival has continued until the present, and its success (unlike that of the Granada event) inspired a healthy vogue of summer flamenco festivals held throughout southern Spain, which have become essential parts of the scene.

The fourth milestone was the establishment in the mid-1960s of a flamencology research center in Jerez, the Cátedra de Flamencología y Estudios Folklóricos Andaluces (CAF), which has hosted a library, published a journal, and funded conferences and other events that have provided legitimacy to flamenco studies and inspired other sorts of institutional support elsewhere in the country (see, e.g., Gamboa 2004, 166–67). These events thus inaugurated what could be regarded as four of the most essential activities in the modern flamenco scene: recordings, festivals, flamencological publications, and institutional support.

Several other developments further revitalized the genre. One was the emergence of peñas, or flamenco clubs, consisting of small or medium-size venues funded by dues-paying connoisseurs, that host regular performances. While Granada's peña La Platería—still a fine venue—was founded in the 1940s, it was from the late 1950s that the peñas really came to proliferate and become focal institutions of flamenco in an era when flamenco was discouraged or officially prohibited at taverns. La Platería, Málaga's Peña Juan Breva, and Torres Macarena in Seville are among the hundreds of clubs that have constituted invaluable centers for performance, documentation, and general promotion of the art. Unfortunately, many of the peñas were exclusively male domains until recent decades.

Yet another significant development was the boom of tourism and of new venues—the *tablaos*—that, somewhat like latter-day versions of cafés cantantes, began presenting flamenco in family-friendly clubs to mixed audiences of locals and tourists. The flow of tourists had been interrupted by the vicissitudes of the Spanish Civil War, followed by World War II and the stagnation of the next decade, but from the late 1950s the influx resumed with vigor. The Franco regime, eager for both revenue and legitimation, promoted the tourist boom in various ways, including infrastructure and publicity. As Holguín documents (2019, ch. 7), in advertising Spanish tourism the regime found itself in a bit of a quandary, having to reconcile its puritanical dislike of flamenco with the tourist demand for it; the basic policy included a *nacional flamenquismo* comprising a gingerly promotion of sanitized versions of the art and the festive image of "Spain of the castanets." In any case, independent of state policies, dozens of tablaos sprang up in Madrid, Andalusia, and elsewhere, proffering flamenco stage shows to sunburned, freely spending visitors who knew nothing of the art but were eager to see a dance-oriented version of it in respectable establishments where they could sip sangria and take photos.[6] The tablaos typically featured a set of "in-house" dancers (a *cuadro)* and a featured artist, also usually a dancer.

The tablaos have often been disparaged for their touristic orientation, their emphasis on dance spectacle rather than solo artistry, their uneven standards, and a penchant for hiring female dancers for their looks rather than their talent. However, since their inception, the tablaos have played important roles in flamenco. From the early 1960s, they were providing steady, salaried employment to hundreds of performers in safe rather than seedy contexts. Female dancers and singers were valued and remunerated (albeit poorly) and were not regarded as disreputable as they might have been in the cafés cantantes. Moreover, while the cafés cantantes mostly presented flamenco only alongside other popular entertainment, the tablaos have focused on flamenco. They have also served as training grounds where legions of singers, guitarists, and dancers learned to perform in compás, mastered the full range of cantes, and became polished and experienced stage artists. Many performers recall the tablao scene of the 1950s–1970s fondly, with special affection for venues such as Madrid's La Zambra and Café de Chinitas (see Murillo Saborido 2017). The artists were often top-notch and included not only "orthodox" performers but also innovative figures such as Diego Carrasco and Enrique Morente (Gamboa 2005, 155–61). Artists—both men and women—would typically reconvene after the show at some local tavern for spirited informal fiestas that would last until dawn. Like some spectacles presented as long ago as the early 1800s, the tablao audiences often included not only tourists but also many knowledgeable and appreciative locals (see, e.g., Moore 2015, 172). Meanwhile, throughout the 1960s, flamenco continued to be performed for private patrons at roadside ventas like the Casablanca in Seville. Patrons, whether a set of señoritos or a man and his girlfriend, could rent a room for the evening and hire either the resident cuadro—that is, a set of musicians and dancers—or other performers who might be on call.

In speaking of foreign interest in flamenco, mention must be made of the activities of Donn Pohren (1929–2007), an American flamenco enthusiast who in 1965 purchased a small ranch near the town of Morón and turned it into a flamenco center of sorts, catering primarily to foreigners—especially American guitar students. Guests would stay for various lengths of time, paying modest fees, while enjoying the town's ambience and attending the regular juergas that the fun-loving Pohren staged, which featured local, mostly Gitano performers, especially guitarist Diego del Gastor (1908–1973). Gastor, discussed below, was much beloved both by the foreigners and local flamencos, both for his playing—at once original and old-fashioned—and his famously congenial temperament. Over the decades of its operation, the *finca* (ranch) hosted many dozens of visitors, several of whom became fanatic devotees and proselytizers of Gastor's playing and of flamenco in general. Pohren himself authored four informative, entertaining, and unabashedly opinionated books on flamenco (1962, 1980, 1988, 1992), which were by far the best publications on the subject available in English during his time and well afterward.

The final landmark of this period's revival was the production of a remarkable set of one hundred half-hour, black-and-white documentaries about flamenco, collectively titled *Rito y geografía del cante flamenco,* which aired on Spanish National Television between 1971 and 1973. Produced by a set of young, progressive cinematographers with the collaboration of top flamencologists, these films provided a comprehensive portrait of the flamenco world, covering history, cantes, regions, and especially singers, from stars like Manolo Caracol to lesser-known, mostly amateur Gitanos like "La familia de los Perrate." Definitively opting for realism instead of the saccharine, prettified nacional flamenquismo approach, the shows typically presented interviews with and performances by artists not on stage but seated comfortably in local taverns or private homes, in front of wine-laden tables and surrounded by friends and family. With the artists clearly feeling relaxed, many of the performances were superb, often leading to spontaneous dancing and providing glimpses of what Gitano family fiestas were like. In a period of suffocating state control of the mass media, the producers of the series envisioned their project not merely as a documentation of flamenco but also as a subtle subversion of the regime's negation of any form of grassroots regional culture (Molina 1998). The *Rito* series—now available on the internet—has remained an extraordinary gold mine for students and scholars of flamenco.[7]

Mairena and Mairenismo

An essential concomitant of the flamenco revival was the emergence of a host of brilliant performers, including singers, dancers, and guitarists, both male and female and Gitano and non-Gitano. Many of these were at once reared in traditional flamenco households while able to take advantage of the new opportunities that the renovation offered. Some of the most outstanding cantaores will be mentioned further below, but special attention must be paid to the impact of the most influential artist of the period, Antonio Mairena (Antonio Cruz García, 1909–1983).[8]

Mairena was born in the Andalusian town Mairena del Alcor, whose name he eventually adopted as a sobriquet. His father and grandfather were blacksmiths, and the family was part of the town's quintessentially poor but cohesive and proud Gitano community, which included many accomplished singers and dancers. Although his formative years coincided with the Marchenista fandango vogue, he grew up steeped in cante jondo, whether the martinetes sung in the family's forge or the siguiriyas and soleares sung by Manuel Torre, Joaquín el de la Paula, and other veteran cantaores at local Gitano reunions.[9] He had to abandon school after three years to assist his father at the anvil but eventually took up singing and dancing and by his teenage years was earning recognition. With Torre as his model, he developed a keen sense of a dichotomy between the traditional cante jondo rooted in Gitano communities like his own and, by contrast, what he regarded as the lighter music—especially fandango variants—of non-Gitano singers like Marchena and Manuel Vallejo, as well as the commercial ventures of his primary rival, Manolo Caracol. Mairena survived the 1930s–1950s singing professionally in and around Seville and Madrid, all the while energetically learning all the repertoire he could from elderly cantaores. Offered a recording contract in 1941, he resented being obliged to sing light fandangos and *cuplés por bulerías* rather than cante jondo. In 1952 he had the good fortune to win the country's lottery, enabling him to devote all his energies to flamenco. In 1962 he was granted a lucrative "Golden Key Award" (*La Llave de Oro del Cante*) in a competition that, though seen as prestigious by some, was also essentially arranged for him by his admirers.

It was in the early 1960s that he undertook the public campaign for which he became known: to codify and propagate the cante jondo repertoire, to dignify flamenco and rescue it from maudlin marchenismo and the seamy world of señorito juergas, to legitimize and celebrate the preeminence of Gitanos in flamenco, and to inspire the younger generation of Gitanos to maintain that repertoire and the venerable traditions of the community in general. In 1963 with Ricardo Molina he coauthored the book *Mundo y formas del cante flamenco,* which, despite problems, constituted an unprecedentedly informative history and taxonomy of flamenco cante. Equally valuable were the sets of 1960s anthology recordings, either sung or edited by himself, which featured the traditional "cante gitano-andaluz" that he successfully sought to revive, especially soleá, siguiriyas, tangos, and tonás, including various obscure cantes and estilos that he had assiduously collected and in some cases refashioned.

Together, this book and record anthology served as veritable bibles for a generation of aspiring singers, and even today many vocalists use the records to learn cantes and estilos, especially lesser-known forms. They have been supplemented by two books elaborating his compilations of traditional estilos—namely, *Antonio Mairena en el mundo de la siguiriya y la soleá* (Soler Guevara and Soler Díaz 1992) and *El cante jondo de territorio a los repertorios: Tonás, siguiriyas, soleares* (Lefranc 2000). Flamencologist Norman Kliman's website (http://canteytoque.es) provides audio samples of most of these estilos, serving as yet another valuable resource for singers.

Meanwhile, Mairena performed and proselytized widely, exerting considerable influence on contemporary styles and repertoires and inspiring a veritable school of worthy followers, including his brothers Curro and Manuel as well as José Menese and Curro Malena. He also energetically promoted the careers of younger singers such as María Vargas and La Perla de Cádiz (Antonia Gilabert Vargas) and made known to the broader public veteran juerga performers such as Juan Talega and Anica la Periñaca. In 1976 he published a readable memoir, *Las confesiones de Antonio Mairena,* in which he further elaborated his ideas. Among flamenco historians, there is unanimous agreement that he made an extraordinary contribution to the art form. Accordingly, the term "*mairenismo*" came to denote what during the 1960s and 1970s was perhaps the dominant ideology in flamenco, comprising a *gitanismo* and the belief that the flamenco repertoire was essentially complete and was only to be developed rather than expanded.

However—a word that anyone familiar with flamencological literature will be expecting around now—by the mid-1970s mairenismo was also coming to be seen in many circles as stifling, reactionary, and excessively gitanocentric. Among the less important criticisms of Mairena were the ambivalences about his singing, which, though indisputably solid, was enjoyed and respected by some people but deemed cold and didactic by others (e.g., Camacho Galindo 1977, 85). Another relatively minor criticism concerned his project of tracing genealogies of soleá and siguiriyas estilos, attributing their authorship or popularization to various known or less-known singers of previous generations. Mairena could be said to have made these attributions in order to document in print those that were current among elders and cognoscenti, to highlight the role of Gitanos as composers rather than "mere interpreters," and to bestow on flamenco a deserved sense of actual history instead of a hopelessly murky evolution. While many of the attributions—for instance, the siguiriyas of Silverio—were plausible, in an orally transmitted genre where tunes were freely altered over the generations, several of the attributions were dubious and were dismissed as such by skeptics such as Pastora Pavón and Manolo Caracol. Moreover, it was clear that in some cases Mairena had simply heard some fragment somewhere and then elaborated it into a full-blown estilo, which he then presented with a dignified genealogy—for example, "the soleá of Charamusco" (see, e.g., Grimaldos 2010, 120–21). More than a few flamencologists have noted the irony that while Mairena claimed to be merely documenting a canonic, traditional repertoire that was not to be expanded, he in fact was effectively composing several estilos.[10] To add to the confusion, he claimed to be the author of various traditional lyrics while, conversely, attributing to legendary past singers other lyrics that were evidently of his own invention.

A more substantial objection to mairenismo involved what many saw as his explicit conception of flamenco, and especially cante jondo, as a fundamentally Gitano art form, to which non-Gitanos have contributed in only a secondary fashion. As noted above, the relation between Gitanos and non-Gitanos in flamenco history and character is extremely complex and contentious. In his writings and other forums, it was Mairena who most explicitly propounded the gitanophilic view of the art form. In doing so, he could be said to have been motivated by an awareness of the history of persecution of Gitanos, the tension he may have felt as the only Gitano in his elementary school class, the pride and cohesiveness of his own community, and a desire to instill in younger Gitanos an appreciation of cante jondo and their contribution to it. As the first Gitano flamencologist (and one of the first Gitano "organic intellectuals" in Spain), he saw himself as playing an important role in celebrating and legitimizing the role his community had played in Spanish culture. A broader context for his activism was the crisis befalling the Gitano community during this period as such traditional occupations as blacksmithing and horse-trading evaporated. During this period, many Gitanos acquired education and managed to move into the lower-middle classes, and flamenco performers certainly found new opportunities, but on the whole, the same modernization process that was uplifting the Spanish economy wreaked a new sort of havoc on Gitano communities.

There were several aspects to Mairena's gitanismo. One, evident in his writings, was a disparagement of non-Gitano singers like Chacón and Marchena and of the supposedly lighter cantes, such as peteneras, fandangos, and cantes of the Levant (Gamboa 2004, 169). Another was his advocating of the dubious "hermetic theory," discussed above, which claimed that cante jondo evolved in private Gitano households in the early 1800s and then became diluted and Andalusianized in the cafés cantantes. Most questionable was his promoting of the notion of *Razón Incorpórea* (Incorporeal Reason), a term that sounds no more elegant in Spanish than in translation. This was a kind of mystical, nebulous spirit of timeless Gitano law, pride, and tradition that appeared to him one night in the form of a goddess of sorts and bestowed upon him the honor and duty of inspiring his people (Mairena 1976, 186). As might be expected, this notion has inspired mostly cynicism and eye-rolling and certainly has not been perpetuated by subsequent generations.

The most fundamental criticism of mairenismo concerned the way it promoted an orthodoxy in terms of repertoire and style and a general spirit that prized fidelity to tradition rather than creativity and innovation. Mairena had sought, through his research, recordings, and publications, to establish a canonic and codified repertoire of flamenco cantes and estilos.[11] He clarified that this repertoire was complete and was not to be expanded and that subsequent progress and innovation were to consist only of development of this melodic corpus. It should be acknowledged that in asserting, "*El cante está hecho*" (the cante [repertoire] is complete), Mairena was in some respects simply stating an established fact; even now, half a century later, there have been no additions to the basic repertoire of cantes, and innovations, while substantial, have comprised elaborations of, rather than additions to, the existing repertoire. However, the neo-traditional orthodoxy of mairenismo promoted an aesthetic of xenophobia and hostility to innovation that by the 1970s was coming to be resented by younger musicians. At the same time, mairenismo also effected a dictatorial sidelining of worthy elder singers who were tainted as populist *fandangueros*. From Timothy Mitchell's perspective, mairenismo constituted "a reactionary artistic revolution to the right, that is, the reimposition of hierarchy, small-group dynamics, ritualism, archaic singing styles, and self-conscious ethnicity" (1994, 16).

Since Mairena's passing, the legacy of mairenismo has been mixed. As discussed previously, the hermetic theory is no longer in favor among most flamencologists, though it continues to pop up here and there and is elaborated in Pedro Peña's volume *Los gitanos flamencos* (2013). For its part, a general gitanocentric conception of flamenco persists and perhaps will never cease to be debated. Since recent decades, the term "mairenismo" has had mostly pejorative connotations, as indicating a stuffy, narrow-minded conservatism, and *mairenista* is most commonly deployed as an epithet for someone who opposes innovation and disparages anything but Gitano-style cante jondo.[12]

Musical Developments: Neo-Classical Consolidation

The period of the 1950s–1960s was not marked by such conspicuous and tangible changes in terms of repertoire and style as were previous decades. Regardless of one's opinions of mairenismo, the maestro's assertion "el cante está hecho" was largely correct in that the basic repertoire of cantes and, to a large extent, estilos had been established and consolidated by this period and was not further expanded. With a neoclassicism replacing the Marchena vogue, most prominent vocalists sang in a more or less traditional style. However, fandangos continued to be sung, though often in an elaborate, deeply expressive, rather than hackneyed, fashion that exhibited its own sort of *jondura,* or depth. During this period, for example, Manuel Agujetas (1939–2015) and Fosforito (Antonio Fernández Díaz, 1932–) regularly sang fandangos, and Chocolate (Antonio Núñez Montoya, 1931–2005) became well known for his soulful renderings of tarantas (a fandango form).

This period was in some ways a felicitous one for the art in its particular conjuncture of traditional community values and modern mass media and performance opportunities. As in previous generations, there were many artists who were raised in traditional, especially Gitano households where flamenco was performed regularly, whether by children or elderly aunties, constituting a part of the fabric of life. At the same time, as of these decades an unprecedented number of these home-trained musicians and dancers were able to take up professional careers, typically starting in tablaos and ideally graduating to the festival circuit.

It would be pointless to attempt to cite all the distinguished singers who flourished primarily in this era, or to try to sum up their particular contributions in pithy phrases, but aside from those mentioned previously or in the next chapter, some of the most distinguished ones include the following (in no particular order): Terremoto (Fernando Fernández, 1934–1981), Aurelio Selle (or Sellés, 1887–1974), Juanito Varea (1913–1985), Porrina de Badajoz (José Salazar Molina, 1924–1977), Fernanda and Bernarda de Utrera (Fernanda and Bernarda Jiménez Peña, 1923–2006 and 1927–2009, respectively), and the aforementioned Agujetas, Fosforito, and Chocolate. Particularly prominent was Manolo Caracol, whose expressiveness and flair contrasted with Mairena's rather arid style. Accordingly, the world of hardcore flamenco fans and performers was to some extent divided into the two camps: of *caracoleros* and *mairenistas* (both of whom might disparage the unmentionable third camp, of *marchenistas*).

The era was also a dynamic one for guitar playing.[13] With the passing of Ramón Montoya in 1949, Niño Ricardo, whose records were more widely available, became the most popular and imitated guitarist. Like Montoya, Ricardo was active more as an accompanist than a soloist, and his playing could sometimes be a bit *sucio* (dirty, rough), as if his fingers could not keep up with his ideas and energy. (He is said to have had fingernail problems.) Nevertheless, his prodigious repertoire of original falsetas, in all palos, was assiduously learned by almost all aspiring guitarists, including the young Paco de Lucía. Meanwhile, as an accompanist he was rivaled by Melchor de Marchena (Melchor Jiménez Torres, 1907–1980), favored sideman of Antonio Mairena. In general, guitar solos had not achieved the popularity in Spain that they would in the hands of Paco de Lucía and others in the 1970s. While guitarists remained relatively rare in towns like Lebrija and Utrera, Jerez continued to produce gifted Gitano artists such as Paco Cepero (b. 1942), Parilla de Jerez (Manuel Fernández Molina, 1945–2009), and the Morao dynasty, which included Moraito (Manuel Morao, b. 1929), his brother "Moraito Chico" (Juan Moreno, 1935–2002), and the latter's son—also, confusingly, "Moraito Chico" (Manuel Morena Junquera, 1956–2011).

The nearby town of Morón was home to the aforementioned Diego del Gastor, who was celebrated both for his unique playing and his quintessentially bohemian disinterest in fame or fortune. Gastor composed many artful and distinctive falsetas and was a favored accompanist for several local singers, despite his relatively modest technique and repertoire and a generally "stripped down" (*cuerda pelá*) style. Gamboa (2004, 367–70) characterizes his playing as the product of a "time tunnel" through which a few local guitarists had transmitted the archaic style of Paco de Lucena (d. 1898). Gastor continues to be revered, though it must be said that his style is not widely imitated and sounds a bit quaint by modern standards.

In quite a different category were three guitarists who enjoyed careers mostly as soloists in the Americas and whose music was consequently not well known in Spain. The most brilliant of these was Sabicas (Agustín Castellon, 1912–1990), who with dancer and partner Carmen Amaya fled the Spanish Civil War and subsequent dictatorship to perform together in Latin America and the United States. In 1955 Sabicas settled in New York, where he became best known as a solo guitarist, releasing a series of albums (especially *Flamenco Puro* [1959]) that established new standards for technique and brilliance of falsetas. Guitarists would note specific technical advances, such as six-string arpeggios, but most unprecedented was the extraordinary clarity of Sabicas's dazzling picados and other effects, which could be said to contrast with the somewhat rough playing of Niño Ricardo.

Another contemporary who settled in New York was Mario Escudero (1928–2004), who, with a distinctively classical orientation, was best known for etude-like compositions such as "Ímpetu" (a bulerías of sorts) rather than *por derecho* ("straight-ahead") flamenco playing. Escudero himself was particularly inspired by flamenco guitarist and composer Esteban de Sanlúcar (Esteban Delgado Bernal), who had settled in Latin America. More renowned—whether deservedly or not—than these among American audiences was a third New York immigrant, Carlos Montoya (1903–1993), a nephew of Ramón. Montoya, skillfully promoted by his American wife, brought solo flamenco guitar to the most prestigious American concert venues over the course of his lucrative career and, indeed, helped make that idiom (which had no language barrier) considerably more popular than it was in Spain. His solo career was buoyed by the advent of LP records, of which he eventually made more than fifty. Although Montoya had formidable technique and could be inspired (as perhaps in his versions of granaínas), he was not highly regarded by connoisseurs, especially because of his frequent disregard for compás and his showy mannerisms. The latter would include playing extended *legato* passages with the left hand only (hammering-on and pulling-off) in a manner that would be regarded as gimmicky by mainstream flamenco standards. His playing, however, was certainly more orthodox than that of Manitas de Plata ("Silver Hands," Ricardo Baliardo, 1921–2014), a French Romani who enjoyed a lively career on the Riviera and elsewhere playing his own flashy and jumbled version of flamenco. Manitas could be said to have helped popularize flamenco, or a facsimile of it, on the international circuit. A dandy, flamboyant showman and a ladies' man, in his occasional encounters with real flamenco guitarists he was insistently apologetic about his playing, telling Paco de Lucía, "Cousin, I don't know how to play the instrument, but I have twelve children to feed" (in Gamboa 2016, IV:379).

The guitar solos recorded by Sabicas, Montoya, and a few others during this period were mostly strings of falsetas rather than structured compositions. The falsetas themselves could be played independently or recycled in other solo cuts on records. The recorded solos would usually be given titles evocative of the palo, such as "Ecos de la mina (tarantas)." The primary exceptions to this practice were some pieces by Sanlúcar (such as "Panaderos Flamencos") and Escudero, especially his bulerías "Ímpetu," which, with its recurring "theme," had a more structured character and, accordingly, was learned and played faithfully as a concert item by many other guitarists, including Paco de Lucía.

The "Revolutionary" 1970s

If the 1960s in Spain was a period of belated economic renaissance, cultural awakening, and revival of flamenco, the 1970s saw the full fruition of these trends, further enhanced by the end of the Franco regime and the advent of democracy. The economic boom engineered by the regime's "technocrats"—against the inclinations of the narrow-minded despot himself—was in full flower, with dramatic expansions of tourism, manufacturing, and commerce. Equally striking was the cultural aperture encompassing education, mass media, and the arts, with the nation moving past the decades of censorship, xenophobia, isolation, and domination of the reactionary Catholic Church. The awakening involved both avid consumption of foreign developments—comprising everything from rock to miniskirts—as well as blossoming of local cultural production, including cinema, theater, literature, and all kinds of music, from classical concerts to revivals of regional folk song. Meanwhile, the regime's gradual relaxation of censorship around the beginning of the decade became definitive with Franco's death in 1975, and the country successfully transitioned to democracy and the contention of a healthy range of political parties.

During this decade many people continued to associate flamenco—"*lelolai* music"—with both kitsch tourist shows and a seedy lumpen underworld, and the new scourge of drug addiction tainted popular perceptions of urban Gitanos and their flamenco-tinged pop groups like Los Chunguitos. Nevertheless, flamenco's public image was changing, as it increasingly came to be seen as a legitimate and even fashionable art form. The flamenco scene was booming, with lively extension of the trends of the previous decade. Tablaos, peñas, stage concerts, and summer festivals proliferated and thrived, as did commercial recordings and flamencological publications. The summer festivals were especially dynamic, as Andalusian towns competed with each other to present serious cante by the best singers, wooing them away from the tablao circuit. In some circles a mairenista orthodoxy prevailed, comprising at once a healthy cultivation of a wide range of traditional cantes and a sense that the repertoire was thus complete and that innovation constituted a threat to this delicate art form that had struggled for so long merely to survive. However, despite the persistence of this conservatism, the flamenco scene simmered with an extraordinary amount of innovation and experimentation, whether in style, performance contexts, lyric content, or sheer numbers of gifted performers. The boom also provided genuine livelihoods to legions of Gitanos, especially since the "informal sector" of performing music and dance was consistent with their traditional values and way of life.

A concurrent development was the foregrounding of flamenco in popular cinema, which was emerging from decades of stagnation under Franco. In the transitional 1970s, flamenco items were introduced in dramas, as was the popular bulerías of Lole y Manuel, "Todo es de color" in the 1976 film *Manuela* by Gonzalo García Pelayo. In the 1980s such trends intensified, especially in the "Flamenco Trilogy" by Carlos Saura (b. 1932), consisting of *Bodas de sangre* (Blood Wedding, 1981), *Carmen* (1983), and *El amor brujo* (Love, the Magician, 1986), followed in 1995 by his documentary *Flamenco* (see, e.g., Cordero Sánchez 2014, ch. 2).

Nuevo Flamenco

In the realm of repertoire and style, there was a veritable explosion of new forms that fell under the umbrella category of "nuevo flamenco." This "new flamenco" has comprised such a vast diversity of idioms, personages, and agendas and has come to constitute such an extensive and lively part of the cultural scene that it merits full book-length study. As such, this volume makes no attempt to provide a proper survey of nuevo flamenco. In style and structure, much nuevo flamenco lies fairly unambiguously outside the boundaries of flamenco per se, being more in the realm of other commercial popular music genres (rock, pop ballads, etc.). (Also outside the realm of flamenco would be various songs, whether coplas or pop rumbas, whose flamenco tinge consists of no more than a vocal flourish or the odd Andalusian cadence.) At the same time, however, the boundaries of flamenco as a genre are blurry and are the subject of ongoing and often heated disputation; accordingly, much nuevo flamenco would generally be acknowledged as lying within the borders of flamenco, even as narrowly defined, and even if many lovers of the art prefer more traditional cantes and estilos.

Since its very inception, flamenco as a genre has existed as part of a fluid continuum comprising various other genres of popular song. Many café cantante and subsequent *ópera flamenca* presentations were variety shows featuring a potpourri of flamenco and other types of performances. Many flamenco cantaores themselves, from Manuel Vallejo to Manolo Caracol, have sung both traditional flamenco as well as contemporary popular genres, such as *canción andaluza* or copla. In that sense, the flamenco-rock fusions in "Catalan rumba" or Enrique Morente's album *Omega* represent merely another chapter in the ongoing syncretism of flamenco with contemporary pop genres. In other ways, however, the nuevo flamenco phenomenon was qualitatively different, especially in the sheer amount of activity and in the new genres involved, especially rock and the pop ballad.

While the heterogeneity of nuevo flamenco makes generalizations about style difficult, one may note two typical features that may situate an item on or outside the borders of flamenco per se. One is the addition of miscellaneous instruments beyond or in place of guitar and the now-ubiquitous *cajón* (a box-like hand drum). Many nuevo flamenco songs incorporate electric bass and perhaps even other instruments in ways that do not disqualify the song as flamenco. In some cases, however, the expanded instrumental ensemble—perhaps in the form of a rock band—lends the song a character that may be much more redolent of rock or pop than flamenco, especially when their presence eliminates improvisation.

The second feature distinguishing much nuevo flamenco—and most pop songs in general—from traditional flamenco involves formal structure. A standard flamenco item—which should not be called a "song"—consists of a series of thematically independent stanzas (coplas) each set to a different preexisting stock tune (an estilo) in a given cante. This form is quite distinct from that of a "song" per se, which typically implies a fixed set of thematically related verses set to a precomposed, original melody (which is not meant to serve as a stock tune in other items). In the realm of flamenco or pop flamenco, such an item, if an original composition, could be called a *canción de autor* (authored song), or a *tema* (lit., theme), or, slightly disparagingly, a *temita*. Typically, it might have a simple (supposedly) catchy refrain (or *coro*) rendered by a chorus of two or three backup singers, who might sing in parallel thirds. Such a song might or might not be regarded as flamenco per se, depending on how closely it coheres to an extant cante in terms of compás or other features. Thus, for example, José Merce's song "Aire" might be regarded as a bulerías or perhaps a *canción por bulerías* (a song in bulerías rhythm). As discussed further in chapter 4, such genre distinctions—whether a song is accepted as "flamenco" or not—are important to some people and not others. Often, the precomposed entity is merely one stanza or tercio within a longer item, in which case (especially in bulerías) it might be called a cuplé—a term that will be used thusly in this book but that, as mentioned earlier, otherwise denoted a genre of popular, typically saucy songs of the 1920s and 1930s. That is, a cantaor like Camarón de la Isla might commence a bulerías with standard verses and melodies (such as a *bulería corta*, described in chapter 5) and segue to a section presenting an original melody that had been composed for him by Pepe de Lucía; this section could be called a cuplé.

The advent of nuevo flamenco brought a prodigious explosion of flamenco-inflected composition, whether within the boundaries of flamenco or not. Outside those boundaries, insofar as they have been generally accepted, would be songs more in the realm of commercial popular music, in the sense of having stylistically evolved in connection with the mass media, through which they were marketed as commodities. Some of these have been akin to rock, or the pop ballad, but sung, to some extent, in an aflamencado vocal style. In the 1970s and 1980s, popular in some circles were pop "rumbas," with flamenco-tinged vocal style and Andalusian harmonies, by Madrid- and Barcelona-based "Gypsy rock" artists such as Bambino, Las Grecas, and Peret, and Gitano groups from Madrid's Caño Roto (broken water pipe) barrio. Representing a more eclectic and arguably sophisticated form of crossover would be such a band as Ketama, active in the 1980s and 1990s, or some disco-flavored songs (e.g., "Voz de Agua") by Tijeritas, who was also a fine cantaor in the vein of Camarón de la Isla. Yet another flamenco-tinged genre was the pop-oriented sevillanas, which would be widely marketed in Seville—including by flamenco singers—on records and cassettes during the vernal Fería season.

A very different sort of "new flamenco" would be represented by some of the productions of Niño de Elche (Francisco Contreras Molina, b. 1985), a unique performance artist whose output is prodigious and diverse. Much of his music is in a singer-songwriter or avant-garde pop vein unrelated to flamenco, while he also sings "por derecho" flamenco. In the flamenco world, however, he may be best known—or most notorious—for productions (especially a concert at the 2018 Bienal de Sevilla and the album *Antología del cante flamenco heterodoxo*) in which he subjected flamenco to various forms of postmodern deconstruction, much to the outrage of critics and purists.

Paco de Lucía and Camarón de la Isla

By far the two most important figures in the flamenco revival were guitarist Paco de Lucía (Francisco Sánchez Gómez, 1947–2014) and singer Camarón de la Isla (José Monje Cruz, 1950–1992). Paco's father, Antonio Sánchez, was a guitarist who supported his wife and five children by working day jobs and accompanying singers at juergas in their town of Algeciras, near Gibraltar. Although not Gitanos, the Sánchez family lived among Gitanos and had amicable relations with them. (Living near the British outpost, they also picked up bits of English.) When Antonio's sons, Ramón (1938–2009), Pepe (b. 1945), and Paco, began to respond well to his musical instruction, Antonio undertook what would turn out to be a phenomenally successful "master plan" of raising a brood of distinguished flamenco musicians, even at the expense of taking Paco out of school at age eleven in order to practice. Ramón, the eldest, became a guitarist, initially in the mold of Niño Ricardo, and toured as an accompanist from his teenage years. Pepe became a gifted singer but opted to devote his professional activities more toward composing songs and flamenco cuplés; both he and Ramón would go on to collaborate extensively with Paco, who, from childhood, distinguished himself as the resident genius, cultivating a ferocious technique and freely altering the Ninõ Ricardo falsetas Ramón taught him.

From his teenage years, the young virtuoso was performing with his brothers, winning local competitions, touring with dance troupes, and recording both as soloist and accompanist. Visiting New York on tour with dancer José Greco in 1963, he met Sabicas and Mario Escudero, both of whom encouraged him to compose his own material rather than relying on Ricardo's. The subsequent landmark event in Paco's career and flamenco guitar history was the 1967 solo album *La fabulosa guitarra de Paco de Lucía*, which contained a mixture of nicely played items in the style of Sabicas, Ricardo, and Escudero, along with original falsetas and technical advances that presaged the dramatic innovations to follow. These latter were fully evident in his next solo album, *Fantasía Flamenca de Paco de Lucía* (1969), which presented the guitarist as a mature virtuoso with his own voice. The listener seeking an entrée to Paco's neo-traditional style can do little better than to listen to the soulful tarantas "Aires de Linares," with its modernist chords and charming tremolo melody, and the bulerías "El tempul," a breathless medley of dazzlingly original falsetas, which were henceforth dissected and practiced by legions of guitarists.

By this time, Paco and Camarón had met, and their friendship cemented as they worked in troupes touring Europe. Camarón, son of a blacksmith in the Gitano barrio of San Fernando, had developed an early flair for cante and, after singing for tips in trolleys as a youth, was performing professionally in tablaos in Málaga from the age of fifteen. Gifted with a solid, pleasantly husky (*afillá*) voice, a prodigious musicality, and a congenial, if soft-spoken, demeanor, Camarón was ideally suited to team up with Paco and his family, who warmly adopted him as one of their own. The two created a sensation in the flamenco world with their debut album, *Camarón de la Isla con la colaboración especial de Paco de Lucía* (1969/1970). Though often referred to by the name of its innovative bulerías, "Al verte las flores lloran," the LP's hit song was the tangos "Detras del tuyo se va," with its catchy, pop-tinged "a-rin-tin-tin" refrain. American flamencologist Paco Sevilla wrote of these two songs, "In place of the rather stodgy 'three-chords-and-you're-out' monotony of the traditional styles came an airy lightness fueled by countertime, new melodies, and innovative chord progressions" (1995, 27).

Over the next twenty years, Paco and Camarón would collaborate extensively, both in concerts and in recordings, whose production they undertook quite seriously as documents of their creativity and achievements. Most of the duo's records were traditional in the sense that, with a few exceptions, they adhered to the established repertoire of cantes and the convention of singing thematically independent, unrelated verse sections. However, on most records the duo would also include a more populist precomposed song in tango or rumba rhythm, with thematically connected verses, a catchy refrain, and perhaps electric bass and cajón accompaniment. Such items included "Rosa María"—well suited for singing in the shower—and the masterful "Como el Agua" (1981), which brought this kind of song to a new level of both popularity and sophistication. These songs were generally composed by Paco, his father Antonio, or especially his brother Pepe. Antonio composed most of the lyrics (several of which, in *gitanesca* tradition, sang of the pride of being a Gitano). Meanwhile, Camarón himself had a keen interest in learning all possible extant repertoire and might even travel to some remote Andalusian town to hear some auntie sing an obscure estilo of soleá. A particular contribution of Camarón's music was the elaboration and further popularization of bulerías, which he recorded over sixty times. While bulerías was certainly popular by the 1960s, in Camarón's singing the variety of melodies was dramatically expanded, such that bulerías became the quintessential cante of modern flamenco. Meanwhile, Camarón also avidly cultivated the less-Gitano-oriented cantes such as tarantas and fandangos de Huelva and played a key role in bringing the tangos and jaleos of Extremadura, as inspired by Ramón el Portugués, into the mainstream repertoire. A typical item on a record, such as a soleá or tango, might feature Antonio's letras set to a mixture of traditional estilos and original tunes (cuplés) by Pepe, all enlivened by Camarón's expressive interpretation and, of course, Paco's brilliant and tasteful falsetas.

Much of the stylistic "revolution" that is accredited to Paco and Camarón was well within the boundaries of flamenco per se, but in its innovative spirit and enhanced repertoire of estilos and guitar sonorities, it was seen as breaking from the mairenista notion that the cante repertoire was "complete" and not to be departed from. Paco stated:

> When I was growing up there was no freedom to compose. You had to repeat the old. The flamencologists and flamenco people regarded as sacrilegious any note outside of what was already established. Camarón and I disrupted somewhat this purist sentiment, which I regard as false. This wasn't purity, it was putting the music in a box and archiving it in a museum. (qtd. in Gamboa and Núñez 2003, 93)

From the mid-1980s, Paco and Camarón largely pursued independent careers. For guitar accompaniment Camarón replaced Paco with fellow Gitano Tomatito (José Fernández Torres, b. 1958), one of several remarkable virtuosos emerging in Paco's wake. For new material Camarón relied on other composers, especially Antonio Humanes, for the album *Te lo dice Camarón* (Camarón Tells It Like It Is, 1986), and Ricardo Pachón for *La leyenda del tiempo* (The Legend of Time, 1979). The latter album, which took many months of preparation, is regarded as a landmark in flamenco history, though it provoked much controversy when released. Combining poetry by Lorca and others, and compositions by Pachón and Kiko Veneno, it mixed neo-traditional items with catchy rock-style anthems like "Volando Voy," following patterns set by rock andalúz groups such as Azahara, Pata Negra, and Triana.

By the 1980s Camarón had achieved a stardom unprecedented in flamenco history, and in doing so, he, with Paco, had popularized flamenco both internationally and among Spaniards who had previously disparaged the music. A flashy dresser, Camarón became a particular idol for young Gitano men, who copied his attire and his sculpted coiffure. At concerts Gitano women would ask him to bless and touch their infants, as if he were a beneficent saint. Unfortunately, at a time when drugs were devastating the Gitano community, many young admirers may have taken inspiration from Camarón's own addiction to heroin. (Camarón also turned to what some regard as another opiate, the evangelical church known as Iglesia de Filadelfia, which has been especially popular among Gitanos.) As his drug habit intensified, his health declined and he missed several concerts (though some of these alleged no-shows were scams by unscrupulous promoters who advertised his presence at concerts without his consent). A low point was reached in 1986 when he fell asleep at the wheel of his Land Rover and rammed another vehicle, killing its two passengers. In 1992 he and Paco reunited for the album *Potro de rabía y miel* (Colt of Anger and Honey), but by this time he was suffering from lung cancer, presumably related to his having smoked four or five packs of cigarettes daily since adolescence. Later that year he succumbed to the disease, leaving his widow and four children.

As with singers in some other genres, it is difficult to specify how much of "Camarón's music" should be attributed to him as opposed to his producers, especially the de Lucía "team." Most of the material he sang was either traditional or was composed for him by collaborators like the Sánchez/Lucía family or Fosforito. (In his final months Camarón complained that he deserved more composition royalties than he had received, sparking a nasty controversy.) In any case, the expressivity of Camarón's singing was indisputable, and his style and repertoire came to be widely imitated, especially by young cantaores such as Duquende (Juan Rafael Cortés Santiago, b. 1965), Rancapino Chico, and Pedro el Granaíno.[14]

In the case of Paco, there is less ambiguity about the extent and nature of his specific achievements (even if it may be unclear whether a song like "Como el Agua" was composed mostly by him, or Pepe, or their father). Many of Paco's most celebrated activities were outside the realm of mainstream flamenco. Prominent among these would be his guitar trio tours and records with John McLaughlin and Larry Coryell and, more extensively, Al DiMeola. These had little to do with flamenco, or jazz, but consisted primarily of mostly diatonic improvisations—in the form of machine-gun single-note runs—over songs like "Mediterranean Sundance." Indeed, de Lucía's hardcore flamenco fans were far outnumbered by guitar-technique fetishists, who would hoot and howl after every lightning sixteenth-note run played in his guitar trio or septet shows. De Lucía himself, who was, among other things, an intelligent, humble, and articulate man, had no illusions about the refinement of such musical tastes, although he found the art of improvising in such contexts to be challenging in its own way. He also commented incisively on the contrast between such ecstatic international reception of the shallower aspects of his music and on the ambivalence or indifference with which flamenco, and especially guitar, continued to be received in Spain itself, the cradle of the art form.

In quite a different vein, Paco, though unable to read staff notation, spent months laboriously learning Joaquin Rodrígo's *Concierto de Aranjuez* and several pieces by Manuel de Falla. Meanwhile, his regular touring group consisted of a sextet that presented a potpourri of a few neo-traditional flamenco items as well as nuevo flamenco songs such as "Sólo quiero caminar" and "Entre dos Aguas"—a light, mostly improvised rumba that Paco dashed off in the studio to fill out an album and soon became a pop hit.

Of greater relevance to this volume are Paco's contributions to flamenco itself, especially, of course, his flamenco guitar playing. One sort of contribution was the sheer prestige that he brought to flamenco, and flamenco guitar, both internationally and within Spain itself. A particular milestone was his 1975 solo recital in Madrid's Teatro Real, a venue previously reserved for classical fine arts. Most important were his novel approach to compás and cante accompaniment, his

Figure 5. Camarón de la Isla and Paco de Lucía (© José Lamarca)

harmonic originality, and his brilliance in technical advances, especially as a composer of falsetas and structured solo pieces.

It would of course be a mistake to evaluate Paco, or any artist, solely or even primarily for their innovations. Much of Paco's playing was more or less neo-traditional in style, and as a composer of fine falsetas, in that vein he was hardly alone among his contemporaries—although he was certainly unsurpassed and the most widely revered and imitated. (Among other fine guitarists of that generation was Manolo Sanlucar [b. 1943], who suffered the misfortune, as it were, of being a contemporary of Paco.) Innovation was in fact extremely important to Paco, who would take several months off from his lucrative touring in order to prepare albums that made fresh statements. Paco described his approach to reconciling creativity with fidelity to the stylistic idiom of flamenco:

> Every time I make a record I want to say something new, create a surprise, so that the guitarist who listens to it will enjoy it and find things to learn, or to experience.... The attitude when composing for a record is always the same ... to try to evolve, take a step forward, without forgetting the tradition. The most complex thing in making a flamenco guitar record is trying to create a new language without losing the *sabor* [flavor], the flamenco essence, because it's very easy to create something new that has nothing to do with that language, that culture.... That's how it was with *Siroco* [1987]—trying to make

a record that was as flamenco as possible, but also as new as possible, which is almost paradoxical, contradictory. (qtd. in Téllez 2003, 486–87)

It is difficult to describe in technical terms—not to mention layman's terms—the specific innovations in Paco's guitar music. Certain particular features could be mentioned, including a greater use of playing positions covering the entire length of the guitar neck instead of just first position; an expanded harmonic vocabulary, including more varied altered chords and modulations from one Phrygian tonic to another; complex arpeggio and plucked chord patterns, often involving non-adjacent strings; triplet *alzapúas*; and a fondness for playing familiar palos in unconventional tunings and keys (e.g., tangos in the granaínas key of B Phrygian). All of these and other features were rendered with Paco's extraordinary technical clarity, command, and good taste. While the guitar trio music was all about flashy runs, Paco's flamenco playing never gives the impression that he is trying to show off; for example, as in all good flamenco playing, Paco would use picado runs sparingly and more for textural variety than display. Accordingly, flamenco guitar playing is commonly divided into "pre-Paco" and "post-Paco" periods, with the albums *Almoraíma* (1976) and *Siroco/Zyryab* (1990) constituting particular watersheds.

While in Cancún escaping, as he often did, from the exigencies of touring and recording, Paco de Lucía died unexpectedly of a heart attack in 2014.

Spanish Names

Given the diverse surnames of the Sánchez/de Lucía family members, this may be an appropriate occasion for an explanatory digression about names in Spanish society and the flamenco world. An initial consideration is that in the Spanish-speaking world, as in several other cultures, individuals may exercise greater freedom in choosing or altering their names than is common in Anglo-American society. In Spain and Latin America, individuals often have two legal surnames, appending the mother's maiden name to the father's name. Various forms could be chosen, such as José Vargas García, or José Vargas y García, or José Vargas-García. Often, the individual opts not to use the mother's name, except perhaps in documents, as in the case of Fidel Castro Ruz. However, if the first surname is very common and the second more distinctive, the latter may be preferred; thus Federico García Lorca is generally known as Lorca (or "García Lorca" but certainly not as "García"). Compound surnames can accumulate, especially when a married woman retains her surnames and adds those of her husband (preceded by "de"). Even first names can be long-winded and are often shortened in practice; thus, mid-nineteenth-century cantaora María Borrico's first name was María de Montemayor de Todos los Santos ("of All the Saints"—certainly more concise than enumerating them; her actual surname was Fernández Fernández). The poet Antonio Machado was actually Antonio Cipriano José María y Francisco de Santa Ana Machado y Ruiz. Meanwhile, however, in traditional and especially lower-class circles, surnames were not widely used except in unusual formal contexts.

In the flamenco world it became common to adopt stage names, often invoking one's hometown. Thus, Paco de Lucía's elder brother became Ramón de Algeciras, Antonio Cruz García became Antonio Mairena, and guitarist Melchor Jiménez Torres became Melchor de Marchena (Algeciras, Mairena, and Marchena being Andalusian towns). The latter's son Enrique, also a prominent guitarist, went through several stage names before eventually coming to be known as Enrique de Melchor. Other performers sharing their fathers' first names might be distinguished, for example, as "Rancapino Chico" or "Moraito Chico"; the latter stage name, however, was confusingly shared by Juan Moreno and his son, Manuel Moreno Junquera. As for Paco de Lucía (Francisco Sánchez Gómez), "Paco" is the standard nickname for Francisco, Sánchez and Gómez were his father's and mother's surnames, respectively, but he chose to adopt his mother's first name (Lucía) as a stage surname. In recent decades, however, stage nicknames have been falling out of use, especially among guitarists.

Among Gitanos the use of nicknames has been especially common, particularly since, in earlier times, even siblings might share the same first name, having been named after different relatives—for instance, after a grandfather and an uncle both named "Juan." Sometimes the nicknames are affectionately whimsical, especially as taken from foods, as in the case of the guitarist Tomatito. Camarón de la Isla (Shrimp of the Island) acquired his sobriquet from his slight build and "blond" (actually brown) hair, with "La Isla" referring to the town of San Fernando. Nicknames, of course, are generally not chosen by individuals themselves; according to some accounts, guitarist Perico el del Lunar (Perico with the Mole) eventually tired of being identified by his facial blemish and had it removed, which only led to his being dubbed, in some circles, "Perico sin Lunar" (Perico without the Mole).

Other Artists and Developments

If Paco and Camarón were the two most prominent figures of the flamenco revival, the phenomenon was a broader movement that encompassed various parallel developments as pioneered by several artists. Enrique Morente (1942–2010) was a particularly innovative (and thus controversial) singer. Better known through recordings than the performance circuit, his more than twenty albums included a flamenco mass; a "fantasy" for voice and orchestra; various fusion projects with rock, African music, and Moroccan andalusí music; and an LP on which he sang over old 78 records of flamenco. Morente was among several cantaores who set to music an eclectic variety of poetry, adapting suitable works by Lorca, his contemporary Miguel Hernández, his friend and collaborator Leonard Cohen, and various modern Spanish poets. (See chapter 6 for further discussion of flamenco letras.) He furthered the links between flamenco and intellectuals—earlier promoted by Mairena—as he often performed at universities and was part of a progressive, leftist circle that included flamencologists José Luis Ortiz Nuevo, Andrés Raya Saro, and Francisco Almazán, along with singers like José Menese (1942–2016), the latter being at once a mairenista and an outspoken political progressive. A different sort of innovative direction was pursued by the photogenic young duo Lole y Manuel (vocalist Lole Montoya and guitarist-composer Manuel Molina), whose most popular album, *Nuevo Día*, featured extended, somewhat dreamy compositions, with original tunes rather than traditional estilos, typically in medium-tempo bulerías with flower-powery lyrics.

If Paco and Camarón eschewed sociopolitical themes, other singers openly allied themselves with current progressive movements. In the final years of the Franco regime, cantaores José Menese and Manuel Gerena pushed the limits of censorship in their openly dissident lyrics. Gerena's concerts were often canceled by the authorities, and his passport was revoked.[15] In composing and publishing his own lyrics, he was as much as a *cantautor* (singer-songwriter) as a flamenco cantaor. Paralleling the movement to democracy was a spirit of regional assertion and pride (though not separatism) among Andalusians who felt that their province had been exploited and abused by Madrid governments ever since the Reconquest. With land ownership concentrated in the hands of a tiny elite and unemployment provoking massive migration to Barcelona and elsewhere, many Andalusians felt that the time had come to demand socialist land reform and state investment and to assert regional pride in the realm of culture. This sentiment had various musical expressions, including a local *nueva canción* movement and, in the realm of flamenco, politicized lyrics by José Domínguez ("El Cabrero") and others and stage productions such as *Quejio* (Complaint, 1972), which dramatized Andalusian history with flamenco song and dance. A concomitant move was to celebrate, rather than disparage, Andalusia's Moorish heritage, as in collaborative concert and recording projects fusing flamenco with Moroccan andalusí music. The album *Dáme la libertad* (Give Me Freedom, 1985), by Juan Peña "El Lebrijano," and the theatrical production and recording *Macama Jonda* (Deep Encounter, 1983), featuring Gitano writer-producer Pepe Heredia and vocalist Enrique Morente, were the most popular of these ventures.

A counterpart to this Andalusian spirit of renewal was a fresh, modernist sense of solidarity, ethnic pride, and self-assertion among Gitanos. As mentioned above, Gitanos benefited little from the economic opening lifting the national economy, as the community was eviscerated by the obsolescence of traditional occupations like blacksmithing and livestock trading, with rampant drug addiction following these setbacks. At the same time, increasing numbers of Gitanos were becoming educated and sociopolitically aware and active; quite a few, of course, were finding gainful employment and respect through flamenco. A few high-profile flamenco projects sought to highlight themes of historical persecution of Gitanos, especially El Lebrijano's album *Persecución* (1976), with poetry by flamencologist Félix Grande, and the flamenco-based theatrical work and film *Camelamos Naquerar* (Caló: We Want to Speak, 1976), scripted by Gitano poet, essayist, and professor José Heredia Maya (1947–2010).[16]

By the turn of the new millennium, these sorts of activist projects had become somewhat less intense, but also more commonplace, as established parts of a lively and heterogeneous flamenco scene that encompassed mainstream cante as well as all manner of pop crossovers and eclectic fusions with jazz, tap dance, Irish step-dancing, and North Indian kathak. With these developments, the art had essentially reached the modern, or postmodern, situation in which it now finds itself, however further impacted by the internet, the intensification of globalization, and other recent developments.

PART II

Structure and Forms in Flamenco

4

Structure

Cante

The basic structural entity in flamenco music, and to some extent dance, is the "cante," which can be roughly translated as "song-type." The word "cante," as noted, also means "singing," as opposed to "toque" (playing, implicitly on guitar) and "baile" (dance). More or less synonymous and interchangeable with "cante," meaning song-type, is "palo" (lit., a suit of cards), although that more recent term is in some senses more applicable to and suggestive of instrumental music and is still disparaged by some. It could be said that there are about twenty cantes that are basic and common and another twenty or so lesser or subsidiary cantes. Some cantes are metered—that is, in compás—while others are free-rhythmic.

Among *flamencos* (flamenco people), the concept of cante is unproblematic and clear enough to those who have occasion to use the word. However, actually defining what a cante is and enumerating its constituent features are difficult, because the distinguishing parameters vary from cante to cante. In fact, the entire structuring of flamenco—and much Andalusian and Spanish music for the last several centuries—around the entity of the cante is quite distinctive in world music.

In general, a cante is more limited in scope than a genre per se, but it is more ramified, flexible, and diverse than a "song." However, some cantes may have originated, and might still have parallel lives, as either genres or songs. Evidence suggests, for example, that the eighteenth-century fandango was primarily a dance genre with typical accompanying music. As this music became stylized and cultivated independently, it took various forms, some of which became elaborated in the nineteenth century as flamenco cantes. For its part, sevillanas is a substantial dance and music genre that flourishes independently of flamenco. However, sevillanas can also be performed in flamenco shows, in which capacity as a music form it could be regarded as a cante. Some cantes—perhaps such as peteneras—may have originated as a song, which was then cultivated in somewhat diverse forms as a stage item and then adapted to flamenco style as a "cante." Conversely, such a form as the caña may have flourished in the early 1800s as a cante-like entity, with several variants, but as most of these were forgotten, it came to survive mostly in a single form, almost as a "song"; hence it is generally referred to in the singular rather than plural.

The distinctiveness of cante as a structural entity is reflected, among other things, in its syntactical treatment, including an idiosyncratic use of singular and plural forms. In common Spanish speech, instead of singing "a bulería" (*una bulería*), one sings "in (*por*) bulerías"—that is, one sings a set of verses, perhaps with different tunes, in features (melodic, rhythmic, harmonic, etc.) typical of bulerías as a form. Thus, one would say, for example, *Voy a cantar por bulerías*—"I'm going to sing in bulerías." In other contexts, either singular or plural might be used—for example, *la bulería es muy festiva* or *las bulerías son muy festivas*. (For their part, English usages, as in this book, are inconsistent; one might say, "Bulerías *is* a festive cante" or "She sang a bulerías.") Somewhat confusingly, there is no standard noun in Spanish for a performance "item"—that is, what in English parlance might be referred to as "a bulerías"; as discussed below, the word "canción" (song) has different meanings and would not be appropriate. The most common term is "*tanda*," meaning set or batch, as in "He sang two tandas of bulerías, before and after the intermission." Alternately, "He sang *por bulerías* twice." But not "*El cantó dos bulerías* [*bulerías es*?]" (He sang two buleríases). The use of the plural can also distinguish flamenco cantes from namesakes in other genres; thus, if a popular singer (such as Rocío Jurado) were to announce, "I will sing a tango" (instead of "I will sing *por tangos*"), a listener might expect an Argentine tango song, such as by Carlos Gardel, rather than a flamenco item; however, the singular might be used to denote a specific estilo—for example, "She sang a tango de Granada" or "Juaniqi composed this soleá."

At a basic level, a cante, as a structural entity, could be said to comprise a repertoire of stock tunes set to a distinctive compás in the case of metered cantes, along with certain other typical identifying features. In practice there are several criteria that can distinguish a cante, all of which might be operant to different degrees and in different ways. These, as discussed in more detail below, are roughly as follows:

Melody. Most cantes, as stated, are distinguished by a corpus of stock tunes, which are often called estilos or "styles" and which are discussed in greater detail below. Thus, for instance, there are a few dozen common traditional estilos of soleares, some of which are known by name to singers (and have been catalogued and documented in written and internet sources). A vocalist can set to these tunes any verse (letra) that fits and is appropriate. Cantes, however, differ in the number of traditional estilos they comprise. Siguiriyas and tangos each have dozens; in malagueñas, only eight or so are common; and granaínas, peteneras, caña, and *polos* basically each have only one or two basic tunes, though these tunes can, of course, be rendered with individual flourishes and variation.

Rhythm. Here the more specifically relevant entity is compás, whose basic musical meaning is "bar or measure" but in flamenco denotes a more particular rhythmic cycle with distinctive points of internal stress. Most cantes are metered, the primary exceptions being peteneras and the languid, free-rhythmic fandango variants, especially tarantas, malagueñas, granaínas, and *fandango natural*. The specificity of relation of cante to compás varies. Thus, for example, tangos, tientos, and tanguillos each have a different, single distinctive compás by which they can be easily recognized. Soleares, alegrías, caña, and *polos* share the same basic compás, though in other respects they are quite different.

Guitar accompaniment. As discussed in more detail below, all cantes (except for those such as saeta, toná, and martinete, which are performed *a palo seco*, without accompaniment) have conventional, traditional guitar accompaniment patterns, which generally include typical guitar tonalities and falsetas. Thus, for example, tarantas is most characteristically performed in the guitar position of F♯ Phrygian, and granaínas in B Phrygian (or transpositions, using a capo); each has a corpus of familiar, conventional associated falsetas, whether derived from oral tradition or from known composers such as Ramón Montoya; an advanced professional guitarist typically composes new falsetas that often retain some features or flavor of the traditional ones. However, the associations of tonalities with palos are by no means inflexible; guitarists have long been fond of using different guitar tonalities for different cantes, often composing falsetas that are quite original and not particularly suggestive of earlier models. In other respects, the conventions are not overtly violated; thus, if a vocalist announces that she is going to sing a tarantas, the guitarist would be unlikely to play an introduction that sounded conspicuously like a malagueñas in E Phrygian (although nowadays, to the dismay of some, almost anything can happen).

Text. Text as a constitutive element involves form, performance format, and lyric content. Cantes can be distinguished to some extent by their texts. In terms of form, several cantes generally use the familiar, venerable form of an octosyllabic quartet (*cuarteta arromanzada*), with lines two and four having assonant or consonant rhyme in the final or penultimate syllables. Siguiriyas, by contrast, uses an altered seguidilla form, with three or four lines of verse, each of six syllables except for the penultimate one, which has eleven. Performance renderings and repetitions may be distinctive; in the fandango forms, for instance, the second text line of the five-line verse is generally sung first and then repeated after the first line; thus, there are six musical lines (tercios), with the text lines being 2–1–2–3–4–5.

Thematic content is a less typical criterion, except for certain general conventions. Lyrics of alegrías (lit., "joys") are typically (though not always) upbeat, while those of siguiriyas are lachrymose. Songs lamenting the hardship of mining life are most likely to be encountered in *cantes mineros* (tarantas, cartageneras, etc.). In general, however, thematic content can vary widely, which allows individual letras to be freely used, perhaps with modification, in different cantes.

Cante as a structural entity should be understood in contradistinction to such entities as estilo, tanda, cuplé, and canción/tema/"song." These distinctions are familiar to flamenco people, but at the risk of tiring such readers, they are worth belaboring for those who are new to the genre. A standard flamenco item, consisting of a series of estilos with thematically unrelated coplas, has few of the essential attributes of a "song" (canción). Although in the case of cantes like soleares there are certain conventions as to the sequence of estilos (including a gradual increase in range and intensity), there is no particular overall structure, symmetry, or design, nor is there any particular form of closure aside from a quick concluding tag (*remate*, cierre, or *macho*). The "title" of an item that appears on the label of a commercial recording is typically nothing more than the first line of the opening stanza, or perhaps a distinctive line from another stanza, rather than constituting a phrase relevant to the tanda as a whole. Further, vocalists need not make any particular attempt to reproduce any particular sequence of coplas and estilos that they have sung previously in concert or recordings, although they might do so.

A typical tanda of tangos, performed on stage, lasting eight minutes or so, might consist of a series of verses set to familiar estilos that cognoscenti could recognize—for example, as a *tango del Titi*, a *tango de La Repompa*,[1] or one of the several *tangos de Granada*. A singer might insert, amid these, a precomposed passage with a distinctive text and tune, not conforming to an extant estilo. This passage might be a composition of some acquaintance or composer, or it might be an adaptation of an old or new popular song. (The guitarist would have to be familiar with the item in order to accompany it properly.) In flamenco parlance, this inserted entity, especially in bulerías, could be called a cuplé. Thus, for example, "Camarón sang a bulerías estilo popularized by La Perla de Cádiz, and then he sang a cuplé consisting of a setting of a verse from the Mexican song 'La cigarra' and then another cuplé composed for him by Pepe de Lucía." The tunes of these cuplés are not expected to become stock tunes—that is, to be used for other song texts—and in that sense they would not properly be called estilos. However, there is no doubt that over the generations, the tunes of several precomposed popular songs—especially in tangos—have come to be adopted as stock tunes, becoming estilos.

A distinct entity is the precomposed song—a canción or tema. A cantaor might adapt a preexisting song, in part or in full, to flamenco style. Thus, "María de la O," a popular 1920s song (a copla, not to be confused with Ernesto Lecuona's "María la O"), has been sung by various cantaores in bulerías form—that is, in bulerías compás and flamenco vocal style. Such a setting could be referred to as a "canción por bulerías"—for example, "Manuel Vallejo sang 'María de la O' por bulerías." A singer might render such a song, or part of it, as one section of a longer tanda. A related entity would be a song that is written specifically for a flamenco singer, such as "Como el Agua," composed by Paco de Lucía and family and sung by Camarón de la Isla. Such a precomposed, pop-flavored entity might be regarded as marginal to traditional mainstream flamenco but has become increasingly common in the nuevo flamenco era. "Como el Agua," set to a tango/rumba rhythm, could be called a *canción* (or *tema*) *por tangos*. A singer might even insert a verse from that song in a tanda of tangos, in which case it might be said to constitute a cuplé.

The status of such cuplés in flamenco is somewhat ambiguous. Although less likely to be heard in such contexts as a formal competition, they are quite common in other contexts, especially as somewhat light items set to bulerías or tangos. Even if an Antonio Mairena might disapprove, there is little point in declaring that they are not flamenco. As repertoire, they may be popular songs, originating outside flamenco, but they are sung and accompanied in flamenco style, set to a flamenco compás, and typically performed in a flamenco setting, such as a tablao. However, as more instruments are added and improvised vocal and guitar flourishes disappear, such items, especially as recorded, may be better characterized as *aflamencada* (flamenco-tinged) commercial popular music rather than flamenco.

The centrality of the entity of the cante—or similar forms—in flamenco and Andalusian music, as mentioned, is a distinctive and unique feature, with few counterparts elsewhere in world music culture. This structuring of musical forms could be said to have roots in Renaissance Spain, when much vernacular and even salon music was based on song-types such as the folía, the zarabanda, or the *Guárdame las vacas* chord pattern. Much instrumental music consisted of variations (or diferencias) on these patterns, especially in order to accompany dance. Accordingly, some entities, such as the zarabanda and eighteenth-century fandango, were best regarded as dance forms with typical accompanying music; some, such as the seguidilla, were verse forms. It can be assumed that some of these forms, as vernacular musical entities, comprised a corpus of familiar tunes to which new or old lyrics could be set. However, they were more than mere stock tunes, since they, like flamenco cantes, were also constituted by particular conventional rhythms, chord patterns, and verse forms.

By the late eighteenth century (well before the flamenco era), it was customary to refer to some such entities in the plural—for example, by mentioning a vocalist singing *las playeras*, or *unas playeras* (some playeras), or *unas coplas de playeras* (some verses of playeras). The same phrasing could also be used for instrumental music, as in a concert featuring "las playeras played on guitar." By the 1860s, in flamenco discourse, the word "por" was coming into modern usage, as in "Silverio sang *por siguiriyas*" (*in* siguiriyas). Meanwhile, in accordance with the ambiguity of these entities as forms, they were referred to or described in a variety of ways, as continues to be the case. Hence, for instance, one finds an entity like the playeras referred to as a *canto,* a *cantar*, a *canción*, a *tono* or *tonada*, or in English, a modality, a form, a piece, a style, a species of verse, a class of melodies, and other terms, none of which adequately characterizes the somewhat ambiguous entity of the cante.

Stage dance items have their own formal structure. In most basic terms, they consist of three parts, referred to as letra, falseta, and zapateado, concluding with a *remate*. More specifically, a dance item typically commences with the vocalist singing an opening *salida* (roughly, entrance, such as in alegrías, the *tiritrán tran tran*), during which the dancer may stroll (a *paseo*) and end with a dramatic cierre (closing, cadence). The cantaor then sings one or two coplas, with the dancer marking the compás in various ways, especially through graceful hand and arm gestures (*braceos*) and punctuating *desplantes* and *llamadas* (lit., "calls"). Then comes the "falseta" section, in which the dancer, accompanied by the guitarist, again emphasizes grace and expression rather than virtuoso display. After a segue to the faster *castellano* comes the zapateado or *escobilla* section, in which the dancer performs thunderous footwork, demonstrating his or her rhythmic talent and virtuoso technique, typically accompanied only by palmas and perhaps the guitarist strumming *a tapao*—that is, muting the strings with the left hand. After accelerating to a climax, the musicians join in for a climactic *remate* or cierre in fast tempo (in siguiriyas, a "macho"); in alegrías or soleá, this typically consists of a major-key bulerías de Cádiz (though it might be in Phrygian or even minor key, as in Fosforito's popular "Plaza de la catedral").

Such a format applies only to "presentational" stage dances, not to an informal bulerías or tangos that might occur at a family fiesta or be spontaneously shouted out with palmas by a *corrillo* (informal group) of boisterous youths in the street. For such festive occasions, individuals might take turns singing verses and perhaps dancing solo. Slow-paced cantes like soleares and siguiriyas would be less likely to be heard on such occasions, and even if intoned, they would not inspire dance.

Estilos

The estilo as a formal component of flamenco merits some further explication here. The basic cantes or palos may be regarded as general frames or molds, distinguished by the criteria outlined above, that accommodate a variety of more specific stock tunes. These latter are referred to by most musicians as estilos, whose direct translation as "styles" is inaccurate. An estilo is a stock tune that, although allowing some scope for variation, contains certain identifying features and can accommodate any copla or verse that fits. A typical tanda of soleá, for example, might comprise from three to six thematically unrelated coplas sung in different estilos, punctuated by guitar falsetas. (Two alternate terms for estilo that are occasionally encountered are *camino* [road] and *cuerpo* [body], as in competition guidelines: "Each vocalist must sing *dos cantes de tres cuerpos cada*" [two cantes, each of three cuerpos].)

As mentioned above, cantes vary in terms of the numbers of estilos they include. Soleá and siguiriyas each have many (though they tend to be similar), while granaínas basically consists of a single tune, however flexibly it may be rendered. Most of the repertoire of estilos was established by the first decades of the twentieth century. In theory, anyone could compose an estilo, but it would not properly achieve the status of an estilo unless it entered general circulation as a stock tune, used by other singers, and sung to various coplas. In fact, few estilos have come into common usage since Antonio Mairena's time; a prominent exception ("proving the rule") is a fandango tune of Enrique Morente recorded by Camarón and others. Instead, the sung repertoire consists mostly of these older established estilos, adaptations of coplas and other songs, and new compositions (the latter two thus constituting "cuplés").

Luis Soler Guevara and Ramón Soler Díaz, in their 1992 book elaborating on the encyclopedic recordings and research of Antonio Mairena, enumerated almost a hundred estilos of traditional soleares and siguiriyas, discussing their presumed origins and histories. However, since the book provided no transcriptions, the taxonomies and discussions are somewhat inscrutable unless the reader is able to identify and access some of the particular recordings that the authors cite as examples.[2] American flamencologist Norman Kliman made a prodigious contribution to this taxonomy by preparing an erudite website (http://canteytoque.es) that presents these estilos with embedded audio examples (but still no staff notation). Most of the estilos are named after singers (e.g., La Serneta) or places (e.g., soleá de Alcalá); several are further classified—for example, the soleá estilos include "La Andonda 1," "La Andonda 2," and so on. Most cantaores would not use or be familiar with such precise enumerations but would most certainly know the traditional named attributions, which, whether historically verifiable or not, serve as handy designations.

Hence, if a singer and guitarist were performing without rehearsal, the cantaor might mention to the guitarist, "I'll sing a soleá de Triana." (In theory, competent guitarists should be able to adapt to any estilo, but foreknowledge may certainly ease their task.) As Kliman notes, while the labels are convenient, the attributions they imply should not be regarded as entirely canonic, and there may be ambiguity as to whether a supposed estilo is a genuinely distinct entity or merely a variant of another estilo.[3]

The extent to which estilos are flexible can be a subject of controversy, and estilos themselves may vary in this regard. Certain sorts of spontaneous flexibility are not only common and tolerated but are also appreciated if they are expressive and effective. On the other hand, an estilo is typically distinguished by certain particular identifying features that should supposedly be present. In my discussion of specific cantes in chapter 5, I show, for example, how in certain estilos of malagueña and Levant cantes, where each copla comprises six tercios (sung lines), each tercio follows a pattern determined by the estilo, including such features as its final cadential note, its general contour and range, its manner of proceeding—whether directly or after a cadential pause—to the next tercio, the extent to which melismas may be introduced, and perhaps certain other features, such as a distinctive melodic leap or scalar passage. The singer enjoys considerable license in terms of pacing, improvised melismas, and other features, as long as the identifying features are honored. Similarly, in my discussion of soleares estilos below, I note that a singer can start a given estilo around beat one or alternately around beat six; she may repeat a text line or not; she might extend a certain melisma for as much as a full compás, but the estilo could be regarded as intact, and faithfully rendered, if the general melodic framework and certain key details are present. Perusal of the Kliman website affords some idea of the sorts and degrees of liberties that can be taken.

Some purists insist on closely rendering the established estilos without significant variation. Such orthodoxy may be institutionalized, especially in the competitions; for example, in order to win the Lámpara Minera in the prestigious Concurso de La Unión, one must sing mineras exactly in the established style of seminal figures Antonio Piñana, Encarnación Fernández, or Pecho Cross (Calahorra Arjona 2018, 262). Others criticize this conservatism as stultifying "mairenismo." Innovative cantaor Enrique Morente disparaged the stuffy purism of the señoritos who dominated flamenco patronage until the 1960s: "If ever they would see a singer depart for a moment from a detail of 'La Trini' or 'El Canario' [malagueña estilos] they would denounce him and throw him down—as if I have to spend my whole life without changing even half a note!" (qtd. in Pérez Paíz 2018, 15). A common view is that alteration of estilos can be ventured only by those who are well steeped in the standard versions. Cantaor David Pino articulated this view:

> I've heard Enrique Morente sing a malagueña de la Trini, in his own version, in peñas like El Rincón del Cante, and people loved it. But of course, it's that he knows that malagueña perfectly, and it shows. Recently I was at a concurso and I saw singers who were clueless. How can you tell? Because they start out singing a malagueña of Chacón and then next thing they are doing something from that of Canario. They have no foundation, they are starting from a point of ignorance. If you innovate, it has to be beautiful, and if you do it well, there's no problem. I've invented my own malagueña and people have liked it. But you can't just do whatever you feel like without knowing. You've got to start from a position of knowledge. (qtd. in Calahorra Arjona 2018, 382)

A key argument in favor of respecting the estilos would be that the common and canonic ones have proven their beauty, internal logic, and aesthetic worth by withstanding the test of time. Alfonso Cid, one of quite a few professional cantaores who actually took lessons during one period, relates how his teacher, Rocío Márquez, worked with him extensively to render a certain granaína melisma of Chacón "just right." One might think that in an oral, roughly improvisatory genre like flamenco, such precision should not be important, but astute listeners (or those who some might regard as nerds) would in many cases be able to distinguish a skillful and accurate rendering of a particular distinctive melisma from one that is "fudged."

Vocal Technique

Flamenco vocal style is one of the most distinctive features of the genre as well as one of the most difficult to render for those who have not been extensively trained or who lack the ability to sing with proper intensity. A pleasant voice and an aptitude for singing in tune may be prerequisites but in themselves fall far short of what is needed to sing convincingly. Several characteristic features of flamenco singing can be enumerated. Perhaps most conspicuous is its impassioned, dramatic delivery, which requires a certain artistic temperament and perhaps even personality type. While some vocalists have tended to sing in a natural voice, more current in modern times has been a more hyper-expressive style, perhaps especially associated with Jerez singers. Flamenco singing—like Indian classical singing—also lends itself to being accompanied by gestures, and almost all vocalists gesticulate emphatically as they sing. Facial expressions are often anguished and strenuous; cantaor Alfonso Cid relates that he was trained to frown in order to achieve the proper vocal intensity. Despite the ability of the cantaor to relax during guitar entrecoplas, the process of singing, whether a siguiriyas or a malagueña, is usually strenuous, and a cantaor is often drenched in sweat after a single item.

Various particular techniques contribute to the hyper-dramatic effect. One is the controlled and artful use of brief falsetto breaks (*romper la voz*) called *jipío*. These can be introduced at specific points, serving both to generate an effect akin to sobbing and, more prosaically, to articulate notes in a melisma. The use of this technique is commonly associated with Gitanos, many of whom acquire it more or less naturally by singing informally beginning in childhood. However, some Gitanos do not sing it—perhaps because they lack the falsetto range—and many non-Gitanos master it perfectly well. Skilled and experienced vocalists may sing it more or less intuitively, but most have practiced it and make conscious choices about where to effectively place the technique in a given melodic line. A similar technique—at once articulating certain notes and imitating sobbing—is a sharp, plosive exhalation, an *ataque soplado* (blown attack). Still another articulation technique is *bebeo*, in which a syllable is repeated non-lexically to extend a line or create a stammering effect; thus, *mi saber* can become *mi sabe-be-be-ber*, and *cuando* becomes *cuando-wo-wo-wo*.[4]

Another distinctive feature is melisma, whose prominence, as mentioned earlier, presumably derives from Moorish tradition. Singers vary in the fluidity with which they perform melismas. Some, such as Pepe Marchena or, in modern times, Israel Fernández (b. 1989), are able to sing scalar melismatic passages with great speed and agility, almost like Indian classical vocalists, and with a similar articulation technique of approaching each note from below. However, such virtuosity, though appreciated, is not essential, and a cantaor like José Mercé can enjoy great popularity despite having a relatively heavy and slow-moving voice. In any case, the melismas—like picado runs on guitar—are generally used judiciously and economically at certain points rather than being foregrounded as displays of virtuosity for its own sake, as was the case in the *ópera flamenca* period. Some modern singers—especially those who train at the Cristina Heeren Fundación—practice scales and exercises in order to acquire such agility, as part of "voice therapy," but this may be a largely recent phenomenon.

Another component of the flamenco vocal aesthetic is a fondness for a timbre that is husky or raspy—in flamenco parlance, "afillá" (*afillada*, named after nineteenth-century singer El Fillo). This sort of voice is again quintessentially associated with Gitanos, as exemplified by singers such as Camarón, José Mercé, and, among women, Fernanda de Utrera. Gitano vocal cords, of course, are not congenitally different from those of other humans, so the afillá timbre is cultivated rather than simply inherited; presumably, if José Mercé had grown up in different social circumstances and aspired to sing classical lieder instead of flamenco, he would have learned to sing with a clear (*redondo*) tone. The husky vocal timbre may be regarded as expressive, but like Louis Armstrong's voice, on a purely musical level it is also acoustically rich in overtones and can be seen as felicitously complementing the clear timbres of the guitar.

In general, the more a cantaor's voice is husky and jipío-laden, the more "flamenco" and *rancio* (roughly, authentic) it will sound. However, genuine expressivity is by no means proportional to the amount of jipío, gravelly rasp, and histrionic effects, and connoisseurs do not hesitate to criticize singers who overuse these techniques or constantly "shout." Many popular vocalists simply do not have raspy voices, and a John Fogerty–type attempt to affect a gravelly timbre can sound forced and artificial. Vocal quality in early flamenco records, by such Gitano singers as Manuel Escacena, was clear and nearly operatic rather than rough and husky, and it is possible that the fondness for the afillá voice may date only from the 1940s. Estébanez Calderón, in his aforementioned 1830s account of a pre-flamenco event in Seville, quoted El Planeta chastising El Fillo for his raspy voice, saying, "El Fillo, I tell you that this rough voice is crude and unappealing, and in terms of style it is neither fine nor Spanish-sounding."[5]

Vocal range in itself is not necessarily an important criterion, and most of the cantes and estilos can be presentably sung with a modest range (although, for example, peteneras and soleá apolá require a wide range). Juan Talega sings the soleá shown as example 5.1 within the gamut of a single octave. Other singers, such as Pedro el Granaíno, have extensive ranges, such that, for example, in singing material of Camarón he is able to add further flourishes in the higher octaves. Some cantaores, like Talega, have low voices, and others, from Manuel Vallejo to Israel Fernández, have high ones, and a few of the latter, such as Tijeritas, are almost Michael-Jacksonesque in their androgynous timbre; what is important, however, is expressivity and skill rather than one's particular range. Such expressivity is mostly in the realm of nuances, involving spontaneous modulations of dynamics, ornamentation, and flow, which would be almost impossible to analyze or notate but are ultimately the most important criteria for excellence. They are arguably more important than the basic melodic material one sings; thus, for example, Duquende sings much material of Camarón, and audiences certainly enjoy hearing echoes of that deceased cantaor, but Duquende's excellence and popularity rest on the spontaneous flair and the expressive nuances of his singing rather than his simply rehashing his mentor's songs.

Rhythm and Compás

Spanish music and dance, especially flamenco, have long been recognized and celebrated for their distinctive and uniquely dynamic rhythms. A few flamencologists (e.g., Castro Buendía) have argued that rhythm is the most basic and distinguishing feature of flamenco as a music genre. There are, of course, many distinctive aspects of flamenco rhythm, such as in many vocal lines a consistent stress on off-beats; a general fondness for syncopation; the combination, or juxtaposition, of free-rhythmic singing and metered accompaniment; flexibility in terms of numbers of measures in phrases; and a predilection for triple meter and distinctive forms of hemiola.

The single most salient entity in flamenco rhythm is the compás, which, as mentioned, constitutes a defining feature of metered cantes, comprising a metrical cycle with characteristic internal accent points, especially as articulated by guitar strumming, dance, or palmas patterns. Some compás patterns present unique challenges to analysis and have thus inspired endless discussion and debate, as well as diverse sorts of notation, description, and counting that could be variously regarded as complementary or contradictory. Many vocalists, especially of previous generations, sang entirely by intuition and feel and might not even be aware (or interested to know) that, for example, siguiriyas can be counted in twelve beats.[6] For their part, guitarists and dancers have had their own sometimes idiosyncratic ways of counting beats that, though logical, may be in some ways unsystematic. Meanwhile, since the latter nineteenth century, guitarists preparing pedagogical materials and composers penning stylized versions of flamenco items have had their own diverse "academic" ways of notating compás in palos such as soleares, often in contradiction to each other. Finally, modern flamencologists (whether institutional academics or learned amateurs) with some training in Western music have presented their own interpretations and notations, again often in disagreement with one another.

A basic taxonomy of compás types would group them as binary, ternary, or "amalgamated"—that is, hemiola-based (e.g., Berlanga 2014, 7). The most popular and familiar duple-metered cante is tangos, whose basic ostinato pattern also illustrates some typical features of flamenco compás as an entity. This pattern, which could be played as an entrecopla or ritornello (that is, between verses), or during initial parts of certain copla melodies, can be schematized as in example 4.9. It is a two-bar pattern, but during vocal passages (obviously the more important part of an item), numbers of measures in phrases may often be uneven and irregular as the singer freely extends melismas and the like, and the guitarist follows accordingly. The first bar could be regarded as "acephalic" ("headless") in that the first beat is accented (i.e., felt as a downbeat) but is unstressed or even silent. Typical of some compás patterns is that phrases typically end—often with a dramatic guitar strum or *remate*—on a beat prior to the downbeat (in tangos, beat three of the second bar).

A second category of compases would be those in ternary meter. As with tangos, basic compás patterns may exhibit a tendency to form two-bar phrases, but in fact phrases of uneven numbers of bars are common. Such is the case in related traditional genres such as folk verdiales, and if a reader visits any

YouTube site showing a *panda de verdiales* and attempts to count beats and bar lengths, these turn out to be highly irregular, as guitarists and bandurria players freely follow the singers and even change chords in seemingly unpredictable and unsystematic places.

A basic building block of ternary-metered compases is the aforementioned abandolao strum ("bum biddy-bum biddy-bum bum . . .," as stylized in Ravel's "Bolero"). A staple of much nineteenth-century Andalusian music, this strum pattern underlies flamenco verdiales and verse sections of fandango de Huelva. While the abandolao rhythm poses no analytical problems, by contrast the basic entrecopla pattern of the fandango de Huelva is in some ways enigmatic. This pattern, notated in example 5.8 in chapter 5 (whether played in flamenco or by amateur groups in Huelva) comprises two bars of 6/4 oscillating between Am and E (iv and I, in E Phrygian), with guitar golpes ("g") on beats one and four. (Guitarists traditionally count the pattern as "one two three four five [pause], one two three four five [pause] . . .").

beat:	1	2	3	4	5	6	/	1	2	3	4	5	6
chord:	E7	E7	Am	–	–	–		G	F	E	–	–	–
	g			g				g			g		

The rhythmically distinctive feature is that the accented chords—the Am, preceded by two beats of E7, and the E in the second bar, the target of the iv–III–II–I Andalusian cadence—occur on the weak beat three rather than on strong beats one or four. (I confess that when I was initially studying flamenco guitar, I found this ostinato highly confusing and heard it incorrectly for months until finally realizing my error and having to retrain my ear.) This syncopation has led some flamencologists (e.g., Jiménez 2015, 129–32; Fernández Marín 2005) to argue that the compás is *cruzado* (crossed), or what others might call polyrhythmic, combining in its basic structure the 6/4 meter shown above and a binary 3/4 meter placing the accented chord changes on accented beats, as could be schematized E7 E7 / Am Am / Am – / G F / E – / E –. This characterization, however, would apply better to the entrecopla pattern than to the verse sections, which might be played as an unsyncopated abandolao pattern. Certainly guitarists, in their falsetas and variations, introduce patterns that, in articulating binary accents, set up ephemeral polyrhythms.

In some cases the syncopations involve accents suggested by the chord changes, which may contrast with accents suggested by dynamic stressing (that is, in terms of volume) of other beats. In the traditional guitar *entrada* (entrance) to sevillanas, for example, most of the strumming could be heard as suggesting a 6/4 meter, except that the chord change on the "and" of beat two could be heard as suggesting 4/4, a binary meter. Alternately, it could be seen as 6/4, with the first half syncopated and the second half not. For its part, the cajón, if present, plays a pattern quite clearly in 4/4. For readers unfamiliar with such meter counts, the difference can be understood as two different ways of counting—and especially *feeling*—twelve fast pulses, as either in four (4/4, "four-four," with each beat containing three fast pulses) or six (6/4, "six-four," with each beat containing two fast pulses):

4/4: *one*-and-a-*two*-and-a-*three*-and-a-*four*-and-a
6/4: *one*-and-two-and-three-and-*four*-and-five-and-six-and

The ambiguities in sevillanas rhythm, like those in bulerías, have led guitarists and others to propound and employ a prodigious variety of analytical and notational schemes, even if dancers and their teachers favor a resolutely logical norm. One can sympathize with the confusion felt by a guitar student consulting some online guru who insists, "Sevillanas is counted *twelve-one-two-three-four-five*, even if everyone incorrectly counts it as *one-two-three-four-five-six*," or, "Sevillanas is a bar of 2/4 followed by one of 4/4, with no threes at all, although everyone counts it in three."

The third compás category comprises the "amalgamated," hemiola-based meters, a few of which are fairly straightforward and some of which are not straightforward at all. Among the former are guajiras and peteneras. While the latter of these (as popularized by Pastora Pavón) is typically rendered in a relatively free rhythm, the "I like to be in Ame-ri-ca" hemiola pattern is quite clear in guajiras. As mentioned earlier, guajira was adapted in some form from Cuban music in the eighteenth century, and its hemiola pattern, schematized in example 5.20 in chapter 5, resembles that of earlier Latin American–derived forms such as the sixteenth- and seventeenth-century zarabanda.

If guajira presents no particular analytical problem, the notation and interpretation of soleares, the metrically similar alegrías and bulerías, and of siguiriyas have been the subjects of endless disagreement and discussion. A fundamental challenge has been to understand and interpret—and be able to transcribe accordingly—these compás patterns in ways that reflect their internal accent structures while also acknowledging, to some extent, customary vernacular ways of doing so.

As noted above, evidence suggests that the soleares of the café cantante period may not have had a strong hemiola character, instead more typically outlining a ternary rhythm (two bars of 6/4 or one of 12/4), perhaps with abandolao strumming, cadencing on the tenth beat. However, in the early 1900s—perhaps influenced by the guajira—a distinctive sort of twelve-beat hemiola pattern became standard. The essence of this, as articulated on guitar, is what could be called the "three-ten axis," involving a move to the Phrygian dominant (II♭, or F in the key of E Phrygian) on beat three, resolving to the tonic on beat ten, roughly as shown here:

beats:	1	2	3	4	5	6	7	8	9	10	11	12
chords:	(I	I)	**IIb**	–	–	–	(**IIb**	**I**)	IIb	**I**	–	–
(in E:)	(E	E)	**F**	–	–	–	(**F**	**E**)	F	**E**	–	–

The first beat, although not functioning as a strong downbeat, retains importance as a standard starting point for guitar falsetas, dance steps, and vocal phrases. The stress pattern is typically understood as: one two THREE four five six SEVEN EIGHT nine TEN [pause pause]. For those who find mnemonics useful, this could be verbalized as "I want TO live on a CHICK-EN FARM in SPAIN (pause pause)." The rhythm could be regarded as a 3+3+2+2+2 hemiola, except that the accents do not fall on the first beats of each subgrouping, but rather on beats three, six or seven, eight and ten. Typical guitar renderings of this compás can be seen in example 4.1. (In order to facilitate reading, I have opted to use dotted bar lines to subdivide each compás into threes—that is, 3+3+3+3—with the caveat that these subdivisions do not coincide precisely with the aforementioned accents.)

Since the latter nineteenth century, various formally trained composers and flamencologists have used notation forms that seek to match bar lines with the internal accents (as reflected in the chord changes) and map the structure onto the more familiar "I like to be . . ." hemiola pattern. Strategies have varied, but one technique—used, for example, by Castro Buendía (2014a, II:1130)—has been to retain the traditional count pattern but shift the starting point to beat twelve: (12) 1 2 / 3 4 5 / 6 7 / 8 9 / 10 11. As he notes, this interpretation renders the soleá compás "acephalic," since the initial beat (number 12) is not stressed and is in fact often entirely silent.

When well-informed and astute analysts propose dramatically different notation schemes for a musical entity, it could be said that there are two different ways of regarding such divergences. One is that the different forms do not necessarily represent contrasting conceptions or understandings of the pattern but rather are simply proposing notations that are envisioned as easier

Example 4.1. Basic soleares compás patterns

to read. Alternately, the divergent notations could be said to be proposing fundamentally distinct ways of hearing and conceiving the music. Anyone who attempts to notate such an entity as the bulerías compás, in deciding where to place the bar line, is making a fundamental interpretation.

The logic of the "12–1–2–3 . . ." system may be apparent, and the erudition of its advocates is unquestionable, although its problems are equally evident. Among the latter are the issues of basic terminological intelligibility, as when the authors proposing this system refer to, for instance, "the first beat" (which is that?) and the unfortunate reader is immediately lost. A more fundamental interpretive problem is ascribing special salience to beat twelve as the first beat in this notation when actually that beat has no importance at all in soleares, whether as a phrase beginning or ending point or as the site of a chord change or other form of accentuation. Hence, the meter is "acephalic" only if one insists that it starts on an insignificant beat rather than the beat that musicians and dancers have generally claimed that it starts on. It is in no way comparable to tangos, whose first beat is clearly felt as a downbeat even if it may be unstressed. Meanwhile, many dance teachers as well as several flamencologists use a different counting pattern for these palos, highlighting the cadential character of beat ten, 1–2–3–4–5–6–7–8–9–10–1–2.

Notation and conceptual problems intensify with bulerías, where beat twelve does indeed have a salience it lacks in soleá. Dancers, guitarists, and others have traditionally counted this palo the same way as soleares, in accordance with the obvious similarities between the two cantes. These affinities would include the basic three-ten axis, typical melodies, and their standard underlying guitar chord progressions (e.g., oscillation between II♭ and I, perhaps with a move to iv, and the III7–VI climactic cambio in the penultimate line on beats eight and ten). However, offsetting these similarities is a significant difference in that, for example, if a dancer and accompanists accelerate from soleá to bulerías, at a certain point beat twelve acquires accentuation—through a subtle guitar "kick" as well as palmas and dance steps—and beat one accordingly drops out of salience. As such, a solid case could be made for claiming beat twelve to be the starting point of the cycle, as does Castro Buendía, such that it thus forms something closer to the standard guajiras-type ("I like to be in Ame-ri-ca") hemiola. Doing so, however, would provoke the same confusion of enumeration and obscures the significant structural affinities with soleares. Actually, the bulerías compás represents a metrical cycle that has a distinctive internal accent structure but lacks a strong sense of downbeat or starting point. There may be no ideal or perfect way to transcribe such an entity. Further, even the three-ten axis can be obscured by passages accenting twos, threes, sixes, or other patterns, all of which accord the palo much more variety than has the superficially similar guajiras when rendered in fast tempo. To make matters more complicated, in bulerías, and occasionally in old-style alegrías, the guitarist, following the singer's phrasing, may often play a six-beat half-compás instead of the standard twelve beats. In chapter 5 we will examine a representative passage of bulerías to explore how these passing syncopations and recurrent patterns can interact.

For its part, the siguiriyas compás presents its own analytical enigma. In its 2–2–3–3–2 pattern, it could be regarded as a sort of displacement of the standard hemiola (3–3–2–2–2), although with its own set of internal tensions and accents and its unique traditional "vernacular" counting: "one [pause] two [pause] three [pause pause] four [pause pause] five [pause]." The acephalic "headless" interpretation again rears its head—for example, in the analysis of Castro Buendía (2014a, II:972, counting it as 2–2–2–3–3)—but in claiming a silent, unstressed beat to be the downbeat, this approach is again at odds with conventional enumeration and perceived accentuation, as shown in example 5.5.

At a certain level, dance, singing, and the instrumental dimensions of flamenco can all be said to be governed by the same general set of rhythmic principles and aesthetics. One obvious distinction, discussed below, is that much singing, even in metered palos like bulerías, is free-rhythmic in character or perhaps alternates free-rhythmic phrases with points of particular rhythmic punctuation. A typical example would be an extended, more or less rubato melisma in bulerías that, after some meandering, concludes quite precisely and dramatically on beat ten, the customary *remate* point.

Rubato phrasing may also be conspicuous in guitar playing, especially when soleares, siguiriyas, and tientos are rendered at slow tempi. Among flamenco connoisseurs, opinions about such elastic playing may vary. In general, it could be said that rubato playing affords scope for certain kinds of rhythmic expressivity, while maintaining a steady pulse affords different sorts of potential. Certainly elastic rhythm is workable only in the very slow tempi that came into vogue, especially under the influence of the dancer El Güito (Eduardo Serrano Iglesias, b. 1942) in the 1960s. Indeed, it is ironic that maintaining a steady pulse in a palo like soleá is generally quite essential for dance accompaniment, but as guitarists and singers became accustomed to rendering such palos very slowly, when performing without dance they often came to render their rhythms with an elasticity that might otherwise be unsuitable for dance.

Alternately, if flexibility and elastic rhythms may be pervasive in some contexts, in others vocal phrasing may be quite systematically off-beat, effectively offsetting the on-beat guitar and palmas parts, as in example 5.6b. Those familiar with Latin music, such as salsa, may note some affinities in the use of off-beat phrasing, though Latin rhythms are more typically governed by the two-bar clave pattern, with a stressed downbeat on the "two" side alternating with off-beats.

Some modern flamenco musicians have experimented with expanding and elaborating rhythms such as those of bulerías and soleá in various ways, ideally while retaining the basic feel and structure of the original models.

Modality and Tonality

Flamenco employs three or four tonalities: major, minor, what could be called "altered Phrygian," and, arguably, a fourth tonality that could be characterized as idiosyncratically Mixolydian (that is, major scale with a flat seventh degree). Each of these has its own associated repertoire of basic chords, chord progressions, and typical melodic patterns.

Major tonality is found most overtly in alegrías, cantiñas, the verse sections of most fandango forms, and such cantes as guajiras, tanguillos, and most bulerías de Cádiz. Minor tonality occurs in farrucas, milonga, *vidalita*, and in some estilos of tangos and bulerías. The chordal vocabulary of both major and minor tonality in flamenco is basic, consisting primarily of tonic, dominant, and subdominant chords, perhaps voiced on guitar with some coloristic added notes. These forms of tonality present no particularly distinctive or analytically challenging features.

The most characteristic and distinctive flamenco tonality, shared with much Andalusian music in general, is what most flamencologists refer to as "Phrygian," though that term, as noted earlier, must be used with some equivocation. Other flamencologists refer to it merely as the "flamenco mode" (*modo flamenco*), writing, for example, that a given passage is in "Fa flamenco" (the flamenco mode from Fa). This volume refers to the mode as "Phrygian," with the primary caveat that the third degree is often raised (or occasionally sung neutral) rather than lowered, affording, if played chordally on guitar, a major rather than minor tonic triad. Hence, some flamencologists refer to the mode as "major Phrygian" (and I suggest the term "altered Phrygian"). In this system, as mentioned in chapter 1, the chordal vocabulary derives not from the Western major or minor scales but primarily from the Phrygian or "E" mode (or transposed variants thereof), with the exception that the tonic E chord is major rather than minor. This tonality is best regarded as a sort of modal harmony in the sense that it has clearly evolved as a harmonization based on scale degrees of a modal system rather than a tonal one per se.

In Andalusian altered Phrygian harmony, the chordal vocabulary derives primarily from the pitch resources of these modal resources, affording major chords on the second, third, and sixth degrees (in E: F and G, and C) and minor ones on the fourth and seventh degrees (Am and Dm). In E Phrygian the role of the "dominant"—that is, the chord that demands resolution to the tonic—is thus played by a major chord on the lowered second degree—here, F major. The Western dominant chord—a B7—is not functional in this system, except as a coloristic passing sonority; thus, for example, in a bulerías in A Phrygian, if a singer descends to rest on a B natural, the guitarist will take it as a signal to play an E7 chord, but this functions not as a dominant but as a coloristic predominant typically segueing to a B♭ chord and then to the tonic A major.

Andalusian Phrygian tonality is epitomized in the common Andalusian cadence Am–G–F–E (iv–III–II–I, La–Sol–Fa–Mi). In Western music this could be heard as i–VII–VI–V in the key of A minor, but in Phrygian tonality E serves as the unambiguous tonic and stable resting point. However, the iv chord (Am) can serve as a sort of secondary, momentary tonic, with a certain amount of temporary stability, paralleling the similar function of that fourth degree in Hijāz and Bayāti maqāms. Lola Fernández (2005, 91) refers to this move as an "inflection" to the iv chord. A deliberate semicadence on this iv chord can be followed, depending on context, by a iv–III–II–I descent to the tonic or by a more circuitous progression through the cycle of fifths—that is, iv–vii–III–VI–II–I (Am–Dm–G7–C7–F–E). The Andalusian cadence has the sort of centrality that the IV–V–I cadence has in Western common-practice tonality (or that the ii–V–I progression has in mainstream jazz). In its descending contour, it parallels the descending character of most flamenco vocal and guitar melodies.

A distinctive feature of the Phrygian mode in flamenco—which also differentiates it from the aforementioned otherwise similar eastern Mediterranean systems—is the instability of the third scalar degree, which accords with its variability in chordal accompaniment; for example, in E Phrygian, the tonic E major chord has G♯, while the G and C chords (III and VI) have G natural. In general, in flamenco melodies the third scalar degree is relatively weak, encountered mostly in passing, and, if rested on, is variable in its intonation (see Valenzuela Lavado 2016b, 9–10). Often, whether in passing or in a warm-up salida, the note is intoned in a neutral fashion, somewhere between minor and major third (e.g., between G and G♯, in E altered Phrygian). This neutral intonation is not, however, as systematic as that encountered in Arab and Turkish traditional music. Further, at the risk of crudely generalizing, it could be said that in the core cantes of soleá, siguiriyas, and bulerías, melodies tend to ascend to between the fourth and seventh scale degrees (in E Phrygian, between A and C above it) and then descend relatively quickly to the tonic. In many cases, if a singer does come to rest on the third degree, it may be taken as a special signal to the guitarist. For example, if in a bulerías in A Phrygian, the cantaor sings an introductory "ayayay" ending clearly on the C natural (the minor third degree), the guitarist may interpret that as a signal to play an A minor chord, in a shift to A minor tonality, or perhaps a C chord. By contrast, such a phrase ending on a sustained C♯ might indicate either a continuance of A altered Phrygian (with its A major tonic chord) or, alternately, a shift to A major tonality, which would be confirmed by introducing a B natural (rather than B♭), perhaps in the course of a quick descent to A. Similarly, in tangos (in A Phrygian) a clear C natural sung at the beginning of a copla might cue the guitarist to play the F7 chord opening the *coletilla* (refrain, tag) of the *tango extremeño* shown in example 8.6. Often, however, the lowered third degree (for example, a C natural in A Phrygian) contrasts with the raised third (C♯) in the guitar chord, just as might happen in American rock or blues tonality (although with a different generative logic).

My use of the term "tonality" here implies a system of chordal harmony, which in the case of flamenco Phrygian tonality, derives from the characteristic mode used, thus constituting a form of modal harmony. However, cantes such as the unaccompanied toná, martinete, and saeta are fundamentally modal rather than based in any sort of "tonality." These latter cantes have no harmonic element, and even in siguiriyas, the chordal harmonies played on the guitar are arguably decorative and rhythmic rather than harmonically structural, serving as ornamented, pulsed versions of a drone. Soleares could similarly be heard as fundamentally modal rather than "tonal" except insofar as one regards as structural some of the guitar harmonies, such as the frequent move to the minor iv chord. One could even regard the entrecopla sections of fandangos as modal rather than tonal, depending on the guitar treatment (Fernández Marín 2011, 38).

It remains to be considered what may constitute a fourth form of tonality, found primarily in the cantes of the Levant, especially tarantas, cartageneras, and mineras (and also the fandango de Lucena, from the southern part of Córdoba province). These are fandango forms, conventionally rendered with the entrecopla in F♯ Phrygian and the coplas in the relative major key of D—at least in early recordings of these, such as those by Chacón. However, as these cantes matured and decelerated in Chacón's wake, the standard copla chord structure became obscured, and the lowered seventh degree of C natural became far more prominent in melodies than the C♯ of a normal D major tonality. Guitarists enhanced this tonal ambiguity by rendering the tonic and subdominant chords as seventh chords (i.e., D7 and G7) and deploying an E7 chord as a predominant.

The resulting enigmatic tonality has been interpreted in different ways by flamencologists. Some might say that the tonality remains D major, with an exaggerated but basically coloristic use of the C natural. Others hear a persistent

F♯ Phrygian modality, such that, for example, an A7 chord is heard as III of F♯ Phrygian rather than the dominant of D major. Still others may hear the copla sections as essentially D Mixolydian, in which the C natural is an inherent scale degree that does not necessarily suggest tension (e.g., as of a D7 chord demanding resolution to a subdominant G chord). Indeed, the flatted seventh degree is found in various southern Spanish folk songs, especially archaic modal work songs (Livermore 1972, 149). Some flamencologists claim that the copla sections are bitonal; French analyst Philippe Donnier, for example, suggests that the singing is essentially in G major while the chordal accompaniment is in D (1996; see also Torres 2004, 147–73).[7] In modern Western art music, bitonality (and polytonality) is a compositional technique that was used by Béla Bartók, Darius Milhaud, and others. However, as an analytical and descriptive concept, its utility is contested, as various composers and theorists have argued that one cannot hear two tonalities at once, any more than one can understand two people speaking simultaneously. What is generally agreed upon is that the sense of tonicity in these cantes is studiously ambiguous and that this ambiguity has its own charm and flavor and lends the cante its own sort of richness and depth. For me, it is as if the chords and the dissonant melodic lines lack a clear sense of inherent directionality but seem to float in a sort of haunting, eerie limbo, eventually resolving to the F♯ Phrygian chord, which has its own strange dissonance, being flavored by the extraneous notes G, B, and E.

In discussing mode, some mention must be made of the notion, repeatedly voiced by some flamencologists, that microtonal intervals are common in flamenco singing. As noted above, the third degree in the flamenco Phrygian mode is often rendered in a neutral, half-flat intonation, and Jerez-style cantaores are known for singing the sixth degree in certain phrases—especially in bulerías—in a neutral manner.[8] Intonation in unaccompanied cantes such as martinete or toná may be conspicuously untempered, including as rendered by vocalists like Camarón who otherwise sing consistently "in tune" (see, e.g., Beyhom 2021). However, aside from these specific cases, intonation in flamenco is consistently diatonic, and the exaggerations made by certain flamencologists may derive from a tendency to hear as microtones any unfamiliar or exotic-sounding melismas or ornamentation.

Harmony

Flamenco harmony, quintessentially as rendered on guitar, is one of the most distinctive, rich, and appealing features of the genre as a whole. The flamenco harmonic system, though strikingly similar in its structure to aforementioned counterparts in Balkan and eastern Mediterranean musics, has been elaborated by generations of guitarists into a tradition of remarkable complexity, uniqueness, and expressivity, continually being expanded and enriched by innovative guitarists and, recently, eclectic jazz pianists.

Harmony as Structural or Merely Decorative?

In its basic structure, flamenco harmony may seem to be fairly straightforward and amenable to analysis and description. However, like so many elements of flamenco, some fundamental aspects of its function are ambiguous and even subject to earnest disputation among flamencologists. A primary question involves the extent to which chordal harmony (typically as played on guitar) constitutes a structural rather than a dispensable and coloristic aspect of the music. The question is most apparent in relation to core flamenco cantes such as soleares and bulerías. On the one hand, in most formal and professional performance contexts, singers of these cantes are accompanied by guitar; audiences are accustomed to guitar accompaniment, and many listeners feel that the guitar, with its conventional chord progressions at certain points, provides an essential component of the music. On the other hand, at present as in the past, there continue to be many contexts—especially but not only informal sessions—in which guitar is not only absent but is not necessarily desired, and many listeners and performers find the unaccompanied singing to be perfectly satisfying. The question thus involves whether melodies can function as purely modal entities, or, alternately, do they imply and at some level require chordal accompaniment for their flow, logic, and manipulations of dynamic tensions and resolutions?

In addressing this question it should first be acknowledged that there are different types of listeners, with different sorts of aesthetic sensibilities and expectations. On the one hand, there are many who are accustomed to hearing (and singing and dancing) flamenco at informal reunions of family and friends in which guitarists are often absent, and one should not necessarily assume that those present are imagining chordal accompaniments in their heads. As mentioned earlier, in chapter 2, many such people might even regard guitar accompaniment in such contexts as distracting and intrusive; accordingly, a few cantaores grounded in such reunions and juergas—such as Juan Talega—even chose to make commercial albums without guitar accompaniment. On the other hand are the more typical flamenco enthusiasts who apprehend the genre in stage performances and recordings, in which guitar accompaniment is standard; many such people prefer hearing cante with guitar, and when hearing the occasional soleá or bulerías rendered a palo seco, they might even imagine the standard chordal accompaniment in their heads as they listen.

A different sort of continuum pertains to the cantes themselves. Several cantes, such as saeta and martinete, are sung unaccompanied; this tradition is not merely a quaint, archaic custom but is reflected in the form of the melodies themselves, which are entirely modal and do not suggest any chordal accompaniment. At the opposite end of the continuum are, for example, fandangos de Huelva, most of whose verse melodies suggest—in some cases, quite clearly—the "standard" fandango chord progression (I–IV–[V7]–I–V7–I–IV) in the relative major key, with its internal dynamic flow, and also the climactic conclusion as it modulates to the Phrygian tonicity of the ritornello. (Such cantes also tend to be more syllabic [rather than melismatic] in style, rhythmically regular, and "hummable.") Typical in this sense are the fandango melodies shown in examples 5.8 and 5.9, which clearly suggest the accompanying harmonies (indeed, to the extent that guitar accompaniment is almost dispensable). Nevertheless, some flamencologists contend that such melodies should be regarded as modal, not harmonic (e.g., Sánchez Garrido 2015, 13–15), and others (e.g., Ortega 2011, 2012) transcribe them simply as monophonic melodic lines, without guitar chord indications. However, it could well be argued that these cantes are better regarded as flexible compositions for voice and guitar, in which the guitar chords structurally influence the directionality, relative stability, and consonance of the notes. Omitting chord harmonies from such notations is distorting their very sense of logic, tonality, and teleology. For example, listeners assuredly hear a C sung over a C chord in the copla section of a malagueña or fandango de Huelva as a stable tonic note, not a dissonant sixth degree in the key of E Phrygian, seeking to resolve to B. Consequently, it may be misleading to write that the copla section of such a fandango is in the "E [or Mi] Phrygian mode" when its tonality is likely to be heard as C major (Do) (see, e.g., Fernández Marín 2011).

Listeners might hear cantes such as soleares in different ways. Flamencologist and guitarist Faustino Núñez (personal correspondence; hereafter, p.c.), for example, likens hearing an unaccompanied soleares to singing an opera aria, or any popular song, in the shower, in which case one is imagining the instrumental and especially chordal accompaniment, which constitutes an essential structural aspect of the song, informing much of the dynamic logic and expressivity of the vocal melody. By contrast, various people, including cantaores, insist (if asked) that the melodies of soleá and bulerías have their own dynamic flow, which might be enhanced by but is not dependent on any chordal accompaniment, real or imagined. The ambiguity is conspicuous in the climactic cambio moment in the penultimate tercio, which a guitarist typically accompanies with a decisive III7–VI (Sol–Do, in E: G7–C) semicadence, followed by a iv–III–II–I Andalusian cadence to the tonic. It is noteworthy that in the melody at this point there is nothing to suggest this particular III7–VI chord progression nor, for that matter, any chord progression at all. Essentially, then, the guitar is serving to intensify, in its own conventional way, the drama of the moment. (Accordingly, in bulerías the chords of the cambio can actually be reversed to no ill effect—that is, VI–III instead of III–VI.) However, there is no doubt that for many listeners, the guitar accompaniment, with its climactic cambio, has become such a familiar part of the fabric of a soleá that its absence is undesirable (and may inspire the listener to imagine the accompaniment). For that reason, it could well be argued that soleares evolved not as a modal entity to which guitar chords were subsequently added but rather as an idiom developed collaboratively by singers and guitarists in professional contexts, especially the cafés cantantes.

Chords and Progressions

The flamenco chordal vocabulary basically coheres with the tonalities discussed above—that is, common-practice major and minor, and Phrygian. The most distinctive feature of flamenco harmonies is the prominence of altered chords with non-triadic tones. These are typically open strings on the guitar, indicating how closely linked that instrument has been to the evolution of flamenco form itself. Different palos, as played on guitar, exploit the various sonorities obtained by open strings on that instrument. Thus, soleares and malagueñas are most typically played in the finger positions of E Phrygian ("por arriba"), bulerías and siguiriyas in A Phrygian ("por medio"), tarantas in F♯ Phrygian, and granaínas in B Phrygian (or transpositions of these keys if a capo is used). Some typical altered tonic voicings are shown in example 4.2; note that the non-triadic tones in the tarantas and granaínas chords are open strings. The enhancement of the modal tonic chord with non-triadic tones, especially the 7th and 9th degrees, does not imply any instability or demand for "resolution" to the iv chord.

If tonic voicings may contain coloristic non-triadic notes, dominant II♭ voicings vary even more (like dominant chords in jazz). Example 4.3 shows various voicings or variants of the dominant II♭ chord in that key. Of these, the first three voicings of B♭ chords are entirely traditional, with the non-triadic G

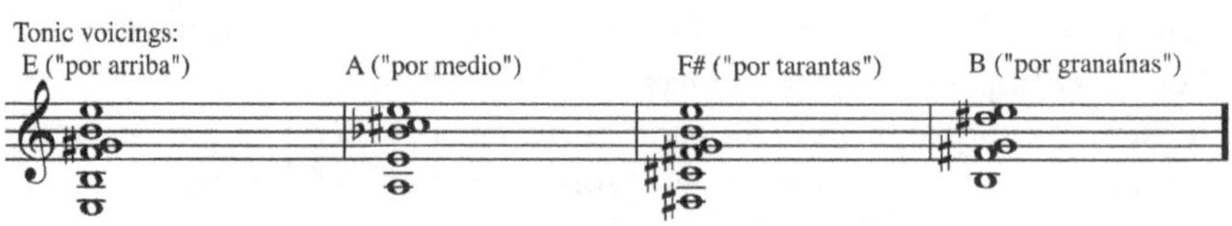

Example 4.2. Typical tonic guitar voicings: E, A, F♯, B

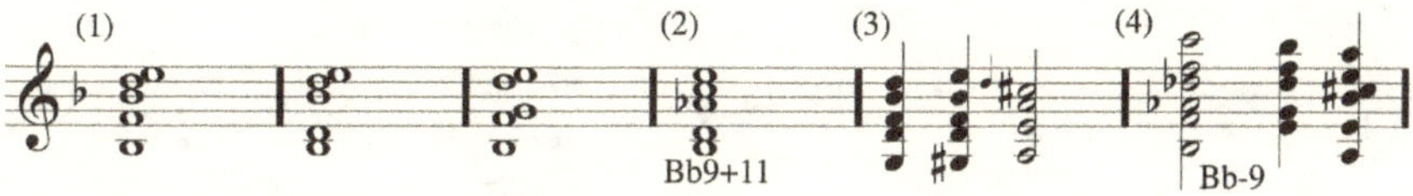

Example 4.3. Dominant II♭ (B♭) chords and patterns in A Phrygian

and E tones being open strings on the guitar. The fourth voicing (#2), although quite familiar nowadays, is a distinctively modern-sounding B♭ sonority, which jazz musicians might regard as a B♭9+11. Number 3 shows another common pattern, in which the A Phrygian tonic chord is approached from below—that is, via the G minor vii chord (a dominant substitution in A Phrygian common from the 1970s), with a passing chord substituting a G♯ leading tone for G in the bass. Most such chords, though effectively serving as dominant substitutes resolving to the tonic, do not lend themselves to any sort of common-practice or even jazz-informed analysis, having a different generative logic than would be operant in mainstream jazz. Thus, in the first B♭ chords shown in example 7.3, the E functions not as a "♭5" but as a sort of an appoggiatura, or drone—an atavism from flamenco's roots in purely modal music. Finally, the last bar in this example shows another modern flamenco sonority, in which a minor 9th chord on the flat second degree (here, a B♭ minor 9 chord) substitutes for the standard II♭ chord. The B♭ minor 9 chord fits easily with the tonality, since its D♭ (= C♯) and C natural are both present in the Phrygian flamenco scale.

In the music of Paco de Lucía and the innumerable gifted guitarists in his wake, the harmonic vocabulary further expanded to include a greater variety of chords, including ninth chords, half-diminished chords, and other sonorities. Some of these resemble counterparts in jazz, though few flamenco guitarists have more than a superficial knowledge of jazz. (Flamenco jazz pianists, by contrast, have dramatically exploited the affinities and compatibilities between the two genres; see Manuel 2016.) Another modern technique involves modulations; these might be parallel moves—for instance, from A Phrygian to A minor or A major—or modulations from one Phrygian tonic to another (e.g., from A to C). (The latter can pose some technical difficulty for the flamenco guitarist, who, accustomed to playing basic Phrygian tonic and II♭ chords in first position, in the new key may need to devote his index finger to barring the tonic fret in order to generate basic chords.)

Some typical modern flamenco harmonies are shown in example 4.4, a falseta in tangos, notated in A Phrygian.[9] Visible here are the substitution of a $D^{7\flat 9}$ for a Dm (i.e., a $IV^{7\flat 9}$ chord in place of a minor iv chord); the somewhat unclassifiable descending chords in measures 5 and 6 preceding the II♭ dominant; and the substitute dominant chord in bar 9. While this could be

Example 4.4. Modern tango falseta

labeled as a D♭$^{\Delta7}$ chord, it is more coloristic than teleologically functional, and it works well in the Phrygian flamenco context with its combination of both C and D♭ (= C♯); this chord can also be "planed" upward as shown in the final appended bar.

Form

Formal structure in mainstream "por derecho" flamenco cante and even solo guitar is relatively consistent and straightforward. Essentially, a flamenco item or tanda consists of a series of coplas (verses) sung to various melodies, typically stock estilo tunes. In lyric content, the coplas are thematically independent and complete statements, with no relation to each other; accordingly, their sung renderings are also independent musical entities and need not structurally relate to each other. The length of a tanda is thus quite flexible (unless, for example, conditioned by external factors, such as the context of a recording or an accompanying dance). A soleá sung on stage typically lasts around six to ten minutes. A tanda of bulerías might easily go on for fifteen minutes if the singer is inspired. In an informal setting such as a fiesta in a Gitano household, "item" lengths may vary even more, with a bulerías or tangos extending almost indefinitely as different friends and family members take turns singing—or even boisterously shouting out—whatever coplas come into their heads, with those present perhaps arising to dance as they are moved to do so. Similarly, at an informal gathering of fandango enthusiasts at a peña in Huelva, a set of fandangos might last twenty minutes, as different amateurs alternate singing coplas while one or more guitarists accompany.

Due to this loose structure, it would not be appropriate to call such a tanda or item a "song" or canción, since those terms imply some sort of structured entity, with elements of symmetry, recapitulation, and closure (as in the familiar 32-bar *AABA* popular song). Rather, the atomistic form is more typical of premodern Western genres, traditional folk and especially dance-music idioms, and various traditional non-Western genres. An example of the latter is the *ghazal*, a poetic form common in Urdu and Persian, consisting of a series of thematically independent couplets linked only by rhyme and prosodic meter; as a musical genre, ghazal (e.g., in Urdu) reflects this form in comprising a series of sung couplets that, though sharing a same basic melody, are independent poetic-musical units.

Various factors and conventions may, however, provide a certain limited sense of form and structure to a tanda, though not to the extent that it would acquire the character of a "song." Many flamenco tandas achieve some sense of closure by means of a final, short verse, sung as a tag or coda, that could be called a coletilla (little tail) or *juguetillo* (or in siguiriyas, a macho). In bulerías and soleá (as in example 5.1), these often modulate to the major key. A tientos typically segues to faster tangos, whether for a full rendition of one or more coplas or simply a compás or two appended as a concluding tag.

A tanda of soleares typically exhibits a conventional ordering of estilos that can lend it some sense of structure. It commences with a four-line *cante de inicio* (such as Joaquín el de la Paula) that is limited in range and does not involve a temporary guitar move to the minor iv chord. After a guitar falseta, the next estilos are usually "transitional," with a range extending beyond the fifth degree and an iteration of the iv chord. The tanda concludes with a short macho or cierre but still retains the character of a loose, non-teleological string of coplas.

A few palos, such as caña (discussed in chapter 5), are (or have become) somewhat ossified in their internal structure, acquiring the predictability of a "song." Formally distinctive in another way are some of the free-rhythmic cantes—especially malagueña or tarantas, whose rendering can often consist of a single copla stretched out to last three or four minutes, preceded by a leisurely guitar introduction. Tandas of most traditional cantes would not accurately be described as strophic, since they normally comprise a series of different estilos rather than reiterating the same melody.

Flamenco Guitar

Flamenco guitar constitutes an instrumental idiom of remarkable richness and contemporary vitality. As a musical tradition, its status is unique in that while its origins lie in a sort of urban folk music and its practitioners articulate little in the way of a standardized theory, it has the variety, sophistication, and technical virtuosity of an art music. Indeed, given the rather modest size of the classical guitar repertoire, flamenco guitar could well be argued to be the richest genre of acoustic guitar music in existence. Thus, flamenco guitar has been the subject of a fair amount of literature, from pedagogical materials to interviews with performers, though scholarly writings have consisted primarily of historical studies rather than synchronic analysis.[10]

Technique

Flamenco guitar, like classical guitar, is played on nylon and wound strings with the bare fingers. However, most flamenco guitarists strike the strings with their nails, which must be grown longer, rather than the soft skin of their fingertips. Nail maintenance is a major concern for guitarists, especially for those who have naturally soft cuticles. Long nails are a perpetual annoyance in daily life, and if broken or otherwise defective they must be artificially reinforced, whether by such techniques as parts of table tennis balls appended with superglue or by thick extensions applied at a nail salon. Through the first half of the twentieth century, most flamenco guitarists held the instrument more upright than would other guitarists, obliging them to bend the right hand at a sharp angle; modern guitarists have abandoned this practice, and many feel free to use foot rests—formerly disparaged as somehow "not flamenco."

Flamenco guitar playing can be regarded as comprising a finite set of specific techniques, especially rasgueado (rasgueo, strumming), arpeggio, alzapúa, picado, and tremolo. The most basic kind of folk, vernacular, or "stable-boy" Spanish guitar playing could consist only of rasgueo and thumb strokes as needed for accompanying dance or song. As flamenco evolved, it incorporated the other techniques. Rasgueo patterns are particularly important. A basic technique is pinky down, ring finger down, middle finger down, index finger down, index finger up; repeated quickly, this could be used to achieve a percussive machine-gun effect or, alternately, a more constant, unbroken flurry.

Whenever possible, a downward stroke by the index finger hitting two or more strings is executed by snapping the tip of the finger off the joint of the thumb, as if flicking some drops or debris off one's finger; the technique affords a sharp, percussive attack. In rhythmic palos such as tangos and bulerías, a "power chord" effect is certainly operant when such a vigorous stroke is used with chords (such as A or B♭, in A Phrygian) whose third degree is barely audible.

Alzapúa (*alzar*: to raise; *púa*: plectrum) is a basic traditional technique in which the thumb is used with both up- and downstrokes to generate fast, rhythmically driving, repetitive passages. Example 4.5 shows two typical alzapúas in tangos (in A Phrygian, por medio); note the chromatic E♭ in the second, allowing for an exact intervallic replication of the descending sequence: half step, whole step, whole step (F–E–D–C, E♭–D–C–B♭). (All guitar notations in this volume are descriptive rather than prescriptive; guitarists seeking details of playing technique should consult other sources.)

Example 4.5. Alzapúa

Picado denotes a single-note run, generally played with alternating strokes by index and middle fingers. Picados most typically consist of scalar passages that descend, sometimes circuitously, to the lower tonic (as in examples 4.8 and 5.2). Competent flamenco guitarists are able to play picado with dazzling speed, although they generally use such passages sparingly as part of achieving a general balance between strummed and plucked textures. In that sense, their intent is not comparable to that, for example, of fast single-note runs in jazz, which are designed to be melodically complex, intricate, and varied. Some flamenco guitarists, especially of the pre-Paco generations, have not cultivated picado technique at all. It is quite unfair of certain non-flamenco critics of modern playing to dismiss it (as did Segovia) as a torrent of showy picado; rather, it is quite common to hear an entire set without any picado, or perhaps only a single, electrifying picado run, thrown in as a flourish.

Arpeggios also vary in form, though they are primarily played on the top (in terms of pitch, not placement) three strings. In some cases they can be regarded as quick, ephemeral decorations of a melody that is played by the thumb, as in example 4.1; in other cases, as in the lush repeated arpeggios often played in malagueñas or granaínas, they are foregrounded in themselves (see examples 5.12 and 5.14).

In flamenco and classical guitar playing, tremolo denotes a melody articulated by fast repeated notes mostly on the high first string, accompanied by arpeggios played by the thumb on lower strings. Flamenco tremolos use four sixteenth quintuplets between each thumb stroke, in contrast to the standard classical technique of three sixteenth notes. Depending on a player's intent or general style, a tremolo can have its own sort of percussive intensity, or, perhaps more often, it is used to present a cantabile melody over the steady arpeggio accompaniment picked by the thumb. In either style the technique does not lend itself to reinforcing rhythmic drive, so it is seldom heard in bulerías or tangos. Many

Example 4.6. Tremolo

traditional tremolo patterns are fairly short and simple, but skilled guitarists use the technique to present charming, lyrical mini-compositions of their own creation, especially in the otherwise free-rhythmic palos of tarantas, granaínas, and malagueñas. Flamencologists have often regarded tremolo technique as having been adopted from classical playing by Ramón Montoya, though more recent research has revealed tremolo to have been cultivated by El Murciano in the 1840s, no later than its usage in classical playing (Martínez and Manuel 2016). Example 4.6 shows part of a popular tremolo falseta in soleares by Sabicas.

Flamenco guitar playing is further distinguished by the use of golpes ("blows," or fingernail taps, usually by the ring finger) on the face of the instrument, often in combination with other plucking or strum patterns, and often in ways that are essential to compás patterns rather than merely decorative. Most traditional flamenco playing is done in or near first position, allowing the player much use of hammering-on and pulling-off techniques on open strings. In general, the flamenco guitarist plays with a more forceful and vigorous touch, and perhaps less variation of volume, than the classical player.

The cejilla, or capo, is widely used by flamenco guitarists, especially to accommodate singers at their preferred ranges. Whether or not cantaores have any formal understanding of pitch, harmony, or guitar playing, they must have learned through experience to be able to instruct an accompanist, before singing, where to put the capo. Typically, before commencing a given item, the guitarist will look for guidance at the singer, who might say "tres" (indicating to put the capo on the third fret) or perhaps merely flash three fingers. In some cases, the singer might also specify the tonality—for instance, "bulerías, cuatro por arriba." Guitarists playing solos may also use the capo, perhaps on the first one or two frets, to give the instrument a brighter sound, but positioning it much higher limits their range at both upper and lower registers. In recent years, some cantaores have taken to having the guitarist move the capo (typically upward) in the middle of a given item in order to sing particular estilos in more comfortable ranges.

As mentioned above, guitarists accompany cantes in specific conventional tonalities that have their own character, especially in association with the open strings and the non-triadic tones with which tonic chords can be enriched. Thus, for example, tarantas is conventionally accompanied in the guitar tonality of F♯ Phrygian (or, with capo, a transposed version), in which the open G, B, and E strings add much flavor to the modal tonic chord. This guitar tonicity is intrinsic to the character of the cante in general. Similarly, siguiriyas is almost invariably accompanied in A Phrygian por medio, as is soleá por bulerías. Bulerías and tangos, by contrast, though typically in por arriba A Phrygian, are flexible, and guitarists are fond of playing these in different tonalities. For the popular rumba/tango "Como el Agua," by Camarón and Paco de Lucía, two guitars accompanied, one playing por medio and the other, with the capo two frets lower, por granaínas; the effect of the latter is audible in the non-triadic high G♭ heard in the strumming of the tonic D♭ chord. Fandangos are most commonly rendered por arriba (in E Phrygian/C major) but can also be accompanied por medio, especially to accommodate a singer's range (and also give a more "folkloric" sound). A "proper" rendering of a granaínas is invariably in B Phrygian/G major, but a concert malagueña de Mellizo—announced as such—may be preceded by a granaínas, accompanied by the same E Phrygian por arriba tonicity, which is seen as a warm-up item and would be recognizable as a granaínas only by its vocal melody rather than its guitar accompaniment.

Falsetas

Mainstream flamenco guitar playing may crudely be regarded as comprising either standard accompanimental or time-keeping patterns, or distinctive, precomposed, relatively short passages called falsetas, presented as foreground entities preceding or punctuating sung verses. (A modern guitarist like Gerardo Núñez may dislike this dichotomy and attempt to play in a more seamless fashion.) In metered cantes such as tangos and bulerías, the accompaniment may consist of conventional compás patterns oscillating between tonic and II♭ chord, with occasional other chord progressions (often, an Andalusian cadence, or the III7–VI cambio). In free-rhythmic cantes, the accompaniment typically comprises relatively standardized patterns, though rendered in a loosely improvisatory manner.

While providing sensitive and skilled accompaniment to sung passages can involve great artistry, the falseta is the vehicle for the guitarists to foreground their virtuosity and, in many cases, compositional creativity. Historically, falsetas can be seen as related to the variations or diferencias that constituted the basic building blocks of Spanish Baroque guitar music. On a more vernacular level, one can imagine the proverbial eighteenth-century stable-boy guitarist

Example 4.7. Patiño soleares falseta

who strums accompaniment patterns to a fandango or verdiales and then, in between sung verses, plays some other pattern that he has picked up from somewhere. In the nineteenth century, and especially in the café cantante context, as guitar playing became more professional and elaborate, the falsetas became dramatically more intricate, numerous, and varied, and their composition came to be earnestly cultivated by guitarists in open competition with each other.

Falsetas vary considerably in length, style, and general character, although a few generalizations can be made. Some falsetas may be very short, such as the patterns shown as c. [compás] 22 (at 1:50), and c. 27, each lasting only one compás, in example 5.1. Others—especially, for example, tremolo melodies—might last almost a full minute. A few falsetas, or sequences thereof, have acquired informal names, such as Sabicas's "*las tres hermanas*" (the three sisters) in soleares.[11] Many falsetas, especially traditional ones, have an *aab* "question-answer" structure—that is, a phrase is played, then repeated (perhaps with slight variation), and then a contrasting phrase concludes the passage. A primordial example of this form is the soleares falseta presumably composed by Maestro Patiño in the mid-1800s, shown as example 4.7.

Other falsetas in this volume illustrating this form include those in example 5.5, in siguiriyas, and example 4.4, in tangos. In the latter, a phrase is played in the tonic chord of A Phrygian; then it is reiterated, in abbreviated form, in an altered form of the iv chord. Then follow two harmonically unstable, chromatic bars, a concluding descent to the tonic, and then a reiteration of the first chromatic chord of c. 5, functioning as a substitution for the standard II♭ dominant chord. This falseta structure bears an obvious affinity to the typical verse forms in soleares and other cantes: a line of verse is sung and then repeated, and then second and third verse lines are sung, linked, in a contrasting melody. In other cases, climax and closure may be achieved by an accelerated pattern or the introduction of a dramatic picado run landing on the lower tonic.

Many falsetas outline descending patterns, especially diverse articulations of the iv–III–II–I Andalusian cadence. Example 4.8 shows three short (two-compás) falsetas in bulerías, using different textures to outline the descent. The

Example 4.8. Bulerías falsetas

first, a picado, segues from a sequence to a chromatic descent ending, in typical fashion, on beat six followed by a *remate*—cadential rasgueo. The second ends with a traditional six-note tag instead of the strum. While both of these start on beat twelve, the third falseta starts on beat one, ending with chromatically descending chords.

The free-rhythmic cantes offer different sorts of possibilities to guitarists. Falsetas tend to be relatively long, with much use of lush arpeggios and with a languid, ruminative character, punctuated by artful pauses.

Accompanying Cante

Flamenco guitar solos have been performed on stage since the 1860s, and solo playing has evolved into a formidably sophisticated art, but there is no doubt that flamenco guitar evolved primarily as an accompaniment idiom and in most contexts remains secondary to the vocals. As any well-rounded guitarist will attest, accompanying is an art in itself, in many ways distinct from solo playing. The primary job of the guitarist is to make the vocalist sound good, even in the broad sense of having some falseta material to play while the singer is catching his or her breath between coplas.

An initial requirement is to know the cante repertoire well, including the lesser-known palos. Thus, while a singer might achieve a professional level knowing only eight or ten cantes, a guitarist must be ready to accompany any singer. If a vocalist embarks on a caña, or a fandango de Lucena, it is not satisfactory for the guitarist to attempt to fake their way through by playing soleares or fandango de Huelva accompaniment patterns, respectively. Meanwhile, in performance the guitarist must also know how to respond to any cues and spontaneous trajectories the cantaor may undertake. We have mentioned, for example, that while bulerías is most often in A Phrygian, "por medio," the guitarist must be alert to switch to A minor or A major tonality if there is any such indication, however subtle, from the singer—especially, singing a major second (B natural) in combination with C or C♯. In a set of fandango de Huelva, most of the coplas will be in the relative major key of the Phrygian entrecopla (e.g., C, if the copla is in E Phrygian), but the guitarist must be ready to switch to A minor or major if the cantaor opens the copla with a phrase of the fandango of Cabezas Rubias, for instance. In soleares, as noted above, if the singer departs from the "textbook" phrasing—especially by starting a line around beat seven instead of beat one—the guitarist must know how to adjust the chords, including the cambio, to fit the cante while maintaining the compás. In any of the metered cantes—such as tangos, bulerías, or fandango de Huelva—the singer may melismatically extend certain phrases, passages, or notes, and the guitarist must adapt accordingly, perhaps reiterating the chord in question (typically a dominant) rather than mechanically proceeding to the next one.

On another level, the guitarist must be constantly interacting with and complementing the cantaor's phrasing and dynamics, filling in gaps and pauses with quick riffs or rasgueos and sensitively complementing the singer in various ways, as by tailoring dynamics, intensity, and even tempo to particular passages, anticipating phrases, knowing when to be assertive and when to lay back, and generally intensifying the vocalist's mood. Guitarist Adrian Alvarado nicely articulated his conception of accompanying Alfonso Cid: "You have to provide a clear tonal center for the singer, but I also like to surprise him sometimes, but without derailing him" (p.c.). (Estela Zatania observes, "Nowadays guitarists may lead singers around by the nose anticipating chords not yet signaled by the melody" [p.c.].)

Most playing is fairly forceful, even if often economic, such that a timid, uncertain strumming accompaniment will not sound good. Although the guitarist's falsetas are precomposed, the ongoing extemporized flourishes and variations lend the guitar playing a flavor of looseness and spontaneity. A skilled singer and guitarist will sound like a single organism—breathing, pausing, surging, ebbing, and flowing in perfect synchrony with each other. Much of the responsibility for achieving this effect lies with the guitarist, who must respond to the singer's cues. Guitarists may be especially likely to feel as if they are on the hot seat when accompanying an unpredictable or less than entirely competent cantaor, who might start singing on the wrong pitch, enter at the wrong moment, or sing lines out of order. An unfortunate occasional occurrence is when, after the guitar introduction, a cantaor—perhaps accustomed to singing from a particular key or to singing without guitar—enters on a completely different tonality from that of the guitarist, who either doggedly proceeds, hoping the vocalist will find his or her bearings, or else fumbles around, attempting to figure out the singer's pitch. Guitarists also often have to contend with singers who stray from the compás in metered cantes; as Enrique de Melchor noted, "Eighty percent of them get lost sometimes, even the big names, so the guitarist's job is to make it so that no one notices, not even the singer" (qtd. in Curao 2008, II:186). In many cases, a guitarist and singer may have performed together extensively, or perhaps they have had occasion to rehearse a few items, such as a precomposed cuplé. However, in both theory and reality, a competent guitarist and vocalist are able to perform most items together well without any such rehearsal.

Accompanists also solo, playing one or more falsetas at the beginning of an item and in between coplas. The guitar introduction to a song serves, on a basic level, to set the pitch and tonality for the singer, to establish the mood of the cante, and, in the case of metered cantes, to set the rhythm. Although this introduction traditionally consists of one or more straightforward falsetas, many modern guitarists (to the annoyance of some purists) play extended, meandering preludes in which the identity of the cante only gradually becomes evident. In general, audiences come to hear the cantaor rather than the guitarist, but good guitarists are certainly appreciated, and skillful playing can elicit thunderous applause. The lengths of guitar interludes are flexible but governed by convention and good sense. A typical stage presentation of a free-metered cante such as tarantas or malagueñas might last around eight or nine minutes, of which the guitar introduction might easily last four minutes and the subsequent entrecopla playing another full minute. Thus, around half of such an item may consist of solo guitar playing. Hence, whether or not a guitarist aspires to be a soloist, an evening's performance will afford plenty of time to occupy the foreground. When concluding his opening solo, the guitarist may look at the singer and play an entrada pattern, such as the basic compás pattern, effectively inviting the cantaor to sing. If not preferring to sing just then, the vocalist will look elsewhere, and the guitarist plays a bit more.

The amount of foreground guitar playing may, of course, vary. At informal reunions—which might feature some excellent singers—there are many amateur guitarists who might have only modest technique and a limited repertoire of falsetas but who are adept and sensitive accompanists and might be particularly attuned to the predilections and repertoire of the local singers. Such vocalists, indeed, might well prefer such a "background" guitarist—or might prefer to sing unaccompanied—rather than sing with some stranger from out of town who can play flashy falsetas but has little idea how to accompany a diverse range of cantaores. A different sort of player was Diego del Gastor, whose interludes between coplas might go on for several minutes, until he would eventually remember the vocalist and provide a proper entrada. As his nephew Paco related, this habit was enjoyed or accepted by some local singers but not by those such as Antonio Mairena, who preferred short, unobtrusive guitar entrecoplas and avoided singing with Diego (qtd. in Curao 2008, V:154).

Accompanying Dance

Accompanying dance is an important part of flamenco guitar playing. The main professional or semiprofessional activity of many guitarists consists of accompanying dance classes and their occasional performances or playing at tablaos, which foreground dance. Even if the guitarist is not the featured artist in such contexts, the guitar is an important component, and many top-level guitarists attest to the invaluable experience and insights that accompanying dance can provide. Further, guitarists do enjoy the scope afforded by some parts of a dance show, such as the *silencio* section of an alegrías, where the guitarist plays slow falsetas, usually in minor key.

Most important, however, is the guitarist's ability to enhance the baile by following cues, establishing tempos, and leading sections when appropriate, following the dancer's fluctuating tempo in other moments, and, ideally, complementing the dancer in various subtle and spontaneous ways. Whether playing vigorous rasgueos or ornate arpeggios, the guitar must strongly maintain the compás; the guitarist also learns that some falsetas work well in dance contexts, and others, however suitable for solo playing, are less effective.

During much of a typical dance item, the cantaor is singing, such that the guitarist is primarily accompanying and following that performer. However, other aspects of accompaniment are unique to the dance format. Several sections, such as the silencio and escobilla of alegrías or the double-time *redoblao* of soleares, have no singing and are thus played by guitarists only in dance contexts; even "copla" sections might be performed without cante in certain contexts, whether dance class rehearsals or performances by such students if no singer is available. During the footwork-oriented escobilla sections, the guitarist typically plays variations on a basic compás pattern in a way that ideally supports and coheres with the dancer rather than showing off or regurgitating elaborate falsetas.

The guitarist must also play various particular flourishes and passages to accompany specific dance moves. Most important and basic of these are forms of llamada. The llamada is a short cadential dance move cohering with the compás. Perhaps most typically, it starts with the dancer bringing his or her arms, with fists closed, toward the chest (as on the first few beats of a compás of alegrías or soleá) and then stepping clearly to end on a dramatic pose, accompanied by a guitar and palmas cierre or corte (lit., "cut"), usually on the cadential beat ten in the case of a twelve-beat compás or seven in an eight-beat, two-bar cycle like tangos. Dancers might punctuate or end a passage of footwork with such a llamada, or perhaps having sat or strolled through an introductory paseo during the first sung verse, they might do a dramatic llamada to announce that they are starting to dance in earnest. In either case, the guitarist should recognize the llamada and accompany it with matching rasgueo patterns (which may be the same sort of pattern that the guitarists might play to conclude a falseta or punctuate a sung verse). Somewhat more elaborate, from the guitarist's perspective, is the desplante, a longer pattern in which the dancer commences with the llamada-type closing-arms movement, takes a few steps backward (in the middle part of a twelve-beat compás), and then does some percussive footwork, often in *contratiempo* (e.g., stressing beats 12–2–4–6, etc.), to a dramatic pose on a cierre (usually on beat ten in the twelve-beat compás). As with a llamada, the guitarist should accompany the pattern closely.

Not all llamadas and desplantes are identical or easily predictable. Basilio Georges, a prominent New York–based guitarist, relates the following:

> One dancer I work with likes to do a two-compás pattern in alegrías between the first and second letras, where she does a dramatic stop on beat six, followed by a pause, and then she comes in a bit slower, and I can recognize when it's coming and play along. And now I've been accompanying for thirty years and I've seen so many little tricks like that such that I can anticipate them even with dancers I don't know. But it's hard to keep up, because with every generation of new dancers—whether it's Sara Baras or Rocío Molina or whoever—they keep making the dance more complicated, with new theatrical moves, tempo changes in odd spots and the like, and the younger dancers don't even know the dance styles that I grew up accompanying. (p.c.)

One sort of challenge involves accompanying an inexperienced dancer who does not articulate llamadas and other moves properly, or whose tempo is uneven, or who attempts to perform a fixed choreography without having mastered it, and the guitarist, as always, must try to help make the dancer look good, whether by following or judiciously leading. In most contexts, a skilled guitarist knows what to expect and is able to accompany a dance performance without rehearsal. Usually it will suffice for the performers to have a brief "talk-through" before an item, in which they clarify, for example, if the vocalist will sing either one or two letra sets before the escobilla. Often even such a brief exchange is unnecessary. Rehearsals are only necessary in the case of a pre-choreographed, theater-style *baile montado*, whether an item by a dance teacher for the students or an elaborate, programmatic *espectáculo* prepared by a troupe for a special stage show.

Guitar Solos

Although the primary function of the guitar has always been to accompany cante or baile, guitar solos have occupied a niche in flamenco since the 1860s, and the idiom of solo guitar has developed into a rich art form—even if most of its core audience may consist of other guitarists, whether Spanish or international. From the 1960s, Carlos Montoya, Sabicas, Manitas de Plata, and a few other performers successfully marketed their versions of solo guitar outside Spain—where the language barrier limited appreciation of cante—but it was not until the early 1970s that Paco de Lucía legitimized solo guitar concerts in Spain. Even there, guitar solos have only a secondary presence in the mainstream circuit of festivals and peñas, which are devoted mostly to cante and, secondarily, dance. For their part, tablao shows invariably feature one guitar solo in providing a mixed fare for their tourist-heavy audiences. Various sorts of solo guitar performances do occur occasionally in Spain, and top guitarists can do their best to arrange foreign tours, but even virtuosos like Gerardo Núñez lament the limited market for their talent.

Recordings have paralleled this general trajectory. Ramón Montoya and, subsequently, Niño Ricardo recorded a few solos, but they were career accompanists and did not extensively cultivate solo playing. Carlos Montoya, Sabicas, and a few other emigres also recorded many dozens of solo albums in the 1960s, but again it was Paco de Lucía who legitimized the solo album in Spain itself, even if sales for these were seldom substantial.

The guitar solo itself has had a rather ambiguous status as an art form. The traditional guitar solo would generally consist of a series of falsetas—such as would normally punctuate vocal stanzas—without any particular overarching formal structure or design. Within this loose format, the guitarist would naturally try to introduce a measure of variety, perhaps, for example, by including an extended melodic passage played in tremolo style. These falsetas might be the same ones that the guitarist plays separately while accompanying, and they could thus be detached and played independently by other players. The guitarist, if recording this sequence, might give it some quaint title but might or might not attempt to reproduce it verbatim again. An early departure from this informal approach was represented by Ramón Montoya's rondeña, which he recorded in 1937 and later in a nearly identical form; more exemplary are various pieces by Mario Escudero, such as his aforementioned 1960s "Ímpetu," a tightly structured bulerías with the character of a classical composition.

Since the 1970s, guitar solos by leading artists like Paco de Lucía have generally been presented as extended compositions, with evocative titles, that are rendered in more or less the same fashion in successive performances. (In order to be a top-ranking guitarist today, one must not merely play well but also compose original and artful falsetas.) Even these pieces, however, continue to consist essentially of strings of falsetas, which are freely disassembled and copied individually by imitators, and even their originators, such as Paco de Lucía, may play falsetas independently. Post-Paco guitarists have endeavored to structure some of their pieces more coherently, as in Vicente Amigo's "Morente," an item (which could loosely be called a granaínas, for its tonality) whose initial theme recurs at the conclusion, or items on Manolo Sanlúcar's *Tauromagia*. Such innovations notwithstanding, most guitar solos heard in tablaos and elsewhere continue to consist of strings of falsetas and invariably adhere to the inherited body of traditional cantes. Thus, modernization and innovation have consisted not of adding to the repertoire by the creation of new cantes but of expanding and enriching the cantes from within by using more varied, adventurous, and eclectic styles and harmonies.

The relation of guitar solos to the cantes themselves, however, is often flexible and loose, since the cante's foremost distinguishing element—the vocal melody—is absent in instrumental performance. A rendition of a metered cante (such as soleares, bulerías, or siguiriyas) will naturally adhere to the distinctive compás of the cante in question. It will also generally employ the most conventional key used to accompany that cante, as discussed above. However, especially in the wake of Paco de Lucía's *Siroco*, guitarists have avidly experimented with different tonalities, as in Gerardo Núñez's rendering of soleá in C♯ Phrygian with rondeña retuning of strings (D–A–D–F♯–B–E). If guitarists use such tonalities to accompany singers, as for example, Vicente Amigo has done with José Mercé in a soleá, the cantaor must either accustom himself to the distinct sound or sing newly composed melodies.

The relation to the traditional cantes can be especially ambiguous in the case of free-rhythmic cantes, such as granaínas and tarantas. Here, since neither vocal melody nor compás is present, it is only the conventional guitar key and perhaps the use of a few typical falsetas that identify the palo as such. In effect, guitar solos in these palos have the character of free fantasias exploring the possibilities of a given guitar key. If a modern guitarist such as Dani de Morón plays a solo in one of these palos—modulating about, avoiding traditional falsetas and voicings, and exploiting the full range of the neck rather than favoring first position and its characteristic sonorities—there may be little that identifies the palo at all, except, perhaps, a concluding chord or *remate*. Connoisseurs may have mixed feelings about such unrecognizable items, which are innovative in their avoidance of conventional phrases and cliches but may also dissatisfy listeners who would like to hear what a creative guitarist can do precisely with the established conventions. (An analogy could be made to an innovative jazz musician whose radically "outside" rendering of a standard such as "Round Midnight" felicitously eschews hackneyed phrases but essentially ignores the chord progressions and the challenges and opportunities they present to the interpreter.)

Spain has an extraordinary number of gifted flamenco guitarists and, needless to say, an exponentially greater number of earnest amateurs from whose ranks the professionals emerge. Through the 1960s, the standard performance context for professional or semiprofessional guitarists—as for singers—would be the circuit of juergas, taverns, baptisms, and weddings mentioned earlier. In that decade, however, tablaos also began to proliferate, and by the 1970s the summer festivals and peñas were also thriving throughout Andalucia; together they provided new opportunities for flamenco performers and liberated them from the perversities of the juerga life.

Guitarists have operated in various ways in this modern period. Many teach, or accompany dance classes, and many of the better players have enjoyed regular gigs at tablaos. In the 1970s–1980s heyday of the all-night summer festivals, four or five guitarists would be engaged for an event and would spend the occasion either relaxing backstage or accompanying a cantaor, with no need for rehearsal. Such ad hoc arrangements were largely satisfactory, and guitarists remember the festivals fondly, though Enrique de Melchor recalled having to accompany six or seven singers on occasion and then at another festival passing the night without playing at all, for whatever reason (Curao 2008, II:194). Other guitarists would be professionally paired up for extended periods with singers, enjoying a different kind of stability; such duos would include Tomatito with Camarón, Pedro Bacan with Calixto Sánchez, Ramón de Algeciras with Juanito Valderrama, and Paco del Gastor with El Cabrero. The record industry provided supplementary income for some performers, such as Manolo Sanlúcar, who served as a "house guitarist" for the recording label Philips. Several guitarists, including Paco Aguilera and Antonio Arenas, operated as effective producers for records of cante, even selecting the featured singers. Unfortunately, it remains difficult for even virtuoso guitarists to earn a decent living playing flamenco.

Palmas and Jaleo

While flamenco is often described as comprising cante, baile, and toque, the custom of understanding the latter as synonymous with guitar playing omits an element that has long been recognized as essential to metered cante—namely, palmas, or rhythmic hand-clapping. Especially in bulerías and tangos, palmas constitutes an intrinsic rather than optional or merely decorative element of the rhythmic texture. The importance of palmas and the artistry involved have been commented on by flamencologists from González Climent (1955) onward to the recent dissertation by Jiménez de Cisneros (2019).

Rhythmic hand-clapping, especially as performing interlocking hocket patterns, is found in various music genres worldwide. In Javanese gamelan music, it is called *keplok*. Geographically and culturally somewhat closer to flamenco is the clapping, called *fijri*, of Bedouins in Kuwait, providing basic rhythms to song forms *arabi*, *leywa*, and *saut*. While any sort of historical link between these genres and flamenco would be highly speculative, the term for such music sessions, *samrah*, as also used in North African Arabic, is certainly cognate with the "zambra" of Granada. More assuredly related is the Amazigh ahwash tradition of Morocco's Atlas Mountains. In the ahwash (examples of which can be seen on YouTube), men and women in separate lines alternate singing verses to the accompaniment of percussion instruments. At various points the men clap vigorously in unison, generating a lively 12/8 hemiola polyrhythm in combination with the drumming. A historical connection with Andalusian music is likely, since Amazigh dynasties ruled Moorish Spain in the eleventh and twelfth centuries, and Amazigh constituted around a quarter of the region's population during this period.

If the tradition of "doing palmas" (*haciendo palmas*) may be centuries old in Andalusia, it has acquired considerably more importance, standardization, and sophistication in the modern period. As Jiménez documents, palmas patterns on early twentieth-century recordings were fairly simple, but with the advent of the LP and greater recording fidelity in the 1950s, more sophisticated palmas patterns became standard in both recording and live performances.

Palmas provides several functions, as Jiménez discusses (2019, 159–60). At informal family reunions—again, especially but not only Gitano—palmas provides a socially integrating role, as everyone from children to octogenarians not only enriches the musical texture but also becomes active participants instead of passive onlookers. Children, with the encouragement of elders, soon acquire an intuitive grasp of the rhythmic flow of bulerías, tangos, and other festive cantes, learning when to intensify their clapping, when to lay back, and when to conclude a phrase with a forceful *remate*. On the musical level, palmas serves to articulate the basic pulse and the specific compás and to intensify the dynamic ebb and flow generated by the singer and to some extent the guitarist. Finally, the palmeros, both with their clapping and their shouted jaleos, encourage and inspire the soloists.

Palmas are arguably more indispensable than the guitar in informal music sessions, whether a domestic reunion or an ad hoc street corrillo formed by groups of rowdy youngsters who burst into a bulerías in which people take turns shouting out verses while everyone else does palmas. In the tablaos, a standard format for a cuadro is a singer, a guitarist, a dancer, and two backup dancers who provide palmas. In stage shows, the palmeros may either stand or be seated at a table, which they may rap with their knuckles when not clapping. Such palmeros, needless to say, are professionals, and since the 1980s some duos and trios have acquired considerable renown and demand. On some occasions they insert elaborate routines they have prepared (allowing the cantaores to catch their breath).

Palmas can be executed either *sorda* (mute) or *abierta* (open, or *clara*, clear). In a sorda clap, the cupped palms meet, with the thumb and other four fingers straddling the thumb of the other hand, producing a lower-pitched, muted sound. In an abierta clap, the three or four fingers of one hand strike the palm of the other, generating a dry, sharp, higher-pitched "crack." Each of these two basic techniques can be done in a few different ways, producing varieties of volume and timbre (such as might be variously labeled *lisa* [plain], *seca* [dry], *sonora* [resonant], etc.).

Palmas patterns typically comprise two parts, the *base*—usually a quarter-note pulse on the beat—and the *contra*, or contratiempo, involving claps on off-beats; together they produce a composite pattern via hocket technique. Such patterns can reinforce and duplicate rhythms such as the basic tangos compás or a falseta being played by the guitar. Alternately, they can complement voice or guitar phrasings, such as concluding a vocal phrase with a cadential tag called cierre, or *contestación* (response). Example 4.9 shows a basic tango pattern with palmas accompaniment. During the singing, the palmas base and contra combine to produce the standard compás pattern and then join to answer and conclude the final phrase with a cierre/contestación. This pattern is identical to the three-two clave of Latin music, although while the latter is an ongoing ostinato, the cierre is a cadential phrase, more akin to "shave and a haircut, two bits."

Clapping basic compás patterns in tangos is easy enough, and when several audience members in a medium-size venue like a peña are doing so along with the music, the effect is felicitous. Doing palmas with bulerías, however,

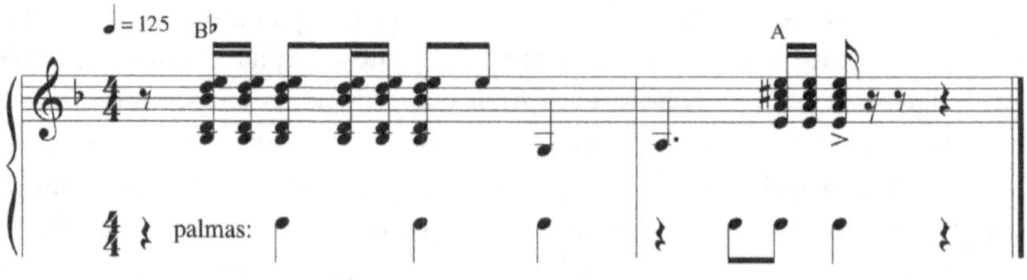

Example 4.9. Tango with palmas

requires genuine expertise and is best left to the palmeros on stage or, in the case of an informal reunion or street corrillo, the tight core of knowledgeable participants. Moreover, it is only such a relatively small cohort that would be capable of executing crisp *remates* and especially intricate hocket patterns. Patterns may come in and out of fashion, such as the fast triplets popular in tangos of the 1950s–1970s, which are currently regarded as old-fashioned and too reminiscent of castanets (Jiménez 2019, 256). Styles may also vary according to locale; Jerez patterns tend to be fairly straightforward, while those of Seville—perhaps because of the abundance of dancers in that city—are often elaborate and syncopated and are sometimes executed in combination with zapateo (Jiménez 2019, 307).

Those who attend tourist-oriented tablaos are likely to have witnessed an unfortunate occurrence: during a bulerías, a singer or dancer stands facing the audience and commences doing palmas vigorously, which the spectators misinterpret as a signal for them to applaud, which they then do, drowning out the proper palmas. Generally the palmeros decide who will do the steady base and who—usually a single palmero—will do the more variable and syncopated contra. The palmeros must work together organically in response to the phrasing or cues from the singer or dancer. Particularly effective, when used judiciously, are sixteenth note double-time passages, in which the contra palmero claps off-beat eighth notes, generating a composite machine-gun effect.[12]

Palmas can be regarded as one component of jaleo, the other consisting of shouts of encouragement. Jaleo is done by those on stage—such as palmeros, dancers who are seated while their colleague is dancing—or by the audience. Jaleo is especially common, and indeed essential, in the festive cantes of bulerías and tangos. The most common expression is "olé"; others include *eso es* (that's it, pronounced "soé"), *vamos allá* (let's go there, pronounced "amayá"), and *arsa* (from *alza*, or lift). These vocalizations may occur after any expressive passage or dance move, but they are almost obligatory at certain moments, such as immediately after a dancer's desplante, in which the dancer completes a vigorous sequence by halting in a statuesque pose facing the audience. In bulerías, such a desplante, or the cadential remate of a singer's or guitarist's passage, generally comes on beat ten and is answered by the audience reflexively shouting "olé" on beat three, as if performers and audience were a single, breathing organism. It is dispiriting for artists to perform, whether at a tablao or outside Spain, for foreign audiences who may applaud vigorously at the end of an item but sit like cadavers when they should be shouting jaleos at specific points.[13]

Other Instruments: Cajón, Piano—and the Dancer

In 1977 Paco de Lucía, touring South America with his accompanists, attended a function at the Spanish Embassy in Peru at which a local group included in the ensemble the cajón (lit., "big box"), a hand-played wooden box drum used in Afro-Peruvian music. Paco and his percussionist Rubem Dantas were intrigued by the instrument, and Paco acquired one, returned to Spain with it, and was soon incorporating it into his sextet. Within a decade the cajón came to be widely incorporated into flamenco, constituting yet another contribution made by de Lucía to the art form. As he explained, the instrument was well suited to flamenco in that its timbre could resemble that of the dancer's zapateo, or the traditional rapping of knuckles on a table, and that unlike most hand drums it did not sound a specific pitch, the likes of which could interfere with the guitar. The Spaniards soon altered the instrument's construction, adding a set of guitar strings behind the front panel that served as a snare, lending a crisp tone to the bass, slap, and muted ("ghost") timbres available. They also soon developed conventional ways of accompanying the metered palos, especially bulerías and tangos. While the cajón is neither indispensable nor ubiquitous, it has become extremely common, whether at tablaos, festivals, or informal sessions. Students can now avail themselves of a vast array of pedagogical materials, from books and DVDs to online tutorials. While the cajón is not without its detractors, its players have learned to accompany in ways that tastefully complement the guitar rather than drowning it out (especially if the guitar is adequately amplified). Performances nowadays may even feature cajón solos, whose rhythmic aesthetic and style may be said to resemble that of the dancer's zapateos.

A different sort of addition to the flamenco instrumentarium is represented by the piano, which made its first appearances in the 1950s and 1960s when Manolo Caracol would sing to the accompaniment of his son-in-law, pianist Arturo Pavón (1930–2005). While Pavón established a certain niche for the instrument, pianists face the disadvantage that so much of the very language of flamenco has been bound to the guitar, with its unique harmonic palette and its inimitable techniques of rasgueo, *ligado*, alzapúa, and other textural and timbral effects that simply cannot be rendered on a piano. A flamenco pianist must somehow retain the flavor of flamenco while exploiting the particular capabilities of the keyboard rather than merely trying to imitate the guitar. With the dramatic expansion of conservatory education since the 1970s, the number of skilled pianists has increased, and several of them have taken up flamenco and legitimized their instrument in different ways, in certain contexts, though it will never replace the guitar (Troncoso 2011). One approach is represented by María Toledo (b. 1986), who is perhaps primarily a singer, and a gifted one at that, but who often performs seated at the piano, which she uses primarily to enrich and complement the other instruments accompanying her.

The most prominent flamenco pianists have in fact expanded their stylistic approaches into other genres or have forayed into flamenco from them. David Peña Dorantes (b. 1969), born into a prominent flamenco dynasty of Lebrija, is best known for playing solo, or with bass and drums, in his own idiosyncratic style. Other pianists have taken up flamenco jazz, and, indeed, it is piano, rather than guitar, that is the most prominent instrument in that genre, primarily because there are relatively few flamenco guitarists familiar with jazz. A few flamenco-jazz pianists come from flamenco backgrounds, such as Diego Amador (b. 1973), who, like Dorantes, hails from a prominent Gitano flamenco family. Most, however, approached flamenco more from jazz backgrounds—perhaps especially the music of Chick Corea—while growing up well familiar with flamenco; such has been the case with Chano Domínguez (b. 1960), Alex Conde, and Pedro Ojesto. (For further discussion of flamenco jazz, see Manuel 2016.) Mention should also be made of the flute, which has been introduced into flamenco ensembles, especially in providing precomposed refrain parts or jazz-oriented solos.

It remains to be considered how dancers constitute percussive musicians in their own right. This aspect of performance is especially obvious in the escobilla sections of an item, in which the singer and guitarist drop out and the dancer performs rhythmic patterns—especially as rendered by footwork, or zapateado—rather than expressive upper-body movements. Until the mid-twentieth century, percussive zapateado was considered unladylike and was performed mostly by men; however, especially in the wake of Carmen Amaya, this bias has declined, and nowadays any well-rounded dancer, whether male or female, is expected to be able to demonstrate their fundamentally musical (rather than strictly choreographic) talent in the escobilla.

Like any percussionists, dancers have a finite set of timbral techniques at their disposal. Primary among these are the various zapateado or *taconeo* forms, the most basic of which are golpe (striking with the whole foot), *tacón* (striking with the heel), *planta* (striking with the ball or front part of the sole), and *golpe de puntera* (striking with the toe). These, of course, can be performed with varying degrees of force and volume. Dancers have standard ways of marking the compás (that is, in steady eighth-note patterns) in escobillas in the different palos (see, e.g., Pablo and Navarro 2007, 108–116). Prominent in other patterns are 3–3-2–2-2 hemiolas, with the subdivisions marked by the aforementioned different kinds of foot strokes and also repeated off-beats (as in the pattern xx–x–x–x–x . . .; see, e.g., Weich-Shahak 1992). Meanwhile, zapateado can be combined with other percussive techniques—namely, palmas, finger-snapping (*pitos*), and *palmadas*, or slapping one's chest, knee, or raised foot.

Flamenco Musicians, "Theory," and Audience Connoisseurship

In the analytical portions of this volume, the question may naturally arise as to the extent to which the terminology and concepts employed here relate to those used by flamenco performers themselves. In other words, do flamenco musicians (including dancers) "have theory," in the narrow sense of the word "theory" as implying an explicitly articulated set of terms and concepts describing abstract entities such as mode, harmony, and meter?

In general, it could be said that there has always been something of a continuum in terms of level of theoretical articulation among flamenco performers. At one end of this continuum would lie the majority of performers, who would be essentially innocent of formal theoretical knowledge, having learned their art informally, perhaps as a domestic inherited tradition. Singers are particularly likely to fall in this category, as well as almost all musicians before the twentieth century. (Until the last few generations, quite a few Gitanos avoided school and remained illiterate.) We may picture, for example, a traditional vocalist who has solid command of all the major cantes but who is unaware that siguiriyas could be counted in twelve beats.

At the other extreme, we may take an educated, middle-class amateur flamenco guitarist, who may have also studied a bit of classical music; aside from avidly copying recordings, he or she makes abundant use of pedagogical books and websites that describe and discuss cantes in abstract analytical terms and that provide transcriptions, in both tablature and staff notation, of guitar falsetas. Rafael Marín's aforementioned guitar manual of 1902 was aimed at such players.

In modern times, most flamenco musicians might fall somewhere between these extremes. On the whole, theory, in the sense defined here, is not extensively developed (or necessary) in flamenco. Singers are especially less likely to be able to verbalize theory, such as harmonic and rhythmic concepts, in comparison to guitarists; however, many singers also play guitar to some extent. In any case, there might be little need for such verbalizations, aside from being able to tell the guitarist where to place the capo.

Practically all guitarists—and teachers of dance—would be able to tell someone, such as a student, that soleares is generally counted in twelve beats. However, they might feel more comfortable using traditional idiosyncratic counts for such palos as siguiriyas, whose 2+2+3+3+2 form might be verbalized something like "one-and-two-and-three-ee-ee-four-ee-ee-five-ee." Traditional chordal vocabulary, insofar as it exists, derives mostly from guitar fingerings and basic solfège. A typical guitarist might describe a G minor chord as *sol menor*, and if trying to convey the concept, would have to demonstrate it on the instrument, and might refer to it as a *postura* (posture, fingering) rather than an *acorde* (chord). The F♯ Phrygian tonality of tarantas, with its distinctive tonic chord, would be described as *tono de tarantas* rather than, for example, "F♯7 with a flat nine and thirteen, and no third degree." B Phrygian might be referred to as *tono de granaínas* and C major as *tono de caracoles*.

Most audience members at a typical flamenco concert, as in other concert arts such as jazz or classical music, vary in terms of their formal knowledge. Probably many attendees at a concert might be able to tell the difference between a bulerías (festive, rhythmic) and a siguiriyas (slow, serious), though in general most would not know one cante from another. However, such listeners might certainly be discriminating connoisseurs in their own way, well able to distinguish good from mediocre flamenco (and also able to provide appropriate jaleos). Meanwhile, the audience may contain a small but not insignificant minority of knowledgeable musicians—such as amateur guitarists—along with present or former dance students who have their own sort of familiarity with and appreciation of the art but whose knowledge of flamenco music per se may be spotty. Then there would be a good number of serious fans who, though not knowing music theory in formal terms, would have cultivated a detailed knowledge and would recognize, and perhaps relish, for instance, when a cantaor is singing a *granaínas por bulerías*, in imitation of Arcangel, who himself was inspired by such-and-such a cantaor, who recorded such an item in such-and-such a year, and so on. From perusing internet forums one can get a sense of the intense (and sometimes competitive) connoisseurship in the flamenco world.

5

The Flamenco Repertoire: Description and Analysis

Despite the dramatic stylistic evolution of flamenco over the course of recent generations, the musical repertoire, however innovative it may be, has continued to conform, with only a handful of exceptions, to the set of cantes that was established by the early twentieth century. A few singers have attempted to expand the repertoire by inventing new palos, as Juan "El Lebrijano" did with his "*galeras*" and Camarón with "*canastera*," but these have not been taken up by many other performers. As mentioned previously, many contemporary guitar solos are so adventurous that their palo designations, as on CD labels, may be quite arbitrary, and some modern guitarists—along with singer Enrique Morente in some cases—have dispensed with such labels on their recordings; nevertheless, cante items continue to adhere, however innovatively, to the existing repertoire of forms.

Most of the performed repertoire consists of about a dozen common cantes—namely, alegrías and cantiñas, bulerías, fandangos (de Huelva and *natural* or free-metered), granaínas, malagueñas, peteneras, siguiriyas, soleares, tientos, tangos, and tarantas. However, another twenty or so cantes exist that, although "lesser" in some way, are certainly performed and should be known by any well-rounded singer (and accompanying guitarist).

Flamencologists have grouped the cantes in various ways, ideally in categories that reflect logical affinities and historical connections. Such relationships between the cantes have often been depicted in graphic form, especially as in a genealogical "tree." Another approach involves a map of boxes with connecting lines. However, such graphic illustrations have their problems and limitations, and since the relationships are often complex and intricate, the more precise such diagrams become, the less intelligible they are.[1] Ambiguities emerge as to whether they are illustrating historical or synchronic structural affinities.

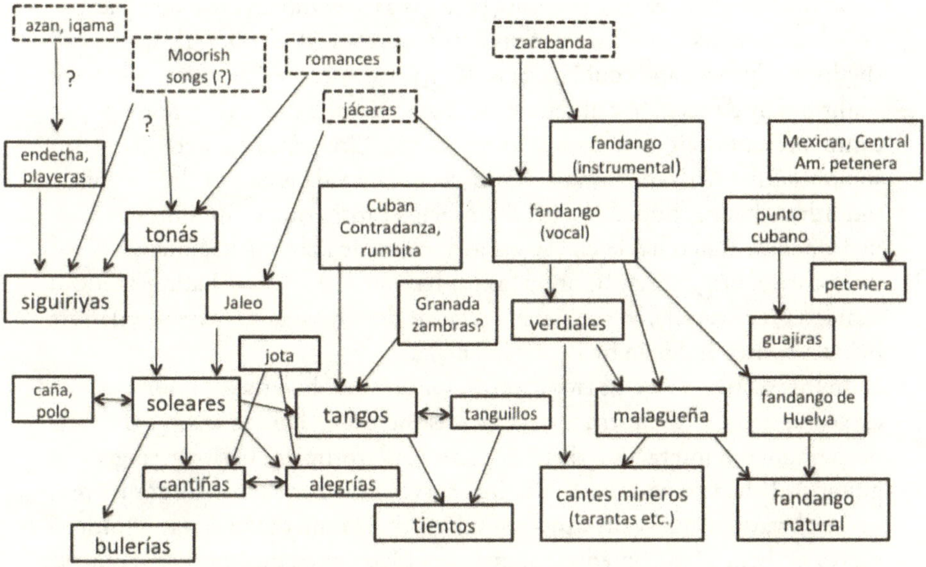

Figure 6. Historical and structural cante relationships

For example, caña and *polo* are older than soleá and share the latter's compás, such that "tree" diagrams often show soleá emerging from caña and *polo*, but that is not necessarily what transpired. Moreover, "tree" genealogies typically show all flamenco forms ramifying historically from a single trunk (perhaps "tonás"), which is quite misleading. Such considerations notwithstanding, for those who find visual representations useful, figure 6 presents one sort of simplified graphic scheme, proceeding historically from top to bottom and omitting many minor genres and cantes. Items in dotted-line boxes are effectively extinct in Spain.

Actually, there is no single ideal or obvious way to classify or organize cantes. Some schemes make a distinction between the serious "cante jondo" forms (especially soleá and siguiriyas) and the more festive palos such as bulerías and tangos. Others might lump soleá and bulerías together because of their structural affinities. An overlapping and not unproblematic grouping is that of the historically Gitano-associated palos (again, soleá, siguiriyas, and, supposedly, tangos) and other "Andalusian" forms, such as the fandango variants. One might also make distinctions between the metered and free-rhythmic cantes and between the Phrygian-mode ones and those in major tonalities (such as alegrías and guajiras). Yet another distinction could be made between cantes that are more or less "hummable," with relatively fixed and catchy tunes (such as fandangos de Huelva or many tango estilos), which could even be sung by more than one singer on occasion (perhaps as accompanying dance), as opposed to those, like soleá and siguiriyas, that are more difficult, melismatic, and rhythmically loose and could never be sung in unison. Further, many cantes are traditionally danced, but others, such as granaínas, are generally not. Various cantes present their own taxonomic problems. Granaínas has been classed in some schemes with the Levant cantes, since Granada is east of the "triangle," but others have grouped it with the Málaga cantes due to its affinities with malagueñas. Tango has been classed as a "cante de ida y vuelta," but whatever its historical origins may be, it no longer has much particular Latin American character; conversely, colombianas certainly does have such character, despite being invented in Spain by Pepe Marchena.

In this section I discuss two forms—soleares and bulerías—in some detail, exploring some of their structural nuances and using them to analyze the sorts of spontaneous interaction that can occur in performance between singer and guitarist. I then provide a less detailed survey of other cantes. Just as there is no ideal way to classify the cantes, similarly there is no obvious way to order a survey of them. I have opted to commence with soleares, the "mother of cantes," proceed to the rhythmically related bulerías and alegrías, and then go on to the remaining jondo styles—that is, siguiriyas and the unaccompanied cantes. I then discuss the tango family, the fandango family, and ida y vuelta cantes.

Soleares

Soleares (soleá) enjoys a certain preeminence among cantes. It is sometimes referred to as the "mother of cantes"; it has certainly been a primary source for the evolution of bulerías and perhaps tientos, and its compás has been adopted for palos such as caña and *polo*. However, although its origins are to some extent obscure, it is not as old as such forms as caña and *polo*, and its development has no particular relation to that of other cante categories such as the fandango. In general, its "maternal" status would appear to rest on its inclusion in almost any flamenco concert, on the way it seems to epitomize the structural features of the cante jondo category, and on its obligatory role in the repertoire of any aspiring singer, dancer, or guitarist. Most serious flamenco fans and performers would probably cite soleá as their most cherished and indispensable ("desert island") cante. As a cante, soleares is constituted by its compás (essentially shared with alegrías), its Phrygian tonicity (typically rendered "por arriba" E Phrygian by guitarists), and its repertoire of estilos, most of which conform to a shared general contour and structure.

In chapter 4 we discussed the soleares compás, which is best regarded (and typically counted, e.g., by dance teachers) as a twelve-beat cycle with accents on beats three, six (or seven), eight, and ten; thus, one two THREE four five SIX SE-VEN EIGHT nine TEN (eleven twelve). Essentially the same compás and the same moderate tempo (mm. ca. 110) are used in alegrías, which, however, is in major key rather than Phrygian tonality, and whose lyrics are correspondingly light rather than tragic in character. A more fundamental structure is the aforementioned "three-ten" axis, often marked guitaristically by a dominant II♭ (F) chord on beat three, resolving to the tonic on beat ten:

beats:	1	2	<u>3</u>	4	5	6	7	8	9	<u>10</u>	11	12
chords:	(E	E)	F	–	–	–	(F	E	F)	E	–	–

As mentioned above, flamencologists have notated this compás in various ways; in this text we have notated it as 12/4, with dotted bar line subdivisions that do not, however, correspond with structural accents of the compás.

Soleares is generally performed at a tempo of around mm. 100–120. In the first half of the twentieth century, typical tempos were considerably faster, around mm. 130, but often as brisk as mm. 170. The soleá analyzed below as example 5.1, recorded by Juan Talega (or Talegas, 1891–1971) in 1962, is at 140. From the 1960s to the 1970s, it became common to sing soleá slower, at around 90. This deceleration may have been in order to accord with dance, especially as promoted by El Güito, but was then adopted by singers for its own expressive potential. At this tempo, guitarists might play with a markedly elastic rhythm, often compressing some beats while retaining the structural accents. Regional approaches also differ: Jerez musicians tend to render the compás more freely than those in Utrera, and a metronomic pulse is naturally more appropriate if accompanying dance.

A typical formal rendering of soleares might consist of four or five coplas punctuated by guitar falsetas. The coplas are set to different estilos, generally drawn from the repertoire of forty or so forms established by the mid-twentieth century (and described in the aforementioned book by Soler Guevara and Soler Díaz and supplementary website of Kliman). Most of the estilos are similar in contour and form. They consist of three or four lines of verse that are set to two basic melody lines, which may actually themselves be quite similar, even if verse repetition patterns differ. Typically, the first line ascends from the tonic to the area around the fifth degree, during which the guitar essentially sits on the tonic E chord or oscillates with the dominant F (II♭). Alternately (but not in an opening estilo), the line semicadences on the fourth degree, and the guitar moves to that degree (Am) and then returns to the tonic. The second melodic line, sung to the last two verse lines, ascends to around the fifth and descends to the tonic, often closely resembling the first melody line; however, the penultimate verse line, though not melodically striking, constitutes a sort of dramatic climax, which the guitar marks by a dramatic III7–VI (G7–C, Sol–Do) semicadence, usually on beats seven-eight and nine-ten, and then returns to the tonic by the iv–III–II–I Andalusian cadence. As mentioned, guitarists, especially outside Spain, use the all-purpose term "cambio" (change) to describe this III7–VI move. The melody line then returns to the tonic, and the dramatic intensity tapers off and is dispelled. As noted earlier, there is nothing in the melody to suggest the particular cambio chords, nor is there any feature, such as a melodic peak or flourish, that would overtly mark that point as climactic. Nevertheless, the moment is felt as climactic, and the guitar cambio serves to reinforce a sense of intensity that trained listeners would feel even when guitar accompaniment is not present.

Example 5.1 presents the first two coplas of a soleares tanda sung by Juan Talega.[2] This well-known recording (accessible on YouTube) has been notated and analyzed by a few flamencologists, partly because it nicely illustrates not only the "classic" form and style but also a few representative departures from that form. This transcription, like others in this volume, is descriptive rather than prescriptive and is especially imprecise in its representation of free-rhythmic vocal phrases and of passages—notated as rests—where the guitar is playing softly and indistinctly. I have chosen to notate the item in E Phrygian, transposed a minor third down from the actual key (which the guitarist achieved by using a capo on the third fret).

The first copla, of four lines, is a characteristic flamenco lament, in which the singer hyperbolically relates his anguish, leaving its causes to the listener's imagination. The second and fourth lines rhyme but only approximate rather than adhere to the conventional octosyllabic length:

A quién le contaré yo,
La' fatiga' [las fatigas] que estoy pasando
Se la' voy a contar a la tierra
Cuando me estén enterrando.

To whom will I tell my sufferings?
I'll tell the earth when they are burying me.

The estilo of this verse is attributed to Talega's uncle, Joaquín el de la Paula (1875–1933), though as mentioned earlier, it was notated fairly accurately by Eduardo Ocón in 1874, and it became a standard melody for an opening copla, an *estilo de inicio*.

The first few tercios of this estilo rendering conform closely to the "textbook" (or "squared-off," "square-box") model of soleares, in which the vocal line, while not pulsed, reflects the compás by beginning on or around beat one, perhaps pausing around four or six, and either finishing around beat ten or somehow leaving a gap for the guitarist to emphasize that beat and perhaps beat three as well. (In the first lines, this occurs in c. (compás, bar) 1 on "yo," c. 2 on "-do," and c. 5 on "-do.") At the same time, the rendering of this copla also illustrates the sort of variation that can occur. The most notable departure occurs from the start of the line "Se la voy a contar . . ." in c. 6. Normally (in "square-box" format), after finishing the last rendition of the second verse line, the singer would promptly begin singing at the start of the next compás. Here, however, Talega has extended the last note of the preceding line (". . . -do") such that it overlaps the beginning of c. 6, and then, rather than have a complete empty compás, he starts the next tercio ("se la voy") halfway through the compás instead of at the beginning. This obliges guitarist Eduardo de la Malena, who adheres like a rock to the compás, to adjust some of the standard chord accents to fit Talega's melody. In particular, he essentially marks time for the rest of this compás and then performs the G7–C cambio on beats three and four of the next compás instead of the usual seven-eight and nine-ten; a strong, accented E played on beat ten then reasserts the "normal" stress pattern of the compás. Talega's displacement of the verse illustrates the sort of flexibility that is not only tolerated but also even appreciated in certain situations in flamenco. (However, this practice is less common nowadays than in Talega's time, and dancers certainly prefer vocalists to sing in "square-box" form rather than confusing them with variations.) Talega then starts the final rendition of the last text line in more standard fashion, at the beginning of the compás.

Aside from such adjustments, Malena's chordal accompaniment largely follows the patterns of the schematic model above, oscillating between I and II♭ (E and F) during the first melody lines (c. 1–6), climaxing at the cambio in the third melody line (c. 7, repeated at 9) and returning to the tonic via the Andalusian cadence of iv–III–II–I (Am–G–F–E) at the fourth melody line (c. 10). As indicated by the chord names above the staff, the guitar progressions tend to stress beats three and ten of the compás. The guitar falseta following the first copla, lasting one compás (c. 12), is highly conventional in its arpeggiated Am–G–F–E descent cadencing on beat ten of the compás.

The second copla (c. 13–15) is of three verse lines, with a rhyme between the first and third lines and a loose adherence to the standard octosyllabic length. This verse's estilo ("Joaquín el de la Paula 2") is a typical "transitional" one in its semicadence on Am (iv), then proceeding to a G7–C cambio and the tonic E. There is no repetition of text lines, such that the entire copla is rendered in only three compases. The familiarity of the copla—which appears in Francisco Rodríguez Marín's 1882–1883 anthology—allows Talega to omit what would otherwise be an essential word, "dices."

[Dices] que no me quería'
y cuando [d]elante tú me tienes
el sinti'o te [d]esvaría'

[You say] you don't love me
but when you've got me in front of you
you get all flustered.

Example 5.1. Soleá: “A quién le contaré”

Example 5.1. continued

In singing a soleá—or for that matter, almost any cante—the vocalist (unless accompanying a dancer with a fixed choreography) enjoys much liberty in choosing the sequence of estilos. The first is typically an opening estilo de inicio, with a relatively small range, and the tanda ends with a light juguetillo, but the bulk of the item consists of a series of estilos whose number, order, and form are flexible. Generally, the vocalist aims for some variety by, for example, not singing two closely similar estilos in succession. A cantaor might plan the sequence ahead of time, but competent singers have a great number of estilos and letras at their fingertips and can choose and sing them spontaneously, perhaps making that choice during the guitar falseta.

As mentioned above, a given estilo is distinguished by particular features of its melody. A singer might extend a melisma, repeat a line, play with the rhythm, and, of course, sing any letra that fits, while maintaining the defining elements of the estilo. Many soleá estilos closely resemble one another, though a few are distinctive. "Andonda 1," for instance, starts with a conspicuous G♯–B–D arpeggio before descending; a few other estilos, such as "Paquirri 2," ascend dramatically to the higher tonic or even above.

When performed as a dance item, soleá corresponds to the basic pattern outlined earlier—that is, one or two letras are sung; then the dancer is foregrounded during the "falseta" section; and then comes the footwork-dominated escobilla, which may accelerate; and then the item concludes with a brisk, major-key macho sung in bulerías de Cádiz form.

Bulerías

If soleá is the "mother" of cantes, bulerías enjoys its own preeminence, even though it can make no claim to antiquity. Bulerías is a conventional, almost obligatory finale for any concert, yet it has a richness that makes it a pièce de rèsistance rather than a light dessert. It is at once "festive" but also capable of being a vehicle for intense, passionate expressivity, whether pathetic or jocose. It is also omnivorous in accommodating all manner of innovations and non-flamenco songs.

In previous chapters we sketched the evolution of bulerías, including its presumed origins as an accelerated *remate* conclusion to soleá and, in Cádiz, to alegrías and the jota. The cante did not really take shape until the 1920s, and even then it was regarded as a light dance item until the 1960s, when it was enriched and legitimized by Manolo Caracol, Terremoto de Jerez, and Antonio Mairena. In the next two decades, Camarón further expanded and elaborated the genre. Meanwhile, bulerías had become, along with tangos, the core festive cante at Gitano reunions. Gitanos such as Pedro Peña have related that they were raised to the soundtrack of bulerías, such that its compás became an intrinsic ethnic identity marker, beating in the Gitano heart and body, a "consubstantial part of existence . . . ruling the universe" (2013, 148–49).

The bulerías compás is indeed an enigmatic and captivating entity, whose description and analysis have been subjects of endless debate by flamencologists. As discussed in chapter 4, the basic compás is best regarded as a twelve-beat pattern, akin to that of soleá and alegrías in its three-ten axis, with the guitar (if present) typically moving to the dominant ($II^{\flat}$) on beat three and resolving to the tonic on ten, as shown in example 4.1. This compás differs from that of soleá in being faster (usually around mm. 250), and usually accompanied in the A Phrygian por medio guitar position. Most importantly, the first beat, which is a clear starting point in soleá, essentially disappears in bulerías, which instead features an accent on beat twelve. The resulting stress pattern, if counted from beat twelve, affords the familiar "I like to be in America" hemiola, **12**-1-2-**3**-4-5-**6**-7-**8**-9-**10**-11. Hence, as previously noted, some flamencologists opt to notate the pattern thusly, which also accords with the prominence of beat twelve as a starting point for most guitar falsetas. Such a notation, however, can be confusing and obscures the affinity with soleares. For this reason, many performers and analysts correctly stress that the bulerías compás is a cycle with internal accents—especially the three-ten axis—and lacking clear points of beginning and ending; as such, any linear notation is potentially misleading, and several flamencologists have pointed out that a clock-like circle more accurately represents the compás. Even the affinity with the standard hemiola should not be exaggerated. Much of the flavor and structural richness of bulerías lie in the way that it accommodates subdivisions into twos and threes. A dancer may step in twos (12-2-4-6 . . .) while clapping in threes (1-2- -4-5- -7-8 . . .) and may alternate moves that are phrased in twos with others phrased in threes. Guitarists might well play patterns suggesting threes while tapping their feet in twos. These off-beat accents, often forming polyrhythms with the palmas, make bulerías much more complex and variable than, for example, a fast-tempo guajiras, which would adhere unambiguously to the "I like to be . . ." pattern.[3]

Musicians and flamencologists have notated bulerías in various ways, none of which can claim to be uniquely and obviously "correct" or superior. Even those who show the compás starting on beat one (as does this book) may notate it as 3/4, 6/8, 12/4, 12/8, or various combinations of these. In this volume I notate it as 12/4, with the proviso that the tempo is typically *prestissimo*.

This syncopated compás pattern was originally associated with Jerez but has become the pan-regional norm. It can be contrasted to some extent with the traditional bulerías of the nearby town of Lebrija, whose traditional style tends to subdivide into threes more than twos, with palmas on beats three, six, nine, and twelve, and, sometimes, "ah!" exclamations on beats twelve and six.

Bulerías, being a relatively young cante, does not host as many traditional estilos unique to it as do soleá and siguiriyas. Much of the standard repertoire consists of soleares estilos (such as Andonda, Frijones 2, and Mellizo 1 and 2), which are adapted to the faster tempo but retain the same basic melody, line repetition pattern, and chordal guitar accompaniment pattern. (Some dancers might refer to such renderings, or to old-fashioned medium-tempo soleares, as "soleá por bulerías," though this term is not common unless used interchangeably—and arguably incorrectly—with "bulerías por soleá.") Thus, these estilos are coplas of three or four lines, the first or first two of which ascend to the area of the fifth degree, while the guitar either oscillates between tonic and dominant or rises to the iv minor chord and then descends. The second half of the penultimate line is the dramatic climax, marked by the III7–VI cambio.

Bulerías also features a few estilos that, while following these basic structures, have sufficiently distinct melodies as to have acquired names. The estilo named "María la Moreno" is recognizable by its C♯–D–E–F–E (Sol–La–Ti–Do–Ti) ascent followed by an extended (and variable) melisma. "Sorda la Luz" is especially effective as a finale, with its dramatic opening on the high seventh degree, perhaps ascending further. (Examples of both, in bulería por soleá, are found on the Kliman website.)

Example 5.2 shows forms of two other common bulerías estilos, called *bulería corta* (short) and *bulería larga* (long), from a well-known recording by Manolo Caracol ("No quiero na contigo"), accessible on YouTube. The guitarist, Melchor de Marchena, accompanies with the por arriba E Phrygian position, with the capo at the third fret, such that the actual tonality is G Phrygian; in this transcription, however, I transpose the key up a whole step to A Phrygian in order to accord with the more typical por medio tonality referenced elsewhere in this section. As the vocal phrasing is free-rhythmic, its transcription here is approximate rather than precise. Further, the guitar is notated only schematically, and in snippets, and the palmas parts are omitted. Finally, I have opted to use dotted bar lines only to show the six-beat half-compases, to facilitate reading.

The transcription starts around 1:05 in the recording, with the first copla. This is a typical bulería corta, comprising a three-line stanza, in which the cantaor indicates a move to the iv (Dm) by stressing the scale degrees iv and vi (D and F). Marchena rests on that chord during Caracol's long initial melisma, which, though stylistically free-rhythmic, opens by stressing the structurally important beat three ("yo no *quie*-ro") and concludes, in typical fashion, a few beats before a subsequent beat three, such that Marchena can punctuate the passage with a sharp strum on that beat. Caracol then repeats the first line quickly and proceeds to the second and third lines, sung twice; each time, the second half of the second line is accompanied by the soleá-like III7–VI cambio.

Yo no quiero na' contigo
que a puñalaitas te maten
que eres mi mayor enemigo.

I don't want anything to do with you
You should be beaten with fists,
You're my worst enemy.

After a brief guitar falseta—a picado run ending with a strummed *remate*—Caracol commences the second copla, conforming to the standard bulería larga form. As mentioned in chapter 4, he verbalizes the familiar text imprecisely, omitting the key word "no" in the first two renderings. Here, as is typical in this estilo, there is no move to the minor iv chord. Instead, the first tercio ascends to the fifth degree and then returns back down, starting, in conventional fashion, around beat one or two and lasting about ten beats. At this point, however, anyone who is closely following the compás—which is going by very quickly—notices a departure from the twelve-beat norm: immediately after the end of the first tercio, Marchena, instead of segueing to the next compás with a customary energetic II♭ (B♭) chord on beat three, effectively drops (or adds) six beats—half a compás—by marking time for a few beats, playing a beat-ten-type *remate* (the A major chords), and only then proceeding to the next compás with its typical II♭ (B♭) chord on beat three. (This passage could be notated in different ways; here, I have rendered the first "ay que doble" bar as in six beats [6/4], which allows the subsequent bar to resemble a standard twelve-beat compás, with the guitar *remate* on beat ten. Equally satisfactory—or unsatisfactory—would be to notate the "ay que doble" bar as 12/4 and the next bar as 6/4.) Though Marchena could have easily maintained the twelve-beat compás, Caracol "goes with the flow," adapting to the new phrasing by commencing his next rendition of this verse line just after beat one of the new compás sequence.

The remaining lines are performed in the distinctive bulería larga fashion. After the second tercio, Caracol adds an extraneous half line—"reina no era"—which is not part of the traditional three-line letra. This sort of snippet (which Kliman calls a "zero verse") is essentially filler, consisting either of a semantically insignificant expression such as *compañera de mi alma* (soul mate) or a superfluous phrase such as that added here. The addition of this phrase can be seen as disturbing the twelve-beat structure, since it tends to straddle beat one rather than fitting nicely into a single compás. The guitarist has two options here: either maintain the twelve-beat compás and shift the cambio by six beats (as might be done in a soleá) or perform another half-compás, which is what Marchena does, marking time during what I have notated as the 6/4 half-compás and resuming the typical twelve-beat accentuations in the next bar.

> (A) *Ay qué doble de campanas (. . . no doble . . .)*
> (B) *creyeron que era una reina*
> (–) *reina no era*
> (C) *que era una probe [pobre] gitana*
>
> Don't ring the [church] bells
> They thought it was the queen coming
> but it wasn't the queen,
> just a poor Gitana

It should be noted that in bulerías, twelve-beat compases are the norm, but six-beat "orphan" half-compases are sufficiently common that they are not regarded as anomalies. In many passages where the cantaor is reiterating a verse line and embellishing it with melismas, the guitarist and palmeros may be essentially marking time in sixes for quite a while, until the cantaor is clearly concluding the tercio and they smoothly segue to a *remate*: seven-eight-NINE-TEN (pause—"ah!"). In this sense, bulerías differs from soleares, where, by convention, the guitarist should maintain the twelve-beat compás even if having to adjust his accompaniment to the singer's phrasing.

Insofar as bulerías can be regarded as a compás, rather than a specific repertoire of melodies, it can accommodate virtually any tune or song that can be made to fit, in a way that would not be possible with, for example, soleares or any fandango form. (Conversely, a fandango, with its letras and chord progression, could be sung *por bulerías*—that is, in bulerías compás.) As mentioned earlier,

Example 5.2. Bulerías by Manolo Caracol

in the context of a bulerías tanda, the adaptation of an existing popular song would be called a cuplé. Over the decades, various songs have been adapted as cuplés. Aside from aforementioned adaptations of the copla "María de la O," Camarón integrated various songs, such as the Mexican huapango "La cicada," and in recent years, several singers have popularized a setting of the copla "Romance de Juan Osuna." In these adaptations, the rhythm and harmonies are freely changed to suit bulerías style, while the tune, letra, and original tonality are retained; thus, "María de la O" would be sung in La minor (A minor fingering), perhaps returning to Mi Phrygian for the final cadence. (If one of these melodies were to be used with different lyrics, it could qualify as an "estilo.")

Example 5.2. continued

As mentioned earlier, the term "cuplé" can also denote a new composition set to a flamenco compás. Since the era of Camarón—who was backed by teams of composers—it has been common for a tanda of bulerías to include one or two original cuplés. Any bulerías on an album by a major singer is likely to either include such a cuplé, composed especially for that person, or consist entirely of a newly composed song rather than a mere reiteration of traditional estilos. These cuplés, which allow scope for expressive singing, need not be regarded as contaminations from pop music, although some elders disapprove of their prevalence. In general, the bulerías repertoire can thus include (1) specific bulerías estilos, such as bulerías largas and cortas; (2) accelerated soleares estilos and fandangos; and (3) precomposed "song"-like cuplé items, whether new or old.

Extremadura has its own regional cante called "jaleo," which is best regarded as a sibling or variant of bulerías (see Lozano 2006; López Godoy 2008). The *jaleo extremeño* may have derived in some fashion from the nineteenth-century jaleo, and until the mid-twentieth century it retained its distinctive rhythmic feel, in a moderate tempo with a stronger accent on the first beat. In subsequent decades, however, a Jerez-style compás became adopted, to the dismay of some Extremaduran purists, but the local jaleo retained its own distinctive set of six or seven estilos, as performed and popularized by cantaores such as Porrina de Badajoz, Juan Cantera, Ramón el Portugués, and La Marelu, to some extent associated with towns, or more properly, with Gitano neighborhoods therein (especially Plaza Alta in Badajoz) (Lozano 2006; López Godoy 2008).

Bulerías de Cádiz, in major key, is most typically used to conclude a dance set of alegrías or cantiñas or a standard *bulerías de Jerez*. A cantaor might switch, for variety, to a major-key bulerías in the middle of a tanda, typically cueing the guitarist with a vocal phrase that not only rests briefly on the major third degree (C♯ in A Phrygian) but also, more tellingly, then descends to the tonic via a B natural rather than B flat.

The distinctive rhythmic style of singing bulerías merits comment, as it is at once perhaps the single most important criterion of singing well and the most resistant to analysis. To sing bulerías well is to "have compás" (or *soniquete*), meaning to have a feel for the flow and rhythmic possibilities of the compás, to ride it like a bucking bronco, to direct it with spontaneity and expression, with an artful combination of free-rhythmic and rhythmic phrasings and off-beat passages alternating with punches on key accent points. Much of the singing—such as the melismatic passages in example 5.2—is essentially free-rhythmic, floating over the pulsating guitar and palmas and perhaps touching ground on beats three or ten. Very often, however, the phrasing is more regular but consistently off-beat.

Bulerías por Soleá

A hybrid cante of sorts is *bulerías por soleá*, implying a bulerías sung to the compás of (medium-tempo) soleá. In the past this has also been called "soleá por bulerías," or *bulerías pa' escuchar*—implying a listening- rather than dance-oriented bulerías, or *bulerías al golpe*. The latter term, however, is also—and perhaps more appropriately—used as a rough synonym for the Lebrija-style *romances por bulerías*, or bulerías romanceadas, mentioned earlier. "Bulerías al golpe" could also denote (especially in Jerez) a bulerías or bulerías por soleá sung unaccompanied, with those present rapping their knuckles on a table, or with the guitarist merely striking the face of the instrument or strumming with the strings muffled by the left hand (*a tapao*, or *apagado*). Because of these ambiguities, the cante discussed here is mostly referred to in modern times as "bulerías por soleá." It bears obvious resemblance to the old-fashioned soleás typical of the first decades of the twentieth century, rendered around mm. 150, which is considerably faster than subsequently became the norm. However, bulerías por soleá differs from these up-tempo soleás in that it is conventionally accompanied por medio, in A Phrygian fingering. The form accommodates familiar estilos of both soleá as well as bulerías, especially the bulería corta, bulería larga, the two estilos of María La Moreno, and the upper-ranged, concluding estilo of Sorda La Luz.

A dancer performing bulerías for soleá might, in the escobilla section, accelerate the rhythm and at a certain point might switch from soleá to bulerías compás by stressing beat twelve such that beat one effectively disappears; guitarist and singer may be anticipating this move and follow the dancer accordingly.

Alegrías and Cantiñas

Cantiña is a category of major-key, Cádiz-derived cantes, set to a medium-tempo twelve-beat compás like that of soleá, with coplas generally consisting of a four-line stanza followed by a three-line juguetillo. Alegrías is the most common cante in this family, which also includes *romeras*, *caracoles*, *mirabras*, and a few other miscellaneous styles. Terminology, however, is inconsistent, and the word "cantiñas"—which came into vogue relatively recently—can also be used to denote the cantes that are not alegrías, while, conversely, an item announced as "alegrías" might in fact consist of or include cantiñas. Alegrías, as its name ("joys") implies, is light in character, with jocular or even nonsensical lyrics, expressing the proverbial penchant of Cádiz residents for fun and frolic. Cantiñas melodies evolved from various sources, but as noted in chapter 2, the basic alegrías estilos derived quite clearly from jota tunes, being adapted in the café cantante period to flamenco style and a soleares-type compás. Alegría/cantiña as a dance item is especially popular and indeed indispensable in any tablao show. To some extent, alegrías per se may be more often performed without dance (*para escuchar*) than are cantiñas, with estilos such as that of El Pinini (1863–1930) being especially popular for dance.

The structure of alegrías is quite standardized, with the basic estilos being more rhythmically regular and song-like than, for example, those of siguiriyas.[4] Guitarists generally play alegrías in A major (por medio), E major (por arriba), or C major ("Do"), the latter of which is shown in example 5.3 here (and which is especially common in caracoles and is regarded as particularly sweet and *gaditano* ["Cádiz-like"] by many cantaores). In the solo guitar llamadas and entrecopla sections, the basic pattern resembles soleá in moving to the dominant (here, G7) on beat three and resolving on beat ten:

1	2	**3**	4	5	**6**	7	**8**	9	**10**	11	12
I		V7							I		
C		G7							C		

The first line of example 5.3 shows the basic guitar accompaniment (here, in C) for this pattern, with "P" and "G" indicating "palmas" and "golpe" (finger tap), respectively. Once the singing starts, the pattern changes, with the main chord change falling on beat ten and persisting for a full compás (except for the first tercio).

The cantaor commences with a salida, consisting of a standard jota ditty sung to the nonsense syllables "tiritrán tran tran." (Cantiñas estilos—aside from alegrías—have their own, distinct salidas.) This salida may begin either just after beat ten, stressing beat twelve, or (especially in Cádiz) after four, with the initial stress on six; if the latter, the guitarist might adjust by playing a six-beat half-compás. In any case, it commences either with the notes G–G–G–E–G–E, as notated in example 5.3, or from the upper tonic: c–c–c–A–B–G. The subsequent four-line cuarteta opens (like a fandango) with the second verse line (unless one interprets that as the first verse line, though the syntax often suggests the contrary); after the second tercio, that line then repeats, and the cuarteta is then completed either as five or seven tercios, depending on whether the last two lines are repeated; thus, verse lines 1-2-3-4 are sung either as 2-1-2-3-4 or 2-1-2-3-4-3-4. As in soleá, the vocal style is largely free-rhythmic but in one way or another generally accents the key beats, especially three and ten; in particular, tercios typically begin anacrusically around beat one to stress beat three and end around beat ten of the same compás. The singer often emphasizes beat three by landing a stressed syllable on it and beat ten by finishing the tercio just before it, such that the guitar stroke on that beat provides closure. A skilled singer like José Valencia may naturally play with the meter and vary phrasing considerably, especially if singing "para escuchar" rather than for dance.

The guitarist accompanies the tercios by alternating between tonic and dominant chords. The first tercio typically commences over a V7 chord and descends to rest on a tonic-chord note—typically the third degree—as the guitar resolves to the tonic chord on beat ten. The second commences over a tonic chord and descends to a dominant-chord note—such as the fourth, second, or lower seventh scalar degree—accompanied by a V7 chord on beat ten. The third tercio is sung like the first (with the same text), the fourth like the second, and the concluding tercio like the first and third except cadencing more conclusively on the lower tonic note.

The four-line copla proper usually segues to a thematically unrelated coletilla (or juguetillo, actually a cantiña), which continues the I–V7 alternations and possibly moves via a I7 chord to the subdominant. The tune often resembles that of the salida, entering just after beat ten. The coletilla's two text lines can be rendered in various forms, although a typical pattern is 1-2-2-2-1.

Subsequent coplas may employ different estilos, with the final *letra valiente* extending to the upper octave, but all with the same tonic-dominant alternation. Guitarists familiar with basic jazz chords can make the potentially tedious I–V7 seesaw—accompanying the singsongy alegrías tunes—more interesting by introducing altered chords, such as ii7–V9–I progressions (e.g., Dm7–G9–C). The salida and a common alegrías estilo (of Enrique Butrón) are schematized very roughly in example 5.3 (based on the recording "Que miraras en ello" by Aurelio Sellés).

> *Grande locurita es negarlo*
> *Es verdad que te he querido*
> *Pero tú pa mí acabaste*
> *Así viviera cien años*
>
> *Que en la mar tiré un tiro*
> *cayó en la arena*
> *y confianza en el hombre*
> *no hay quien la tenga*
>
> What madness it is to deny
> that I truly loved you
> But you for me are finished
> Even if I live a hundred years
>
> I shot a bullet into the sea
> but it fell in the sand
> No one should have faith
> in mankind/humanity.

An alegrías not sung for dance will conclude with a light juguetillo in more or less the initial tempo. As a dance item, traditional alegrías would roughly follow the standard three-part form mentioned earlier, with the "falseta" portion typically (or especially outside Spain) featuring a "silencio"—which is not silence, but a guitar-and-dance section in slow tempo, often in minor key. Alfonso Cid (p.c.) relates what a particularly voluble dancer might say to the singer and guitarist before an alegrías (although normally such instructions would be unnecessary):

> You sing the vocal intro, then I'll do a llamada, then we'll do two letras, then another llamada, then I'll do a *subida* [acceleration] and a cierre, then silencio, then I'll do a *castellana* and escobilla; the guitarist will strum a tapao [muted], then I'll do a subida, then open the guitar [*abre la guitarra*], do a cierre, then we do two letras of bulerías de Cádiz, then a *juguetilla*.

Example 5.3. Alegrías

While there are only five or six alegrías estilos, there are many forms of cantiñas, which have the character of "songs," including caracoles, romeras, mirabrás, *rosas*, las Mirris, and cantiñas de Córdoba (a few of which, however, have been called "alegrías"). Often they have seguidilla verses (with lines of five and seven syllables).

Some cantiñas forms, such as the cantiña de las Mirris, extend well into the upper octave and are relatively long-winded, such that they might be regarded by some people as less suitable for dance. Accordingly, a cantaor might opt to sing such an estilo in a lower register; Alfonso Cid, for example, likes to sing that cantiña *al cuatro por Do*—that is, with the C major fingering and the capo at the fourth fret, affording a concert pitch tonality of E major. In singing for dance, he tells the guitarist to play *al dos por arriba*—that is, in the E major fingering at the second fret, giving a concert tonality of F♯.

Caña and Polo

Caña and polo are two similar somewhat "lesser" cantes. Although melodically unrelated to soleares, they are sung to the same compás and share some of its general character. They were popular Andalusian song-types in the early and mid-nineteenth century, performed both in music theater and, in a more gitanesca style, by singers such as El Planeta before being stylized as flamenco cantes by El Fillo, Silverio, and Antonio Chacón (Castro Buendía 2014a, I:565, 678). If several estilos of caña and polo may have been sung in the early café cantante period, in the modern period they are each basically sung only to one estilo and usually with one familiar set of letras, such that they each have something of the character of a flexible "song."

Caña and polo share a fairly distinctive melodic contour, situated mostly in the upper tetrachord, unlike most soleá estilos. However, the most recognizable feature of the two cantes is their set of *lamentos*, or *ayes,* a four-note motif usually sung six times in caña and five in polo. These can be tedious and dirge-like, especially if done slowly, in free-rhythm, but the two palos can have their own appeal. The standard structure for a caña—partially shown in example 5.4—is salida, lamento, copla, lamento, copla, lamento, macho (usually three lines, the first of which reiterates the salida melody and the last of which repeats the final

Example 5.4. Caña

copla line), and then perhaps a segue to a soleá apolá of Triana, in the relative major key (C major, if rendered por arriba). Not shown in detail is the guitar accompaniment, whose conventional and structurally essential *contestaciones* and chord progressions (moving to VI, iv, and III) are quite different from those of soleá.

> *Y a mi me pueden mandar*
> *a servir a Dios y al Rey* [lamento #2]
> *pero dejar a tu persona*
> *eso no lo manda la ley* [lamento #3]
>
> They can order me to serve God and the King
> But to stop loving you—no law orders it.

Siguiriyas

Siguiriyas (*seguiriya*) is one of the most basic and important cantes. In its slow pace, tragic lyrics, and general air of pathos and solemnity, it is the quintessential form of cante jondo, occupying the other end of the flamenco's affective spectrum from the festive and rhythmically driving tangos and bulerías. Siguiriyas is also popular, at least among dedicated flamenco audiences; though less suited to the touristic, dance-oriented tablaos, at stage performances of cante it is indispensable and much appreciated.

As discussed above, its evolution is poorly documented, and as a musical form it has little connection to etymologically related forms of seguidillas or even nineteenth-century "seguidillas gitanas" (though these share the use of the seguidilla poetic form); like soleá, it has no obvious counterpart in any form of traditional Spanish folk music. In its modal (rather than harmonic) character and melismatic, dramatic rendering, it is strongly "Moorish" in a way traditionally (albeit perhaps stereotypically) associated with Gitanos and with male rather than female singers.

A distinctive feature of siguiriyas is its twelve-beat compás, which can be seen as a displaced version of the familiar 6/8–3/4 hemiola, generally counted as 2+2+3+3+2, or ONE-two-ONE-two-ONE-two-three-ONE-two-three-ONE-two. Guitarists might verbalize this as "one and two and three and a four and a five and" (perhaps written as "1& 2& 3&a 4&a 5&"), and one might even encounter the mnemonic *un y dos y tres y morcilla, morcilla* [blood sausage].) The general feel is short-short-long-long-short. The compás is clearly articulated in typical guitar patterns, as shown in example 5.5 (here, with accent marks rather than dotted bar lines indicating the subdivisions). As with soleares and bulerías, flamencologists and musicians have interpreted and notated siguiriyas in different ways, while generally agreeing that feeling the flow and accents is more important than choosing a counting or notation format. Some performers count it as 8-9-**10**-11-**12**-1-2-**3**-4-5-**6**-7.

Cante tempos may vary, from around mm. 190 to a languid 120; however, phrasing renders even the faster cante renditions solemn and serious rather than sprightly. At slow tempi, the guitar rhythm may be highly flexible. Indeed, one might speak of three approaches to rhythm in siguiriyas: a metronomic one suitable for dance; a slow but still metronomic one for *pa'alante* singing; and, lastly, a slow, rubato-laden version whose rhythm can be so flexible that it has almost the character of a cante libre. Finally, as a dance item, siguiriyas accelerates to a dizzyingly fast tempo but maintaining the 2-2-3-3-2 compás.

Another distinctive characteristic of siguiriyas is its seguidilla text form, consisting of four, or less often three, lines, in which the penultimate line is of eleven syllables and the others of six—or thereabouts, given the elisions of vowels and occasional insertion of phrases like *ma're de mi alma* (mother of my soul). The long line can be treated as two hemistiches—of five and then six syllables—the first one of which may be repeated.

The volume of the Solers (1992), following Mairena's enumeration, and the supplementary website of Kliman (http://canteytoque.es) present around sixty estilos of siguiriyas (and the related, major-scale *cabal*). It may be said that most of these are quite similar in form and contour, differing primarily in nuances—that is, they exhibit much less melodic variety than do estilos in, for example, tangos. Also in contrast to such palos as tangos, they are not catchy and "hummable," instead being free-rhythmic and melismatic in style. Their range is also quite limited, typically extending only from the tonic up to the flat sixth degree. The estilos of Juan Junquera and María Borrico are two exceptions, with the former starting prominently on the upper seventh degree, being thus suitable for a dramatic conclusion.

A tanda generally commences, after a guitar introduction, with a salida/*temple*, sung either to the vocable "ay" or the syllables *tiritirí*—originally an imitation of the cornet, calling the audience's attention, derived from music theater. The "ay" typically descends from the fourth or sixth degree to the tonic or ascends to the fifth and descends, in a manner similar to the first phrase of the common Islamic *azān and iqāma in maqām Rāst.*

The structure of the sung copla is fairly standardized, with the four lines of verse, with repetitions, rendered as eight sung lines, as shown here:

(AAAY AAAY AAY)

(1) *Qué desgracia yo tengo*
(2) *ma're en el andar*
(3) *qué desgracia yo terelo*
(2) *ma're en el andar*

(3) *como los pasos que para a(de)lante yo echo*
(4) *se me vuelven atrás*
(1) *qué desgracia yo terelo*
(2) *ma're en el andar*

What misfortune I have, O mother, in walking
Every step forward I try to take, I end up further back.

Of these eight sung lines, the first, third, and seventh lines and the second half of the long line usually feature what Kliman calls an "arc," in the form of an ascent to the fourth or sixth degree and then down. The other lines are less dramatic and serve as "reset" points for the singer. As in the other Phrygian cantes soleares and bulerías, the third degree is unstressed, often heard only in passing. Notable exceptions include a few of the old Triana estilos (such as that of Frasco el Colorado), whose prominent minor third degree clashes with the major third of the A chord, thereby perhaps suggesting that the siguiriyas cante evolved before the guitar came to be added.

A siguiriyas tanda usually starts with a *siguiriya corta* (short), which is archaic-sounding in that its range does not extend beyond the fourth degree above the tonic. After this cante de inicio and a guitar falseta would follow one or two coplas of more melismatic *siguiriya larga* (long), extending a bit further in range and eventually concluding with a macho, which often moves to iv, I7, and then VI–III–II–I. Standard machos in use are those of María Borrico, Juanichi el Manijero, and Manuel Molina, with the latter of these, commencing *No me des más pena*, often requested by dancers.

Example 5.5 represents a popular siguiriya larga estilo ("Francisco la Perla 2"), roughly as sung in a 1928–1929 recording by Manuel Torre, using the copla outlined in the preceding paragraphs. The vocal style is largely free-rhythmic; hence the notation is approximate rather than precise, though one can see how the sung lines generally begin on the first beat of the compás. The guitar accompaniment on the recording is barely audible, aside from the strums on beat four, as represented by accent marks in the score. (The guitarist plays por medio with a capo on the first fret, such that the actual tonic pitch is A♯, a half step above what is shown here.)

Siguiriyas is almost invariably played in por medio A Phrygian, with the guitar accompaniment foregrounding rasgueos on the tonic and 4–3-2–1 descents that, however, are characteristically dyads rather than full Dm–C–B♭ chords. In general, the guitar style reflects the mostly modal, and in some respects archaic, character of the cante; the patterns can be regarded basically as decorations of the tonic A oscillating with B♭ (II♭). Unlike in soleares, there is no typical movement to the iv chord nor even a passing III7–VI cambio, except for in the concluding macho. In keeping with the solemn character of

Example 5.5. Siguiriyas

the cante, the guitar style is restrained and "primitive," consisting mostly of thumb strokes and arpeggios and avoiding picado, tremolo, and any kind of technical display. In example 5.6, the initial rasgueos serve as a llamada; the 4-3-2-1 pattern (c. 4), repeated, as a sort of ostinato, could serve as accompaniment to a sung tercio or salida, whose end would be marked by a strummed *recogida* (pickup). A falseta, such as that from c. 5, would punctuate coplas.

Siguiriyas comprises not only diverse estilos but also the subcategories *liviana* and *serrana*, which are typically performed in sequence, often segueing to the siguiriya of María Borrico. These are set to the siguiriya compás but are usually accompanied by guitar in por arriba (E Phrygian) rather than por medio position. The liviana was a song of sorts, extant from the 1820s, that was incorporated into flamenco by Silverio as a prelude to the more demanding serrana (as suggested by one etymology of "liviana," meaning "lead mule"); both forms enjoyed greater popularity in that century than at present. The liviana's

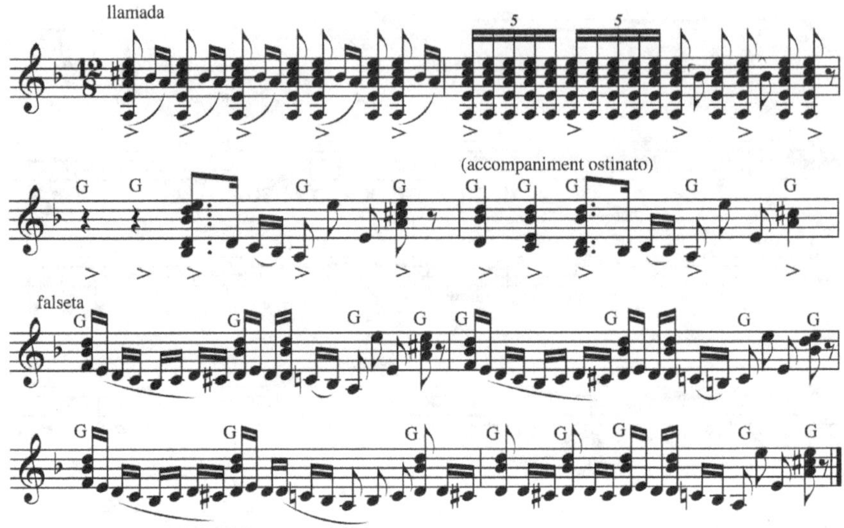

Example 5.6. Siguiriyas guitar

text, deriving from the *seguidilla castellana*, consists of four lines, of 7-5-7-5 syllables, sung in the sequence A, B, pause, B, B, B, pause, C, D. As suggested by an alternate theory of liviana's etymology (meaning "light" or "easing up"), it is light in the sense of having a relatively fixed melody, sung in a syllabic rather than melismatic manner. This melody itself could be characterized as nondescript—rising to the fifth degree and down a few times—though the repetition of the B line comes to rest prominently on the third degree (G), accompanied by a G major chord.

The subsequent serrana (lit., "highlands") is more dramatic in character and strenuous for the singer. Its lyrics are often about highland flora, fauna, and the like in accordance with its supposed origins in hilly regions such as Ronda and Huelva (though these are not close to each other). The text is a seguidilla of five alternating short and long lines of seven and eleven syllables, respectively. As in the liviana, these are rendered in a relatively fixed scheme: A, A, B, pause, B, C, pause, C, C, D, pause, D, E, pause, E, ayy, ayy, ayy, E. From the first line, the melody ascends to the upper tonic and then to the third or fourth degree above that. (Hence, to accommodate the cantaor's range, it is sung in a lower key than siguiriyas, as enabled by the por arriba, E Phrygian guitar position.) Also as in the liviana, and in contrast to siguiriyas, there are clear chordal moves, especially to the VI (C); another distinctive recognizable feature is the downward arpeggio e–C–A, suggesting an A minor chord. The concluding "ays" (or "o's") are also distinctive, the first ascending to the second degree, the next to the third, and the last rising dramatically to the third and fourth degrees of the upper octave.

The serrana often segues to a major-scale cabal, or to the siguiriya of María Borrico, of four lines. Perhaps its most recognizable feature—not found in other siguiriyas styles, with their narrow range—is the initial ascending phrase with the notes (in E Phrygian): A–B–C–D–e–D, and so on.

Unaccompanied Cantes

Comprising a distinct category of cantes are the toná, martinete, debla, carcelera, saeta, *trilla*, and *pregón*, which are sung without guitar accompaniment, a palo seco. Archaic in character, these would not have existed in such nineteenth-century theatrical or salon versions as might have been notated, and as such, their early history is undocumented. Flamencologists disagree as to whether some of their modern forms are ancient or are twentieth-century creations. Presumably their evolution was linked to other oral-tradition unaccompanied folk songs, including *romances*, work songs, wandering minstrel songs, and lullabies (nanas).[5] The cantes were little known even in the nineteenth century, though they enjoyed a modest recuperation in the twentieth, being documented, in old and modernized forms, on recordings and through the efforts of such singers as Antonio Mairena. They are occasionally heard, and appreciated, in stage performances, and the saeta has its own performance context during Holy Week processions. None of them was traditionally danced, though theatrical dance troupes have taken up the martinete.

Although flamencologists and others have enumerated several estilos of tonás and other unaccompanied cantes, singers have tended to mix elements, and terminology is inconsistent. The term toná (from *tonada*, "melody") has been sometimes used (especially by Mairena and Molina 1979, 159–65) as an umbrella term for all the unaccompanied cantes, but in modern parlance it more often designates a specific cante. All are sung in free-rhythmic style, with coplas consisting of four or five octosyllabic lines, perhaps with a three-line macho/estribillo.

The *toná chica*, as its name implies, is relatively brief and undemanding. Although its text is a cuarteta like that of the *toná grande*, it is sung syllabically, typically with two melodic phrases, each commencing around the fourth degree of the Phrygian mode and descending to the tonic. It may be sung as a prelude to the toná grande, which is more elaborate, with extended melismas, larger range, and a strenuous performance style. Melodies vary, though a particularly distinctive one is that attributed either to nineteenth-century cantaor Tío Luis el de la Juliana or to Antonio Mairena, who mixed supposed revivals of lost styles with his own inventions (see Castro Buendía 2014a, II:1614–17); this toná commences dramatically on the seventh scale degree above the Phrygian tonic, and then descends.

The martinete (cf. *martillo* [hammer]) is associated with Gitano blacksmiths, who sang it while relaxing. The standard practice of singing martinetes to the accompaniment of an anvil, nowadays hammered in siguiriyas rhythm, is a stage tradition, though dating back as far as the eighteenth century (Blas Vega 2006, 31). Most martinete styles are in major rather than Phrygian mode. In the *martinete natural* (Castro Buendía's "Type #1"), the first tercio or tercios commence on the tonic, ascend to the fourth, and after elaborate melismas but no verse repetitions, cadence on the second degree; the last tercio starts similarly but eventually concludes on the tonic. Carceleras—with lyrics about prison life—are musically identical to martinetes.

The debla is a lesser cante, about whose origin there is little consensus. Mairena and Molina (1979, 166–67) claim it has deep Gitano roots, as reflected in the occasional concluding tag phrase *deblica barea*, allegedly from "debla," Caló for "goddess" (and cf. Hindi, *bara* [big, great]). Flamencologist Romualdo Molina, by contrast, claims that this phrase originated as a catchy nonsense refrain in music theater (in Castro Buendía 2014a, II:1591–92). For his part, Faustino Núñez asserts (in http://flamencopolis.com) that it came from "de Blá," referring to Blas Barea, its supposed inventor. Meanwhile, Castro Buendía opines that the cante was created by Tomás Pavón (1893–1952). In any case, the version occasionally heard at present may be a relatively recent rather than ancient invention.

The debla exists in only one melodic form, which is quite distinct from the other unaccompanied cantes; its opening phrases, stressing Do–Ti–La (C–B–A), suggest La minor (A minor) tonality, though it ends by descending to Mi (E), as in Phrygian tonality. Often the following text is sung:

> *En el barrio de Triana*
> *ya no hay pluma ni tintero*
> *pa yo escribirle a mi mare*
> *que hace tres años que no lo veo.*
>
> In the Triana neighborhood,
> there is neither pen nor inkwell
> for me to write to my mother
> whom I have not seen in three years.

In the flamenco repertoire, the saeta is unique in its explicitly religious lyrics and performance context. The saeta is associated with Holy Week (Semana Santa) processions in Andalusian towns, when brotherhoods (cofradías) take statues of Christ or the Virgin Mary, mounted on elaborate platforms, out of churches and slowly parade them through the streets while a brass band plays a somber dirge. Some of the accompanying cofradía members may wear pointed canvas hoods (which, for Americans, bear an unfortunate resemblance to Ku Klux Klan regalia). At certain points the men bearing the figures halt, the band stops playing, and a singer, perhaps hired by the cofradía, sings a saeta, whose typically devotional or lachrymose lyrics pertain to the image—for example, the Crucifixion. (Several clips of such events can be seen on YouTube.) From the early twentieth century, if not earlier, it became popular to engage flamenco singers (whether amateur or professional) for these occasions. If possible, the vocalist sings from a balcony, addressing the throng below. Many of the listeners—who need not be flamenco enthusiasts—may be moved to tears by the singing. (Meanwhile, there are some traditionalists who disparage the showy professionalization of saeta singing.) Flamenco saetas are also occasionally performed on stage.

Although some have argued for Arab or Jewish origins of the saeta, there is little evidence for this theory. The lyric tradition, commemorations of the Passion, and some version of saeta recitation date from the 1500s, especially as promoted by Franciscan friars (Klostermann 1976). The existence of the saeta as an Andalusian musical form is further documented from the early nineteenth century. This *saeta vieja*, as surviving in certain locales today, is typically a text of four or five octosyllabic lines, which are sung syllabically, in free rhythm, in Phrygian mode, with some characteristic liturgical melodies (see Castro Buendía 2014a, II:1707–716).

The flamenco saeta, as taken up by cantaores from the decades around 1900, can be regarded as comprising two categories. One consists of "flamencoized" versions of the saeta vieja, adorning those settings with typical cante jondo melismas and a dramatic vocal style. The other category—more common in modern times—does not derive its form from the saeta vieja but instead draws primarily from other cante jondo styles, especially siguiriya and martinete. These may exhibit a degree of melodic variety, especially in their melismas, and they may be either in Phrygian or major modes, but many of them follow standard patterns (see Kramer and Plenckers 1998). Most lines commence by approaching the modal tonic from below; the first few lines center on the tonic and the minor third scalar degree, while the concluding lines may ascend to the fourth and fifth degrees, all with elaborate melismas sung to "ay."

Tangos

Tangos constitute one of the most popular and basic categories of cante. Since tangos are basically defined by their rhythm and compás, almost any kind of suitable melody and chord progression can be set to tangos, such that the cante is accordingly diverse. Tangos, in fact, have flourished in several forms since at least the mid-nineteenth century, including the zarzuela "tango americano" and a parallel Andalusian vernacular style that evolved into a flamenco cante, suitably "orientalized" with Phrygian tonality, flamenco vocal style, and a distinctive syncopated basic compás. These render the flamenco tango so unlike anything in Latin America that it can be quite misleading to regard the tango as a "cante de ida y vuelta."

Flamenco tangos are uniquely heterogeneous. Tangos, with bulerías, are the mainstays of informal Gitano fiesta song and dance sessions, often sung collectively, and in that sense they illustrate how flamenco is not merely a professional stage art but, in such contexts, a living, community-based "urban folk" genre. Tango is also the most basic palo of nuevo flamenco, and any modern album is likely to contain two or three original tangos—that is, newly composed songs, typically with a catchy refrain, set to the compelling tango rhythm; many such tangos can be regarded as commercial popular music insofar as their style has evolved in connection with commodified mass media marketing. And, finally, there is the mainstream flamenco tango.

The basic tango compás is a two-bar pattern, as shown in example 4.9 in chapter 4. In accompanying dance, the two-bar, eight-beat structure may be maintained relatively consistently, but in "cante pa'alante" contexts, singers feel free to depart from this pattern, obliging guitarists to follow their phrasing. (Tango, in this sense, is unlike clave-based Afro-Cuban Latin musics, with their consistent two-bar structure.) Rhythmic cadences—including the cierres or contestaciones punctuating sung tercios—typically land on beat three or, rather, the penultimate seventh beat of the two-bar pattern, perhaps preceded by a sixteenth-note rasgueo. Such cierres are built into the structure of several tango estilos, including as shown in example 5.7. A tango copla typically segues to a catchy coletilla, often with nonsense lyrics. Certain copla-coletilla pairs are conventional and almost obligatory, while other coletillas (such as the "yali yali" shown in example 5.7) could be appended to diverse coplas.

Aside from newly composed tangos, the corpus of traditional tangos estilos is diverse and rich and includes many contributions from Extremadura and Granada, which are outside the cante jondo "triangle." Example 5.7 schematizes some familiar tangos estilos, all in the key of A Phrygian (as would be accompanied by a guitarist playing por medio). All of these can be sung and accompanied in variant forms; the cantaor may add melismas or pauses that alter the measure counts, and the guitarist is not bound to the chord changes indicated in this notation.

The first estilo shown is a "classic" *tango de Cádiz*, associated with Pastora Pavón. A typical tanda of tangos is likely to include this estilo (or perhaps a variant in which the first tercio starts around the fifth degree and descends). In this form, the first two tercios are sung over a II♭–I (B♭–A) ostinato, while subsequent tercios typically ascend to iv (Dm) and then descend via the Andalusian cadence, perhaps with a sharp III7–VI (C7–F) cambio, and the last line resumes the II♭–I oscillation. This structure bears an obvious affinity with that of soleares and conventional bulerías. This similarity, and the popularity of tangos in informal Gitano fiestas, presumably inspired Antonio Mairena to insist on the fundamentally Gitano origin and character of tangos, though this view is not universally accepted by flamencologists. For its part, the *gurugú* vocable of the refrain is often cited as a legacy of the communities of African slaves in Andalusia.[6]

If most soleares and siguiriyas estilos tend to follow quite similar contours, many tangos estilos have distinctive melodies, as in the popular tangos of La Repompa (1937–1959), a Málaga-based Gitana singer who achieved considerable popularity in her short life. Example 5.7b shows two familiar tangos popularized by her. The *yali yali* (or *yeli yeli*) coletilla is often sung by Gitanos at weddings and can be appended to various coplas, especially of Granada and Málaga; many Spaniards might recognize it from its cameo appearance in Rosalía's 2018 hit "Di mi nombre." This tune exhibits a feature typical of many tango melodies in that the vocal tones consistently fall on off-beats (the "ands").

Some of the most familiar and catchy tango estilos, such as that shown in example 5.7c, come from Granada, where, with their simple, tuneful character, they can be sung collectively, whether at an informal reunion or a cave tablao for tourists. This tune is typically sung either with the verse shown here or that commencing *Yo quiero vivir en Granada* (I want to live in Granada).

Another crucible of tangos estilos is Extremadura, especially the Gitano barrio of Plaza Alta in Badajoz. The category of tangos extremeños includes both traditional estilos—also often sung collectively—as well as some fashioned or stylized by the region's most renowned singer, Porrina de Badajoz. Juan Pedro López Godoy (2008) categorizes around a dozen traditional estilos of Plaza Alta and another dozen or so created or refashioned by Porrina and Ramón el Portugués (Ramón Suárez Salazar, b. 1948).[7] The best known of Porrina's tangos (which López Godoy labels "Plaza Alta 1") features a distinctive sinuous melisma, the *tirabuzón* (corkscrew) *de Porrina*, which became a trademark not only of his singing but also of the tango extremeño in general. This chromatic melisma, with its prominent E♭ (mostly over an F7 chord preceding a B♭ chord) occurs on the penultimate syllable of the first tercio, as in c. 4 of example 5.7d, #1; the distinctive E♭ (which Spanish flamencologists call *medio tono*) also appears in 5.7d, #2 (labeled by López Godoy as "Plaza Alta 6").

Letras of example 5.7 are as follows:

A la Virgen del Rosario
velitas le he prometido
si hace que tu me quieras
como yo se lo he pedido.

I promised to light candles for the Virgin of the Rosary
if she makes you love me, as I asked her.

La que quiera madroños, vaya a la sierra
¡Ole morena! Vaya a la sierra
porque se está secando mis madroños
¡Ole morena! Mis madroños.

Whoever wants strawberry bushes,
Go to the hills, O sweetheart
Because my strawberry bushes are getting dry.

Ay mama, mama, no quiero eso
que yo solo quiero que venga a verme
ay, de tu propia voluntad.

O mama, I don't want that,
I only want you to come see me
if it's of your own volition.

Que no me quieres te alabas
quien no te quiere a ti soy yo
¡Ay! tronco de tan mala rama.

You brag that you don't love me
I'm the one who doesn't love you
You're just a log of rotten wood.

No te metas con la Adela
La Adela tiene un cuchillo
pa' quien se meta con ella.

Don't mess with La Adela
La Adela has a knife
for anyone who messes with her.

Pensabas, tonta, pensabas que por ti me moría
y era por entretenerte hasta que la otra venía.

You thought, silly girl, that I would die for you
but I was just amusing you until another woman came along.

Example 5.7a: Tangos de Cádiz

Example 5.7b: Tangos de la Repompa

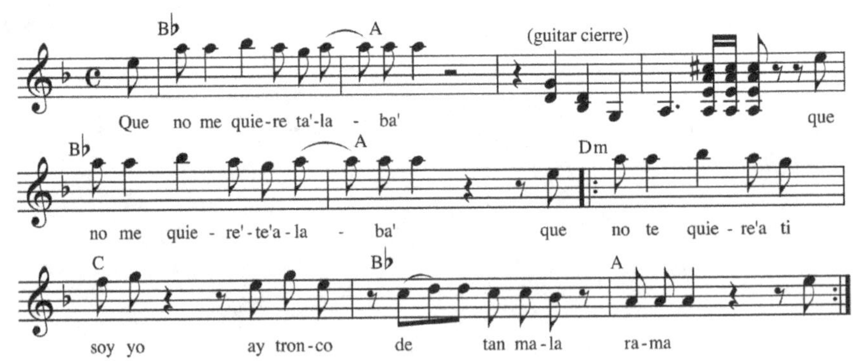

Example 5.7c. Tangos de Granada

Example 5.7d. Tangos extremeños

A few of the most popular tangos estilos are not in Phrygian tonality. The tango of El Piyayo alternates between A minor and A major, with a guajiras-tinged tune reflecting that singer's years as a soldier in Cuba. Clearly in A minor is the tangos del Titi, the best-known Triana estilo.

Tientos

Tientos is like a slow tangos, although with the guitar affording a triplet rather than strictly duple rhythmic feel, more akin to the tanguillo discussed below. At around mm. 55 instead of mm. ca. 160, it lacks the catchy, kinetic drive of tangos but has its own sort of solemn dignity, and when sung with appropriate jipio and other effects, it acquires a certain depth. Most flamencologists believe that tientos evolved as a decelerated version of tangos, as popularized by El Mellizo and subsequently Chacón, though some speculate that the reverse process occurred, with a tanguillo-informed tientos, with its 6/8 feel, being the source for the faster and festive tangos.

Tientos, unlike tangos, is purely a flamenco cante, having little presence in pop. Although several estilos have been extant, most tientos follow a single standard basic pattern, that of the tango de Cádiz, presented as example 5.7a. The first two tercios may have various melodies, sung over the II♭–I ostinato, the next tercio usually ascends to iv, and then the last tercios descend to the tonic by a circle of fourths (Dm–G7–C–C7–F–B♭–A). If the C7–F (III7–VI, Sol–Do) progression is interpreted or played as especially structural, it has something of the character of a cambio, as in soleá, with which tientos has clear affinities. As Zatania (2021) notes, until the 1960s or so, tientos had its own concluding cierres, but since then, insofar as tientos lacks estilos unique to it, one could argue that it is not a cante per se but a different way of rendering tangos de Cádiz (including use of the same letras, such as *rejas de bronce*). Tientos, however, does have its own repertoire of conventional guitar falsetas, which are suitable for its slow tempo and would not work in tangos. Meanwhile, tangos can also be performed in the slow tempo of tientos, in which case the two palos would be distinguished by the triplet feel of tientos.

Tanguillo and Other Tango Variants

Related to the tango and tientos is the tanguillo, or *tanguillo de Cádiz*, which in its traditional form has been a light song performed by Carnival groups in that festive city. The flamenco-style tanguillo is a more direct stylization of the Carnival song, retaining its simple, folksy tunes in major or minor tonalities (or both, as in the familiar song "Aquellos duros antiguos"), sung syllabically, without dramatic effects, with frivolous lyrics and a distinctively syncopated rhythm. The loose affinities of this rhythm to various hemiola-laden Latin American genres justify its customary inclusion in the ida y vuelta category.

The tanguillo rhythm, however, is not really a hemiola but rather a basic strum pattern—mostly alternating A and E7 chords—that, in accordance with its particular phrasing, can suggest syncopated forms of either 4/4 or 6/8 meter. Depending on the length of the first stroke, it could be played either in duple meter: ♩ ♪♪ ♩ ♩, or in compound form, 6/8: ♪♪♪ 2/4: ♩ ♩, in each case with a characteristic stress on the second strum, an upbeat. The guitarist may articulate the first beats as an eighth note followed by either a loose strum or two clear sixteenth notes or two eighth notes. The latter distinction may depend on the presence or absence of a micro-rhythmic pause after the first note; the presence would push the rhythm toward 3/4 or 2/4, while its absence suggests 6/8. Often the guitarist deliberately plays the rhythm (including the pause after the first beat) in an "in between" manner, achieving a distinctive *meneo gaditano* or "Cádiz swing." However, in recent decades this syncopation has become less common, giving way to a duple feel (Jiménez 2015, 164–65).

Also in the tango family is the garrotín, a playful ditty in rumba rhythm, said to be derived from a tango of Granada transplanted to the north and, more remotely, from a threshing song. Adapted to flamenco in the early 1900s, it later enjoyed some popularity as danced by Carmen Amaya. Another lesser item more known as a dance idiom than a cante is the farruca, a theater dance adapted to flamenco in the first decade of the twentieth century, somewhat like a minor-key tangos (Molina and Espín 1992, 69–75).

Fandango Forms

The fandango family of cantes includes all forms of malagueñas, granaínas, and cantes mineros as well as entities named "fandango." It constitutes the largest single category of flamenco cantes, accounting for around a fifth of the performed repertoire. On the level of traditional vernacular music as well, the fandango constitutes a uniquely popular, durable, and versatile form that became the single most prominent traditional song and dance genre throughout Andalusia and other parts of Spain as well.

As we have seen in previous chapters, some form of the fandango, evidently imported from the Americas, took root in Spain in the early eighteenth century as a popular dance with conventional music accompaniment. From as early as the 1830s, soloistic forms of malagueñas and rondeñas—conforming to a fandango musical form—were being cultivated by professional singers, including Gitanos, for audiences of connoisseurs. With further elaboration and incorporation of flamenco vocal style, these became core items in the newly standardizing idiom of flamenco.

If eighteenth-century keyboard fandangos consisted of endless Dm–A ostinatos, the structurally important part of the flamenco fandango forms is the copla, with its six tercios sung over a standardized chord progression, most typically in the relative major key: I–IV–(V7)–I–V7–I–IV, with the final chord serving as a pivot to the Phrygian tonality, of which it is the dominant II♭ chord. (In por arriba tonality, the entrecoplas would be in E Phrygian, with the reiterated Andalusian Am–G–F–E cadential ostinato, and the coplas would follow the progression C–F [G7]–C–G7–C–F–E.) The final F–E cadence (the *caida*, or fall), transitioning from major to Phrygian tonality, is the dramatic climax of the copla section, usually intensified by a melisma. The verse itself generally consists of a five-line *quintilla* of octosyllabic verse in the rhyme scheme *ababa*. The second line of verse, or a part thereof, serves as the first sung tercio; that verse line is then repeated, constituting the third tercio (usually with more or less the same melody). Thus, if the five verse lines are numbered sequentially, they would be sung as 2-1-2-3-4-5. (If the letra is a four-line cuarteta, the tercios proceed as in a quintilla, but the last tercio uses one of the preceding verse lines.) The typical scheme, with chords, is as follows:

tercio	chords
1	I
2	IV (V7)
3	I
4	V7
5	I
6	IV (= II of relative Phrygian tonic, to I and entrecopla)

The copla and entrecopla scheme could be represented as below, in the key of C major/E Phrygian:

	entrecopla						copla							entrecopla					
(chords:)	//:	Am	G	F	E	://	C	F (G7)	C	G7	C	F	E	//:	Am	G	F	E	://
E Phryg:	//:	iv	III	II	I	://						II	I	//:	iv	III	II	I	://
C major:							I	IV(V7)	I	V7	I	IV							

As mentioned earlier, the various fandango forms are generally accompanied by distinct conventional guitar positions or fingerings; thus, guitarists generally use the E Phrygian/C major position to accompany malagueñas, fandangos de Huelva, and *fandangos naturales*, the F♯ Phrygian/D major position for tarantas and other cantes mineros, and B Phrygian/G major for granaínas. These distinct guitar tonalities, with their particular chord voicings and open-string sonorities, lend the particular fandango forms much of their individual characters. They can also be seen as strategies that accommodate different melodic-chordal ranges within the same absolute pitch range (without moving the capo about). To clarify with an example: Most malagueña melodies center on the tonic note in C major, extending about a fifth below it (down to around F) and a fourth above it (up to the higher F). Granaínas melodies, by contrast, center on the fifth degree of the tonality. However, since the granaínas verse is sung in G major, that central fifth degree is D—only one note removed from C; thus, the approximate range of melodies, in absolute pitches, is roughly the same as in malagueñas. Using different guitar tonalities for these cantes allows a vocalist to sing in the same comfortable range.

Modality, Harmony, and Nomenclature

Spanish flamencologists generally describe fandangos as being in "the mode of Mi," which would be E Phrygian in por arriba guitar fingering. Accordingly, those who notate fandango forms often omit chord symbols, implying that harmonic progressions played on the accompanying guitar are not structural elements of the music. Such writers might point out that some folk fandangos are traditionally performed without guitar, as in forms of fandangos of Huelva accompanied only by flute and percussion. They also sometimes refer to notes as scale degrees counted from E; thus, the note C is degree VI, and if a B♭ occurs (as accompanied by a C7 chord resolving to an F chord), it is described as the "lowered fifth degree" ("*V> rebajado*"), or "lowered dominant scale degree," and, in solfège, as *Si bemol*, in the tonality of Mi (Phrygian). (As mentioned, another term for this note is "medio tono.") Although one cannot dispute the erudition of these scholars, this practice is arguably misleading and confusing. The copla sections are not in Phrygian tonality, nor in a Phrygian "mode of Mi" or E, but typically in common-practice major tonality, with its basic harmonic vocabulary of I–IV–V7 (tonic, subdominant, dominant) chords; in the por arriba position used in malagueñas, fandangos naturales, and most fandangos de Huelva, these chords would be C, F, and G7. The major-key tonality is explicit in many fandango melodies, such as that of the Huelva *cané* notated in example 5.8, with its clear chordal arpeggiations. Thus, for example, in that fandango, a C note sung over a C major chord is a stable and consonant pitch and does not seek "resolution" to a more stable note as it would if it were the sixth degree of an E Phrygian mode. Similarly, a B♭ functions as a lowered seventh degree in this C tonality, not as a flatted fifth degree or "lowered dominant" of E Phrygian. The fact that fandangos may be sung without chordal accompaniment need not imply that chords are not structural features, any more than such would be implied when some Gitanos sing pop songs by Conchita Piquer or Niña Pastori without guitars in their informal reunions. The structural importance of chord progressions in fandango forms such as the verdiales also limits the extent to which their origins can be traced, as some flamencologists have sought to do, to Moorish or even Tartessian roots.

In this survey we shall proceed eastward from Huelva, which is at least partially logical insofar as the malagueña/verdiales complex is in some respects ancestor to the granaínas and cantes mineras of the east. Flamencologists categorize malagueñas, granaínas, and cantes mineros as forms of fandangos because of their structural affinities. However, only certain groups of cantes are specifically and traditionally referred to as "fandangos" per se. The many dozens of estilos of these are customarily grouped into two categories, although in two distinct manners that overlap but do not precisely correspond.[8] One taxonomy divides these "fandangos" into metered cantes—especially but not only the fandangos de Huelva—and the free-metered forms, most often called "*fandango natural*" ("natural" in the Spanish sense of meaning "belonging to [somewhere or someone]"), or less often, *fandango libre*, *fandango grande*, or *fandango personal*.[9] An overlapping approach distinguishes between *fandangos locales*—traditional, folk-derived fandangos associated with specific places rather than singers—and the flamenco fandangos naturales or fandangos personales created by known singers. Almost all of the estilos in the latter category are free-rhythmic; however, the *fandango de Gloria,* notated as example 5.9, is sung in the fandango de Huelva rhythm, though it would not properly be called a "fandango de Huelva" except insofar as that term could denote a rhythm rather than a traditional repertoire. In the following discussion we will use this "local versus *natural*" approach.

Fandangos Locales

Most of the *fandangos locales* originated in the province of Huelva, which has been the crucible of a remarkable variety of fandango forms, constituting the primary genre of traditional song in that province. These presumably evolved in the eighteenth and nineteenth centuries and would have had a special dimension of meaning when they were embedded in community life in an era when there were no mass-mediated musics available. With modernity their status may have changed, but they are still performed and heard at various occasions and in various forms and contexts. (In the Franco era they were also promoted, in somewhat sterile forms, by the Sección Femenina's Coros y Danzas.) In towns such as Alosno and Almonaster la Real, certain fandangos are sung at religious festivals and pilgrimage days; there and elsewhere, other fandangos are sung and danced in peñas, by school choruses and folkloric groups, or as solo items rendered by skilled amateurs at stage concerts, and on the mass media, in most cases accompanied by guitar. Like the verdiales popular in Málaga province and the east, these have no particular associations with Gitanos. However, their urban solo forms are very close to flamenco and have come to be commonly sung in flamenco style; Paco Toronjo (Francisco

Antonio Toronjo Arreciado, 1928–1998) played an important role in popularizing and refining them as flamenco items. Cantaores from all parts of Spain sing fandangos de Huelva, but *onubenses* (people from Huelva) take pride in their local tradition and may claim that their singers are the best exponents of it. Fandangos de Huelva, being metered and catchy, are also common dance items in tablaos. Musicians obliged to repeatedly perform fandangos de Huelva in tablaos may maintain their own interest by performing different local estilos, a practice that of course felicitously perpetuates the survival of these variants. Guitarists must be sensitive to the particular syncopated melodies of fandangos of El Cerro and Cabezas Rubias, which as flamenco items call for specific accompanying patterns.

Example 5.8 presents a well-known fandango de Huelva, the aforementioned "cané," which is the single most familiar form of the town of Alosno, itself the cradle of several tuneful fandangos. The cané is ideally sung by a chorus, which might consist of the audience at a peña or whoever happens to be standing around at an outdoor religious festival. In a flamenco concert anywhere in Andalusia, if a cantaor sings it with familiar letras, the onubenses in the audience will join in, and the item takes the character of a cherished hymn celebrating their beloved home province. Note that what can be regarded as the first tercio consists only of a single word of the second text line (*sabes*). The climactic caida ending and transition to Phrygian tonality are marked here not by a melisma but by a leap to the upper tonic.

(sabes)
Cada vez que hablo contigo
tiene celos quien tu sabes
eso será mientras vivas
porque tu tienes la llave
de mi alma y de mi vida.

Every time I talk to you
you know who gets jealous.
It will be that way as long as you live
because you hold the key
to my soul and my life.

A few "deviant" fandangos de Huelva do not follow the familiar relative-major chord progression. The fandango de Cabezas Rubias (another town), if rendered por arriba, oscillates between a tonic Am and dominant E7 (La minor and Mi7, with Am–G–F–E entrecopla). The fandango of Calañas is in A (La) major, and that of Santa Eulalia and a form of Santa Barbara alternate A major and minor (see, e.g., Valenzuela Lavado 2016b, 11–13). The profes-

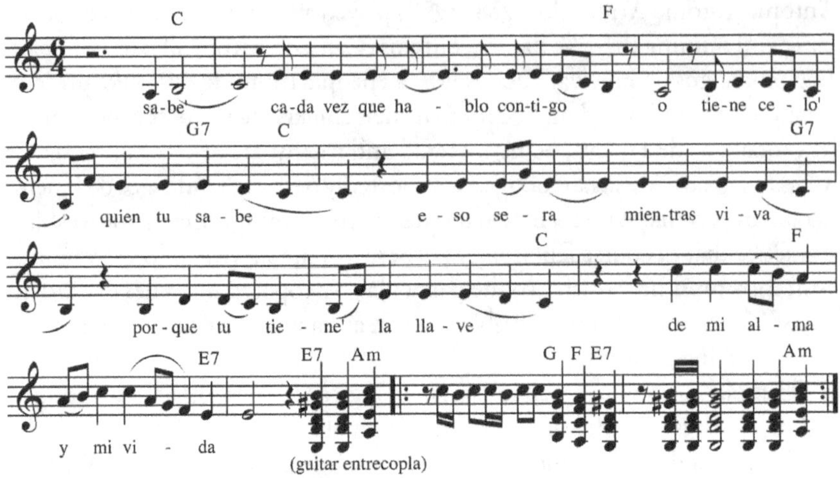

Example 5.8. Fandango de Huelva: Cané

sional guitarist should of course know these forms and, for example, would segue immediately to the Cabezas Rubias chords upon hearing the singer's opening E–G♯–B–D phrase (which, arpeggiating an E7 chord, also clearly indicates that the copla is in A minor rather than "the mode of Mi").

A distinctive *fandango local* not associated with Huelva is the fandango de Lucena, from a town midway between Córdoba and Málaga and standardized by Cayetano Muriel (1880–1948). As noted in chapter 4, the fandango de Lucena uses primarily the flatted seventh degree (B♭, or Si-flat), as if it were an archaic survival of Mixolydian mode rather than being in common-practice major key. This feature lends it certain affinities—and reflects likely historical links—with the cantes mineros that evolved in the Levant, to the east.

The fandango de Huelva is in ternary meter but is syncopated in a way that is potentially disorienting to a non-onubense, as the main chord changes, both in the entrecopla and the copla, as well as many phrase endings, tend to fall on the unstressed beats three or six, as in the entrecopla pattern discussed in chapter 4 earlier. This form of syncopated basic entrecopla rasgueo pattern (shown in the final bars of example 5.8) is standard for all renditions of fandangos de Huelva, even in traditional "folkloric" forms and contexts.

The ternary-metered fandango de Huelva is actually not the only form of metered fandango, as any fandango tune can also be sung, with the typical chord progression, in the compás of soleares—as a *fandango por soleá*—or even *por bulerías*.

The *Fandango Natural* (Fandango Libre, Fandango Grande)

Flamenco-style fandangos achieved unprecedented popularity in the 1920s when they became the mainstay of the repertoire of the *ópera flamenca* variety shows. Traditional metered fandangos comprised part of this repertoire, but more common were new fandango estilos, composed by known singers, sung in a free-rhythmic style that allowed scope for showy melismas and other effects. As sung by Manuel Vallejo, Pepe Marchena, and a host of "Niños," these fandangos became widely popular, though they were disparaged as insipid by purist lovers of cante jondo, especially in the orthodox mairenismo of the 1960s. However, some cantaores, such as Manolo Caracol, had continued to sing the *fandango natural* with great lyricism and power, and since the 1970s the genre has become accepted as a legitimate cante with its own potential for expression and depth.[10]

In terms of melody and guitar accompaniment patterns, the typical *fandango natural* bears some affinities to fandangos de Huelva, although it would be inaccurate to regard it as simply a free-rhythmic version of one of the latter. Further, while some fandangos de Huelva, as noted earlier, have distinctive chord progressions (such as that of Cabezas Rubias), the *fandango natural* always follows the "standard" chord pattern shown earlier. Some *fandangos naturales* could be set to Huelva-style accompaniment, such as that notated in example 5.9; this is the *fandango de Gloria*, a familiar and attractive estilo popularized by Niño Gloria, though perhaps composed earlier by Rafael Pareja (see, e.g., Molina 2001, 435–41). This item demonstrates the typical relation of letra lines to tercios and chord progressions, with the dramatic concluding melisma. (The concert pitch is as notated, in E Phrygian, but the guitarist sought a brighter sound by accompanying por medio with the capo at the seventh fret.)

(llores por mi querer)
Te tienes que llegar el día
que llores por mi querer
con un llanto tan profundo
que tienes tú que aborrecer
a quién más quiera' en el mundo.

The day will come
when you will weep for my love
with a cry so deep
that you'll have to hate
the person you love most in the world.

Example 5.9. Fandango de Gloria

Example 5.10 outlines a fandango copla of Manolo Caracol ("Veneno me dejaste," accessible on YouTube) that is more representative of the free-rhythmic fandango libre style. In this style, as in the other free-rhythmic fandango forms of taranta, malagueña, and granaína, the guitar typically answers the vocal tercios with conventional phrases rather than simultaneously accompanying the singing with strummed chords; hence the abbreviated form of notation employed here. Needless to say, staff notation cannot capture the expressive nuances, such as the powerful transition from full-throated "shouting" to a plaintive, sobbing-like rendering of the last line. The fandango libre, though melismatic and leisurely in its way, is generally more compact than the long-winded malagueña and tarantas; thus, Caracol's copla lasts about fifty seconds, whereas a typical malagueña or cante minero copla might easily go on for three minutes.

(¿Por qué ponías)
los labios sobre los míos?
Mujer, ¿Por qué me ponías?
que veneno me dejaste
que me tienes consumío
Mujer, ¿Por qué me besaste?

Woman, why did you put your lips on mine?
What poison have you given me
that I am so consumed?
Woman, why did you kiss me?

Example 5.10. Fandango natural (Manolo Caracol)

Although the typical guitar accompaniment to *fandango natural* resembles that of malagueña in its por arriba position (unless the singer's range forbids it) and basic structure, the standard patterns are different. A few fandango estilos of relatively recent invention have entered the general repertoire, including one by Enrique Morente recorded by Camarón as "Ni que manden a mí" and an innovative modulating estilo by José María de Lepe.

Malagueñas

Malagueñas could be said to constitute the single most historically important category of Andalusian regional fandangos, especially insofar as they formed models for the cantes mineros and granaínas that took shape in the decades around 1900. As noted in chapter 2, malagueña presumably evolved as an urban counterpart to the danceable, ternary-metered folk verdiales.[11] Estébanez Calderón's 1830s account of the Triana fiesta he attended indicates that by that time malagueñas were being performed for connoisseurs as solo showpieces by renowned professional specialists in what would soon be called "cante flamenco." From the 1870s, Juan Breva was captivating audiences with his versions of the cante, and from the next decade, new estilos were being composed and codified as fully free-rhythmic cantes, especially by Enrique el Mellizo and

Antonio Chacón (neither of whom were from Málaga). Flamboyant renderings of these became mainstays of the *ópera flamenca* period, and after being marginalized during the mairenista orthodoxy of the 1960s and 1970s, the malagueña, like the *fandango natural*, regained its status and popularity as a flamenco art song.[12]

Around eight or nine estilos of malagueña are common and popular, including five or six of Chacón, and one each of Mellizo, Canario, La Trini, and La Peñaranda. Flamencologists (especially Martín Salazar 1998; Ortega et al. 2019) have catalogued another forty-some lesser-known estilos.[13] Most of these share certain distinctive features, some of which, however, also can be found in other cante categories—especially cantes mineros—blurring taxonomies. On a general level, malagueña roughly adheres to the chordal form of the fandango, though the "structural" move to the subdominant (here, F major) at the end of the second tercio is often obscured, or skipped entirely in the case of the malagueña of Mellizo, which is best regarded as distinct from the Málaga line of malagueñas. The expansive, melisma-laden style is in its way leisurely but requires considerable exertion on the part of the cantaor. In early twentieth-century recordings, guitarists often accompanied malagueñas in the tarantas or granaínas positions (F♯ and B Phrygian, respectively), but both before and since that period it has been customary to accompany it in the por arriba tonality of E Phrygian for the entrecopla and C major for the copla.

Most malagueña melodies tend to center on the upper tonic (C) note. A particularly characteristic feature—shared with folk and flamenco-style verdiales—is the ending of tercio melodies on the dissonant fourth degree above the root of the immediately forthcoming chord, such that the guitar must effectively "resolve" the note to that harmony. Thus, the first, third, and fifth tercios lead to tonic C major chords but often conclude by descending to the note F, which the guitar must resolve (often by the V7–I figure: F–D–B–C). Similarly, in some estilos the melody of the second tercio, leading to an F chord, ends on B♭, as if it were the seventh degree in a C7 chord, which the guitarist then resolves by sounding the F chord. (Several cantes mineros forms adopted this feature, which, however, is not common in the fandango libre or fandango de Huelva estilos. Some flamencologists [such as Berlanga 1998, 188] interpret this as indication of the modal rather than chordal basis of the melodies.)

Example 5.11, schematizing a *malagueña de la Trini* (adapted, with emendations, from Valenzuela Lavado 2016a, 104), highlights the dissonances between the cadential notes of certain tercios and the guitar chords (shown in triangles) to which they resolve. The first tercio ends on F, a non-chordal tone in the tonic C chord that immediately follows; the second tercio ends on B♭ as if part of a C7 chord resolving to the subsequent F chord; the third tercio recapitulates the first, and the fifth tercio ends with the same dissonance.

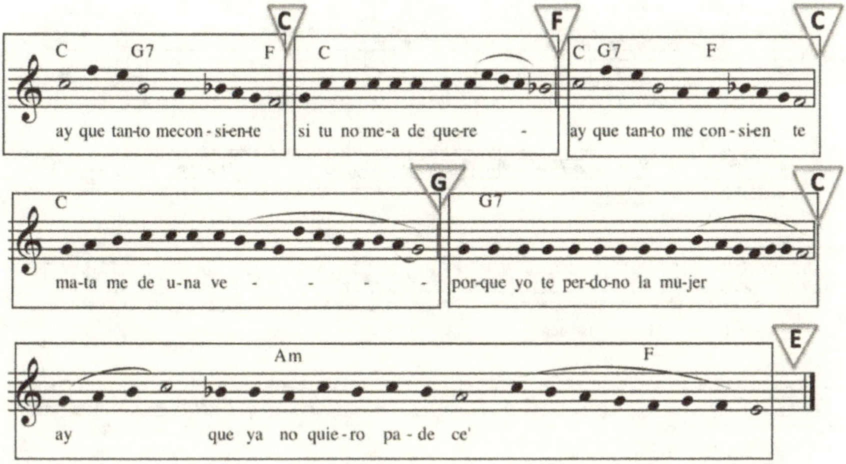

Example 5.11. Malagueña de la Trini (roughly as recorded by Enrique Morente, 1977)

A typical malagueña (like a tarantas or granaína) might be six or seven minutes long, with a guitar introduction lasting two or three minutes, then a leisurely vocal salida lasting about a minute, followed by a guitar falseta, and then, from around halfway through the item, the copla. The salida usually starts on B, descending circuitously to A, and then down to E, with the guitarist playing a corresponding Am–G–F–E descent. A malagueña de Mellizo might be preceded by a less demanding granaína; a cantaor would not sing more than two coplas of malagueña, and usually one is sufficient.

Example 5.12 schematically represents the malagueña (*doble* rather than *chica*) of Mellizo (whose composition was said to have been inspired by a Gregorian chant he heard at church, though this notion is questionable [see Moore 2012]). Though the style is melismatic and there is considerable flexibility and scope for improvisation, several features are structural, including the general melodic contour, as well as such specific features as the initial, deliberative ascent to C; the fixed position (at least in modern times) of the "ayes," which function almost like tercios in themselves; and the only partial rendering of the second text line in the first tercio. The ascent to high F in the second and fourth tercios is typical, but the singer may instead descend to rest on A, which the guitarist would accompany with an A minor chord; similar moves to A minor might occur on the fourth text line and subsequent "ay." As mentioned, the malagueña of Mellizo departs from the "standard" fandango form in that instead of moving to an F chord at the close of the second tercio, it essentially sits on a tonic C chord. In general, the guitarist must follow the singer's melismas, extensions, and suggestions of chords such that the "textbook" harmonic

Example 5.12. Malagueña de Mellizo

structure of the fandango, as described above, is often obscured. At the same time, as mentioned, the guitarist plays an important role in completing certain tercios, especially those ending *llamarme* and *nuestra madre*, both of which end hanging, as it were, on the non-chordal note F, which the guitarist resolves to the C chord. (This notation does not show the salida, which, however, is a structural component of the estilo.)

> *(a llamarme)*
> *Eran/serian las dos de la noche*
> *cuando vino mi hermano a llamarme*
> *levántate/despiértate por Dios hermanito mio*
> *que nos ha muerto nuestro padre/nuestra madre*
> *y nos quedamos solitos.*
>
> It was around 2:00 a.m.
> when my brother came to awaken me
> [saying] Get up, for God's sake
> our mother/father has died
> leaving us all alone.

Although in theory a letra can be sung to any cante that fits, certain lyrics are strongly associated with particular palos or estilos, especially in the fandango family. Thus, in malagueñas of Mellizo, aside from the letra shown here, it is

Example 5.13. Malagueña guitar

common to hear the letras that commence *Hincaito de rodillas, a mi Dios me encomendé* and *Toíta la noche yo me llevo, sentaíta en mi balcón*. Conversely, for example, it would be unusual to hear the letra *Del convento* sung to anything but the malagueña of Chacón with which it is associated.

The malagueña guitar toque, in E Phrygian "por arriba," is particularly rich in conventional patterns and falsetas (which differ, it can be noted, from those that would be played accompanying a harmonically compatible *fandango natural*). As notations of El Murciano's rondeñas/malagueñas indicate, many of these were in place by the 1840s if not earlier. As example 5.13 illustrates, some typical features are the lush arpeggiated F/Dm chord combined with legato effects, leading to the llamada cadence on E. For whatever reason, modern guitarists seldom play malagueña as a solo.

Related Forms: Verdiales and Rondeñas

Traditional verdiales, discussed above, is a folk dance and music genre with accompaniment on a *panda* ensemble of violins, guitars, tambourines, and perhaps the traditional laúd. The songs are structurally fandangos in ternary meter with guitar strumming in straight eighth notes and, usually, melodically "unresolved" tercio endings in the aforementioned manner of the malagueñas. The flamenco verdiales is a stylized version of the folkloric model, preserving its melodies, chordal structure, and certain letras. Its tempo, however, is slower, the strumming pattern is abandolao rather than eighth notes, and the entrecopla pattern features a signature progression—namely, in 6/4: E–E–E–E–E–E / F–F–F–G–F♯–F, repeated. In flamenco a malagueñas might segue to an abandolao verdiales or similar jabera, which could also be used in dance items. However, some singers insist that such a sequence is only appropriate for malagueñas of Málaga and never for the malagueña of Mellizo.[14]

In the mid-nineteenth century, rondeñas was an abandolao fandango variant similar to the contemporary malagueña, in ternary meter. Its por arriba guitar toque was the same as that of malagueña, such that the two names were sometimes used interchangeably. But while the malagueña evolved dramatically, the rondeñas remained essentially as it was, and it now has the status of a somewhat obscure ternary-metered fandango distinguished by its particular vocal estilos (the "grande" and "chica"), somewhat similar to jabera. Confusingly, "rondeña" also came to denote a guitar palo, with altered tuning, in D♭ Phrygian (possibly fashioned in some form by Miguel Borrull Sr.) and codified and popularized by Ramón Montoya, even though that creation bore no relation to the cante by that name nor to fandangos in general. Another idiosyncratic tradition is that of the *rondeña gitana* performed and recorded by Carmen Amaya and Sabicas, allegedly deriving from an estilo popularized by Miguel Borrull but roughly corresponding to what would eventually be called taranto (see, e.g., Gamboa 2016, II:315–28).

Granaínas and the "Zambra"

Granaína and its sibling, media granaína, comprise a popular and distinctive pair of fandango variants, nominally associated with Granada and presumed to be a contribution of that city to the flamenco repertoire. They do not compare in number to the several malagueña estilos or to the dozens of tarantas forms associated with Málaga province and the Levant, respectively. The city of Granada and its environs did generate a variety of abandolao folkloric fandangos, which in the nineteenth century could be referred to as "granadinas." However, for whatever reason, these were not elaborated into flamenco estilos, with the exception of two lesser forms associated with Frasquito Yerbagüena (1883–1994) and Paco el del Gas.[15]

Antonio Chacón and Ramón Montoya were the primary figures in the codification of granaína as a flamenco form. (Although they may not have recorded the cante until 1928, Rafael Marín, in his 1902 guitar manual [p. 20], cites Chacón's centrality.) The B Phrygian/E minor guitar tonality had been popular in the nineteenth century in eastern Andalusia, including Granada, and became a trademark of granaínas by 1900 (though in early recordings guitarists also used it to accompany malagueñas). Some flamencologists (such as José Blas Vega [1986]) claim that Chacón learned the granaínas cante, or an early version thereof, from Africa Vásquez, a Granadan cantaora whom he heard in Silverio's café cantante in the late 1880s. Chacón himself spent several months in Granada in 1890. Other historians, however, doubt that his creation had any particular relation to traditional music of Granada and believe that is better regarded as a variant of malagueña (see, e.g., Martín Salazar 1998,

85–91, 94, 106). By contrast, Yerbagüena's fandango (such as "Un sereno se dormía") is a flamenco-style adaptation of a traditional *fandango del Albaicín* (the old barrio of Granada, opposite the Alhambra).[16] In any case, Chacón's 1928 recording of the familiar granaína "Viva el Puente de Genil"—eulogizing, like many granaínas letras, the picturesque city of Granada—became canonic, along with other recordings of the cante that he made that year.

Chacón designated his recordings as "granadina" and *media granadina* (literally, "half granadina"), stating that the latter name was intended to indicate an estilo that resembled but was not identical to the former.[17] After Chacón's time, for various reasons the two names came to be used inconsistently, though there is presently some consensus (at least outside Granada) that they are now to be used in the opposite manner as did Chacón. Thus, "granaína"—corresponding to Chacón's "media granadina"—is a less adorned estilo that often precedes "media granaína" (Chacón's "granadina"), which extends more to the upper octave and is more melismatic and long-winded. Like malagueñas and tarantas, from the *ópera flamenca* period some singers have used it as a vehicle to display their virtuosity, especially via showy concluding melismas that some listeners find annoying and meretricious; Chacón himself made a point of eschewing such theatrical effects (Martín Ballester et al. 2016, 224).

Example 5.14 notates, in schematic form, a granaína. As can be seen, it follows the basic fandango chordal structure, with six lines, following the chordal structure (here shown in G major): G–C–(D7)–G–D7–G–C–B, leading to the entrecopla in B Phrygian. A distinctive and easily recognizable feature is the fourth line's concluding descent to the second scale degree (here, A) and the next line's commencement (*y rosa*) with a leap from that note up to the fifth, D.

(Fue porque no me dio gana)
Rosa, si yo no te cogí
fue porque no me dio gana
al pie de un rosal dormí
y rosa tuve por cama
y de cabecera un jazmin.

Rose, if I didn't pluck you
it was because I didn't feel like it.
I slept beneath a rose bower,
had a rose for a blanket
and jasmine for a pillow.

The use of the B Phrygian/G major guitar tonality in granaínas may have been codified by Ramón Montoya, who also contributed a wealth of now-canonic falsetas. Actually, the introduction and entrecopla tonality is best

Example 5.14. Granaínas

characterized as B Phrygian/E minor, since guitarists like to take advantage of the open-string sonorities of the E minor chord to emphasize that key; indeed, guitar solos in granaínas often end with that chord rather than its Phrygian relative. Granaínas is particularly popular among guitarists. Its signature features include the lushly arpeggiated Phrygian tonic B chord enriched with non-triadic tones, and a concluding glissando from F♯ up to B, serving as a llamada to the singer or, in guitar solos, a punctuating phrase. Example 5.15 shows these features, as well as a common alternate form of llamada, adorning the F♯ and B with hammered-on and pulling-off legato notes.

Cádiz singer Aurelio Sellés popularized the practice of preceding a malagueña of Mellizo with a less demanding granaína, which would of course be recognized by its melody rather than its malagueña-style toque.

While on the subject of Granada, mention should be made of the "zambra," a word that, like "jaleo," has denoted a variety of entities over the centuries. The term clearly derives from the Arabic *zamra*, which designates various song genres, or flutes, in the Arab world. By the 1800s, if not earlier, Gitanos of Sacromonte were using it as a general term for their music and dance festivities, and the word continues to be used in this loose sense, especially in reference to touristic shows. These generally include some of the tangos for which Granada is famous and some traditional folk songs and dances of the Sacromonte Gitanos, especially the *mosca*, cachucha, and alboreá. Curiously, although the "zambra" is often romanticized as being Moorish, as musical forms these have very little Arab or even distinctively Gitano flavor; instead, they are simple tunes (one might say ditties), sung syllabically in major key, accompanied by a guitar strumming tonic-dominant chords, to which women do a characteristically Gitano dance, moving in a circle with cartwheeling arms and other gestures.

Meanwhile, guitarists such as Sabicas and Niño Ricardo composed fantasia-type items that they called zambras, intended to be evocative of Moorish Spain. In a similar vein were some idiosyncratic "zambras" by classical composers such

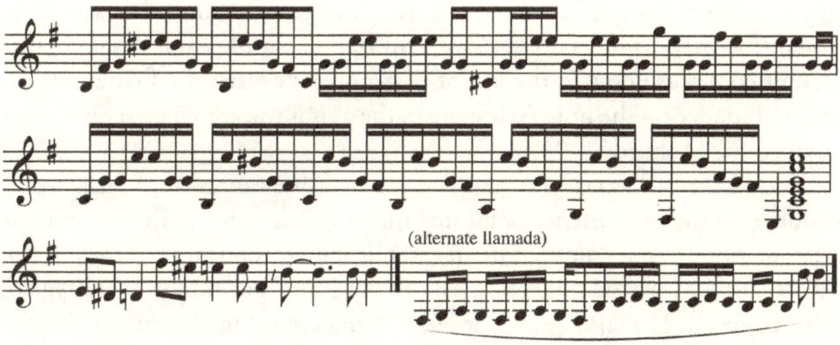

Example 5.15. Granaínas guitar

as Llobet and Isaac Albéniz. To confuse matters further, Manolo Caracol used the term to designate some popular songs of his, such as "Carcelero carcelero."

Cantes Mineros—Cantes of the Levant

The cantes mineros constitute a particularly distinctive and important part of the flamenco repertoire. The cantes are known as "mining songs" because of the substantial number of coplas dealing with the mining life and, more rigorously, because they all evolved in connection with the mining towns emerging from the mid-nineteenth century in southeastern Spain (the "Levant"). As discussed above, that arid and infertile region had been sparsely populated until the advent of lead mining in the 1840s, which attracted tens of thousands of migrant workers, especially from other parts of Andalusia. The populations of Murcia, Cartagena, La Unión, and other towns grew exponentially, and from the 1870s, dozens of cafés cantantes were established, presenting, as elsewhere, popular songs and dances, including flamenco, as performed by local artists or others visiting from the west.

The cantes mineros comprise the numerous estilos of tarantas, and the lesser cantes of cartageneras, mineras, levanticas, and murcianas—all in free rhythm. All are constituents of the fandango family, with entrecoplas in flamenco-Phrygian mode and coplas arguably in the relative major tonality (ending with a caida to Phrygian mode). Most bear structural similarities to malagueñas, from which they derived to some extent. A general similarity to malagueñas is the leisurely, melisma-laden rendering, with the cantaor not commencing the copla until around halfway through the item, after the extended guitar introduction and vocal salida. A more specific resemblance to malagueñas is the way that, in many estilos, tercio melodies cadence on the dissonant fourth degree above the root of the immediately subsequent chord, such that it is the guitar that then completes the movement to that chord. Thus, if one regards Levant coplas as being in the key of D major, very often the first and third tercios cadence on the note G, leaving to the guitar the anticipated resolution to the tonic D chord.

Two factors, however, distinguish the Levantine cantes from malagueñas (aside from the prominence of mining themes in the letras). The first is their customary guitar accompaniment, established by Ramón Montoya in the 1920s, in the "tono de taranta," meaning the guitar position of F♯ Phrygian, with coplas in D major (more or less). A trademark of this tonality is the Phrygian tonic F♯ chord, with its coloristic non-chordal tones of G, B, and E rendered on the open strings. (Malagueña, it will be recalled, is typically played in the por arriba E Phrygian/C major position.) This sonority is an essential, unique, and distinctive feature of the Levantine cantes, whose importance illustrates how they are best regarded as duets in which both voice and guitar play essential roles.

The other distinctive feature is the prominence of the C natural, affording D7 chords where the "textbook" fandango form and supposed D major tonality would call for tonic D chords. The use of this lowered scalar degree occurs in other cantes, such as the malagueña de la Trini and the fandango de Lucena, but it has a unique preeminence in Levantine cantes, where it is often highlighted as a cadential note of tercios. As mentioned earlier, flamencologists do not agree on the psycho-acoustic function of this note (see also Galán 2017). Most refer to it not as a flat seventh degree in the key of D but as a "lowered fifth degree" ("V> rebajado") in F♯ Phrygian—a designation that, as mentioned, may be misleading insofar as it implies that the copla is in the same Phrygian tonality as the entrecopla, which is especially dubious in the case of malagueña or fandangos de Huelva or Lucena. Possibly the note survives as a vestige of Mixolydian modality (Castro Buendía 2011, 124; Torres 2004, 168–69); however, the Mixolydian flavor accorded easily with the documented traditional predilection of Levantine guitarists for seventh chords. As Castro Buendía notes, the use of the lowered seventh degree is documented in malagueña notations from 1857 and later (2015, 3). Eventually, the note, and the D7 chord played by the accompanying guitarist, came to function as V7/IV—that is, a dominant seventh chord of the subdominant G chord to which it invariably resolves. What is unique about the Levantine cantes is that this C natural in the melody, with its accompanying D7 chord, is far more common than the C♯ and the unaltered tonic D chord, such that the cantes acquire a tonal ambiguity that has its own haunting flavor and depth.

In chapter 4 I discussed the question of whether chordal guitar accompaniments function in a structural or merely decorative manner in various cantes.

This issue is particularly pertinent in the Levantine cantes, with their distinctive tonal ambiguity. José Ortega's interpretation (2012, 113) may be especially astute:

> One only need listen to the earliest recordings of these cantes to note how on many occasions the guitarist doesn't really know how to accompany a tercio, such that he falls silent or just timidly strums, as if he doesn't want to interfere. These suggest that in these cantes the melody is one thing and the accompanying chords are another. But it's also true that certain chord progressions, following a logical treatment of certain melodic habits, have ended up, by force of sheer repetition, constituting harmonic patterns that have clearly come to constitute points of departure for the creation of new cantes.

Rafael Chaves and Norman Kliman (2012, 248) identify some forty-one estilos of tarantas, of which some are naturally more common than others. Example 5.16 schematizes a copla of one well-known tarantas, popularized by Camarón de la Isla and subsequently others, that illustrates the aforementioned features of the cante.[18] As can be seen, the chordal sequence bears some resemblance to the "standard" fandango form—that is, I–IV–(V7)–I–V7–I–IV–Phrygian tonic, which in the key of F♯/D major would be D–G (A7)–D–A7–D–G–F♯. However, the C♯ is heard only in passing (in lines 2 and 3), otherwise being replaced entirely by the prominent, repeatedly stressed C natural; further, while a typical tarantas would feature a brief appearance of the "tonic" D major chord at that point, in this case only D7 chords are heard, intensifying the sense of tonal ambiguity and instability. These features are further intensified by the malagueña-type ending of the first and third tercios (and lines) on the G, which is dissonant with the subsequent D chord. Indeed, some listeners—including guitarists—do not hear a D major tonality at all, instead perceiving the A7 chords less as the dominants of D major than as the third degree in F♯ Phrygian.

(En la boca de una mina)
a una mujer vi llorar
en la boca de una mina
ay con dos niños chiquititos
que solo decía papá
y había muerto el probecito [*sic*].

At the mouth of a mine I saw a woman weeping
with two infants who cried out, "Papa!"
Alas, the poor man had died.

Tarantas is popular among guitarists, especially for the rich palette of sonorities that can be obtained through the open strings. The G, B, and E can enrich

Example 5.16. Tarantas

Example 5.17. Tarantas guitar

the tonic F♯ chord and also provide the grounding for extended passages on an arpeggiated, Lydian-flavored G major chord.

Alongside the numerous tarantas estilos is a set of other Levantine cantes; any of these might be combined in a given tanda (and might be generically labeled "tarantas"). Example 5.18 outlines the basic contours of cartagenera (grande), mineras, levantica, and murcianas, showing in particular the structurally definitive cadential notes of their six tercios (separated by bar lines). These are presented as in the key of D major (concluding with a caida to F♯ Phrygian), in accordance with their guitar positions. The guitar chords shown are also conventional, though they are certainly subject to variation. Opening salidas are not shown; horizontal brackets indicate linked (ligado) tercios.

Cartagenera grande (as opposed to the less elaborate *a secas* form, and often with the letra "*los pícaros tartaneros*") somewhat resembles a malagueña, especially in the way the first tercio has a caida on the sixth degree (B), usually with an accompanying B minor chord (equivalent to A minor in malagueña); however, the prominent ascents to high E in the first two tercios are distinctive. As in the model recorded by Chacón, there is no opening salida. The most common form of murciana (often with the letra "*Échase usted al vaciaero*") features less of the Levantine C natural, and its first and third tercios cadence on the consonant F♯ (over a D chord) rather than the "unresolved" malagueña-style fourth degree of that chord. Unlike most fandangos, the fourth tercio does not cadence on the dominant (here, A7). The leaps at the beginning of the first, third, and fifth tercios, and from E to A in the fourth, are distinctive.

Levantica, in its most common version, is perhaps most easily recognized by its commencement on the upper F♯ and subsequent leap down to B, which recurs in the (basically identical) second and fourth tercios; as shown by the brackets, the second tercio proceeds ligado to the third, as does the fourth to the fifth. Finally, the most typical minera starts with a leap from A to the upper tonic D, and the fourth tercio opens with a scalar ascent up to E. Minera, as a cante, should not be confused with the somewhat obscure guitar toque of the same name, which is played in the key fingering of G♯ Phrygian (*sol sostenido*),

Example 5.18. Cantes mineros

exploiting the sonorities of the open strings. A minera cante could be accompanied in this position, though the F♯ tarantas fingering is more common.

The taranto was a free-rhythmic estilo of taranta that was then adapted to dance, in duple meter. Some tarantos were originally recorded under different names, as in a 1928 "taranta" of Manuel Torre and a "minera" of Chacón, but the designation "taranto" and its danceable metered form were standardized in the 1950s by Fosforito and other such singers as José Salazar, Chocolate, Antonio Mairena, and Camarón (Soler Díaz and Torres Cortes 2018, 328).[19] In fact, "taranto" can be used rather loosely to designate a dance form that could accommodate a variety of Levant cante types.

As mentioned earlier, lyrics of Levant cantes typically portray the hardships of the mining life, but verses on this theme should not be assumed to derive from actual miners; more typically, they are penned by a modern urban poet such as José Luis Rodríguez Ojeda, who, in his published anthology of letras, would designate such lyrics to be sung as cantes de Levant.

Peteneras

Peteneras is a popular ida y vuelta cante. In some respects, it is in a category of its own; it is neither festive, like tangos and bulerías, nor is it structurally linked to the core cante jondo forms soleá and siguiriyas, and although the *petenera grande* is free-rhythmic like the fandango libre variants, it is unrelated to them. As discussed in chapter 2, it derives from nineteenth-century namesakes in Guatemala and Mexico, where it existed in various forms. Some of these have disappeared, but "La Petenera" has remained a popular *son huasteco*—that is, a traditional song-type of Mexico's Huasteca region. It would also be categorized as a huapango for its distinctive *jarana* (or guitar) rhythm, in 6/8 with muted strokes on the first and fourth beats: x- - x- - . . . Although this *son* is justifiably referred to as a "song" or "canción," its melodies may differ, and these serve as strophic stock tunes to which various traditional verses can be sung. Versions invariably feature the 6/8–3/4 hemiola of the melody (even if the jarana plays a steady huapango strum), the Am–G–F–E (La–Sol–Fa–Mi) Andalusian cadences, and the passing move to C (Do) in the third sung line.

The flamenco peteneras comprises two estilos: corta (short) and the more common and dramatic grande. An obvious affinity both have with the Mexican namesake is the hemiola pattern played by the guitar in the opening introduction and in the final tercio (although as noted, the huapango articulates the hemiola in the vocal melody rather than the accompaniment).

Example 5.19 outlines the petenera grande, roughly as sung in a well-known recording by Pastora Pavón (though the estilo is attributed to El Niño de Medina). Like the Mexican song, its harmonies basically oscillate between Am

Example 5.19. Peteneras

and E, with a clear move to C in the third tercio; its sense of tonicity is also ambiguous, with both Am and E having their own sorts of stability (as in the pendular tonality discussed in chapter 1). The hemiola is audible, as mentioned, in the guitar pattern and also in the final tercio. At the same time, however, its melody is quite different from that of the *son huasteco*. Its copla, instead of four text lines, is of five lines (or six if one counts the "filler" or "zero line" "*mare de mi corazón*"); with repetitions and melismas, the Mexican song is of ten tercios, and the flamenco verse is of twelve. Most obviously, of course, the flamenco peteneras is languid and free-rhythmic, except for the rendering of the last line, in slow hemiola. The vocal style is accordingly dramatic, melismatic, and expressive, and the lyrics are often tragic, unlike that of the huapango (see also Hernández Jaramillo 2009, 94–108). In order to sing it with proper flair, a cantaor should have an extensive vocal range, specifically from low Mi (E) to La (A) an octave and a half higher.

> *Quisiera yo renegar*
> *d'este mundo por entero*
> *volver de nuevo a habitar*
> *mare de mi corazón, ay*
> *por vé si en un mundo nuevo*
> *encontraba más verdad.*
>
> I want to renounce this world altogether
> and return to it later [. . .]

to see if in a new world
I can find more truth.

For its part, the *petenera corta* is sometimes sung as a *cante de preparación* for the more demanding petenera grande. In its more regular rhythm and phrasing, it bears somewhat closer relation to its Mexican namesake. It does not extend to the upper range and lacks the dramatic ascending melisma in the latter's second tercio.

A curious superstition pertains to peteneras, which many Gitanos have associated with bad luck. Even today, some refuse to perform it.

Guajiras

Guajiras is, like peteneras, another cante de ida y vuelta, though derived from Cuba rather than the western Caribbean Basin and of quite a different character. If peteneras, in both lyrics and style, is plaintive and pathetic, guajiras is light and dreamy, with a drowsily lilting rhythm and lyrics romanticizing Cuban women and pastoral scenes. Sob-like jipío and anguished gestures have no place in guajiras, which was especially popular as a Marchena-style cante chico. In modern times, its popularity has declined, though it is still performed, including as a dance item.

In guajiras the 6/8–3/4 "I like to be in Ame-ri-ca" is a persistent isorhythm in the guitar accompaniment, typically as shown in example 5.20. This pattern, in its hemiola and Do–Sol (here, A and E) chordal oscillation, recalls the ritornello sections of the Cuban punto, which was the primary source of the flamenco guajiras. However, the chordal positions are reversed, as in the punto the Do chord (here, A) falls on the initial 6/8 bar and the Sol on the 3/4 bar. Moreover, the punto exhibits the aforementioned dual tonicity in which the two chords have relatively equal weight; in fact, all cadences, both internal and final, are on the Sol chord, which thus should not be called "the dominant" (see Manuel 2002); the flamenco guajira, by contrast, is in straightforward major tonality (here, A major). Meanwhile, in Cuban punto the aesthetic emphasis is on the décima text (ten octosyllabic lines in the scheme *abbaaccddc*), quintessentially as improvised by the vocalist (accordingly called *poeta*, or *repentista* ["improviser"]), while in the flamenco guajira the focus is on the melodious singing. Hence, in the Cuban punto the melodic form closely coincides with the décima verse structure, which the flamenco guajira does not. Accordingly, flamenco singers sometimes omit verses or render them incorrectly (Manuel 2004; Cid Lucas 2019), disrupting the rhyme scheme, and the same, somewhat hackneyed two or three décima texts are reiterated endlessly in performance af-

Example 5.20. Guajiras guitar

ter performance.[20] One of these, shown below, only approximates décima form, and singers often skip one or two of the middle lines, as in example 5.21, which schematizes the most common guajiras tune. The vocal style is free-rhythmic, as notated. The guitar, not shown, reiterates the ostinato shown in example 5.20.

A mi me gusta por la mañana
después del café bebido
pasear por La Habana
con mi tabaco encendido.
Luego me siento en mi silla
en mi silla o silletón
y saco un papelón
de esos que llaman diario
y parezco un millonario
de esos que son la población.

In the mornings, I like,
after drinking my coffee,
to stroll about Havana
with my cigar lit,
then I sit in my chair
in my big chair
with one of those big things of paper
that they call a newspaper
and I look like one of those millionaires
that they have around here.

In dance contexts, the guajira typically accelerates to the tempo of a bulerías. In its alternating major-key tonic-dominant chords in hemiola rhythm, it sounds somewhat like a bulería de Cádiz (especially if one hears the bulería beat twelve as corresponding to beat one of guajiras). However, this similarity itself also reveals the distinctive features of the bulería compás; the fast guajiras compás, though syncopated in its way, is very straightforward and has none of the cross-rhythms and varied emphases on twos or threes that make the bulerías compás so rich and endlessly productive.

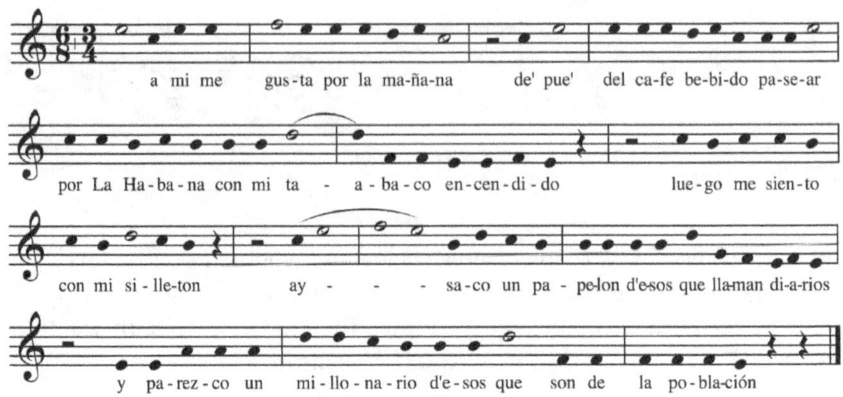

Example 5.21. Guajiras

Rumba

Rumba is another ida y vuelta cante of flamenco, especially pop flamenco, deriving from Cuban popular music. In Cuba, traditional rumba is an Afro-Cuban music and dance form in which an ensemble of voices and percussion (usually three congas, clave, and *palitos* sticks), with no other instruments, accompanies dancers (two in *guaguancó* and *yambú* and one in *columbia*). Flamenco historians typically assert that this folkloric form of rumba is the source for the flamenco namesake, but in fact the latter comes from a quite distinct genre. In the decades around 1900, Cuban popular music theater (*teatro vernáculo*) and cabaret shows often featured items in which white performers, typically in blackface and wearing frilled shirts, would dance to up-tempo songs featuring syncopated 3-3-2 rhythms based on those of the *son* and *guaracha*, with varied instrumentation such as piano, guitar, horns, timpani, and the like. In subsequent decades these items, called "rumba," went on to become standard tourist fare in cabarets. From around 1915 these were adopted as light flamenco items by Manuel Escacena and Pepe el de la Matrona, both of whom traveled in Cuba (see, e.g., Molina and Espín 1992, 88–94). The flamenco rumba, or *rumbita*, went on to enjoy considerable popularity, often closely resembling and even borrowing directly from contemporary Cuban songs. In the 1960s it flourished as a pop genre in the hands of the Madrid-based Bambino (Miguel Vargas Jiménez, 1943–1999) and Peret (Pedro Pubill Calaf, 1935–2009), a Gitano of Barcelona who led the *rumba catalana* vogue. These were light songs with the characteristic Cuban 3-3-2 syncopation, with conventional guitar rasgueo patterns combining strums with golpes evoking the sound of the bongo. With the addition of drums, bass, and perhaps electric guitar, they became essentially light pop-rock songs with little flavor of either flamenco or Cuban music. Since the advent of nuevo flamenco in the 1970s, "rumba" has become a generic term for the catchy pop songs in duple meter that are included on many flamenco albums. More flamencoized rumbas were popular tablao items until displaced by bulerías in the 1970s. Since then, rumba in Spain has been exclusively a pop-fusion entity and would seldom be heard at flamenco peñas, festivals, or competitions.

Vidalita, Milonga, and Colombianas

A somewhat infrequently heard cante attributed to Argentine origins is the vidalita, believed to derive from a song adapted to flamenco by Manuel Escacena and elaborated by Antonio Chacón (Molina and Espín 1992, 140–45). Vidalita is sung in free rhythm, with plaintive lyrics, and chords alternating between the minor tonic and dominant seventh (Am and E7 fingerings, usually). Internal phrases in some versions might cadence briefly on A major. A few melodic variants exist, though these tend to share general contour as well as mood. Opening phrases, though differing in initial ranges, usually pause on E, descend to B, and then to the tonic A after a quick return to E. Although vidalita is not common, in recent decades it has gained some fresh currency due to a powerful recording (on *Querencia*, 2000) by Mayte Martín (1965–). The third copla of her version well captures the melancholy character of this minor but potentially moving cante.

> *Anoche mientras dormía, del cansancio fatiga'o*
> *no sé qué sueño dora'o cruzó por la mente mía*
> *soñaba que te veía, y que me estabas mirando*
> *y yo te estaba contando, mi vida triste, muy triste*
> *y te desapareciste, al despertarme llorando.*
>
> Last night as I slept, exhausted
> I don't know what golden dream came to me
> I dreamt that I saw you, and you were looking at me
> And I was telling you of my sad, sad life
> And then you disappeared, as I woke up weeping.

Another ida y vuelta cante derived, in some fashion, from Argentina is the milonga. The original milonga was an Argentine song form, itself derived from the *yaraví*-influenced *triste*, which became stylized in Buenos Aires in the late nineteenth century. In the early 1900s it was adapted to flamenco by Pepa de Oro (Josefa Díaz), who in her youth had toured parts of South America with her father, a bullfighter. It was then popularized by Chacón, Escacena, and Pastora Pavón and subsequently became a staple of the *ópera flamenca* repertoire as sung by Manuel Vallejo, Pepe Marchena, and other agile-voiced "Niños." It subsequently fell out of vogue. The languid flamenco milonga came to bear little relationship to its twentieth-century urban Argentine namesake, which is an up-tempo dance song (in 2/4, mm. ca. 100), like a fast tango.

The milonga, even more so than the similar vidalita, does not have a particularly distinctive melodic contour, which may partially explain its lack of popularity in the modern period. While the guitar softly reiterates minor tonic-dominant chords (Am–E7) in a medium-tempo habanera beat, the melody, in free-rhythmic style, mostly sits on the upper fifth degree (E), perhaps ornamenting it with Marchena-style melismas, or leaping briefly to the upper A or even C, and then descending to the lower tonic A. Lyrics (such as the aforementioned "Juan Simón") are lachrymose and sometimes maudlin in a manner uncharacteristic of terse, epigrammatic cante jondo letras.

Also out of vogue in recent decades is another ida y vuelta cante called colombianas. Though its name suggests an origin in Colombia, it was created by Pepe Marchena around 1931, inspired by a few Mexican songs that cantaor had encountered (Molina and Espín 1992, 153–56). In the colombianas, Marchena gave free rein to his penchant for decorative melisma, such that specific resemblances to these original songs are not clearly audible. Nevertheless, the cante, set to a major key in moderate duple meter, has a certain Latin American flavor qualifying it as an ida y vuelta entity.

A survey of ida y vuelta forms must briefly mention the tango del Piyayo, mentioned along with the other tangos above. Its creator spent several years in Cuba and popularized a tango estilo with texts often in décima form and a melody somewhat redolent of Cuban guajira music.

Finally, passing mention must be made of sevillanas, which is not a flamenco cante per se, especially as its vocal style is primarily syllabic, with little scope for melisma or personal expression, and guitar accompaniment mostly consists of vigorous rasgueado in conventional patterns. Often it is sung in unison by two or three vocalists. Its choreography is also relatively fixed, consisting of four sections in which a couple executes a standardized sequence, each of which ends with the statuesque, raised-arms, *bien parao* (nicely stopped) pose. Many Andalusian families either teach their children sevillanas informally or, especially with girls, have them take lessons to learn the basic sequence. Sevillanas can be performed on any festive occasion; it is especially popular during annual pilgrimages to El Rocío (in Huelva), and during Seville's Feria, when enthusiasts set up tents (*casetas*), whether for the public or for family and friends, and dance sevillanas through the evening and night. Virtually all flamenco dance students learn sevillanas in their classes, and tablao shows often commence with a sevillanas.

6

Flamenco Lyrics

Flamenco is typically spoken of as comprising cante, toque, and baile—singing, guitar playing, and dancing—yet the cante itself embodies a fourth art, namely, poetry. The lyric dimension of flamenco may not have the overt prominence of the other three components but certainly has its importance, and given the relative ease of writing about verse—as opposed to music and dance—flamenco poetry has long been a topic of study and documentation. Indeed, the first scholarly writings about flamenco—the aforementioned works of Demófilo and Schuchardt—were primarily compilations of verses with commentary.

Like several other aspects of flamenco, thought about letras (lyrics) has been marked by controversy. A primary argument has concerned whether flamenco lyrics are mostly products of the unlettered masses or fragments that trickled down from the educated upper classes. Advocates of the latter notion would argue that the bohemians among whom flamenco emerged—especially Gitanos—would have been mostly illiterate and hence incapable of composing poetry and instead made do with bits of verse acquired, in one way or another, from literary tradition. Others would counter that this argument is an elitist conceit that ignores the oral and popular, rather than academic, nature of flamenco verse and the overt distinctions between such schools of poetry. Another dimension of the controversy involves the extent to which Gitanos in particular have authored letras, expressing their own sensibilities and experiences, and, accordingly, whether a distinctive category of Gitano verse has existed. The controversy and the relation between lettered and unlettered social milieus are made all the more complex by the hoary Spanish tradition of elites composing verse in imitation of vernacular—including Gitano—styles.

Many flamenco letras were derived from song lyrics that circulated well before the advent of flamenco per se, as well as from other diverse contemporary genres. As Soler Díaz (2020) and others have shown, flamenco singers, in oral tradition fashion, freely adapted verses from folkloric fandangos, *romances*, villancicos, seguidillas, lullabies, zarzuela songs, and Cuban décimas, as well as the oeuvre of lettered poets. Most such adaptations and borrowings were in the form of fragments, as flamenco verses are short and concise—generally of three to six lines—rather than constituting extended narratives. Nevertheless, quite a few letras can be seen to derive from long-winded *romances* predating flamenco by several centuries. Gitanos had long been known for their expressive renderings of these *romances*, many of which were transmitted among the galley workers enslaved in the port of Santa María in the sixteenth through mid-eighteenth centuries. Many Gitano families in Cádiz, Lebrija, and elsewhere were known for singing fragments of *romances* as lullabies, wedding songs, or even the single line often used as a warm-up *temple* in tonás: *Trin, trin, que a la puerta llaman* (Suárez Ávila 1989; 2010, 291, 303–304). Pastora Pavón was known for her rendering, as a bulerías, a cuarteta—relatively meaningless in itself—adapted from the medieval *romance* of *Bernardo el Carpio*:

Entré yo en este castillito
Que joven y sin pelo de barba
Y ahora que salgo de él
No hay quien me mire a mí a la cara.

I entered the castle, young and beardless,
And now that I leave it, no one looks me in the face.

An early document relevant to debates about authorship is Cervantes's aforementioned novella *La Gitanilla*, which portrays the amorous relationship between a charming Gitana professional singer, Preciosa, and an aristocratic suitor. The writings of Cervantes, in general, provide a gold mine of material for the historian, although they are of course fiction and must be interpreted with caution. For the flamencologist, the passage of interest occurs early in the story, when a nobleman's lackey gives Preciosa some pages of his poetry (a *romance*) for her to sing with her troupe, for which she pays him. This passage provides an early indication of something verifiably documented in later centuries—namely, that although Gitanos and aristocrats may have been at opposite ends of the socioeconomic spectrum, living in quite different worlds, they may nevertheless have had certain sorts of occasional links, especially insofar as members of the elite patronized Gitanos or took some interest in their art and services. The story further implies that since Gitano performers would be interested in having fresh material to sing, it would not be uncommon for them to acquire lyrics from some educated patron. The related argument would be that much flamenco poetry originally trickled down in this fashion, over the centuries, from upper-class or at least written sources. Opponents of this notion assert that Preciosa (who turns out to be of noble parentage) is an unrealistic character, that precious few (as it were) Gitanos would have been literate in 1600, and that Cervantes may not have had much familiarity with Gitanos and their performance culture.[1]

The next informative—or misinformative—document comes some two and a half centuries later, in the form of George Borrow's 1841 book, *The Zincali: An Account of the Gypsies of Spain*. In his illuminating text, Borrow, an English Bible salesman, combined astute firsthand ethnographic observations, typical disparagements of Gitanos (as a vile and indolent race of thieves), and various dubious assertions gleaned from hearsay—all of which must be regarded with interest, but circumspection, by the historian. Borrow described the genre of spurious "Gypsyesque" poetry written by elite poetasters, which had no presence among Gitanos themselves, and, more relevantly, he culled from Gitano informants hundreds of short stanzas (mostly of two to four lines) that circulated via oral transmission. He regarded many of these as constituting a distinct Gitano corpus of verse, with Caló words and depictions of typical Gitano events and concerns (2015, 80–81, 84–85).

Also dating from the 1830s were Estébanez Calderón's essays describing the pre-flamenco presentations he witnessed in Triana, whose musical aspects have been discussed earlier here. Of interest at this point is his reproduction of the *romances* he heard recited at these events and his situating this lyric content in the tradition of the ballads, sermons, and other miscellany marketed in chapbooks traditionally hawked by blind buskers who sang excerpts from their merchandise, displayed hanging from a string (hence the term *pliegos de cordel* [sheets from a cord]). Other literary precedents for flamenco coplas would be jácaras and assorted songs associated with tonadillas and other forms of light theater. Several flamenco lyrics derive from early nineteenth-century polos, malagueñas, rondeñas, and cañas, and many closely resemble vernacular song verses dating back to the fifteenth and sixteenth centuries, at once orally transmitted and documented in *cancioneros* (songbooks) from that period (see, e.g., Carrillo Alonso 1988).

Meanwhile, over the course of the nineteenth century, Spanish folklorists and poets collected miscellaneous vernacular short verses that were currently sung as seguidillas, *boleras*, tiranas, and polos, and published them in songbooks.[2] These compilers were inspired by a costumbrista interest in local vernacular culture and a Romantic idealization of such popular poetry as a simple, direct expression of common folk, in contrast to the belabored rhetoric of neoclassical Spanish poetry such as that of Gongora. (In a more general sense, they shared a traditional Spanish elite interest in lower-class culture that was manifest in the tradition of picaresque novels.) Paralleling these anthologies were the works by known poets who imitated the unadorned style of orally transmitted verse and, in some cases, hoped that their lyrics would enter that tradition. Exemplary in this sense was Augusto Ferrán (1835–1880), whose anthologies (especially *La soledad*, 1861) combined oral-tradition poetry with his own compositions. Ferrán wrote:

> As for my poor verses, if someday I hear just one of them sung by a bunch of festive girls, accompanied by the sad tones of a guitar, all my ambition for glory will be realized, and I will have received the most critical evaluation of my humble compositions.

In the next generation, poet Manuel Machado would express the same sentiment about his verses. Another known *cantares* poet of the era was Manuel Balmaseda (1857–1881), whose short life was spent in poverty and toil, in contrast to genteel literati such as Ferrán and the Machados, for whom suffering was a literary theme rather than a lived reality. A handful of coplas by Balmaseda, Machado, and other known poets have been sung by cantaores such as Antonio Mairena, but, as Mairena himself noted, these verses have remained a tiny minority within the repertoire. Further, while singers in Lebrija maintain a tradition of singing *romance* fragments, it should be remembered that *romances* such as that of Gerineldo, Bernardo el Carpio, and the Conde Sol have always circulated in both written and oral forms, and the sung versions do not necessarily trace to written ones.

A landmark publication was folklorist Antonio ("Demófilo") Machado's 1881 anthology, discussed earlier in reference to music. Although of much interest for its prefatory remarks on song, the book is primarily a collection of letras that Machado culled from singers in Seville. The authenticity of these verses is unquestioned, and many of them are sung today, as transmitted orally by generations of flamenco families. However, in his introductory essay Machado exaggerated the extent to which flamenco lyrics constituted a distinctive and older genre of "Gitano poetry," which, like "pure Gitano music," allegedly underwent a process of "Andalusianization" in the cafés cantantes. Machado's contemporary Hugo Schuchardt, free from Krausist obscurantism about racial essences, more astutely recognized that flamenco lyrics represented the opposite process—that is, they were essentially a category of Andalusian vernacular song texts, some of which were "Gypsified," whether by Gitanos for their own reasons or in response to an exoticizing Romantic demand on the part of non-Gitano audiences. Gerhard Steingress (1991, 123–54) explores how the latter form of "gitanesca" verse constituted a modern development cultivated by the urban "avant-garde" flamenco subculture. However, most flamenco lyrics, whether of the present or Demófilo's era, are not distinctively gitanesca, though they may contain sprinklings of familiar Caló words and references to Gitano themes. In general, it is likely that most flamenco lyrics were created and transmitted by members of the flamenco community rather than educated dilettantes.

This point merits further commentary. It is clear that in the nineteenth and early twentieth centuries, throughout Andalusia and elsewhere in Spain, there existed a prodigious fondness for short verse forms, generically called copla, canto, or cantares. These were intended to be sung, whether as work songs, amorous odes intoned by a suitor at the window of his paramour, or—perhaps toward the end of a fiesta—in a more serious flamenco manner, ideally accompanied by guitar if one were present. Gerald Brenan described the popularity of this copla tradition in the town in the Alpujarras Mountains, south of Granada, where he resided in the 1920s:

> I speak of [these coplas] as being alive because not only are they continually sung in the house, in the fields and on journeys, but because new ones are still being invented and made. Anyone who is sufficiently steeped in the medium can improvise one. Perhaps, however, it is misleading to speak of them as poems. Until folklorists began to collect them they were scarcely ever written down. They were intended for singing, and just as Sancho Panza had an unlimited supply of proverbs at his beck and call, so there are many people today who have an unlimited stock of coplas and can go on singing them without repeating themselves for days on end. In Andalusia they are sung in the Oriental-sounding style known as cante jondo, or, more vulgarly, flamenco. . . . They provided a constant background to everyday life. There was scarcely a moment of the day when one could not, sitting on a rooftop, hear someone singing one. (Brenan 1957, 108; see also Brenan 1953, 365–76)

Similarly, José Mercado, in his study of flamenco and pre-flamenco coplas, wrote, "Andalusian common folk used to amuse themselves in lunchrooms, patios, or barn doorways singing coplas of soleariyas, soleares, and peteneras, and seguidillas, but in a plain and simple manner" (1982, 63). Such accounts enable us to situate the flamenco copla tradition in a broader perspective. One conclusion is that the copla tradition of sung versification, in various forms, was widely popular throughout Andalusia. Illiteracy was no obstacle; Brenan notes that in his town of Yegen, very few of the roughly one thousand inhabitants were literate. As this was overwhelmingly an oral tradition, there is no need to presume that a significant portion of the circulating repertoire derived originally from literary sources. The same would apply to the flamenco copla tradition, which can be seen as a particular category of the idiom, cultivated especially (but not only) in the urban subcultures of the Seville-Jerez-Cádiz region. There is no need to imagine, as some writers have, that Gitanos would have been incapable of sustaining the art by composing their own lyrics, such that they must have gotten their repertoire from literate non-Gitano poets.[3]

Gitanos, like other Andalusians, cultivated the copla form, including their own versions of old, inherited coplas, as well as original verses in which they introduced their own characteristic themes, concerns, and occasional Caló lexicon. Then, as the mass media spread, the folk copla tradition described by Brenan largely died out, except in flamenco, where it became part of a thriving professional performance idiom and persisted as a set of family traditions (see, e.g., Fernández Bañuls and Pérez Orozco 1983, 52–53).

Letras as Lyric Poetry

Flamenco letras—except for that small minority adapted from lettered poets such as Machado or Lorca—are created and transmitted solely as song lyrics. As such—unlike such genres as the Urdu and Persian ghazal—they have no independent existence as poetry. Even letras originally adopted from literary sources take on their own life as oral literature, being freely altered by singers who may be unaware of their provenance. Regardless of their origin, flamenco lyrics are certainly significant and amenable to analysis in their own right and, accordingly, have been subjects of studies, from an informative chapter in Mairena and Molina's *Mundo y formas* to books such as the more recent *Las letras del cante flamenco*.[4] Authors of such works typically commence their discussions with the largely apt observation that flamenco letras—like vernacular coplas (as implying sung verses) in general—differ in character from literary poetry. In 1861 the poet Gustavo Adolfo Bécquer, discussing letras, wrote that while there is one form of poetry that is "magnificent and sonorous, . . . there is another that is natural, brief, dry, that springs from the soul like an electric spark, that wounds one's sentiment with a word and then flees, free of artifice" (1998, 27). Such statements are illuminating up to a point, but one should be wary of the tendency to romanticize letras as direct expressions of feeling, entirely "free of artifice." Like any form of verse, they are aesthetic creations rather than unmediated expressions of emotion; they make ample use of familiar poetic techniques of simile, synecdoche, and personification ("the wind said to me," etc.), not to mention rhyme and meter. They have their own set of conventions or, less charitably, clichés. At the same time, they use simple vocabulary, avoid such overtly rhetorical devices as alliteration, and make no attempt to be subtle or erudite. As song lyrics, they need not be outstanding as literary works, and as is often noted, much literary verse would not work well as song lyrics. Most are open and epigrammatic rather than specific in meaning, allowing the listener to imagine whatever scenarios might animate them; as commentators have noted, they are like sketches that the listener fills in (Blanco Garza et al., 1998, 19). Typical in this sense are the following:

Todos mis amigos me dicen a mi
que yo vivo de borrachera
pero ellos no saben los motivos
y si algunos de ellos supieran
también se emborracharían conmigo.

My friends tell me I'm a drunkard
But they don't know why I am that way
And if any of them did
They'd get drunk with me.

El carrito de los muertos
paso por allí,
como llevaba la manita fuera
yo la conocí.

The cart bearing the dead passed by
I recognized her hand dangling there.

A un anciano le pegué
porque me faltó en la calle
y al año, cuando me enteré
que ese hombre era mi padre
gotas de sangre lloré.

In the street I slapped an old man who was rude to me
The year I found out he was my father
I wept tears of blood.

For Mairena and Molina, the important social distinction is that between Gitano letras and "Andalusian" (that is, non-Gitano) ones (1979, 99–100). Certainly many verses are Gitano-flavored in their use of Gitano themes and occasional Caló words (such as *debel*, *undebé* [God], *ducas*, *duquelas*, and *puchar* ["to ask," another Hindi cognate]). However, in the present as in the past, such verses are as likely to be composed by non-Gitanos as Gitanos. A different sort of corroboration for Mairena and Molina's notion might be sought in fandango forms, which are traditionally more associated with non-Gitanos than Gitanos, and in their five-line structure are more likely to be composed by poets of some sort rather than merely handed down or improvised. Hence, fandango singers have tended to rely on poets—in the past, such as Emilio Mezquita or Nicolás Callejon—or in some cases they have composed their own letras, as did El Sevillano, José Cepero, and Pepe Pinto (see Soler Díaz 2016, 611). However, most modern flamencologists would opine that the polarizing distinction made by Molina and Mairena is overly simplistic, and in keeping with the problematic gitanocentricity of their books in general. As we have suggested, Gitano-inflected flamenco lyrics are best regarded as a category of a broader corpus of Andalusian copla.

A basic and distinctive feature of flamenco letras is their brevity, entailing a marked economy of expression. Soleá and siguiriyas coplas are typically of three or four lines; tangos and tientos of four, and fandango of five. In each case, the individual copla is an independent entity, which need not relate in any way to other coplas in a sung item. The structure of a flamenco tanda, as noted before, is thus atomistic: a copla is sung, perhaps generating applause; a guitar falseta is played, and then the cantaor sings another copla, with the sentiment of the previous copla being essentially forgotten and irrelevant. (Many traditional folk genres worldwide, such as Mexican *son* varieties, share this atomistic form. It would be quite mistaken to seek or posit some subtle unifying structure or interrelation in such verses.) This formal structure is quite distinct from that of a canción or "song," whose verses interrelate. As discussed below, much nuevo flamenco does consist of such structured songs, with newly composed, thematically interrelated lyrics, but these are quite distinct from the mainstream neo-traditional flamenco that continues to be standard fare at festivals, competitions, tablaos, and peñas. Similarly, in several cantes, a cantaor often proceeds without pause from one copla to another, inserting nonsense coletillas in between, all thematically unrelated. The effect may sometimes seem jarring when the cantaor is singing a tragic verse in bulerías with great evident expression, only to segue immediately to a nonsense coletilla. (The insertion of such unrelated refrains is long traditional in Spanish music, being documented in seguidillas from the 1700s [see, e.g., Durand-Viel 1983, 16].) For example, in a Lebrija-style bulerías al golpe, a cantaor might sing the following verse:

Tengo en mi casa un almendro
Que to' el que sale y to' el que entra
Que almendrita sigue comiendo

I have an almond tree in my house
Everybody who comes in and out
Keeps eating almonds

This might segue immediately (in "ligado," linked fashion) to the following coletilla:

Ay levanta! No duermes más
Que es mañanita de madrugá

Come on, get up!
It's early morning!

These two verses are each basically meaningless, and when sung together in quick sequence, they are all the more so. No singer or flamencologist would argue for their deep significance, except perhaps as family heirlooms.

Metrically, most letras are in the familiar octosyllabic four-line *romanceado* form. Three-line *tercerillas*, counted 5-7-5, are also common in soleá, bulerías, and as estribillos in tangos; these forms do not place any great demands on the poet nor on the singer who needs to remember them. A prominent exception to these forms is the siguiriyas, akin to the seguidilla, of either three lines (of 5, 11, and 5 syllables) or four lines (6 or 7, 6, 11, 6). A four-line seguidilla in syllable count 7-5-7-5 is sometimes used in cantes such as bulerías and cantiñas (not alegrías). Fandango verses, as noted earlier, are usually of five poetic lines, with the second line, or part of it, sung first and then in its proper position, making six tercios or sung lines. The standard form for sevillanas is a four-line seguidilla followed by a three-line verse, which could be called a *bordón*. Finally, the guajiras typically uses a ten-line décima. The lighthearted cantiñas uses all manner of prosodic forms as juguetillos punctuating coplas. As in Latin American vernacular poetry (including décimas), syllable counts are somewhat flexible, especially with elisions of vowels, such that, for example, *me entro* becomes *mentro*; as noted earlier, lines can be extended by adding filler phrases such as *ma're de mi alma*, by bebeo, and by adding the diminutive *-ito* (rendering *cabeza* as *cabezita*), which should not be regarded as altering its meaning. Even a verb can be "diminutivized" this way, with *m'he enterado* becoming *m'he enteraito*.

Verses generally contain assonant rhyme, in which the last accented syllable—usually the final or penultimate one—matches. Technically, the cuarteta scheme is *abab*, the *redondilla* is *abba*, the copla is *abcb*, and the *terset* is *aba*. (As mentioned earlier, any verse may be referred to simply as a "letra"; "copla," aside from the popular song genre, denotes a complete sung verse or stanza [e.g., of three, four, or five lines], while "tercio" means a line of verse as sung.) Given the characteristically languid, free-rhythmic performance style, rhyme does not have the same rhetorical importance or impact as in many other forms of verse. Indeed, in singing, some words, especially at the ends of lines, may be all but lost in melismas and sob-like bebeo and jipío, especially if the copla is already familiar (as most are) or the line ending is in other ways predictable (see, e.g., Amor n.d.). Even Spaniards unfamiliar with a given verse may have difficulty following such renditions. An uninitiated listener might well be hard-pressed to understand Manolo Caracol, as notated in example 5.2 in chapter 5, when he sings the familiar line *No doble de campanas* (Don't ring the bells) with the rather essential word "no" barely making an appearance: *Ay que doble de campana, ay que doble de campana, campanero, no doble campana, ay que doble de campana*. One flamencologist wrote of siguiriyas, "For the listener who doesn't understand the words . . . it seems that the singer is babbling like a child or a drunkard, and that he is physically struggling, with titanic exertion, to force the words into narrow musical molds" (Mercado 1982, 91).

While most familiar letras are commonly heard sung as one particular cante or another, they are to a considerable extent movable in the sense that they can be sung to other suitable cantes as well. Thus, a four-line, octosyllabic letra, whatever its origin, could be sung in several cantes, including as a soleá, alegría, tango, tientos, bulería, or even a fandango, though quintillas are the norm in that latter form. Almost any copla can be sung as a bulería. A primary exception would be coplas of siguiriya and cantiñas, which, with their distinctive seguidilla syllabic counts, would not work in a cante such as soleá. Meanwhile, some letras—especially in the free-rhythmic fandango forms—are so well known and closely associated with their classic settings that singers would be unlikely to use them in other styles. Such associations may rest on a feeling that the phonetic flow of a particular verse is perfectly suited to the melody to which it has been set; this perfect match, indeed, may explain the popularity of some coplas that are inconsequential in terms of their meaning.

In general, lyrics are pronounced in accordance with Andalusian colloquial speech (whose most distinctive features correspond with Caribbean Spanish as well). Final and preconsonantal "s" is aspirated or elided ("debuccalized"), and "d" between vowels or at ends of words is omitted. (Hence, e.g., *estados* would be rendered as *ehtao* or simply *etao*, and—as I learned in a frustrating exchange with a grocer whom I had to repeatedly ask to identify a fish that I was pointing at—*pez espada* [swordfish] can be pronounced *pe pá*.) "L" and "r" are often interchangeable, and adjacent vowels and diphthongs are truncated such that *mal de amores* would be sung as *mar d'amore*, and *paciencia* becomes *pasencia*. Metathesis is common, especially in the displacement of "r," such that *Gabriela* and *pobre* may become *Grabiela* and *probe*, respectively. Such pronunciation is characteristic of flamenco and would be observed even, for example, by non-Andalusian singers who do not otherwise speak in that accent. Similarly, as in *pasensia*, the lisped "c/z" typical of regions north of Andalusia is generally (but not entirely) avoided.

As Estela Zatania (2007a, 69) has noted, many coplas are constructed in a concise bipartite form of "proposition" (*planteamiento*) and resolution, such as this bulerías/tangos verse:

¿Qué quieres de mí?
Si hasta el agua que yo bebo
Te la tengo que pedir.

What more do you want from me,
When I even have to ask you
For the water I drink?

Many commentators have praised flamenco coplas as sublime poetic masterpieces, although as mentioned, many are essentially nonsense; cantaor Alfonso Cid sees such verses as akin to scat-singing phrases, suitable for playful rhythmic extemporization and release of tension. Other commonly heard letras, even in more serious cantes, are not necessarily deep or expressive but might be appreciated as venerable bits of heritage:

Me llamo Curro Frijones
y no me caso con la Farota
pa' no echarme obligaciones.

My name is Curro Frijones
And I won't marry La Farota,
Because I don't want any obligations.

The best letras—and some flamenco lovers may have their favorites—are concise lyrical gems and can achieve great poignancy and power when sung. It is in some respects surprising that many, by contrast, are inexpressive and trivial, such that the listener who does not attend to their meaning may not be missing much. However, it should be reiterated that what is important is not that a letra be outstandingly brilliant but rather that it can be a serviceable vehicle for evocative singing, acquiring depth and power through the cantaor's expressive rendering and the listener's imaginative reception. Even in a serious cante such as siguiriyas, the lexical meaning of the letra may be less important than its dramatic, pathos-laden rendering. Dancer El Farruco asserted, "In siguiriyas, the letra isn't fundamental; the pain is expressed through the quejios, the vocal breaks (*berríos*), the lament" (in Espada and España 2022, 170).

Some flamencologists, such as Félix Grande (1979, 44), have asserted that the essence of flamenco lyrics is the expression of pain; the mouth of the cante jondo singer, as the saying goes, should "taste like blood" (*saber a sangre*). In fact the thematic content of flamenco letras is much more extensive, even if tending to fall into a set of familiar categories. Mairena and Molina (1979, ch. 4) enumerate some fifteen of these—namely, romance; curses and vilifications; the mother; society; poverty; the futility of wisdom and experience in the face of death and love; moral judgments; death; fatalism; honor and dishonor; religiousness and irreligiousness; humor; vanity regarding worldly possessions; natural phenomena; countryside; and animals.[5] Other topics could be added, such as *piropo* (complimenting a woman), sociopolitical themes (discussed below), and expressions of Gitano (or Andalusian) pride and heritage, such as:

Qué alegría haber nacío
hijo de pa're gitano
canastero y andarrío.

What a joy it is to be born
Of a nomadic Gitano.

This, however, is precisely the sort of lyric that might have been composed by an exoticizing non-Gitano.

Many fandangos celebrate Andalusian towns or regions (such as Huelva or Málaga). Fernández Bañuls and Pérez Orozco (1983, 59–60) note that the imagery and worldview of flamenco letras are primarily urban in character, with the occasional references to rural life or nature being bucolic rather than realistic.

Some typical topics have changed over the generations such that a few coplas, though still heard, may provoke more bemusement than sympathy in their anachronistic values, such as what some call the "laundry" letra:

Desde que murió mi mare
una camisa que tengo
no encuentro quien me la lave.

Ever since my mother died
I have no one to wash my shirt.

(Wash it yourself, you lazy bum!)

By far the most common topic has been romance, especially its vicissitudes and tragedies, including *desamor*, or the end of love.

El cristal se rompe del calor al frío
como se ha roto de alegría y pena
mi corazoncillo.

The crystal breaks from being heated and cooled
Just as my poor heart has broken from joy and pain.

Many letras eulogize the mother figure or lament her death:

En la tumba de mi madre
a dar voces me ponía
y escuché un eco del viento
no la llames, me decía
que no responden los muertos.

At my mother's grave, I cried out
And I heard an echo from the wind,

Don't call out to her, it told me,
For the dead do not respond.

While some letras have been traced back to earlier centuries, the conception of love and personal interaction is essentially modern and Romantic in its portrayal of nuances of relationships between two socially autonomous individuals. The personae are neither the flat, stock characters of balladry, nor are they explicitly embedded in a constricting web of family obligations. However, many letras do involve family members, in a way that can be said to reflect the strength of the family as an institution in Gitano and Andalusian society and certainly contrasts with specifically youth-oriented genres such as rock or reggaeton, where such themes are absent.

Letras typically portray the poverty and social impotence of the narrator:

Desgracaíto él que come
el pan en manita ajena
siempre mirando a la cara
si la ponen mala o buena.

Unfortunate is he
Who has to get food from a stranger's hand
Always looking at that person's face
To see if their expression is good or bad.

Yo no tengo más remedio
que agachar la cabecita
y decir que lo blanco es negro.

There's nothing I can do
But bow my head
And say that white is black.

No pegarle a mi padre
es un pobre viejo y
no se mete con nadie.

Don't hit my father
He's a poor old man who doesn't bother anyone.

However, while soleares and siguiriyas coplas are invariably tragic, more typically festive are those of alegrías and in general of the city of Cádiz, with its proverbially fun-loving populace, as celebrated in this tangos verse:

Si alguna vez vas por Cái
pasa por barrio Santa María

y allí veras los gitanos
cómo se bailan por alegrías.

If you come to Cádiz someday
Pass by the barrio of Santa María
And you'll see how the Gitanos dance to alegrías.

A few letras may be mildly suggestive, but outright ribaldry and obscenity are avoided. However, in the early, dismal decades of the Franco era, when flamenco was especially associated with dissolute señoritos, prostitution, and, in general, *la mala vida* (the low life), many fandango verses reflected the spirit of desperation and decadence, speaking of beatings, alcoholism, women in insane asylums breast-feeding rag dolls, and the like (see Soler Díaz 2016, 63–64). The following is typical:

Mira si ella estaría borracha que hasta la copa de vino
Que tenía en las manos se le caía;
No maltratadla por Dios,
porque yo también tengo una hermana en la vía
Y eso son desgracias que nos manda Dios.

You see how she would get so drunk
that the glass of wine could fall from her hands
But for God's sake don't abuse her
For I myself have a sister living the *mala vida*
These are the misfortunes sent by God.

If most letras—including pre-flamenco coplas that may have been recycled in flamenco—have been amatory and ahistorical, there has been a steady current of those that, if not overtly political, have articulated social commentary of some sort.[6] Many of these, especially from the eighteenth and nineteenth centuries, are expressions of Gitano persecution:

Andando por una calle
he visto una horca
y a mi me habló
guárdate gitano.

Walking in the street, I saw a gallows
and I said to myself, watch out, Gitano.

Los geres por las esquinas
con velones y farol
en voz alta se decían
"¡Mararlo qu'es caló!"

The horsemen at the corners with lamps and lanterns
were shouting, "Kill him, he's a Caló [Gitano!]"

A tós los ojos negros
los van a prender mañana
y tú que negros los tienes
échate un velo a la cara.

They're going to take away all the dark-eyed people tomorrow
With those dark eyes you have, you better put on a veil.

Many depict the plight of prisoners, whether Gitano or not, in a time when wretched Andalusian poverty drove many to steal merely to survive:

Me sacan de un calaboso
y me llevan a otro más oscuro
y allí no podia ni verme
los deitos de las manos.

They took me out of one cell,
and put me in another so dark
that I couldn't see the fingers on my hand.

Aquel que quiere y no puede
gozar de su libertad
no es menester que lo entierren
que enterrao en vida está.

He who wants to enjoy his freedom but cannot—
There's no need to bury him when he dies,
he is buried alive.

Sociopolitical Themes

Some flamencologists—especially Félix Grande (1979) and José Manuel Caballero Bonald (1988)—have argued that flamenco is at some fundamental level an expression, however oblique, of Gitano protest against centuries of persecution. Others have aptly pointed out that flamenco letras invariably lack any sense of genuine rebellion or solidarity and are thus better regarded as resigned complaints, articulated from the persona of a solitary individual. Such resignification can be seen in other themes as well; thus, a traditional verse about Eve's original sin—"A woman was the cause of the first perdition"—was transformed in peteneras into a personal lament: "A woman was the cause of *my* first perdition" (*Una mujer fue la cause de la/mi perdición primera*, in García Gómez 1993, 313–14).

Meanwhile, the lighthearted gaditanos (citizens of Cádiz) would find amusement in any circumstance, as in this theater copla, subsequently recycled in flamenco, mocking Napoleon's 1810 ineffective bombardment of the city with flimsy projectiles:

Con las bombas que tiran los fanfarrones
se hacen las gaditanas tirabuzones.

From the bombs hurled by the arrogant [French]
The women of Cádiz made hairclips.

Invariably, coplas articulated the perspective of the Andalusian common man, worn down by poverty, military service in Spain's endless wars, and capricious domination by local landlords and police.

Cuando se emborracha un pobre
le llaman en borrachón.
cuando se emborracha un rico
"qué alegrito va el señor."

When a poor man gets drunk, they call him a drunkard.
When a rich man gets drunk, they say, "How merry is the good sir!"

Cuatro casas tiene abiertas
el que no tiene dinero
la carcel, el hospital,
la iglesia, y el cementerio.

There are four doors open to he who has no money:
the prison, the hospital, the church, and the cemetery.

Todo lo puede el dinero
porque mucho es su poder
ningún hombre jornalero
puede guardar su mujer.

Money can do anything, such is its power
No day-worker can even protect his woman.

The latter 1800s saw the flourishing of genuinely political coplas, articulating broader social concerns in a spirit of protest and activism. From the stunted Revolution of 1868, the country was wracked with contending battles between liberal Republicans, reactionary Carlists and Isabelists, and armies of assorted caudillos and regions. Still popular is this copla, in which the "Republican" flags can be reworded as "Gitano" ones:

Qué bonita está Triana
cuando le ponen al puente
banderas republicanas.

How beautiful is Triana
when they adorn the bridge
with Republican flags.

From around 1900, Andalusian coplas were coming to express regional resentment against domination and exploitation by Madrid. After the Reconquest, culminating in the 1492 fall of Granada, the imperial Madrid government treated Andalusia as a conquered and occupied territory rather than a region of economic value to be developed. Under Christian rule, irrigation networks collapsed, trade withered, and land ownership became concentrated in the hands of a largely absentee landlord (*latifundista*) elite. Ruinous imperial wars, mass emigration to America, and internal stagnation and repression further devastated Andalusia, causing recurrent famines that persisted through the nineteenth century. While the development of mining in the eastern Levant area provided employment for many landless laborers, it also condemned thousands of workers to blindness, lung disease, and early deaths. Even this, however, was preferable to the fate of the legions of draftees who perished in the colonial wars in the Americas.

Such conditions promoted a sense of regional hostility to Madrid and the landlords along with the spread of socialist ideas. By the mid-nineteenth century, the civic discontent once expressed in *bandolerismo* (banditry) and fatalism was generating strikes, unions, leftist publications, open revolts (as in 1868), and explicit social commentary in flamenco coplas. These were particularly common in the *cante minero* forms documenting the exploitation of miners in the Levant region:

Minero, ¿pa qué trabajas
si pa' ti no es el producto?
Pa' el patrón son las alhajas
para tu familia el luto
y para ti la mortaja.

Miner, why do you work when the profits aren't for you?
For the owner are the jewels, for your family is mourning,
and for you is the funeral shroud.

However, genuinely political commentary in the mining region was more common in trovo vernacular verse and song than in flamenco, which generally portrayed individual, personal drama rather than collective causes and abstract themes. Insofar as flamenco drew from and even supplanted sociopolitical trovo, it tended to depoliticize it, replacing political protest with sentimental laments (García Gómez 1993, 288–311).

The initial decades of the Franco regime brought further misery to the region in the form of famines, brutal political repression, absolute censorship, and a stultifying atmosphere pervading all arts and culture, including flamenco. In the latter 1960s, however, the Spanish economy began its aforementioned belated revival, and a few bold and politically minded flamenco singers began testing the limits of censorship. Most outspoken among these from the early 1970s were Manuel Gerena, Enrique Morente, Pepe Taranto, José Dominguez ("El Cabrero"), and, especially, José Menese, who performed cantes explicitly calling for freedom and democracy.

Political repression and censorship ended with Franco's death and the return to democracy, but Andalusia continued to suffer from state neglect, unequal land distribution, and massive migration to the industrializing cities of the north, especially Barcelona. Many flamenco singers, in tandem with a *nueva canción andaluza* movement, voiced a new sense of Andalusian regional pride and solidarity (see Manuel 1989a).

Since the 1990s, while problems of unemployment and out-migration have continued, the flourishing of democracy and the disappearance of tangible antagonists such as Franco or exploitative Madrid policies have engendered a less charged political scene, such that protest and social commentary are less often heard in flamenco (see Manuel 2017). At the same time, higher levels of education and ongoing concerns about the environment, inequalities of wealth, and other issues have inspired some cantaores to sing and in many cases compose letras that address a wide variety of topics. An example is this fandango verse composed by New York–based singer Alfonso Cid:

La tierra vamo' a dejá
Sequita como una pasa.
Cuando vengamo' a darno' cuenta
Na' má dinero va a quedá
Y eso no nos alimenta.

We're going to leave the earth as dry as a raisin
And when we finally realize
Nothing will remain but money
And that can't feed us.

Gender relations constitute their own form of social politics, and flamenco lyrics can be seen as a forum in which they have been dramatized and negotiated. Gender dynamics are discussed in greater depth in chapter 8 of this volume, but a few basic observations may be made here. From the café cantante period to the 1960s or so, female performers ran the risk of being regarded as floozies and were largely excluded from taverns and juergas, and to some extent even from stage shows. Since the 1970s, however, flamenco has constituted a more neutral medium in which female performers are appreciated and welcomed, and cantaoras as well as cantaores can voice the full range of amatory sentiments, from longing to heartbreak and recrimination, as in this fandango verse recorded by María Vargas:

Frente a frente, díme que no me quieres
dímelo tú, frente a frente
Tú rodea'o de mujeres
y presumes de valiente
¡Qué poca cosita eres!

Tell me to my face that you don't love me.
Surrounded by women,
you think you are so cool.
What a pathetic little thing you are!

Abuse of women may also be commented upon, as in this traditional tango *extremeño copla*:

Si el molinero jugara
A la pelota y perdiera
No le faltarían palos
A la pobre molinera.

If the miller plays ball and loses,
His poor wife won't escape a beating.

Most flamenco letras are not explicitly gendered, so they can be sung by men or women, and even a gendered lyric such as, *Mujer, ¿porqué me besaste*? (Woman, why did you kiss me?) could easily be reworded by a female singer as *Primo mío* (lit., "My cousin," but could refer to any man). Even such rephrasings are not strictly required; cantaor Luis de la Pica was celebrated for his rendering of a bulería beginning *Ayer llegó tarde*, sung from the persona of a woman complaining about her wayward lover.

Male singers have always outnumbered females, especially at the professional level (and there have been scarcely any female professional guitarists), and women have had to contend with various sorts of attitudinal and logistical obstacles in the field. As modern cantaoras such as Rocío Márquez have pointed out, some traditional letras are overtly *machista*,[7] such as the following, which is still sung:

Algunas veces te pego palos
porque me gusta verte llorar

tus lagrimitas me parecen
caracolitos del mar.

Sometimes I hit you
Because I like to see you cry.
Your tears look like little seashells.

Curiously, a canonic rendering of this letra was by Pastora Pavón, suggesting either that she regularly beat her husband, Pepe, or, more likely, that traditional verses can be sung either from the male or female persona, as mentioned above. Another traditional letra is:

La maté porque era mía
A la mujer que yo quise
Y si se resucitara,
Cien veces la mataría
Pa que en este mundo no me engañara.

I killed her, the woman I loved, because she was mine.
And if she were to revive,
I'd kill her a hundred times
because no one in this world deceives me.

Less sociopathic, but chauvinistic in its own way, is this familiar chestnut:

Te voy a meter en un convento
que tenga rejas de bronce
que la gente no te vea
ni la ropita te roce.

I'm going to send you to a convent
that has bronze bars
so that no one hears you
or touches your clothes.

Génesis García Gómez (1993, 313–43) argues for a distinction between Gitano and non-Gitano attitudes toward women as portrayed in flamenco. Several traditional letras in the more Andalusian-associated (rather than Gitano-associated) fandango forms, drawing from conventions of popular verse, articulated a dichotomous virgin/whore view of women as either angels or she-devils, or they have a moralistic tenor or portray the man as a picaresque, womanizing dandy. Such lyrics, she notes, are uncommon in the more Gitano-oriented palos such as siguiriyas, which instead depict the man as hopelessly and often tragically consumed by his love, reflecting the considerable power and autonomy that women can wield.

Traditional attitudes are certainly changing, and most modern cantaores would avoid explicitly sexist letras. Rocío Márquez is one of a handful of modern singers who have penned their own socially conscious lyrics. Another is Alejandro Villaescusa, a gifted singer from Albacete, who, in his letras and YouTube videos, occasionally injects an element of humor into the genre and sings such letras as the following, which he composed for International Women's Day:

Mi mari'o me ha besao
porque mientras él planchaba
le he hecho su cola-cao.

My husband kissed me
because while he was doing the ironing
I made him a hot chocolate.

That copla is a reworking of a traditional one:

Mi mari'o me ha pegao
Porque no le había hecho
Papita con bacalao.

My husband hit me
Because I didn't make him
Potatoes with codfish.

Chocolate sang a particularly poignant fandango letra portraying abuse of women:

Papá, deja la bebía
Que mi mare está llorando,
Sácala de cuando en cuando,
y alegra un poco su vía.
mira que la estás matando.

Papa, stop drinking, my mother is weeping,
Take her out every now and then,
and brighten her path a little.
See how you are killing her.

Oral Transmission and Lettered Poets

While letras constitute a rich corpus of vernacular discourse and certainly play a role in cante, they are not intrinsically valued at the same level as dance, guitar playing, and the art of singing expressively. Among singers and enthusiasts, there is relatively little sense of connoisseurship about letras, and among flamenco people, lyrics are seldom the focus of animated conversation. Moreover, while vast numbers of letras are available in published anthologies and the internet, most singers do not exert themselves to seek out new or interesting coplas that they then set to music. Instead, cantaores tend to sing letras that they have heard before, whether on records, in performances, or, among hereditary flamenco families, from elders. Hence, in a typical evening performance, whether at a peña, tablao, or festival, most or even all of the sung letras may be traditional, and a hardcore flamenco enthusiast may have heard all of them before. Audiences do not seem to tire of hearing familiar letras repeatedly; they do not groan and roll their eyes upon hearing *A tó's los ojos negros* or *Te voy a meter en un convento*, but rather accept and appreciate these verses as heritage.

Direct oral transmission—of letras as well as estilos and dance moves—is in fact valued among flamenco families, especially Gitano ones, in crucibles such as Jerez, Lebrija, and Utrera. Hereditary singers in such families, whether professionals or amateurs, are proud of their local and family lineages, and they cherish letras handed down from elders. Accordingly, they might criticize a local cantaor for singing letras or imitating styles of performers from rival towns. However, most coplas, even if their regional provenance is known, circulate freely as part of a shared repertoire.

Meanwhile, however, there has always been a certain minority of cantaores who take an active interest in letras and incorporate new ones into their repertoire. Such expansion of repertoire was intensified in the 1970s with the spread of 33 rpm LPs, some of which (such as Lole y Manuel's *Nuevo Día*) could be structured as coherent entities rather than random sets of tandas (Martín Cabeza 2016, 105). Much of this output, as noted elsewhere in this volume, has consisted of precomposed songs (canciones), often in some style of nuevo flamenco, and thus on or beyond the margins of the focus of this volume. However, some work by lettered poets has certainly found its way into mainstream flamenco. In recent decades, many singers who record albums select their letras thoughtfully, whether soliciting them from poets or browsing published anthologies.

One kind of source has been literary poets who, like most authors, did not write their verse with the intent that it be sung. One such poet was Manuel Machado, a few of whose lyrics, as mentioned above, have been sung, though well after his lifetime. Another has been García Lorca, whose relation to flamenco merits further discussion than can be presented here. Lorca, a flamenco enthusiast, titled one of his poetry collections *Cante jondo*. He did not, however, envision these poems as being sung but rather saw them as evocations of the spirit of flamenco. Although his interest in and knowledge of Gitanos was in some ways superficial—by his own admission—over the generations, several flamenco artists, including Gitanos, have regarded him as a sympathetic and kindred soul, and some have set his lyrics to song. In recent times, singers have freely adapted verse from a variety of Spanish poets such as José Bergamín (1895–1983) and Agustín García Calvo (1926–2012). Singers such as Vicente Soto and Carmen Linares have also based recordings and shows on verses of well-known poets such as Miguel Hernández and Juan Ramón Jiménez. In adapting such literary poetry to cante, singers may have to contend with the challenge of verse that is not in standard flamenco meter.

A more direct sort of collaboration is involved when *letristas* (lyricists) compose verses for specific cantaores. One prominent example is Antonio Sánchez (father of Paco de Lucía), who composed many lyrics for Camarón to sing on recordings and in concert. Sánchez, though never a celebrated "star," should be appreciated as one of the unsung heroes of modern flamenco, except that his verses were in fact sung. In his guidance of Camarón's LPs, he was a prototype of the modern producer, and his numerous lyrics recorded by Camarón were models of effective, solid, and often original verse.

Another such letrista was Francisco Moreno Galván (1925–1999), a poet and painter who lived mostly in Madrid and his hometown of La Puebla de Cazalla, itself a stronghold of flamenco. If, as we have mentioned, flamenco audiences and singers generally do not seem to mind hearing the same verses again and again, Galván was among those few who envisioned greater depth and variety in letras, stating, "I love cante, but I saw that the letras were always the same, and it bothered me that this Gitano or that other singer never sang anything—pains and joys—that I hadn't already heard" (qtd. in Martín Cabeza 2016, 97). From the late 1950s, Galván was part of a circle of progressive intellectuals and artists, including José Manuel Caballero Bonald and Fernando Quiñones, who were committed both to flamenco and sociopolitical change. In the 1960s he commenced his collaboration with José Menese, who, though in some respects a conservative follower of Antonio Mairena, was fervently committed to using cante as a forum for activism and protest, suffering occasional censorship and persecution by the Franco regime in the process. Together, Menese and Galván used the LP format to expand the thematic content, diction, and imagery well beyond traditional norms, extending to sociopolitical commentary as well as other subjects. A well-known veiled protest lyric of theirs, which was too subtle for Franco's censors, was:

Señor que vas a caballo y no das los buenos días,
si el caballo cojeara otro gallo cantaría.

Sir, you ride on horseback and don't say "Buenos días" to anyone,
If the horse were to limp along, then a different rooster would be singing.[8]

Menese, who spent years doing *rebusca* work, sorting fallen olives on his hands and knees, would be well familiar with the landlord prancing by on his horse and being too haughty to offer the basic greeting that is standard among ordinary Spaniards in all sorts of situations. But if the rider were a poor person on a limping nag, then he would certainly be polite rather than supercilious.

A prominent letrista of the current generation is Juan Carlos Muñoz (b. 1963), whose verses, published in over a dozen books, each dedicated to a single cante, have been sung by dozens of cantaores.

Another category of lyricists comprises those who compose songs—music and lyrics—for particular singers of flamenco and perhaps copla. Especially prominent in the modern era has been Antonio Gallardo Molina (1925–2013), who provided much material for María Vargas, La Paquera de Jerez, Miguel Poveda (b. 1973), Jesús Mendez, Rocío Jurado, José Mercé, and others. Another prolific composer of songs with letras has been Pepe de Lucía, brother of Paco.

Finally, there are letristas who are themselves prominent cantaores, writing lyrics for their own use and perhaps for others. This practice is hardly new, as many of the verses collected by Demófilo in his 1881 anthology were attributed to specific cantaores (see Mercado 1982, 110–11). In the twentieth century, cantaores who sing verses of their own composition have included El Sevillano, José Cepero, Pepe Pinto, and Fernando el de Triana. Particularly prolific has been Fosforito, who has penned hundreds of coplas for his own use and for other singers such as Camarón. Since, on the whole, royalties earned from flamenco lyrics are negligible, letristas like Fosforito often do not bother to register all their verses and feel gratified rather than outraged when they hear, for example, a cantaor sing their letras and claim, if asked, that the verses are traditional (see, e.g., Fosforito, in Curao 2008, III:77–78). A few authors of letras, such as José de la Tomasa, Luis de la Pica, or Manuel Molina (of the duo Lole y Manuel), could be regarded as flamenco versions of "singer-songwriters" (*cantautores*) insofar as their letras portray a consistent personal style.

PART III

Flamenco Culture

7

The Contemporary Scene

Since the "revolutionary" 1970s, flamenco, and the flamenco scene in general, can be said to have exhibited enough stability and continuity that one can regard it as a relatively coherent, unified "modern" period. Various changes and developments have certainly occurred, such as the advent of the internet and the ongoing innovations of nuevo flamenco, but these have unfolded within a broader context of relative stasis. The COVID crisis commencing in 2020 has been catastrophic in its way, but the current form of the pandemic has allowed a new kind of stasis to reemerge in that most cultural life is back to normal, except that people are constantly getting sick. Indeed, by late 2021 much flamenco activity had resumed, although some key venues had closed for good.

The broader context for flamenco's modern period has been that of Spain as a whole, in its general political stability, cultural vitality, and relative prosperity. The Spanish economy, and especially that of Andalusia, have certainly undergone vicissitudes. Prevailing unemployment in southern Spain has led hundreds of thousands of people to emigrate north for the industrial centers of Barcelona, Germany, or elsewhere. Many Andalusian towns seem to be inhabited only by retirees. The 1990s were a period of prolonged stagnation, and a rebound in the early 2000s was cut short by the recession starting in 2008. The recovery from that crisis was slower than in other countries, and many flamenco performers were unable to make ends meet and simply abandoned the profession. A gradual economic revival, aided by the vibrant tourist sector, eventually ensued (see, e.g., Aoyama 2009) but was then steamrolled by the COVID crisis, which bankrupted many more performers, who were dependent on tourism and public performances, and who, being unsalaried, were not aided by whatever social "safety net" could be provided by the state.

Particularly relevant has been the status of the Gitano population. As noted earlier, in the twentieth century Gitanos were hit hard by the obsolescence of most of their traditional occupations of blacksmithing, horse trading, and basket weaving. In the 1980s heroin addiction became endemic, including among such flamenco performers as Camarón. Unemployment remains high among Gitanos, although drug use seems to have declined among flamenco performers, most of whom have adopted an ethic of professionalism, respectability, and reliability. Flamenco in general has largely—though not entirely—shed its former association with a seedy underworld of drug addicts and dissolute señoritos. Newly legitimized, it has been actively promoted by the Andalusian government, and in 2010 it was declared by UNESCO to be part of the "Intangible Cultural Heritage of Humanity." Flamenco has come to account for between 5 and 10 percent of recording and concert sales in Spain as a whole and around twice that in Andalusia (Ruiz and Pérez 2011).

As an art form, flamenco in the modern period can be seen as comprising a relatively stable mainstream style and repertoire that flourish alongside a steady current of innovative styles. It is this "por derecho" flamenco, with its fixed repertoire of cantes and estilos, and its basic format of voice, guitar, palmas, and perhaps cajón, that dominates the circuit of tablaos, peñas, competitions, and festivals. Meanwhile, in commercial recordings and videos and in various sorts of stage shows, performers pursue more eclectic sorts of flamenco, especially in the form of pop-flavored cuplés or highbrow avant-garde projects. (There is an obvious similarity to the jazz scene, in which a basic "straight-ahead" style established in the 1950s and 1960s continues to serve as a mainstream idiom, while many performers undertake various worthy innovations in certain contexts.) As discussed further in this volume, "tradition versus innovation" arguments persist—as they have since the 1880s—regarding the direction flamenco should take; some say that the art must change and evolve in order to remain vital and attract the young, and others insist that the por derecho flamenco core must be nourished and prioritized and that flamenco is not designed to be a mass art and need not try to be so. However, despite the ongoing polemics, dire predictions, and nostalgic elegies of a bygone "Golden Age," even the most pessimistic critic might have to concede that, in general, flamenco is doing well as an art form. It enjoys a stable local and international audience with various sorts of institutional support, it is respected as a legitimate art form and earnestly cultivated internationally as well as in Spain, and the younger generations include a host of remarkably gifted performers.

Performance Contexts

Flamenco, since its very inception, has been performed in two broad categories of contexts—namely, stage shows for a general public and, secondly, more intimate community or domestic gatherings. The latter category itself could be regarded as comprising two sorts of events—that is, informal reunions of families and friends, and private parties (now referred to as "fiestas" rather than "juergas") where flamencos would be hired to perform, whether in a reserved room at a venta or the home of some patron. Through the 1960s such private events provided the most regular source of sustenance for working performers, but in the modern period they have declined dramatically, replaced by tablaos and other public contexts. Flamenco artists may still occasionally be hired for private events, but the era of the paying juerga—whether rewarding or humiliating for performers—is largely over.

Meanwhile, informal flamenco parties have also declined, though for different reasons. Such private reunions certainly persist, especially in places like Jerez, Lebrija, Utrera, or Badajoz, where cohesive communities of Gitano flamenco families host informal fiestas (at which non-Gitano friends may be welcome). Many performers, even of the present generation, have been raised in families where such festivities were common and constituted invaluable training grounds. However, by all accounts, such events have become less common in the modern period. A primary cause has been the displacement of many Gitanos from neighborhoods such as Triana and Sacromonte to dismal housing projects (*polígonos*) like Seville's Tres Mil Viviendas. Triana and other Gitano neighborhoods, despite poverty and crime, were famously convivial and cohesive, with their sets of multigenerational households sustained by economically solvent blacksmiths, artisans, and performers, built around patios that constituted natural spaces for socializing and partying with an easy and amicable mixing of Gitanos and others. The polígonos have proven to be far less conducive to such gatherings, whether because of their very construction or the way that they vitiated settled Gitano communities by relocating them with formerly itinerant and socially maladapted *canastero* (nomadic, lit., "basket-weaving") Gitanos. Sadly, the projects have become better known for unemployment and drug abuse than for flamenco. Guitarist Tomatito (b. 1958) describes his experience of the change:

> The experience that exists now is not like it was. I grew up in a neighborhood, La Chanca de Almería, where people played guitar on the street, in their doorways. Those neighborhoods no longer exist. But now they have YouTube. You can hear whatever you want. Paco de Lucía, click; Vicente Amigo, click; Manolo Sanlúcar, click . . . and there you have it. Different. But that is not enough.[1]

In some cases, the dispersion of tight Gitano communities was caused by specific events, such as the 1963 flooding of Granada's Sacromonte caves, which precipitated the relocation of most of the residents to depressing polígonos. Curro Albaicín related:

1963 was a catastrophic year for Sacromonte, an uprooting, and the community was never the same again. The whole lifestyle was lost—learning flamenco from each other, the young from the old, and with that the barrio died. (qtd. in López López 2015, 541)

The decline of informal flamenco parties, however, has involved more than the dissolution of Gitano neighborhoods and is attested to by many veteran performers, especially as involving the 1970s tablao scene and its after-parties. José Mercé (b. 1955) related:

> That was the golden age of flamenco. I was very lucky to arrive in Madrid in 1969, to be with the greatest artists in the tablaos . . . Paco de Lucía, Camarón, everyone, we were all together. . . . We would go with each other to listen to each other. Today that no longer exists. . . . I remember how we'd leave the tablaos, one from Torres Bermejas, another from Los Canasteros, another from Las Brujas, another from Café Chinitas, and wherever I was from, and we ended up at Venta del Palomar, eating, drinking, and singing to each other, as our own party, to listen to each other. That has been lost, that no longer exists. And that's where you learned, where you drank flamenco, and that's where you fed from that source that was so great.[2]

American-born guitarist David Jones ("Serva") corroborated such reminiscences, adding that for him the ideal context for flamenco was neither the stage nor the noisy party but, rather, "sitting around a table" (p.c.). The reasons for the decline of such gatherings are not clear, aside from such factors as a general intensification of television and computer culture, undermining social life as a whole.

If the late-night, post-tablao party scene declined after the 1990s, the tablaos themselves have remained vital in their way, nourished by the steady influx of tourists for whom a tablao evening is an indispensable part of their visit. The tablaos vary somewhat in size, orientation, and quality. Madrid's Corral de la Morería is like a five-star restaurant with a high-powered spectacle-oriented show. In Granada, Seville, and elsewhere, some venues are humble holes-in-the-wall with fewer than twenty seats. Audiences themselves vary; a few tablaos may attract mixtures of foreign tourists and local flamenco fans; often the entire audience consists of tourists, though in such a scenic locale as Granada's Sacromonte, the tourists may include busloads of visiting Spaniards. Ideally, the artists enjoy performing and have learned how to present a first-class and spirited show even for an audience who knows nothing and who, while applauding vigorously after an item, sit in cadaverous silence after the cadences that should properly elicit vigorous jaleos.

As before, the tablaos serve as indispensable training grounds for flamencos, who learn how to perform with diverse other artists and how to project and communicate to different sorts of audiences. Such skills might well be lacking in, for example, the guitar student who practices assiduously by himself, dissects and masters Paco de Lucía falsetas, but has little experience playing with others and little sense of what works on stage and what does not. Meanwhile, the better tablaos feature first-class artists. Each show includes one or two cante items and a guitar solo, but the emphasis is on dance—perhaps an opening sevillanas, a tango, an extended alegrías or soleá, and a lively bulerías finale.

Since the 1950s, an important role in flamenco culture has been played by the peñas, which number more than four hundred in Andalusia, with several more in Extremadura, Murcia, Madrid, and Barcelona. A peña comprises a venue, a managerial committee, and members who pay a modest fee enabling them to attend the performances that take place, perhaps every month or so. The venues themselves vary in size. A few are intimate rooms where the members sit huddled in a tight circle around the performers, who have no need of amplification. A more typical peña might have a barroom, where members drink and socialize, and an adjoining performance space seating a hundred or so people. The peñas primarily feature cante rather than dance and tend to be conservative ("mairenista") in promoting mainstream flamenco rather than innovative hybrids or pop-flavored cuplé singers.

The peñas can be ideal places to hear cante. The ambience is reasonably intimate, the attendees are hardcore enthusiasts who enliven the event with jaleos, and the performers are typically excellent, even if the peñas cannot afford to bring superstars. The peñas may be especially valuable in the winter months, when there are no festivals and few tourists in the tablaos. Meanwhile, the peñas, in association with one another, contribute in several other ways to the flamenco scene. Some of them organize competitions, summer festivals, and other events such as panels and conferences. A few publish journals, along with occasional books and CDs, collectively enhancing the intellectual study and informed appreciation of the art. A typical institution is the Federación de Peñas Flamencas de Málaga, whose website includes their online journal and information about the various activities of the more than forty associated peñas in the province.

The peñas are not without their problems, especially a disconcerting decline in membership and, thus, in fiscal solvency, leading several venerable establishments to dissolve. There is much concern about the difficulty of attracting younger members, provoking familiar arguments about whether the peñas should depart from the por derecho mainstream idiom and offer more populist fare. Many peñas seek subsidies from private donors, local governments, or the Junta de Andalucía, though such assistance has attenuated in recent decades. Some argue that the peñas should branch out beyond flamenco in order to be seen by young people as attractive cultural centers rather than clubs for gray-haired purists. (Granada's venerable La Platería finds one solution in hosting regular Thursday evening shows open to the paying public; roughly half the attendees are tourists, who help pay the bill, and the remaining locals provide the jaleos.)

The largest audiences for flamenco are reached through the summer festivals that have proliferated since the 1970s. Festivals of Morón, Utrera, Lebrija, and Jerez are especially high-profile, but many smaller towns also take competitive pride in hosting events and bringing the top echelon of artists, who would be beyond the means of the peñas. Like the peñas, most festivals are oriented toward serious, por derecho cante rather than dance or pop. Held in bullrings, town plazas, or other open-air venues, they might go on until the wee hours. As with the tablaos, elder performers recall the 1970s and 1980s as the heyday of the festivals, especially for how they brought together both Gitano and non-Gitano performers and audiences in a spirit of shared love of flamenco. Nowadays, Jerez and other municipalities also sponsor concerts that are free to the public, sometimes to the detriment of events and venues that depend on ticket sales. A major festival in a category of its own is the Bienal de Seville; held in alternate years, it tends to be oriented less toward cante than toward extravagant dance productions, typically with modernist themes. The *ayuntamiento* (*ayto*, municipal government) in a city like Seville or Jerez may spend considerable sums supporting flamenco in various ways; often there is much dispute about how such sums are allocated or misallocated.

While the festival scene continues with much vigor, a similar large concert format is the competition, or concurso, the most renowned of which have been those of La Unión, Córdoba, and Mairena del Alcor. These events are typically organized by the peña federations and are held in large venues, presenting both up-and-coming artists as well as established stars. The concursos are especially useful to aspiring performers, providing tangible benefits to winners both in prize money as well as the concert and recording contracts that follow. (Accordingly, advertisements for festivals proclaim that such-and-such a cantaor is the winner of this or that concurso.) Mayte Martín, for example, is generally regarded as coming to the public's attention when she won the prestigious award at the Concurso de La Unión in 1987. Cantaora María José Pérez asserted, "There are a lot of us involved in this [flamenco], and it's clear not everyone can have the same amount of work. Participating in contests is a way of gaining experience, and also of letting audiences get to know you."[3]

Perhaps like competitions everywhere, the concursos provoke a certain amount of criticism. Some say that they tend to promote dry and stilted performances and that in the current internet era they are no longer indispensable as means of promotion. Flamencologist Manuel Bohórquez wrote in 2015, "Today a kid who sings well records a video, posts it on the Internet and, if it's good, the next day fans all over the world will know about it." Instead of promoting new artists, he continued, many of the concursos have come to be dominated by a stable roster of established artists who are just in it for the prize money. (This consideration may not matter to audiences, who may hear good cante one way or the other.) Meanwhile, the concursos can naturally promote a spirit of rivalry that can be antagonistic, especially when panels of judges have to make difficult decisions that could be seen as involving favoritism based on gender, ethnicity, or other factors, whether or not that is actually the case. Estela Zatania, who has served on several concurso panels, attests that the judging process is often irregular and disorganized, with various idiosyncratic criteria coming into play (p.c.).

Yet another performance context for flamenco, both in Spain and abroad, comprises miscellaneous restaurants that feature flamenco artists, with the dancer performing on a tiny *tarima* (wooden platform) and hoping not to swing an arm into the face of a passing waiter bearing a tray full of food and drink. In the New York area (where I live), there are a few such venues. Often the restaurant is full of diners who jabber and laugh boisterously and for whom the performance, however excellent, is merely background ambience. On occasion, such a large, rowdy group, after ignoring and drowning out the flamenco show, finally departs; the performers and the remaining handful of flamenco fans can at last savor a satisfactory atmosphere, but all are painfully aware that the dedicated fans themselves are too few to make such a show remunerative for the venue. Typically, performers in such venues feel obliged to mix flamenco with more accessible fare such as the Gypsy Kings' "Bamboleo" or Cuban chestnuts such as "Lagrimas Negras." (Chatting with the singer before a show at such a venue during the vogue of the reggaeton hit "Despacito," I remarked, "At least I won't have to hear 'Despacito' tonight," to which he replied, "Well, actually. . . .")

In some respects at the opposite end of the performance spectrum from such modest venues are the elaborate stage extravaganzas—"espectáculos"—consisting of a prominent dance company's flamenco version of some theatrical opus such as *Medea* or *Othello*. These tend to be dark, ponderous productions with entirely precomposed choreography and music, and, as such, their audience may be quite different from those who attend peñas and festivals to hear spontaneous cante. Some top-level dancers complain that impresarios pressure them to concoct such works when they might rather perform por derecho flamenco (see, e.g., El Pipa in Aix Gracía 2014, 422).

Despite the number and variety of professional performance contexts, it remains difficult to make a presentable living performing flamenco, unless one is a star cantaor like Miguel Poveda, or Arcángel (b. 1977). Playing guitar is especially unremunerative. Even a virtuoso guitarist may struggle to make ends meet, playing tablao gigs, teaching, and accompanying dance classes. With little public interest in solo guitar concerts, a guitarist is fortunate if he can secure a steady gig with a dance company (*compañía*). Meanwhile, in flamenco as in many professional art forms worldwide, achieving a successful career may involve more than merely being a talented performer; whether the patronage sources are commercial impresarios or municipal bureaucracies, success may entail ingratiating yourself with the right potentates, having your midday drink with the right people, perhaps supporting the right political party, and so on.

Tourism

As previously noted, tourists have been visiting Spain and seeking out Gitano dances from the early 1800s, and by the café cantante period such visitors were important parts of audiences, with their spending power compensating for their modest numbers. From the 1850s and earlier, ventas and *academías de baile* were staging shows especially for visitors, and flamenco's subsequent evolution was shaped by the touristic Romantic demand for exotic spectacles and the ability of performers to cultivate an art form that could meet that demand and at the same time be rich and sophisticated in its way. However, it was from the 1950s that tourism, as promoted by the Franco regime, reached a genuinely mass level, and since the 1960s, animated by the "Spain is different" slogan, it has constituted a substantial sector of the nation's economy. Spain receives the second-largest number of tourists in the world (after France); tourism has been especially important in Andalusia, which offers both beaches and core flamenco locales, and it constitutes around 10 percent of the state's regional gross domestic product (Aoyama 2009, 86). The ranks of visitors include both those who come specifically for flamenco—especially to take dance classes and attend festivals—and, more numerously, the culture-and-heritage visitors as well as sun-and-beach tourists who attend tablaos and other events. As a result, tablaos tend to be concentrated in sites favored by such tourists, including Madrid, Seville, Granada, and Málaga. Well over half of the attendees of the Bienal del Arte Flamenco de Sevilla and the Festival de Jerez are foreign flamenco enthusiasts, especially Japanese (Aoyama 2009, 96). State, municipal, and federal governments—particularly the Junta de Andalucía—attempt to facilitate and support flamenco tourism by providing infrastructure, coordinating events, and supporting other activities. Subsidies for events like the Bienal and Jerez Festival are more than compensated in terms of revenue by the amounts of money that visitors spend on hotels, restaurants, and other activities.

Tourists support flamenco directly in various ways, including attending tablaos and festivals, taking classes in private academies, and buying dance paraphernalia. Foreign students, including many Japanese, figure prominently in the dance schools that emerged in the post-Franco era. These are especially concentrated in Seville and Madrid; a representative prominent institution is the Fundación de Arte Flamenco Cristina Heeren (subsidized by that American philanthropist), which offers classes in the full range of flamenco idioms and is attended by local as well as foreign enthusiasts of different levels.

The impact of tourism on traditional arts around the world has been the subject of an ample body of literature, and the tourist impact on flamenco has been complex and in some ways contradictory (see, e.g., Calado Olivo 2007; López López 2015; Junta de Andalucía 2004; Aoyama 2009). The familiar negative perspectives on the tourist impact parallel those relating to other world musics—in particular, the notions that many tourists come with naïve ideas about flamenco and Gypsies; that performers deform the art in catering to the exoticizing tourist gaze (especially in favoring dance over serious cante); that those who perform for tourists tend to be second-rate artists; and that tourists deaden the atmosphere at events through failing to know how to provide jaleos and timely applause. (These criticisms can be seen as part of a much more general hostility to tourism in places like Barcelona, where entire neighborhoods have been gentrified and transformed to the detriment of local residents.)

However, a number of rejoinders could be offered to the criticisms of the tourist impact on flamenco. The most obvious point is that tourists financially sustain flamenco as an art form. Today, as since the 1960s, hundreds of artists earn their living largely through tourist revenues, as tablao performers, teachers, and the like. As for the idea that flamencos cheapen their art in proffering "staged authenticity" to the exoticizing tourist gaze, the case of the Granada zambra may be illustrative. The zambras, as performed by the Gitanos of Sacromonte, enjoyed a certain heyday in the 1950s and early 1960s, when they were performed both for tourists and for each other by Gitano cave dwellers who, though not wealthy, enjoyed the benefits of a cohesive community. The shows tended to be of indifferent quality, with much floor sprawling and other theatrics. However, Curro Albaicín, a veteran savant of Granada flamenco and local Gitano life, recalled that epoch fondly, including the interest of tourists:

> It was a neighborhood where 6,000 people lived, who all learnt flamenco, forging, basket making . . . but they dedicated themselves to flamenco. . . . It was beautiful because it was our home and all the tourists that came up the hill stayed to see how we lived. (qtd. in Machin-Autenrieth 2016b, 169)

After the 1963 floods and the subsequent dissipation of the community, the zambra tradition itself largely died out, along with much of the community's social life, except in the tablao-style shows that continue to be presented to tourists in some of the renovated caves. As with other traditions elsewhere, tourism has sustained the preservation—as folkloric spectacle—of an art form that otherwise might be endangered. As López López (2015, 542) and others have noted, tourist interest in flamenco and the conception of Sacromonte Gitanos as quintessentially "authentic" creates a conceptual house of mirrors, in which Gitanos themselves creatively appropriate and rearticulate the exotic image others have of them.

As for the notion that performers at tourist-oriented tablaos are "second rank," many of them—such as the regulars at Seville's Casa de la Memoría—are first rank, and given the extraordinary abundance of talent in Spain, even "second-rankers" may be excellent; in my experience it is unusual to encounter genuinely substandard performers in tablaos. Meanwhile, from the performers' perspective, many tablaos paid reasonably well in the pre-COVID era, though some have exploited artists by contracting them as "waiters" in order to avoid paying benefits. Flamenco performers, like many musicians, have traditionally lacked solidarity and representation, though a new organization, the Unión Flamenca, represents an attempt to bring artists out of the perpetually vulnerable "informal sector."

Learning Flamenco

In the modern period, as before, people have learned flamenco, in its components of cante, toque, and baile, in both informal and formally structured manners, though with a marked increase in the latter. It is generally acknowledged that the ideal way to learn is to be born into a flamenco family where young and old perform flamenco at regular domestic fiestas. Despite flamenco's sophistication, it remains an art that can be learned and mastered informally, almost by osmosis, without formal, structured pedagogy if the family ambience is rich and supportive. On YouTube and other venues, one may find videos of Gitano children singing and dancing with great performativity and flair, to the enthusiastic approbation of elders. Such youths may well be encouraged to pursue the art more assiduously; from performing at informal family festivities, they might move on to various sorts of stage events, and by their teenage years they might be at a professional level, ready for tablao work.

For those so unfortunate as not to be raised in flamenco families, other means of learning do exist, especially for guitar and dance. Cante is the idiom that is least conducive to structured learning, and today as in the past, most cantaores learn informally—through immersion and experience, imitating elders and recordings, and, through performing, acquiring the necessary flair. Miguel Poveda represents one of many examples of a fine singer who did not come from a flamenco milieu. His parents (Andalusian migrants to Catalonia) were not especially musical, and he took no particular interest in flamenco and had little exposure to it until his teenage years. At that point, however, he cultivated an interest, listened and practiced assiduously, and, gifted with a fine voice and abundant talent, soon progressed from singing in peñas, to competitions, and eventually to his current, well-deserved status as a star.

In recent decades it has become increasingly possible for students to study cante in more formal manners. Several singers offer private classes, including online. Their pedagogical methods may vary, as there is no single obvious approach to teaching cante. Singers themselves, of course, may or may not be self-conscious and analytical—as opposed to merely intuitive—about their technique. For example, while a naïve listener might hear some singing of Chocolate as an unmediated expression of pain or passion, that cantaor in fact gave students very specific instructions about such matters as where in a line to take breaths.[4] Often the students in cante classes are dancers (especially women) who desire a more intimate understanding of the cante they are dancing to and who might aspire to sing an item or two in their tablao performances. Only a very few institutions offer cante instruction. Aside from the Córdoba Conservatory, perhaps the most prominent and successful of these is the aforementioned Cristina Heeren institution, where cante classes are structured to cover both repertoire as well as "voice therapy," which includes proper breathing and voice production techniques as well as practicing scales and ornaments in order to develop melismatic agility. Teachers have included top-rank vocalists such as Naranjito de Triana, José de la Tomasa, and Rocío Márquez, herself a Gitana and former student who is also an author of a doctoral dissertation on flamenco voice production. While many students may be beginners or amateurs, a few have been relatively experienced singers seeking to polish their technique and expand their repertoire. Some such students, including Laura Vital, Argentina, Gema Jiménez, and Jeromo Segura, have gone on to enjoy successful careers (Zatania 2019). Recognizing the particular lack of singers outside Spain (where dancers and guitarists may be plentiful), the fundación has offered grants to aspiring vocalists living abroad. One worthy recipient of such assistance was Alfonso Cid (a teacher of mine), who was singing professionally in New York City and spent a productive summer at the fundación. There he learned voice production techniques that enabled him to overcome the polyps he had developed, while expanding his repertoire and getting close, detailed guidance on various estilos. In his own cante classes, he incorporates and uses these methods, guiding students in practicing melismas, placing breaths properly, and other nuances.

Aside from technique, repertoire is another element that can be taught and learned. Naturally, some singers make more of an effort than others to master a wide repertoire. Further, some singers easily learn new material (such as cuplés composed by a producer), while others have difficulty mastering anything beyond the cantes they have grown up singing. Also perhaps obvious, though worth mentioning, is that not all Gitanos come from flamenco families, and many aspiring Gitano performers take formal classes in dance, cante, or guitar.

Flamenco guitar is more conducive to structured pedagogy than is cante, though at present, as in the past, many guitarists raised in flamenco families have learned their art informally, just as many dancers and singers have done. Unlike a classical (or even jazz) musician, the flamenco guitar student need not be able to read music. Ideally, perhaps, one is raised in a family where flamenco is frequently performed at informal reunions. A guitar is lying about the house, an elder sibling shows the youth (usually a boy) basic techniques, and after five or so years of casual playing—which might or might not include self-conscious "practicing"—the lad is competent at rasgueo, alzapúa, and basic arpeggio and perhaps quite adept at accompanying his relatives. If he develops a serious interest, he might practice more assiduously, especially to cultivate picado technique, which requires some genuine "woodshedding." He might then find himself asked to accompany family members and local singers at baptisms, weddings, parties, and other events, gaining invaluable experience in accompanying a wide range of vocalists. The next step is to be engaged at a peña, and then a tablao, which are the ideal training grounds for professional performers.

For those not born into flamenco families—or whose flamenco relatives don't bother to teach them (as is often the case)—guitar instruction may still occur from early ages. Many youths—again, especially boys—take private guitar lessons, and in Andalusia, Madrid, Barcelona, and elsewhere there is no shortage of adequate teachers. The best of these realize the importance of learning to accompany cante and baile and try to provide opportunities for students to do so. Flamenco guitar instruction is also increasingly offered in the curricula of public schools, and also conservatories, which have traditionally concentrated almost exclusively on art music. However, the status of flamenco in these institutions has been in some ways problematic, especially since flamenco guitar—especially in its improvisatory aspects—does not lend itself to formal, institutionalized pedagogy the way that classical music or even jazz do. Attempts to standardize pedagogy may stress learning to read tablature or staff notation, which otherwise is a merely secondary skill in this fundamentally oral art form. The insistence on formal teaching "credentials" may enable even a math or phys-ed teacher to double as a guitar instructor while barring virtuoso guitarists who lack institutional degrees in education.[5] Nevertheless, the amount and quality of flamenco guitar instruction in higher education institutions are steadily increasing.

Novice guitar students may work on exercises in rasgueo, arpeggio, and picado along with basic falsetas, such as those of Maestro Patiño in soleares.

Many students have taken some lessons in classical music, where they learn to read staff notation and tablature, which are far better suited to guitar in showing fingerings. (For example, an E above middle C, shown in staff notation, could be played on either of four different strings on the guitar.) Many amateur guitarists, both in Spain and abroad, reach an intermediate level at which they no longer need lessons and can learn on their own, primarily by mastering falsetas of prominent masters. Those who are able to read staff or tablature notation do this by listening to a recording or watching a video of the falseta and studying a published transcription of it in order to ensure proper execution of it in all its details. Established guitarists naturally perform their own varied renditions of extant falsetas, but students are generally encouraged to learn the models properly rather than approximating them and "fudging" the difficult parts. (Guitarists like Paco de Lucía have voiced their annoyance at such poor renditions of their creations.) Amateur notations of falsetas circulate informally, but professional published notations of the music of top guitarists—especially Paco de Lucía—are also widely available. These may vary in quality and accuracy, with those of Alain Faucher and Claude Worms being among the most widely respected (see Hoces Ortega 2012).

The advent of the internet has greatly expanded the ability of guitarists to learn by imitation. Fee-based pedagogical materials abound, such as the Swiss-produced video series *Encuentro*, which combine notations with detailed clips of masters playing falsetas. (Most students find the videos more useful than the notations.) Meanwhile, aficionados can of course study and imitate videos of live performances as best they can, slowing down passages and trying to see the guitarists' fingerings. Still persistent, however, is the problem of students who learn falsetas but have no experience accompanying cante, which is more important and basic to the art than soloing. Some artists, such as cantaor David Pino, offer online courses in accompanying cante (see Calahorra Arjona 2018).

Aside from learning to perform flamenco, the modern era—and especially the internet—has provided unprecedented scope for learning *about* flamenco. As mentioned elsewhere in this volume, resources include the veritable mountain of books on flamenco, which continue to be generated by publishers such as Almuzara, as well as online magazines and blogs. Such abundant resources partially compensate for the oft-noted decline in informal flamenco parties and gatherings, which as traditional training grounds for artists have now been largely replaced by isolated learning enriched by internet sites.

Recordings

Recordings, as mentioned earlier, have been a significant part of the flamenco scene since the years around 1900. From 1896, cylinder recordings of flamenco were being marketed in Spain alongside other such genres as *pasodobles*, zarzuela songs, and "Gypsy tales" (*cuentos gitanos*). Many of these were unique cylinders rather than reproducible discs, recorded by a singer facing four or five recording devices. Chacón and El Mochuelo are each said to have recorded tens of thousands of such items.[6] By 1901, single-sided reproducible wax discs were being recorded, and two-sided discs became standard from 1910 as marketed by foreign companies such as HMV, Zonophone, Odeon, and Pathé. Most leading singers recorded, providing models for many aspiring artists and, a century later, source material for flamenco historians. The market for recording increased in the 1920s, especially with improved technology introduced by Polydor and other companies. A few top artists, such as Pepe Marchena, Manolo Caracol, and Chacón before them, earned well from recordings, though most performers—paid flat fees rather than royalties—did not and may have regarded recording sessions essentially as routine "gigs" rather than momentous opportunities. While most flamenco did not evolve (or devolve) into a commercial popular music per se (i.e., with a style conditioned for mass marketing), there was a commercially driven preference for lighter cantes such as the fandangos and ida y vuelta songs of Marchena; further, in the 1940s some artists, such as Caracol and Lola Flores, popularized their idiosyncratic forms of orchestrated pop flamenco songs. Despite such controversial tendencies, the spread of recordings, as well as a certain number of radio programs, stimulated many performers to expand their repertoires in order to avoid conspicuous repetition. The advent of microgroove technology and LP format in the 1950s precipitated the production of landmark anthologies—starting with that of Perico el del Lunar in 1954—and coincided with a dramatic revitalization and legitimization of flamenco, as discussed earlier. By the late 1960s, one can speak of an essentially modern period of flamenco recording, with individual artists producing moderately profitable albums in collaboration with major record companies and a few independent labels. In the 1970s, for instance, Camarón de la Isla was recording an average of one album per year, with typical sales of around fifty thousand copies. In the early 1980s, cassettes and then CDs largely replaced vinyl records without significantly disrupting the industry, a certain amount of piracy notwithstanding. Despite some irregularities and abuses, flamenco was assimilated into the modern copyright system, with, for example, its distinctions between traditional public-domain materials and original "protectable" compositions involving publishers' royalties and permissions.[7]

The genuine crisis for the recording industry, impacting flamenco along with much music worldwide, came from around 2000 with the advent of "Web 2.0," neatly bookending the twentieth century as the bygone era of commercially profitable physical recordings. The basic contour of this development is familiar, with p2p file sharing and social media enabling massive free access to recorded music, precipitating a dramatic contraction in the music industry and, for many musicians, a return to an early industrial situation in which livelihoods can only be made from live performance, with recordings serving primarily for promotion rather than direct earnings. Flamenco as an art form has never been dependent for existence and vitality on recordings and the commercial music industry, but the latter did constitute a significant dimension of flamenco culture in ways that have now eclipsed or at least changed significantly. Sales of physical CDs are a tiny fraction of what they might have been in the 1990s. An artist might sell CDs after a stage show, and if a thousand are sold in a series of such concerts, it can be considered a "success" for a small independent producer such as Chemi Lopez's La Droguería Music (Ybarra Ramírez 2021). Meanwhile, as is well known, artist revenues from Spotify and Pandora are negligible. The exceptions are the handful of top stars whose recordings (whether albums or singles) for Sony, Universal, or Warner may do well, such as José Mercé's *Aire* (2000) and *Lío* (2002), both of which sold over one hundred thousand copies.

One obvious development is that many artists who might have aspired to produce a commercial album no longer endeavor to do so. Part of the reason is, of course, that they can promote themselves to some extent through social media, whether YouTube, Facebook, MySpace, or personal websites. Perhaps surprisingly, however, most prominent or aspiring artists do seek to produce albums (whether physical or merely digital), even if these are unlikely to generate profits and may not even recoup production costs. Many performers, aside from the established stars, are obliged to finance their own albums, whether they work through well-known labels or indies like La Droguería. Some artists acquire subsidies from various sources; Antonia Contreras funded an album through a prize awarded her at the Festival del Cante de las Minas,[8] and Mayte Martín raised funds for her album *Tempo Rubato* via crowdfunding. One advantage, of course, of financing and producing your own album, as Martín attested, is that one is free to do as one likes, without any commercial pressure from the label to record pop rumbas and cover versions. A cantaor who wishes to avoid such pressure and sing por derecho cante may also work with a small label like La Droguería that specializes in that idiom, although such labels cannot promote a recording the way a major label can. A "record label," in fact, can nowadays be such a minimal entity that an artist can found one himself, as El Cabrero did (with "Atípicos and Utópicos"[9]). While professional studio time continues to be expensive, new technologies have lowered production costs; hence, for example, Diego el Cigala recorded his album *Picasso en mis ojos* at his home, achieving professional sound quality with his own multitrack equipment.[10] A guitarist in Barcelona, corresponding via email, can have a bass player in Cádiz add a track digitally. (One might think that live albums would be similarly easy to record, but producers insist that they are logistically difficult.[11])

In general, one can speak of two distinct approaches to recording flamenco, constituting antipodes of a continuum. At one end would be a recording of traditional or neo-traditional cante—that is, the established repertoire of palos and estilos and the basic guitar-and-voice format. This can require minimal time and expense and no rehearsal at all: a singer, guitarist, and a few palmeros show up at the studio, do a few takes—or perhaps only a single take—of each item, and an album can be produced in a day or two. In a slightly more elaborate approach, the singer can include some cuplés—that is, original, precomposed songs, usually in tangos or bulerías and usually acquired from some composer. To make the tangos or rumba more marketable, the song can include a catchy "lolailo" refrain sung by two women in parallel thirds. A commercial record company may pressure a cantaor to include at least one such item on an album, bringing it closer to commercial popular music rather than por derecho flamenco. The opposite end of the stylistic continuum is reached when such precomposed songs are enhanced with elaborate arrangements involving ensemble instrumentation (such as bass, drums, violins, flute, or even a full orchestra). This approach is markedly distinct from the por derecho recording in that the recording is not merely a facsimile or exemplar of a live guitar-and-voice performance of traditional cante but rather is a unique and original production, an artistic oeuvre in its own right. Such productions can involve considerably more expense and time and indeed can take months to complete. However, those undertaking such a production may view it as an opportunity to create a singular document in which they explore styles and sonorities distinct from those of the standard live performance.

Thus, these different sorts of recordings involve different relations to live performance. While the basic singer-plus-guitarist format presents no challenges, if a cantaor performs original cuplés that he or she has recorded, then a guitarist accompanying on stage does need to know the proper accompaniment to these items, though learning them may not be difficult. Indeed, a singer may regard producing such an album as an occasion to work up or showcase some new material, including both original cuplés as well as new letras for traditional estilos. However, in the case of more elaborate recordings, the more intrinsic the ensemble arrangements are to a song, the more their live performance will require such an ensemble. In peñas and summer festivals, elaborate accompanying ensembles are generally not seen and might be genuinely unwelcome for the fans of por derecho cante who relish the spontaneous interaction between singer and guitarist. Hence, not all singers want to make a recording that cannot be easily taken to the stage, and not all flamenco fans enjoy such productions, which they may see as frippery and "*musiquita*." Accordingly, it is more in the context of single-artist stage shows that a singer will perform with an ensemble and attempt to reproduce the commercial recording, ideally for an audience that knows what to expect.

The Internet

The advent of the internet, especially its expansion in the "Web 2.0" era, has had dramatic effects on flamenco culture, as on other performing arts worldwide. The initial "Web 1.0" period—with its email and static websites—dated from the years around 1990; the new technologies facilitated communication and marketing and spawned such forums as the 1990s Temple University Listserv, where English-speaking flamenco fans discussed the art form. The true digital revolution took place in the years around 2000 with the advent of social networking and video sharing sites, all of which allowed an unprecedented degree of user-generated content, ease of use, and participation. Especially important among social media has been Facebook, which enables the formation of interactive virtual communities of flamenco fans, scholars, and quite a few prominent performers who choose to participate. Also significant are the several online magazines devoted to flamenco, which feature regular news clips, reviews, interviews, and other miscellany.[12] Supplementing these, and illustrating the prodigious connoisseurship surrounding flamenco, are personal websites and blogs, variously authored by veteran journalists and flamencologists such as Andres Raya Saro, Manuel Bohórquez, and Faustino Núñez. The latter's site, flamencopolis.com presents a cornucopia of information, with audio clips, on cantes and artists. Other sites dig up the scattered nineteenth- and early twentieth-century newspaper mentions of flamenco that flamencologists have so diligently pored over, many of which are now conveniently digitized and easily searchable.

Journalistic reviews of flamenco performances have existed since the early decades of the genre, and the emergence of online magazines such as expoflamenco.com has expanded their number and readership. A look at a typical review, though perhaps digressive, may afford some sense of the connoisseurship surrounding flamenco. Presented here are excerpts from a recent review in an online journal of a concert by a popular cantaora;[13] it follows a fairly standard format in relating the items presented and voicing the reviewer's assessment. The review happens to be scathing but is chosen here mostly because it typifies the sort of aesthetic discourse that critics engage in; it also touches on several points made elsewhere in this volume.

> She spent the whole evening softly toying with the same hackneyed melismas and falsettos, horsing around with jazz-like turns supported by the regiment accompanying her. . . .

She opened with the caña and the polo of Tobalo. Then she sang fandangos of Granada, Lucena, and of Frasquito Hierbabuena [Yerbabuena]. She continued *por tangos* . . . and with two letras *por seguiriya*, the sevillanas "A Lola," "Una espina clavá" [a popular Mexican song] as a zambra, and ended with "La noche de mi amor" [originally a Latin American bolero] and Carlos Gardel's "Volver" *por bulerías*.

She offered a cold assortment of *ojana* [Gitano slang: self-promoting BS], singing without taking any risks, and planting canned, plastic *quejíos* [plaintive vocal breaks]. . . .

The best moments were the solo *por bulería* by one of the guitarists, an *a capella* fandango sung by a member of her group, and a zambra of hers, which is a precious composition when sung at least half-presentably. . . .

However, the seguiriya was one of the worst I've heard lately. Fleeting and sparse in rendering, it was just one letra and then the *remate* of Curro Durse done in a sing-songy manner [*algo acancionado*]. It was ridiculous to see her clenching her fists in a fake, theatrical display of supposedly tragic singing.

She walked off waving her shawl about like a bullfighter's cape [*se fué toreando con el mantón*]—this being the encore demanded by the applause—and without introducing the other musicians, singers, and *palmeros*. . . . If I have to suffer through another performance of hers, I will have to ask her myself who her accompanists are.

A few pertinent observations can be made about this review. It describes a stage concert that was somewhat typical in its mixture of traditional cante, popular songs set to bulerías (and recorded in earlier albums of hers), and a few "zambras"—implying not Granada tangos but medium-tempo Latin-flavored songs à la Manolo Caracol. Variety was further provided by a guitar solo and by another singer's item, which happened to be an a capella fandango—illustrating that fandangos can be sung without guitar, even though, as I have argued earlier, the fandango's chordal structure may tend to be an intrinsic rather than decorative feature. Meanwhile, the reviewer regarded her impassioned gestures and vocal breaks as artificial and criticized her "song-like" (*acancionado*) rendering of a siguiriya estilo, presumably implying a mechanical singing deficient in the sort of free-rhythmic spontaneity that distinguishes a flamenco estilo from a precomposed "song" (canción). He also faulted her for singing merely a single letra and a *remate* in siguiriyas, when a proper tanda of that cante should contain two or three letras.

Video-sharing sites have been dominated by YouTube, whose impact has been prodigious. The range of material available on YouTube itself comprises a vast diversity of content types. An initial category consists of amateur uploads of commercial audio recordings, dating from early twentieth-century cylinder recordings of Chacón and Escacena up to the present. Such uploads might constitute around a quarter of the entire repertoire of commercially recorded flamenco. They constitute a gold mine, especially for collectors of recordings, including foreign enthusiasts who, in the last century, might return from trips to Spain with suitcases full of LPs. Flamencologist Brook Zern was one such collector, whose archive of hundreds of LPs, filling a small room, has since been digitized and can now be accommodated on a thimble-size USB drive. Also posted on YouTube is the entire *Rito y geografía* series of a hundred documentaries; formerly inaccessible, these are belatedly available to all. Many of them have English subtitles, and some have been colorized.

A second category of uploads consists of videos of modern live performances. These range from professionally produced, officially sanctioned videos of stage performances to informal smartphone clips of all manner of events. These latter could include dance classes, intimate peña acts, recycled footage of pre–digital era performances, snippets of tablao shows, private Gitano fiestas, rumbas and tangos at Iglesia de Filadelfia services, and all sorts of informal song and dance sessions.

The ramifications of the existence of such uploads are several and diverse. Most obvious is the sheer bounty that such videos offer to lovers of the art, who, whether based in Osaka or Oklahoma, can spend endless hours viewing an extraordinary range of artists, past and present. At the same time, while the presence of mass-mediated music is sometimes regarded as undermining live performance traditions, there is no evidence that this process has occurred in flamenco. Audiences still relish the spontaneity of live performances and the electrifying atmosphere that can be collectively produced by the artists and an appreciative, responsive audience. The primary exception is the case of sevillanas, since whether in dance classes or casetas at the Feria de Sevilla, recordings often replace live performers.

Meanwhile, online flamenco classes—whether in guitar, cante, or dance—have increased dramatically since around 2020. It is of course coincidental that Zoom technology was developed at the same time that the COVID pandemic struck, but the two developments both contributed to the spread of online pedagogy. A typical case is that of the cante classes taught in New York City by Alfonso Cid; until 2020 these consisted of weekly in-person sessions with about six or seven students (including this author). With the onset of COVID, in-person meetings were canceled, and Cid developed a successful format for teaching via Zoom. Over the next months, a few of the local students dropped out of these online sessions, but through word of mouth many other students were inspired to join; most are located in remote parts of the country, and one is in Japan.

Flamenco as a Global Phenomenon

Flamenco, since its very inception, has enjoyed international popularity, which soon came to comprise not only its attraction to visiting tourists but also the performance of flamenco outside Spain. Since the 1950s and 1960s, flamenco has become a genuinely transnational idiom, extensively appreciated and cultivated in greater Europe, the Americas, Japan, and elsewhere. The global presence of flamenco constitutes a vast and complex subject meriting far more expansive treatment than can be provided in this section, which makes no attempt to present a thorough survey. Further, international flamenco tends to be dominated by dance, which is not the focus of this volume. Hence, the following pages primarily present some general perspectives and observations with an emphasis on musical aspects; the presence of flamenco in New York is then outlined as a representative—and singularly important—case study.

Just as flamenco music and dance have an extended prehistory, so does the genre's global dimension encompass a prehistorical phase, primarily in the form of the popularity of Spanish dance in greater Europe. Spanish court dancing in the Bourbon period had enjoyed some prestige in France and elsewhere, but it was in the 1830s when the cachucha, fandango, and similar items (later labeled "escuela bolera") became hits on European stages as interpreted by eclectic Austrian ballerina Fanny Elssler (1810–1884). Following in her path was the Irish-born, faux-Spaniard "Lola Montez" (Eliza Gilbert, 1821–1861) and, in a different sense, the contemporary ballet choreographers who incorporated elements of Spanish dancing into their theatrical productions (Ivanova 1970, 145–49). In the 1920s, La Argentina (Antonia Mercé, 1890–1936) successfully adapted bolero and *ballet español* to the format of concert dances, with music of Albéniz, Falla, Granados, and Turina; she toured widely with her "Gran Compañia" in Europe and the Americas, basing herself in New York from 1916 until her death.

From the early 1930s, genuine flamenco dance started being presented to large audiences in the United States and elsewhere, especially by Vicente Escudero (1892–1980) and La Argentinita (Encarnación López, 1898–1945), as promoted by impresario Sol Hurok. Although Argentinita's singing was more akin to avian chirping than cante jondo, her flamenco dancing was certainly the real thing, and with guitar accompaniment by Manolo de Huelva and others, she, Escudero, and a few other energetic Spaniards were able to bring unadulterated flamenco (alongside other stage confections) to international audiences. With the outbreak of the Spanish Civil War in 1936, the number of expatriate performers increased dramatically, whether these comprised actual political refugees or, more often, artists who fled the chaos and violence and found that they could enjoy remunerative careers abroad. In the United States, such performers included guitarists Luis Maravilla and Vicente Gómez, but by far the most influential and celebrated was extraordinary dancer (and fine singer) Carmen Amaya (1913–1963), whose troupe, touring North and South America from 1936, featured guitarist and her sometime partner Sabicas.

One can regard the latter 1930s as the time when a fundamentally "modern" international flamenco scene was established, comprising substantial audiences (whether naïve or sophisticated) and a network of touring performers and other artists, whether Spanish or foreign, residing outside Spain. Particularly striking is its popularity in Japan, which hosts a few hundred dance schools, provoking, in some circles, speculation as to whether flamenco aesthetics has some special resonance with the Japanese national character (whatever that might be) (see Aoyama 2007, 107–108).

The international flamenco scene, like most global music scenes, does not merely replicate its Spanish progenitor but has certain distinctive characteristics of its own. One obvious feature is the foregrounding of dance and, secondarily, guitar, neither of which, unlike cante, presents any language barrier. Cante—the most important element of flamenco in Spanish festivals and peñas—thus takes third place in this inverted hierarchy. A related feature is the need to appeal to mixed audiences, which, though certainly including some knowledgeable connoisseurs, may be dominated by people who, though enthusiastic, are not merely ignorant but also inspired by naïve and exoticizing ideas about flamenco as some direct expression of "Gypsy passion" and pathos. Such Romantic fantasies, of course, animated many flamenco audiences from the café cantante period on, but the international scene expands and intensifies this syndrome by attracting audiences who do not even know Spanish. An opulent concert hall in London or Los Angeles is certainly farther removed from the proverbial Gypsy hearth than was a café cantante in Seville, but promoters have often sought to emphasize such affective linkage. Even Carmen Amaya endorsed the evidently mythical notion that she was born in a Gypsy cave in Granada. (The apparent truth—that she was born under a wagon in a Gitano encampment near Barcelona—is hardly less Romantic).

While globalization often entails forms of cultural homogenization and deterritorialization, it also inspires a reactive search for various forms or expressions of traditional place-based identity, offsetting the shallow uniformity of McDonald's and shopping malls; capitalism itself, as has often been noted, operates and flourishes through difference as well as massification. Accordingly, flamenco's grounding in Andalusian and especially Gitano community life has in many ways been celebrated rather than erased in the process of globalization (see, e.g., Aoyama 2007).

It may be useful in this sense to compare the international flamenco audience with those of other transnational genres. There are genres, such as Chinese opera, that may be performed outside their ancestral homeland but whose audience is limited to their specific diasporic communities, as in San Francisco or New York. By contrast, such genres as Western art music—or for that matter, hip-hop—have become transnational entities whose popularity and cultivation do not depend on the presence of some diasporic population. Flamenco invites some comparison with jazz in being recognized as originally associated with a specific ethnic/racial group; however, distinctions would include the way jazz has been hybridized in various ways—such as Latin jazz and Euro-jazz (divested of such features as swing rhythm and blues elements)—while flamenco, despite the abundance of various fusions, has not really generated specific regional or ethnic variants.

International flamenco audiences, it should be noted, are heterogeneous rather than consisting solely of ignoramuses—or narrow-minded purists—and it may be misleading to make sweeping generalizations about, for instance, the "American flamencophile" (as does Heffner Hayes 2009, 16–17). The diversity of audiences is reflected in the typical sorts of performance venues. At the apex—in commercial and demographic terms—are the large concert halls, which tend to feature visiting Spanish stars, especially as presenting large-format dance extravaganzas and thematic "espectáculos." Below these is the circuit of smaller venues, especially supper clubs that present tablao-type acts. Performers at these may tend to be locally based artists (whether Spanish or not), and audiences are more likely to include knowledgeable connoisseurs, including dance and guitar students and miscellaneous cognoscenti. These venues come and go over the years, and individual cities have their ups and downs. Given the finite size of a flamenco audience in a given locale, the presence of a single lively venue—perhaps owned by an enthusiast—can make a significant difference. Such a venue is typically a performance club, but in the case of New York, especially in the 1960s through the 1980s, one such institution was Fazil's Dance Studio (formerly Jerry Leroy's studios), which hosted dozens of dance classes for flamenco and other genres and constituted a convivial meeting place for flamenco fans, teachers, and students. If such a focal venue closes for one reason or another, the vitality of the scene in the whole area may suffer dramatically.

The typical demographic makeup of an area's flamenco base can roughly correspond to the nature of the venues. Often there are a few Spanish performers, teachers, and enthusiasts forming a nucleus for the flamenco community. However, the scene is generally not dependent on a community of Spaniards per se. Few cities outside Iberia host genuinely large Spanish expatriate communities, and such diasporic Spaniards as exist may be neither flamenco fans nor Andalusian. More often, the core flamenco community, both of performers and fans, consists of local enthusiasts, and especially dancers. It needs scarcely be mentioned that many non-Spaniards, whether in Europe, the Americas, or Japan, have become expert dancers and guitarists, quite capable of both teaching and performing at professional levels, and several have performed (especially as tablao dancers) in Spain itself. (Skilled singers remain woefully rare and, even if present, are generally relegated to singing for dance.)

These and other general observations can be seen to be operant in the North American cities that have lively flamenco scenes. A distinctive feature of these cities—in contrast to Europe or Japan—is the substantial presence of Latin Americans (especially of Caribbean background on the East Coast, Mexican and Central Americans in the West and Southwest, and sprinklings of South Americans in both). The Latin presence has been felicitous in various ways. Many of the American performers and teachers are Hispanics, whose fluency in Spanish has facilitated their ability to study in Spain. The Latin element has also generated the flourishing of venues offering a mixed fare of Latin American and flamenco shows, aimed especially at non-Latin general audiences. Such venues were especially prominent in the 1940s through the 1960s in the form of cabarets in New York and elsewhere, which might present an Argentine tango show one night, a Mexican dance troupe the next, and a flamenco group the following night. In the decades before rock and disco, such shows could attract substantial audiences of both "gringos" and miscellaneous Hispanics. If such cabaret establishments are no longer common, Latinos still help fill out both dance classes and the audiences at venues that do offer flamenco.

In other respects the various centers for flamenco in the United States have had somewhat distinctive characters, especially in their formative periods. The flamenco scene in San Francisco (as explored by Dumas 2012) emerged from the late 1950s around a core of bohemian Beat generation enthusiasts based in the North Beach district and its arty club Las Cuevas behind the Old Spaghetti Factory. This community of countercultural cosmopolitans cultivated and enjoyed flamenco alongside American folk music, blues, Japanese Zen, and Native American traditions as embodying a non-capitalist, sublimely artistic ethos free of the taint of commercialism and conformity. Several San Franciscans spent extended periods at Donn Pohren's establishment in Morón, where they savored the friendly, relaxed, small-town ambience and, in the case of guitarist David Jones ("Serva") and several others, became skilled performers, establishing an affective link between the two locales. The San Francisco scene was then reinforced by the activities of a handful of Spaniards like dancer Rosa Montoya (the niece of Ramón Montoya).

For its part, the early flamenco scene in San Diego, like that of San Francisco, was nourished in part by bohemian enthusiasts, such as "beach bum" David Cheney, who, when not surfing, spent several years learning and professionally playing guitar in Sacromonte. Another key energetic individual was guitarist Paco Sevilla (William Stanley), who authored three engaging books on flamenco and from 1977 to 1992 produced and edited an informative bulletin called *Jaleo* (now available online and modeled after an earlier newsletter published by Estela Zatania). The San Diego scene differed from that of San Francisco and other American cities in having a greater presence of actual Andalusian Spaniards. In particular, a few American military personnel had married Spaniards while serving in the 1960s at the U.S. naval base at Rota (near Cádiz) and had subsequently relocated to San Diego, with its large naval facility. Some of these Andalusians were not only flamenco enthusiasts but also competent singers and dancers and could collaborate with local Americans in sponsoring regular flamenco fiestas and performances. (These Americans included John Moore, a skilled guitarist, knowledgeable flamencologist, and linguistics professor, and the source for this information regarding San Diego.)

Flamenco has been cultivated in a few other American cities, including Albuquerque, Miami, and Chicago, but the most active center has been New York City, even if the scene's vitality is in constant flux as venues and artists come and go.[14] As elsewhere outside Spain, public interest in flamenco has largely centered on dance. Appetite for Spanish dance had been stimulated by Fanny Elssler's 1840 visit, and she was followed by Lola Montez and actual flamenco dancers La Cuenca and Carmencita from around 1890; as mentioned earlier, La Argentinita based herself in the city from 1916.

In the 1930s the city's flamenco scene became genuinely dynamic, or at least as dynamic as the Depression might allow any entertainment scene to be. Dancers Vicente Escudero and La Argentinita had settled in the city at the start of the decade and were joined by various refugees from the Civil War, including guitarists Vicente Gómez, Luis Maravilla, and, a few years later, Carlos Montoya. Carmen Amaya and her troupe—a veritable "band of Gypsies" numbering around nineteen people, including Sabicas—had been visiting New York since the 1930s, and they based themselves there from around 1942. From that decade the scene thrived. Focal venues were the tablao club La Zambra, founded by Gómez, and the Liborio and Alameda Room nightclubs, along with various Broadway cabarets offering a mixed fare of Latin bands, flamenco groups, and miscellaneous Latin American stage shows, all attended—like the famous 1950s mambo clubs—by a mixed clientele of Hispanics and Anglo-Americans.

As elsewhere outside Spain, dance was the main attraction, but guitar—and to a lesser extent cante—could piggyback on dance's popularity to establish its own niche, especially in such venues as the "flamenco room" of the Chateau Madrid. Italian-born American dancer José Greco (1918–2000) brought many flamenco musicians, including the young Paco de Lucía in 1964, to the

United States to perform in his shows and both promoted and trained several talented American performers. Meanwhile, New York expatriates Sabicas, Mario Escudero, and especially Carlos Montoya enjoyed prodigiously successful careers as concert guitarists at a time when solo guitar recitals were rare in Spain. Sabicas and Montoya each also recorded dozens of LP records, with the former's *Flamenco Puro* (1959–1960) achieving a biblical status for aspiring guitarists back in Spain. Meanwhile, the city's modest Spanish community and substantial Latino population could enable Sabicas to live there for fifty years without needing or bothering to learn English.

By the 1970s and 1980s, the cabarets, with their extravagant stage shows, had largely closed up, and the flamenco performance scene shifted to a different set of formats. One such stratum would comprise large concert-hall shows featuring visiting artists from Spain; from 1996 the most prominent of these has been the "Flamenco Festival," an annual conglomeration of touring Spanish flamencos who perform at large venues every spring in New York and other East Coast cities. Below this stratum is the handful of clubs, restaurants, dance studios, and other sites that present occasional or regular flamenco shows featuring New York–based performers. These in turn are sustained by dance and (to a lesser extent) guitar students as well as mixed audiences of cosmopolitans, informed flamenco fans, and boisterous diners for whom the flamenco is some sort of festive background noise. The dance classes themselves constitute a substantial stratum. Many students in these classes are cosmopolitans who choose flamenco from the smorgasbord of other sorts of classes offered, such as samba, Afro-Cuban, jazz, modern, and African. For some students it is part of an exercise regimen (often done at home via Zoom) rather than a cultural experience (Aoyama 2007, 111).

As in other American cities, the flamenco performers themselves come from a somewhat standard set of diverse backgrounds. Thus, in New York at present, the resident flamencos include some expatriate Spaniards (singer-flautist Alfonso Cid, cantaor Ismael Fernández, guitarist Adrian Alvarado, and singer-guitarist Juan Pedro Jiménez Relinque), second-generation Spanish Americans (guitarist Pedro Cortes and jack-of-all-trades José Moreno), New York Latinos (dancers Xianix Barrera and Paloma Ríos), Anglo-Americans (several dancers), as well as guitarist Basilio Georges, who with his wife, Aurora Reyes, operates Flamenco Latino, offering classes and performances fusing Latin music and flamenco. These artists are fewer in number than would be found in a Spanish city, but the quality of their performances can be first-rate. Meanwhile, before the COVID era, the energetic Meira Goldberg organized successful flamencology conferences in collaboration with the City University of New York and the Fashion Institute of Technology.

8

Perspectives on Flamenco Culture

The Geography of Flamenco

Flamenco's sociogeographical dimension is complex and contradictory, as the genre is at once transnational in popularity and universal in aesthetic appeal while originating and to some extent still being rooted not only in certain Andalusian towns and cities but also in certain specific neighborhoods and even families therein. This geography, like so many other aspects of flamenco, can be controversial insofar as disparate locales vie for recognition and different conceptions of flamenco's rootedness or, alternately, universality conflict.

The degree and nature of regional heterogeneity in southern Spain have conditioned the genre's sociogeographic character. On the one hand, southern Spain does not have the kind of regional variety found, for example, in much of Italy, where stable communities have resided since the Bronze Age, and until recently residents of neighboring valleys might speak mutually unintelligible dialects. By contrast, after the Reconquest much of southern Spain was settled by migrants from Castille and other northern regions, and Castilian Spanish became the native tongue throughout the region, which was also politically unified. However, other factors—especially the poor transportation network—promoted regional differences and facilitated the cultivation of distinctive performance traditions in different towns and areas. Some of these local traditions contributed significantly to the development of flamenco and continue to exert influence.

It is common in Spanish discourse, for example, to refer to individuals by their place of birth; an article about Paco de Lucía, for instance, might avoid tedious repetition of his name by referring to him as *el algecireño* (the man from Algeciras), or someone from Huelva or Cádiz could be called *el onubense* or *el gaditano*, respectively. Such designations might suggest more than simple happenstance. For example, even in modern, mass media–saturated times, a singer from Huelva—say, Rocío Márquez—is very likely to be raised steeped in the local fandango versions and variants, which would be heard in various formal and informal contexts, from peñas to private parties. These genres absolutely do not flourish as community traditions in other regions, which may instead have their own local idioms. A singer from another region might cultivate an interest in such styles and learn to sing them, and flamenco audiences everywhere might enjoy hearing them, but the "onubense" singer may certainly have a special intimacy with them and be appreciated as such. Such distinctive traditions are especially applicable to a town like Jerez, whose Gitano population is documented as far back as 1438.

Regional differences have various dimensions, of course. Andalusians as a whole are stereotyped by some Spaniards as lazy, unlike the business-minded Catalans, but they are also celebrated as primary creators and exponents of what is by far Spain's most famous art form, which, as a tourist attraction, has made a vast contribution to the national economy. Meanwhile, the Andalusian Spanish accent is different from that of Castile, and slang in Madrid remains very distinct from that of Seville. Even within towns, neighborhoods have had distinctive performance traditions. Flamencologist Romualdo Molina (b. 1934) told me, "Even in my youth, in one barrio of Seville, people had a particular accent, a way of telling jokes, of dancing, and of singing fandango, while in another barrio, five hundred meters away, everything would be different." Another conspicuous example can be found in the Gitano communities of Santiago and San Miguel barrios in Jerez; residents of the former were traditionally seasonal farmworkers who spent several months a year in the countryside, where alongside non-Gitano workers they cultivated their own cante forms and styles that differed somewhat from those of their strictly urban cousins in San Miguel, many of whom were blacksmiths. Similar differences have existed between nearby towns; oft-noted are the distinct styles—especially as performed in private fiestas—of bulerías in Jerez and in nearby Lebrija, with the latter featuring a different palmas rhythm and the frequent use of *romance* passages as texts.

Andalusian towns have always prided themselves on their distinctive song traditions and local interpreters, as articulated in letras such as the following:

La rondeña malagueña nadie la sabe cantar
Sino los malagueñitos, que tienen sandunga y sal.

No one knows how to sing the rondeña malagueña
Except those from Málaga, who have grace and spice.

Such parochialism may be benign or may be disparaged as narrow-minded; Jerez flamencos are notorious for their dislike of singers from any other locale. Singers certainly take local preferences into account when performing; a cantaor invited to sing at the annual cante jondo festival in Mairena de Alcor would be ill advised to sing an item associated with Manolo Caracol, who was the contemporary rival of Antonio Mairena.

The differences between Santiago and San Miguel styles raise the question of whether, or to what extent, flamenco's evolution should be regarded as overwhelmingly urban or whether aspects of it have been substantially nourished by rural folk songs such as the Santiago Gitanos might have acquired in the countryside. If a rural work song, such as a three-line trilla in Phrygian mode, structurally resembles a crude form of soleá, does it represent an ancestor of the latter, a cousin deriving from a common source, or a trickle-down country derivative of soleares? If a farmer in Murcia is recorded in 1958 singing an enigmatic *malagueña de la madrugada*, does that song represent an archaic and seminal regional folk tradition, or did the singer acquire it, directly or indirectly, from a recording by some urban flamenco singer (Sánchez Garrido 2015, 122)?

Estela Zatania's *Flamencos de Gañanía* (roughly, Flamencos of the farmworkers hostel; 2007a) sheds much light on the music culture of the Gitanos of Jerez and Lebrija who spent much of the year working on nearby farms until the 1970s, when mechanization and other changes ended that lifestyle. Life was simple and harsh, with families working from dawn to dusk in the fields, with no schools or medical care, sleeping on straw mats in barracks devoid of any privacy, and subsisting on a diet consisting almost entirely of garbanzo beans. However, Zatania's elder informants recalled the life with great nostalgia and fondness for the camaraderie, the family and community solidarity, and, most importantly, the merry-making; literally every evening, often until the wee hours, they would sing and dance bulerías, tangos, fandangos, and cante jondo, as well as the odd popular song by Conchita Piquer. On at least a superficial level, the milieu was isolated, closed, and primitive; record players, radios, and guitars were unheard of, and there were no workers from other parts of Andalusia, not to mention broader Spain. At the same time, the workers—who were not rural folk but townspeople doing seasonal farmwork—constituted one antipode of a fluid and active sociomusical continuum connected to the juergas and stage shows of the cities and towns. Some of the workers were semiprofessional urban performers who, during slow periods, joined their extended families in the countryside; except for work songs such as trillas, the songs everyone sang in the hostels were the same they sang and heard in taverns in Jerez rather than representing some unique category of isolated rural folk song. However, neither in Santiago nor in the farms would one hear such genres as martinete, a cante of the blacksmiths of San Miguel barrio. "And then," an elder related, presumably of the 1970s, "things changed, new forms arose, people started earning more money, and nowadays children don't respect their parents and the cante isn't what it used to be" (qtd. in Zatania 2007a, 122). If Jerez nevertheless continues to host a lively flamenco scene grounded in festive informal reunions, the comparable vitality that existed in Triana—with frequent festivities in central courtyards (*corrales de vecinos*) of Gitano homes—dissipated considerably when, as mentioned earlier, residents were relocated to squalid housing projects in the 1960s.

The core cantes of flamenco, as well as the general style, can be said to have developed primarily in the Seville/Málaga/Cádiz "golden triangle" of Andalusia, spreading thence to Extremadura and the Levant and, by extension, to Madrid, then Barcelona, and then coming to be cultivated and enjoyed around the world. Needless to say, the story involves considerably more details than this generalization. One regional consideration involves specific contributions to the flamenco repertoire, which can occur in various geographically situated ways. Palos and estilos originating in specific locales may emerge as anonymous entities, such as the tangos of Granada and Extremadura or most of the fandango de Huelva melodies, associated with particular towns. In other cases, entities may be attributed to known creators, as with most of the soleá estilos. Geographical and personal attributions are used interchangeably in some instances, as with the soleás of Juan and Agustín Talega constituting "soleás de Alcalá." Needless to say, despite the mass media and performance contexts promoting pan-regionality, the popularity (or unpopularity) of various cantes continues to correlate with specific locales; hence, fandangos de Huelva are indeed popular in Huelva, and one would be unlikely to hear any free-rhythmic cante in an informal event in Utrera. Nevertheless, cantes associated with specific locales may be enriched by artists from elsewhere; thus, the structural ancestors of the malagueñas may be the verdiales of Málaga province, but the most important creators of the modern cante were Antonio Chacón, from Jerez, and Enrique el Mellizo, from Cádiz. Accordingly, some of the top flamenco guitarists have been non-Andalusian, including Ramón Montoya, Miguel Borrull (father and son), Sabicas, and Mario Escudero. Locales also go through ups and downs; after the violence of the civil war, Seville's early prominence was eclipsed for the time being by Cádiz, which was enriched by the smuggling trade from Gibraltar. For its part, Málaga declined in tandem with the cafés cantantes, only to rebound with the advent of tourism in the 1950s (Soler Díaz 2016, 63).

Since the mid-1900s some locales have earned renown through hosting events or institutions. Jerez's Centro Andaluz de Documentación de Flamenco (CADF), founded in 1959 (under a different name), is one important institution, hosting an archive and occasional events. In a different fashion, the southeastern town of La Unión has garnered special prominence as the site of one of the most important annual festivals, the Festival del Cante de las Minas.

Flamenco's variegated geographic spread was conditioned by the manner in which it came to be cultivated. As outlined earlier in this volume, in the mid-nineteenth century various forms of pre-flamenco music and dance were being performed, whether for tourists or locals, in different Andalusian sites. By the 1830s and 1840s, a few forms, such as the malagueña, though most actively cultivated in their home provinces, had become pan-regional, and even in the absence of published sheet music the guitar styles of El Murciano, of Granada, were taught and enjoyed in Seville and elsewhere. As flamenco matured it came to be performed in professional contexts—the cafés cantantes and private fiestas—and as domestic music and dance among primarily Gitano communities in several towns and cities. Some cities, such as Granada and Seville, attracted tourists who attended the cafés. Other towns, such as Utrera, Mairena, Alcalá, and Lebrija, were outside the tourist circuit but sustained a productive handful of core flamenco families performing for their own community, in taverns, and, professionally, for the señorito elite. The art was spread not only through the circuit of professional performers but also through Gitano livestock traders, who moved regularly around the region and transmitted their versions of flamenco in the fiestas with which they sealed transactions. Commercial records further spread the genre from the turn of the century.

As the art spread, individual locales made their particular contributions. That of Cádiz was animated by its regionally diverse population, such as the jota-loving Aragonese, and from the town's Carnival tradition and pervasive spirit of fun and festivity. It may be quaint and unscientific to characterize major tonality as "happy" and minor (and Phrygian) as "sad," but the Cádiz cantes would seem to bear out this characterization; the bulerías of Cádiz as well as the quintessentially "gaditano" alegrías and tanguillos are all predominantly in major tonality and of light and festive rather than pathetic character.

The primary contribution of Málaga province to traditional music was the abandolao-strummed verdiales, whose popularity extended well beyond the province to the east and the west, forming a structural basis for fandango variants of Granada and the Levant. Málaga native Juan Breva was the first to bring the verdiales-derived malagueña into the flamenco repertoire, although, as noted, by the 1830s that cante had already become a pan-regional, soloistic stage item.

The mining region is regarded as the crucible of the Levant cantes—tarantas, mineras, cartageneras, and so on—although lack of documentation makes it unclear whether their distinctive features derived from hoary local folk traditions, late nineteenth-century modifications of verdiales brought by migrant workers from the west, or flamenco-era innovations by Chacón and Montoya.

As mentioned, some of the same uncertainty pertains to the evolution of the granaína, though Granada—especially the Gitano communities of Sacromonte—is certainly the origin of a distinctive repertoire of estilos in tangos (see, e.g., Navarro García 1993). Granada is outside the triangle that was the cradle of cante jondo, and since the nineteenth century the predominance of tourists as patrons tended to promote an emphasis on dance and lively zambras rather than siguiriyas and soleá. Furthermore, most of the Gitano community of Sacromonte, like that of Triana, was dispersed to polígonos in the 1960s, and the Sacromonte tablao scene has had its ups and downs, though as of 2023 the busloads of tourists are keeping the tablao performers busy. Granada has also long hosted a dynamic tradition of guitarists, including the multigenerational Habichuela dynasty and Juan Maya, known as "Marote" (1936–2002), who, among other things, contributed a triplet rasgueo technique that is now standard among guitarists. For centuries, Granada has also been a center of guitar making and currently hosts over forty-five luthiers, who export top-quality guitars to buyers around the world (Ray 2014).

Flamencologists have commented on the similarity of the nature of the contributions in Granada and Extremadura, on the opposite end of the flamenco region (e.g., Lozano 2006). Extremadura—especially the Gitano community around the Plaza Alta (or Plaza de San Juan) in Badajóz—has contributed its own handful of distinctive tangos estilos, in a way that suggests the early pan-regional popularity of tangos during a period when the jondo forms of soleá and siguiriyas were not intensively performed outside the triangle. The Extremaduran jaleo, though perhaps evolving independently of bulerías, has evolved or devolved, according to some—into a variant of that cante, with its set of distinctive estilos. (Some Extremadurans would insist that their jaleo is distinct from bulerías.) Both the flamenco jaleo and tango of that region were significantly redefined by a single artist, Porrina de Badajoz, who combined traditional songs, flamenco standards, and his own creations in a unique "cocktail" (Lozano 2006, 69). The southern, more distinctively Andalusian part of Extremadura continues to host a lively flamenco scene, comprising peñas, fiestas (mostly in July and October), and concursos sponsored by towns and a fair amount of "street flamenco" in the form of groups of festive Gitanos hanging around Plaza Alta and singing bulerías, tangos, and rumbas.

In the modern period, subsequent to the coalescence of the pan-regional repertoire of cantes and estilos, individual locales are less important as historical crucibles than as performance sites with their particular characters and contours. Cities on the tourist circuit—especially Madrid, Seville, Málaga,

Granada, and Barcelona—have had especially active tablao scenes. Madrid's prominence as a flamenco center started as soon as the genre emerged; in 1880 the city hosted sixteen cafés cantantes, and by the 1890s it had fifty—far more than any Andalusian town (Llano 2017, 19; Blas Vega 1986, 57–59). Madrid has continued to attract top performers from all over Spain, including Extremadura, in various ways detaching them and their art from regional associations.

Barcelona has long constituted another important center for flamenco, in accordance with both its economic dynamism and the presence of tens of thousands of Andalusian migrants and their descendants. The region has sired several top performers, including Mayte Martín, Miguel Poveda, Duquende, Ginesa Ortega, and guitarists Juan Manuel Cañizares and Pedro Sierra. However, the growing movement for Catalonian political and cultural autonomy—and even independence—has problematized flamenco's status for some activists, who disagree as to whether the region should embrace its long-standing flamenco heritage or reject the art as a Castilian-language import from greater Spain.

Meanwhile, in various cities and towns, especially in the Gitano communities of the triangle, flamenco has continued to survive, although in an increasingly diminished capacity, as a living, community-based tradition performed at informal festivities and events such as weddings and baptisms. Jerez is celebrated as the most dynamic in this sense and the most representative of the earlier era when flamenco was firmly grounded in community performance, especially the large Gitano neighborhoods of Santiago and San Miguel. As veteran singer Tía Anica la Pirinaca said of those barrios, "It was very unusual to find a house where they didn't know how to sing or dance" (qtd. in Ortiz Nuevo 2012, 18). The ancient town—strategically located on the Camino Real (Royal Road) between Seville and Cádiz—is also known as a locale whose large Gitano communities are at once vital custodians of flamenco while also coexisting harmoniously with the non-Gitano population. At informal reunions and flamenco parties, Gitanos and others mix on easy and amicable terms. Most importantly, Jerez has produced an extraordinary number of top performers, many of whom continue to reside in the town when not on tour. Many of the artists hail from multigenerational dynasties of singers and guitarists. At the public level, the town hosts a few tablaos and peñas, some more intimate *tabanco* taverns attracting both tourists and Spaniards, various schools of dance and music, some high-profile festivals, and, in recent decades, flamenco institutions sponsored by the local government. Jerez musicians and connoisseurs are fiercely proud of their own flamenco artists. Hence, they have historically preferred local singers such as Terremoto and El Torta to Camarón, who was idolized everywhere else. Similarly, if guitarists throughout Spain have become indelibly influenced and inspired by Paco de Lucía, Jerez players pride themselves on their distinct style led by the Morao and Parrilla dynasties (see Gálvez Jiménez 2018). (Utrera, by contrast, has never had many guitarists, and at an informal fiesta one is particularly likely to hear cantes performed unaccompanied.) The Jerez "soniquete," or style, is also contrasted with the Madrid *escuela* (school) regarded as founded by Ramón Montoya.

The nearby towns of Lebrija, Utrera, and Morón have their own flamenco dynasties, such as the Peña/Pinini family of Lebrija and Utrera. While flamencos of these towns certainly socialize, party, and perform with one another, they also maintain their own local styles and repertoires. Indeed, considerable rivalry, albeit amicable, exists between towns like Lebrija and Jerez, such that at reunions and fiestas they might scrupulously avoid singing material associated with the other town, and Lebrija cantaores would ardently cultivate such things as their distinct bulerías repertoire (Chinoy 2022). Meanwhile, it may be common to hear of the Morón style or school of playing, consisting primarily of Diego del Gastor, his four nephews, and various students and imitators—especially the Americans and other foreigners who flocked to Pohren's ranch and lent the town a certain renown. However, among modern players, Dani de Morón's style, in its verbosity and studied technical virtuosity, is in spirit antithetical to that of Diego.

The extent to which a locale generates performers is, of course, a certain sort of index of its importance. Much data can be gleaned from a 2001 catalog of over a thousand flamenco artists by indefatigable researcher José Manuel Gamboa. Entabulations of these names and their hometowns by Yuko Aoyama (2009, 87–88) show Seville and Madrid each contributing about 15 percent of performers; many of the *madrileños* would, of course, be migrants from Andalusia and elsewhere. In third place is Jerez, whose engendering of almost 10 percent of artists is remarkable considering that the town's population is only .5 percent of Spain's. Andalusia as a whole hosted about 43 percent of the names, although Barcelona's contribution of 4 percent is noteworthy. Roughly a third of the performers are Gitanos, with members of that community thoroughly dominating artist communities in towns such as Lebrija, Granada, and Jerez. Gitanos constitute around 2 percent of Spain's population and 3–4 percent of that of Andalusia (about 250,000, or around 50,000 households).

Institutional developments can have their own geographical dimensions. In the 1960s to 1970s, as mentioned, many Andalusian towns started holding annual summer flamenco festivals, to some extent in a competitive as well as collaborative spirit. On a broader regional level, the regional government of Andalusia (Junta de Andalucía) has undertaken various projects to support the art (see Cruces Roldán 2003, ch. 3). The Junta foregrounded flamenco and the special importance of the region in its creation in a 2007 "Statute of Autonomy," and from 2004 it inaugurated various programs supporting flamenco, complementing a 2010 UNESCO inclusion of flamenco on the "Representative List of the Intangible Cultural Heritage of Humanity." As Matthew Machin-Autenreith discusses (2016a, chs. 3–4), such events, though progressive and benign in their way, provoked annoyance in some quarters, with some Gitano activists as well as Extremadurans feeling that implicitly attributing the art's creation to "Andalusians" was effectively marginalizing their own contributions. Exalting flamenco as an icon of Andalusian regional identity is also awkward in the sense that many, and perhaps even most, Andalusians are not interested in it, and some even resent being identified with it. However, the wording cohered with a sentiment in some circles that flamenco has historically been excessively identified with Gitanos rather than Andalusians and other Spaniards in general.

The statute also provoked controversy in some quarters in its declaration that the Andalusian government assumed "exclusive responsibility" (*competencia*) for regulating and promoting flamenco. This somewhat injudicious and ambiguous statement generated howls of protest from some individuals, while more sober voices pointed out that the polemic was based on an absurd and paranoid misinterpretation of the phrasing (e.g., Téllez 2007). Whether absurd or legitimate, the tempest in a teapot reflected a more fundamental tension between the conception of flamenco as a universal art form versus one that remains indelibly rooted in a particular community.

Purity versus Innovation: The Primordial and Perennial Debate

There may be no music and dance genre in the world where arguments about purity versus innovation and tradition versus change have been waged with such intensity and persistence as in flamenco. Such polemics, of course, are not unique to flamenco. The debut of Stravinsky's *The Rite of Spring* in Paris in 1913 provoked an uproar; American "folkies" were outraged when Bob Dylan performed electrified folk-rock at the Newport Folk Festival in 1964; and white "moldy fig" enthusiasts of Dixieland jazz viciously denounced Black bebop players who in the 1940s dared to turn their backs on the general public and fashion a brilliant new style for hardcore enthusiasts. But debates about purity in flamenco not only predate and have outlasted these other polemics but have also had a unique vehemence due to the particular social dynamics of flamenco culture and the inordinately heavy involvement of intellectuals in it. The advent of social media—especially blogs, Facebook, and YouTube comments—has arguably not merely provided another forum for extant discourse but actually increased the sheer amount of debate.

Arguments about continuity and change in flamenco are in fact complex and multidimensional and overlap with other ongoing controversies. One debate concerns the relative centrality of Gitanos as opposed to non-Gitanos in flamenco. Other aspects of the argument counterpose neo-traditional acoustic flamenco against commercially mass-mediated music, including hybrid forms like flamenco-rock. Particularly relevant is a Romantic ideology of "authenticity" that has conditioned much of flamenco aesthetics from the 1880s until the present. Perhaps the most important factor animating the purity-versus-innovation debate has been the particular—and, in many ways, unique—socio-musical configuration of flamenco culture. From the genre's very inception until the present, flamenco has continued to be performed both as a professional concert idiom, with all the richness and "universality" of jazz or a classical art, and also as a quasi-folk genre in domestic and primarily Gitano contexts, in which songs, dance moves, and other elements are orally transmitted through generations and cherished as ethnic and family heritage. (In this sense, flamenco differs markedly from such a genre as jazz.) Musical features and personnel have consistently traveled in both directions along the continuum between these antipodes, in a manner that is largely productive but also generates a certain degree of tension and a deep apprehensiveness about change and innovation.

As noted in chapter 2, Antonio Machado in 1881 described flamenco—whether accurately or not—as emerging primarily from a tavern-based category of pure "cante gitano" that was then made public and hybridized by Silverio and the entire café cantante phenomenon. Silverio himself, as well as his protégée Chacón, saw authentic "cante gitano" as being bowdlerized by faddish "flamenco"—a term they both resisted. By the 1920s, the ambivalence toward change that Machado expressed was intensified as the genre was increasingly packaged in the context of the "*ópera flamenca*" format and the subsequent vogue of Pepe Marchena, another innovator regarded by purists as cheapening and deforming the art.

The 1950s and 1960s saw a return to orthodoxy, led by Antonio Mairena, with a standardization of the repertoire of cantes and estilos. It is essentially this canonic body of "classic" or neo-traditional flamenco that continues to constitute the mainstream idiom heard in flamenco festivals, competitions, and tourist-oriented tablaos. For many flamenco lovers, this genre (like mainstream, "straight-ahead" jazz for its fans) is sufficiently rich and flexible enough that it can continue to accommodate new artists and attract ardent audiences and is in no particular need of revision or modernization, regardless of whatever worthy innovative styles may flourish alongside it. Moreover, such enthusiasts would feel that while much eclectic or pop hybrid flamenco may be dynamic and meritorious, these latter forms should be kept independent of flamenco per se, both in terms of performance contexts and taxonomic definitions. Accordingly, a Google image search for "flamenco puro" generates many dozens of album covers, concert posters, and other entities, all in supposed contradistinction to inauthentic forms of the art.

In many respects these various subgenres of neo-traditional and eclectic flamenco have coexisted comfortably, and flamenco purists have been reassured by the fact that most of the flamenco-pop singers, such as Pitingo (A. M. Álvarez), have also been gifted performers of mainstream flamenco. Some innovators, such as Camarón and José Mercé, continued to perform in the circuit of festivals, competitions, and tablaos devoted to por derecho cante. An analogy with jazz is again pertinent: the advent of funk, fusion, Euro-jazz, and other hybrid styles from the 1970s did not kill acoustic jazz, which (whether in "straight-ahead" or 1960s modernist styles) continues as a well-established and still vital genre performed in clubs, taught in colleges, and studied and enjoyed by a stable and steadily replenishing set of enthusiasts.

At the same time, the tensions referred to here have persisted in various ways. Given the pressures of the commercial mass media, and flamenco's own history of supposed deformation and vulgarization in the *ópera* and Marchena phases, many lovers of traditional flamenco have felt that the genre is perpetually vulnerable and threatened by commercial pop trends. Such people regularly voice their opinions on social media, as did flamencologist Faustino Núñez in 2020 on Facebook:

> What nonsense it is for some neoflamencos to invoke "evolution" as the elixir that cures all problems. I'm so tired of hearing the same refrain: Whatever doesn't evolve ossifies, so cante, toque, and baile should all evolve. These people seem to forget that flamenco has a classical, century-old repertoire that has a large public, and that many artists are interested only in this repertoire and want to cultivate it without any goal beyond enjoying recreating these treasures that our elders bequeathed us.

Others echoed his sentiments—especially the sense of resentment and hostility against hectoring innovators:

> Few things could be more vanguard than a siguiriya of Silverio or El Nitri.
>
> Ignoramuses with neither brains nor talent nor understanding hide beyond these innovations, but as you said, within a few years one can see which ones are real innovators and which are charlatans.
>
> Some decorate their singing with makeup and call it "innovation," when in reality they don't have the balls to master the classic repertoire.
>
> These fusion mixtures are nothing to applaud, they'll last about as long as soap bubbles.

As if novelty were good for its own sake. Like singing the same cante, but adding a backing track and calling it "evolution."

Occasionally cited is a familiar poem by Juan Ramón Jiménez, which consists in its entirety of the sentence "Don't touch the rose, that's just how it is" (*¡No le toques ya más, que así es la rosa!*).

Opposing such traditionalists are those enthusiasts who, while cherishing traditional flamenco, believe that, like any art form, it will petrify unless it evolves and changes with the times. As they note, flamenco guitar and dance have developed and modernized dramatically since the 1970s, but cante—the core idiom of the art form—has remained essentially static, both in terms of style and the established repertoire of palos and estilos. Essential to such modernization of the art, they assert, is a relatively inclusive definition of "flamenco" that can accommodate, rather than snobbishly exclude, the various innovations and fusions that have been occurring. In this view, articulated in such works as José Luis Ortiz Nuevo's *Alegato contra la pureza* (Allegation Against Purism, 2010), it is the "moldy fig," closed-minded "Taliban," rather than the innovative younger singers, who constitute the grave danger to flamenco.

Despite the stentorian tone of many pronouncements, arguments about tradition versus innovation in flamenco often suffer from a conspicuous lack of specificity. The Facebook commenters cited above might appear to be denouncing any innovation, but presumably none of them would oppose the dynamic modernization and enrichment of guitar playing that has occurred since Paco de Lucía's advent. Or are they merely responding to modernizers who dismiss mainstream flamenco as archaic? Meanwhile, several defenders of mainstream flamenco might confess to enjoying various sorts of aflamencado commercial popular music, be it coplas of Rocío Jurado or "rumba catalana." Further, although Gitano flamencos of places like Jerez and Lebrija have been celebrated as custodians of "authentic" cante jondo, many such Gitanos have been fond of Pepe Marchena and other populists disparaged by purists; moreover, at their domestic fiestas they may happily and "indiscriminately" sing and dance pop rumbas and ballads alongside traditional bulerías and tangos.

Such considerations illustrate how evaluations of flamenco or aflamencado songs often involve defining flamenco and establishing criteria that would either include or exclude innovative or eclectic items. While defining flamenco might seem a profoundly trivial and pointless issue to most listeners, establishing the genre's stylistic limits has in fact been seen as a fundamental task, as reiterated in several flamencological publications. One such declaration was a 1996 "Manifiesto en Defensa del Cante Flamenco," presented by a group of performers and flamencologists, which called for the concerted preservation of cante jondo and urged cultural organizations, mass media, and other spokespersons "not to call these [commercial fusions] 'flamenco,' in order to avoid confusing those persons not well versed in the material" (Casa 1996).[1] Several flamencologists in the journal *Revista de flamencología* also argued this theme, including Bernard Leblon, who wrote in 1995:

> The massive eruption of international-style Western music is at the point of rupturing the precarious balance that flamenco has been able to maintain in its milieu. Until recently flamenco has been able to absorb external modalities into its own system of modes and rhythms. . . . But now, more than ever, we need criteria to distinguish what is inside and outside of the genre. . . . Clearly, the so-called "flamenco-rock" is invariably more rock than flamenco in that it merely takes some superficial elements of flamenco, such as vocal turns or ornaments, and not its deeply Oriental essence. . . . The inversion of terms signifies a rupture of balance. (Leblon 1995, 94)[2]

Various flamencologists have argued that it is pointless to seek or celebrate "purity" in flamenco since it has evolved as an inherently eclectic hybrid, synthesizing Moorish archaisms, Andalusian folk music, Latin American influences, and other elements. However, others might argue that despite such eclecticism, by the mid-twentieth century a stable style and repertoire had been established and "withstood the test of time," such that the cante could, in Mairena's words, be regarded as effectively complete and in no need of being tampered with. Moreover, as Leblon argued, the concern is that a mainstream turn toward pop or modernist experimentation would constitute not merely a stylistic development but also a "rupture" in the social continuum that currently links professional stage flamenco to its quasi-folkloric counterpart in the Gitano community.

The status of fusion and innovative projects can be especially controversial when they are seen to intrude in performance contexts formerly devoted to mainstream flamenco. Opinions were sharply divided, for example, in January 2022 when the new director of the popular Nimes Festival, held in the southern French town, spurned neo-traditional flamenco for innovative fusion projects. Similarly controversial was the aforementioned foregrounding of controversial "provocateur" Niño de Elche in the 2018 Bienal de Sevilla. Yet certainly the most heated polemic in recent decades has pertained to Rosalía Tobella (b. 1993; known simply as "Rosalía"), who burst onto the global pop music scene in 2018 with her flamencoesque album *El mal querer* (roughly, "the bad love"). Rosalía became a Grammy-winning international superstar with her innovative flamenco fusion, dividing much of the flamenco world into opposing camps of those who embraced her music as dynamic and revitalizing and "haters" who reviled her as an interloper whose stardom was undeserved and whose music should not be regarded as flamenco. Social media exploded with furious debates as zealous partisans hurled insults at each other, often posting their diatribes daily on Facebook, YouTube, and other forums.[3]

Particularly pertinent to the Rosalía debate was the idea that innovations within the genre are only truly legitimate and trustworthy if they are undertaken by artists (such as Camarón and Morente) who have earned prior respect as performers of traditional flamenco. Since Rosalía had not achieved such initial status, it is argued, she should be categorized as a cantante (a singer of pop or other genres) rather than a cantaora (that is, a flamenco singer). (Needless to say, most of Rosalía's millions of fans were indifferent to this debate.)

Romanticism, Authenticity, and Biographical Credentials

Occasionally surfacing in the Rosalía polemic was the notion, whether explicit or implicit, that certain biographical credentials are needed to sing "authentic" flamenco (or to sing it well). Some Gitanos as well as non-Gitanos believe that flamenco is fundamentally a Gitano art and that only Gitanos can sing cante jondo properly; however, whenever this notion is voiced on social media, it is roundly shouted down as "racist" by those who point to the significant number of fine non-Gitano cante jondo singers, past and present.

Also occasionally encountered is a more moderate argument to the effect that although one need not be Gitano in order to sing cante jondo well, certain life experiences are necessary in order to perform it with requisite depth and expressivity. Specifically, the familiar maxim is *Hay que pasar fatigas para cantar bien* (One must have suffered in order to sing well). Ideally, one is a Gitano, born in a cave, and enduring poverty and even racist persecution; however, non-Gitanos may also qualify if their formative years have been sufficiently adverse. Several top flamenco performers (especially but not only veterans of the Franco years) did in fact experience horrendous deprivation and poverty as youths. (Examples include Fosforito, El Farruco, and Mateo Soleá.) This argument has a long history, being a running theme in Guillermo Núñez de Prado's 1904 book, *Cantaores Andaluces*, which commences with the assertion "The people who sing the most are those who suffer." Veteran flamencologist Manuel Bohórquez articulated it in a 2020 essay, in which he scoffed at the notion that flamenco could be considered a "universal" art and asserted that modern middle-class singers who sound like the poverty-bred elders are engaged in mere mimicry. Mateo Soleá, an elderly singer quoted by Bohórquez, himself stated:

> The young people of today want to know everything, but they have to learn a lot, and suffer, that this is very important. If you don't suffer, you are not a good

singer. [What about today, with so much unemployment, so many problems making ends meet?] No, suffering was before, sixty or seventy years ago, in the time of [various legendary singers]. . . . Those people who were surviving by singing at a café, earning a few pesos and running home to bring it to their wives to put on the coffee and buy a bit of bread. Today no one suffers. Or having to sing for some patron whether you felt like it or not. . . . You have to go hungry to be a good singer. (qtd. in Múgica 2020)

However, many flamenco connoisseurs and even artists groan and roll their eyes at mention of this notion, which also suggests a very problematic conception of the nature of aesthetic expression in song, much as one might respect Soleá's experience.[4] It needs scarcely be pointed out that many people who have suffered do not sing particularly well, while, conversely, many of the top flamenco singers (whether Gitano or not) did not endure any particular suffering in their lives beyond a primordial and truly universal level of sadness that might occur—for example, when the mother lays her baby down for a nap and turns her back on the child and walks out of the room. The aesthetic process arguably involves a transmutation of emotion—which could include any form or degree of sadness—into artistic expressiveness.

Donn Pohren (1980, 9) refutes the "cry of pain" notion at length:[5]

> We might begin this study by exploding the popular myth that flamenco is the tragic expression of an oppressed people, moving blackly across life's stage amidst great wailing and gnashing of teeth. Poets and other tragedians have successfully presented flamenco in this light, but the fact is that nothing could be further from the truth. I would estimate that within the realm of true flamenco as lived by its exponents . . . light-heartedness is the name of the mood about ninety-nine percent of the time, not only in the art but in the lifestyle as well. The flamencos are traditionally a happy-go-lucky bunch, tireless and inventive in their oftentimes daily efforts to make their existence an enjoyable one.

Accordingly, rather than depending on personal experiences of material suffering, what some vocalists seem to articulate is an expressive process in which they effectively role-play in the sense of envisioning the character portrayed by the lyrics, but they do so in order to generate a sentiment that, with proper aesthetic distancing, can animate their singing. Fosforito articulated the process succinctly, noting both the immersion in the character portrayed as well as the aesthetic distancing: "A singer is a bit of an actor and knows how to put himself in the situation, but if you let yourself get carried away by anguish, by the pains of the day, you can die in that sadness" (qtd. in Curao 2009, 69). In general, modern singers tend to avoid lyrics that are too remote from their own experience and that would require excessive suspension of disbelief for listeners.

Arguably, when a listener such as Bohórquez, quoted above, insists that a singer's biographical suffering is audible in his art, it may be more likely that such a listener is *imagining* that he hears such suffering; he is hearing *as if* their singing were expressing that anguish. Such a willful misinterpretation of a singer's art might enhance the aesthetic experience of some listeners, but it runs the risk of distorting or missing the singer's aesthetic content by using the music in order to indulge in a Romantic fantasy.

Women in Flamenco

The historical presence, roles, and representations of women in flamenco comprise a far larger subject than can be covered in a volume such as this one. A thorough book-length treatment of the theme is Loren Chuse's *The Cantaoras* (2003), and Spanish authors have addressed certain aspects of it (e.g., Arrebola 1994; López Castro 2007). Earlier in this work I briefly discussed portrayals of women and gender dynamics in letras, and here some further sociohistorical perspectives are offered.

Until Spain's dramatic modernization dating from the 1950s and 1960s, Andalusian society was characterized as patriarchal, "machista," and conforming to Mediterranean values of "shame and honor" that restricted women's roles, especially in public life. To some extent, such conservatism might be traced to the Moorish legacy, and even today the word *moro* can be used to denote a domineering and chauvinistic man (e.g., "Her husband is very moro"). The question could arise as to whether the flamenco world has reflected and reinforced such attitudes or, by contrast, has in some ways constituted a distinct social realm in which women have enjoyed greater status and freedom. Some have further wondered if it is productive to contrast Gitano and non-Gitano norms. Gitano society, with its strong institution of the family, is generally regarded as particularly patriarchal, yet ironically this same restrictive attitude toward women's sexual independence may have traditionally allowed some of them greater freedom to work and perform in public. That is, a Gitano family might allow one of their women to perform publicly in the assumption that non-Gitano men, aware of their mores, would be unlikely to make amorous advances toward her—and indeed, according to stereotype, might even fear retribution from her menfolk for doing so. (Historically, it has been rare for Gitana women, however impoverished, to resort to prostitution.)

What is clear is that through the nineteenth century into the early twentieth, Andalusian professional female dancers, singers, and even guitarists were abundant. In the pre-flamenco milieu, such women were prominent in the zambras of Sacromonte, the "academías de baile" of Seville, and other contexts. In the cafés cantantes, they were especially numerous as singers and dancers. Some women, such as La Andonda, La Serneta, and María Borrico, are believed to be the composers of eponymous important estilos of soleares and other cantes, and several nineteenth-century photographs depict female flamenco guitarists (even if in some cases they may have been using it merely as a prop).

As discussed in chapter 3, the café cantante scene declined dramatically in the 1920s, assaulted by the *antiflamenquista* movement, which tarred female performers as floozies, increasingly discouraging women from performing flamenco. Even the more respectable *ópera flamenca* of the next decades featured relatively few female performers. In general, the status of women was much contested in the early twentieth century, with progressive, often socialist modernizers pitted against the Church and reactionaries who wanted to protect Spain from European mass culture. Liberalism triumphed briefly in the Second Republic (1931–1936), which accorded suffrage and many other basic rights to women. However, all such measures were reversed by the Franco regime, which allied itself with the Church and the most repressive elements in Spanish society. Abortion and contraception were banned, wives were declared legal minors, and women were discouraged or prevented from entering the professions. As Franco executed or imprisoned hundreds of thousands of men who were perceived opponents, unprecedented numbers of women were obliged to support their families, leading thousands to turn to prostitution—one occupation that was conspicuously legal and open to them until 1956. Meanwhile, the Franco regime promoted either conservative images of women as wives and mothers or as merry dancers in saccharine "España de la pandereta" films and tourist shows.

As a result, women largely disappeared from the public flamenco scene in the war-torn 1930s and the fascist 1940s. Flamenco was performed mostly in private juergas, whose ambience of booze and prostitutes was not appropriate for respectable women. Those taverns that allowed singing were also exclusively male domains. However, during this period many women—especially Gitanas—continued to sing and dance in their homes and transmit their skills and knowledge to their children.

Conditions for some women started to improve with the founding of tourist-oriented tablaos in the 1950s. These provided work for several gifted singers, including Fernanda de Utrera, María Soléa, and La Paquera; as tablaos, festivals, and other "respectable" venues came to proliferate in subsequent decades, women belatedly found career opportunities performing flamenco. However, women have had to contend with personal obstacles. In this period many husbands forbade their wives from performing; Tia Anica la Piriñaca was able to support her children by resuming her performing career only after the death of her husband. Meanwhile, women almost invariably faced difficulties attempting to pursue performing careers while being obliged to raise their children. (Fernanda and La Paquera, who remained single, were among the few prominent cantaoras of this period unburdened by such responsibilities.)

By the 1970s and 1980s, the definitive modernization of the flamenco scene—and of most aspects of Spanish society and economy—belatedly came to again welcome female singers and dancers, this time in the tablaos, summer festivals, TV shows, and eventually most of the peñas. The outstanding female singers of the modern period are too numerous to enumerate here, but a cursory list would have to include such names as María Vargas, La Perla de Cádiz, Carmen Linares, Remedios Amaya, Aurora Vargas, Tomasa la Macanita, Esperanza Fernández, La Fabi, Niña Pastori, La Paquera, Fernanda and Bernarda de Utrera, and Estrella Morente. Among these, some are Gitanas raised in flamenco families, others are not; some sing only por derecho cante, while others also perform popular genres such as copla. Several are fine singers of siguiriyas, defying notions prevalent in earlier generations that female voices and temperaments are suited only for lighter cantes like fandangos. The numbers of prominent female dancers are, of course, equally impressive. Several successful vocalists, in interviews with Loren Chuse (2003) and Miguel López Castro (2007), said they have never felt any discrimination or sense of being disadvantaged as women, indicating how dramatic the modernization of Spanish society has been since the end of the Franco regime.

The striking and curious exception has been in the realm of professional guitar playing, where even in the present, women are conspicuous by their absence. Facile arguments that women lack the physical strength to play as well as men can easily be refuted by considering the prodigious achievements of women as instrumentalists in Western art music, among other genres. In recent years several skilled female players have emerged both in Spain and elsewhere, but they have continued to face social obstacles. María Albarrán has discussed how unwelcome she has been made to feel in the male fraternity of guitarists, especially among Gitanos:

> Sometimes there will be fourteen or fifteen guys playing guitar, the cajón, having a great time in the dressing rooms. I arrive, wanting to be included like everyone else, but everyone acts strange. They suddenly make excuses why they "have to go because it is really late." I have tried a number of times and it is always the same. (qtd. in Chuse 2003, 213)

Meanwhile, a number of activist women have undertaken specific projects designed to foreground and promote the presence of women in flamenco. A significant production was Carmen Linares's 1996 album, *Antología: La mujer en el cante*, presenting letras and estilos composed by women. A different sort of project was the founding, in the 1990s, of the Peña Femenina de Huelva by a group of women who were fed up with the male-only policy of the existing peñas in that town (Chuse 2003, 216–18). More recently, cantaora Rocío Márquez (herself from Huelva) has been particularly outspoken in promoting female-centered lyrics and attempting to raise consciousness about gender issues in flamenco. Finally, the ever-controversial Rosalía made her own sort of feminist statement on her album *El mal querer*, sung from the persona of a victimized medieval heroine who ultimately rebels against her cruel husband.

In discussing gender issues, mention should be made of the status of gay and lesbian performers in flamenco. Such persons were always present, including a few renowned artists (not to mention García Lorca), and the prevailing lack of contemporary commentary about their proclivities could be taken to have indicated a general spirit of tolerance in the flamenco world as well as a desire to leave such matters unspoken—especially in the Franco years, when the regime vigorously persecuted homosexuals.[6] In recent years a spirit of openness and even proud self-assertion of queer identity in the flamenco world has emerged in tandem with trends elsewhere. Such developments have included scholarly studies (Biddle 2019; López Rodríguez 2017, 2020), a 2017 queer flamenco festival in Madrid titled "Flamenco Diverso," and various dance-oriented theatrical productions.

Glossary

Where relevant, the most common Spanish definition is given, followed by those related to flamenco or music.

a palo seco: without guitar accompaniment
abandolao: related to the bandola lute; using a bolero-like strumming pattern
afillá (afillada): of a voice; raspy, husky (from "El Fillo")
aflamencado: flamencoized, flamenco-tinged
agitanado: "Gypsy-style," Gitano-inflected (as in poetry, or vocal style)
alzapúa: "raising the pick," a guitar technique of playing repetitive patterns with up-and-down thumb strokes
azān (adhān): the Muslim call to prayer; though not regarded as music, it is clearly "musical," generally intoned to a specific maqām or mode.
bandurria: a pear-shaped, mandolin-like lute with six doubled courses (twelve strings), a short neck, and a flat back
base ("bah-say"): base; in palmas, steady clapping on the beat (as opposed to syncopated off-beats)
bebeo (babeo): in flamenco singing, the technique of extending a word by repeating or inserting syllables (e.g., extending "cuando" as "cuando-wo-wo-wo")
bolero: in Latin music, a danceable, slow, romantic song in syncopated duple meter; in Spain, a dance, with accompanying music (especially seguidilla) in 3/4 meter, popular in the eighteenth and early nineteenth centuries
caida: fall; the climactic moment when, especially at the end of a fandango copla, the verse ends and the tonality modulates from major to Phrygian
cajón: "big box"; in Peru, Cuba, and Spain, a wooden box used as a percussion instrument
Caló: the Spanish Romani language
cambio: change; in flamenco, a distinctive and climactic moment, especially in soleares and bulerías when the guitar plays a III7–VI cadence in Phrygian tonality during the penultimate verse line

canción: song, especially implying a structured composition with thematically related verses, as opposed to a loose flamenco tanda

cantante: a singer (of any genre other than flamenco)

cantaor: a flamenco singer (female: cantaora)

cante: flamenco singing; any subgenre or song-type of flamenco (e.g., soleá, alegrías)

castizo: of good stock, racially pure, and authentically "Spanish"

cejilla: capo, a device clipped onto a guitar neck that stops all the strings at a given fret, raising the base pitch

cierre: closing, stoppage; in music, a cadence, especially marked by a break

clave: key (metaphorical); in Latin (Afro-Cuban-based) music, one of a pair of hardwood sticks struck together; the characteristic ostinato (in "two-three" or "three-two" forms) played on these sticks, which may constitute an underlying pattern

coletilla: ("little tail") a catchy, tuneful refrain, often with nonsensical or whimsical lyrics, especially in tangos, bulerías, and alegrías (= juguetillo)

compás: rhythmic meter; in flamenco, comprising a rhythmic cycle with internal structural accents

concurso: a formal competition

contestación: response; in flamenco, a rhythmic cadence or concluding part thereof (= cierre), or a guitar phrase responding to a vocal one

contratiempo: "counter-time," rhythmic syncopation, off-beat pattern (in palmas, as opposed to *base*, on the beat)

copla: poetic verse, especially cultivated as a vernacular idiom; a genre of Spanish commercial popular song, especially popular in the 1930s and 1940s, often with an Andalusian flavor; in flamenco, a stanza of sung verse (e.g., "he sang four coplas in soleares")

costumbrismo: an interest in and celebration of regional, vernacular, ethnically distinctive, and/or lower-class cultural forms, often in an exoticizing and superficial manner

costumbrista: adjective form of costumbrismo

cuadro: frame, painting; a flamenco group (especially in a tablao, comprising a singer, a guitarist, and a few dancers)

cuarteta: quartet; a verse form of four octosyllabic lines in the rhyme scheme *abab*

cuplé: (from French, "couplet") a genre of saucy theater song, especially of the decades around 1900; in flamenco, a precomposed song, or section thereof, perhaps derived from a genre other than flamenco (as opposed to a traditional estilo) sung in flamenco style, especially in bulerías or tangos

décima: a verse form of ten octosyllabic lines, usually in the espinela rhyme scheme *abbaaccddc*

desplante: rudeness; an arrogant posture the bullfighter assumes in finishing a series of passes; in flamenco dance, a sequence, typically commencing with a llamada and segueing through some percussive footwork to a dramatic (*bien parao*—"nicely stopped") pose

diferencia: difference; in Spanish Renaissance and Baroque instrumental music, a short variation on a given chord sequence (such as that of "Guárdame las vacas")

duende: goblin, spirit; in flamenco, an ineffable expressivity or aesthetic rapture

entrada: entry; in guitar playing, the conclusion of a falseta or other passage prefacing the singer's entrance

entrecopla: the instrumental interlude between sung verses (= ritornello)

escuela bolera: "bolero school," the twentieth-century term for the stylized (especially nineteenth-century) form of bolero dancing for stage shows

estilo: style; in flamenco, a vocal stock tune in a given cante to which different lyrics (letras) can be sung

falseta: a short, precomposed guitar passage in a given palo; in dance, a section where the guitar plays, without singing

gachó: (Caló:) non-Gitano (= payo)

gitanesco/a: "Gypsyesque," "Gypsy-style," as in poetry or song lyrics

golpe: blow, stroke; in guitar playing, a rhythmic fingernail tap on the face of the instrument

hemiolia (hemiola): most typically, a rhythmic syncopation involving the alternation of 6/8 and 3/4 meter, as in the pattern *one*-two-three-*one*-two-three-*one*-two-*one*-two-*one*-two (= sesquialtera, "six that changes"); in vertical hemiola, these patterns are superimposed

Hijāz: a mode in Arab and Turkish music distinguished by the lower tetrachord with the configuration half step, augmented second, half step, e.g., D–E♭–F♯–G

ida y vuelta: "going and return," "round-trip," as in flamenco song forms, such as guajiras, derived to some extent and in some form from Latin American ones

jácara: a song and dance form of early Spanish music theater

jaleo: racket, commotion; shouts of encouragement (e.g., "olé!") to a flamenco performer; in Extremadura, a cante related to bulerías; in nineteenth-century Andalusia, the term for a range of ternary-metered song and dance forms

jondo (= hondo): deep, as in "cante jondo," "deep song"

jota: a light dance and dance song in 3/4, especially of Aragon and Valencia, usually with simple major-key tonic-dominant chordal alternation

juerga: a spree, fiesta, or private party, especially with flamenco

juguetillo: a catchy, tuneful refrain, often with nonsensical or whimsical lyrics, especially in tangos, bulerías, and alegrías (= coletilla)

kharja (kharcha, khardja, jarcha): Mozarabic song, written in Castilian but with Arabic or Hebrew characters

laúd: a pear-shaped lute with six doubled courses (twelve strings), a long neck, and a flat back

letra: lyrics, or a specific stanza thereof ("She sang this letra as a fandango")

Levant: Murcia province and eastern Andalusia

llamada: call; in flamenco, a short, cadential dance move used to punctuate a section or announce the commencement of one; also, the corresponding accompanying guitar passage

macho: the short, refrain-like concluding section of a flamenco tanda, especially siguiriyas

majo: in eighteenth- and early nineteenth-century Madrid and urban Andalusia, a sort of swaggering, raffishly attired, lumpen proletarian ruffian

maqām: in Arab and Turkish music, a musical mode, comprising an ascending and descending scale, pitch hierarchy, and characteristic phrases, used as a basis for composition or improvisation

morisco: a converted Moor in a given Spanish region—especially southern and eastern Spain—after the Christian conquest

Mozarabic: relating to Christian inhabitants of Spain under Moorish rule, or their architecture, language, or culture

muwashshah: Arabic poetic form and musical genre in classical Arabic with a refrain, originating in ninth-century Moorish Spain and subsequently cultivated throughout much of the Arab world, including Syria

ojana: (Gitano slang:) self-promoting, insincere posturing

ópera flamenca: a variety show that, in the 1920s through the 1950s, typically featured various music items, including flamenco

palo: stick; a suit of cards; in flamenco, a song-type (= cante)

panda: in Málaga district, a group of musicians performing verdiales, comprising singers, players of laúd, bandurria, guitar, and/or pandereta, and a conductor of sorts waving a stick or a dried bull pizzle

paseo: a walk; in flamenco dance, the stylized walking preceding the dance proper

payo: non-Gitano

plañidera: a woman hired to mourn at a funeral; the stylized lament intoned by such a person

polígono: polygon; an urban housing project or industrial park

por arriba: the first-position guitar fingering in E altered Phrygian, with a tonic E major chord and Andalusian cadence Am–G–F–E

por medio: the first-position guitar fingering in A altered Phrygian, with a tonic A major chord and Andalusian cadence Dm–C–B♭–A

punteado: plucking (of a guitar or other stringed instrument)

quintilla: a five-line stanza, usually octosyllabic (standard in fandangos)

rasgueo (**rasgueado**): strumming (as opposed to plucking)

Reconquista: the Christian reconquest of Spain from the Muslims

remate ("ray-mah-tay"): finishing-off; a short cadential instrumental passage (especially a guitar strum)

ritornello (**ritornelo**): the instrumental interlude between sung verses (= entrecopla)

romance ("ro-mahn-say"): a narrative ballad, typically sung to a simple stock tune; also traditionally sung in flamenco style in Lebrija and Puerto de Santa María

sainete: a short (usually one-act) Spanish (and Cuban) light operetta, often inserted in or following a longer entertainment genre and often depicting vernacular culture

salida: exit; warm-up vocal phrase (= temple); in music theater such as zarzuela, the entrance song of a character

seguidilla: verse form, usually of four lines, with the syllable count and rhyme scheme 7a 5b 7c 5b, or if of seven lines, 7a 5b 7c 5b 5d 7e 5d; one of several kinds of song and dance form using that verse structure, typically in 3/4 meter, with guitar and castanets

señorito: (lit., "little sir") a landlord or aristocrat (often pejorative)

silencio: silence; in alegrías dance, a slow section, usually accompanied by minor-key guitar playing, preceding the more agitated zapateado sections

soniquete: in flamenco, expressive singing or playing (e.g., "she has soniquete")

taconeo: in dancing, heelwork, footwork

tanda: batch; in flamenco, a performed item, i.e., a few coplas in a given cante

tema: theme, subject; in music, a precomposed song or section (in flamenco, as opposed to a loose tanda of traditional estilos)

temple ("tem-play"): temper, mood; the warm-up phrase sung at the beginning of a tanda (usually to the vocables "ayayay")

tercio: a third; in music, a sung line of verse (thus, a typical fandango copla has five lines of verse, with the first repeated such that there are six tercios)

tonadilla: a light theater song, not for dance, especially of the eighteenth century, often inserted between acts of a play or operetta; in the nineteenth century, a short comic operetta

toque: touch, stroke; in flamenco, guitar playing (or instrumental accompaniment in general)

venta: a roadside inn, the likes of which formerly hosted flamenco parties or shows

zambra: a Moorish dance; in Granada, a flamenco fiesta or item, typically consisting of tangos; as popularized by Manolo Caracol, a precomposed, medium-tempo, Latin American–flavored song, in a somewhat commercial popular vein, with ensemble accompaniment

zapateado: percussive heelwork or footwork; also a flamenco dance item and characteristic accompaniment form

zarzuela: Spanish operetta, flourishing in the seventeenth and early eighteenth centuries and then, in a new form, in the latter nineteenth century, sometimes using stylized forms of vernacular music such as habanera and tango (also cultivated in Cuba and elsewhere)

Notes

Chapter 1. Pre-Flamenco Music

1. E.g., by Anglés 1943–64. An authoritative summary of music in Moorish Spain is Wright 1992.

2. *Don Quijote* (II, episode 54) portrays a returned, clandestine Moor who avers that many of his community who spoke Spanish returned to the peninsula after being expelled.

3. In *Consejo del Estado*, cited by J. L. Navarro 1993, 19. It should be noted, however, that such assertions were part of an ongoing attempt by Spanish rulers to solve the "Gypsy problem" by discursively denying their existence (see Leblon 2018, 33). Pedro Peña offers a contrasting perspective of his childhood in Lebrija, noting that among his Gitano community there was no doubt or confusion as to who was an ethnic Gitano and who was not (Peña 2013, 140–41).

4. For example, when flamencologist Brook Zern told guitarist Diego del Gastor that a passage by the latter sounded "Arab," Gastor replied, "Yes, it's a very Gitano *falseta*" (in Zatania 2018).

5. See, e.g., Ferreira 2004; Pacholczyk 1983.

6. Ferreira 2016, 12–13. However, Ferreira, among others, opines that Alfonso's experimental cantigas were idiosyncratic personal projects that were not necessarily reflective of broader musical practices in Iberia.

7. Traditional Spanish musicology (e.g., Rossy 1966) referred to the Phrygian (E) mode as "Dorian" (or Doric), in accordance with early Greek and Byzantine (as opposed to Gregorian medieval) nomenclature.

8. As discussed in chapter 4, flamenco makes no use of systematic neutral or microtonal intervals and in that sense resembles Arab-Andalusian music as well as modern vernacular and commercial popular music of the Maghrib (Morocco, Tunisia, and Algeria). The absence of neutral intervals in Maghribi music contrasts with their centrality in eastern Arab, Persian, and Turkish music. Modern scholars believe that neutral intervals

entered Arab music from Turkish influence, which would not have occurred before the twelfth century, such that the prevailing diatonicity of Maghribi music could represent an archaic survival. (Poche, by contrast, argues the opposite: that the absence of neutral intervals in Arab-Andalusian music derives from Gregorian—that is, European, influence [1995, 45].)

9. The maqām Hijāzi described by Safiuddin in the thirteenth century had a scale quite different from that of its modern namesake. Hijāz with a neutral rather than lowered/flat second degree (i.e., 1 2 3 4) is documented in Arab music from around 1300 (see Wright 1978, 51–52, 2♭). Attempts to attribute the mode-type to Indian origin, as transmitted by Romani, are specious. It does not appear to have existed in Indian *rāg* systems until the late sixteenth century and even today is uncommon in folk music. Its designation as "Hejāzi" (or "Hājiz," "Hejuji") in seventeenth-century Indian treatises suggests that it was introduced from Arabia (Jairazbhoy 1971, 94). Thanks are due to Scott Marcus, Owen Wright, and Jonathan Shannon for offering their perspectives on mode in Andalusia and the Maghreb.

10. Melodies in Bayāti would not lend themselves to chordal accompaniment because of the neutral second degree in that maqām. By contrast, melodies in Hijāz-type modes are easily harmonized, whether in flamenco, Balkan popular music, or klezmer songs. This modal harmonic system is discussed in detail in Manuel 1989b.

11. Melchor de Santa Cruz, in *Floresta Española* (1574).

12. The exceptions, of course, are those Andalusian Gitanos who are olive-complected, whether due to South Asian ancestry or historical intermarriages with Moriscos and Afro-Spaniards.

13. *Vida bona, vida bona, está vieja la chacona, de las Indias a Sevilla, ha venido por la posta* (The good life, the good life, the chacona is old, it came by post from the [West] Indies to Seville).

14. A Mexican song of 1567 refers to Zarabanda as a deity (see F. Núñez 2021, 253). However, a reference from 1612 describes the zarabanda as a Morisco dance (Reynolds 2021, 231). The etymology of the word is actually far from clear. In a Basque dialect, "zarabanda" also means "swing" (verb, *zarandatu*), and some of the numerous Basque colonials in the New World might have applied that word to an extant dance, just as two Castilian words for "swing" (*columpio*, *bamba*) both came to denote song forms (with the latter, as *bambera*). Meanwhile, in Persian music of the fifteenth and sixteenth centuries, *sarband* denoted an actual music genre, specifically, a light, instrumental ritornello (Pourjavady 2019, 236). If it is difficult to imagine how this word might have traveled from Persia to Panama, it is also hard to definitively trace the word to the Congo, although the names of other palo deities clearly derive from that region. Some early zarabanda references identify it as the name of a woman of Campeche, Mexico (Stevenson 1962, 2). To confound matters further, Covarrubias, in his 1611 *Tesoro de la Langua Castellana*, claims that the word derives from the Hebrew *çara*, meaning to sift, ventilate, or walk around (see Ruiz Mayordomo 2003, 288).

15. Some Western musicologists unfamiliar with Spanish music have mistakenly described such pieces, with their oscillation between D (major or minor) and A chords, concluding on the latter, as "ending on the dominant" and, worse, have published editions

and recordings in which they "correct" the endings by adding final D chords. In fact, in such a piece oscillating between D minor and A major (Re minor and La), the ending on A can sound perfectly natural to the Andalusian ear (and is also typical of Latin American genres such as son huasteco, son jarocho, Venezuelan/Colombian *música llanera*, and Cuban punto). Depending on context and style, it reflects either Andalusian Phrygian tonality or an ambiguous pendular oscillation between two chords of relatively equal stasis and weight; the tonality might well be categorized as "D/A." The salon fandango, oscillating between Dm and A chords (in the key of Dm/A), exhibited the same tonal ambiguity, which easily accommodated a tendency toward the altered Phrygian mode on A. The derivative fandangos of Mozart (*Le nozze de Figaro*, Act 2) and Boccherini (4th Guitar Quintet, rearranged from his String Quartet Op. 40, no. 2), who were more firmly ensconced in mainstream Western art music, conclude on the "tonic" minor key. See Manuel 2002 for further discussion of this form of dual tonicity in Spain and Latin America.

16. Sebastián de Covarrubias, *Tesora de la Lengua Castellana Española*. (All translations from Spanish in this volume are by the author.)

17. E.g., Norman Kliman, at http://canteytoque.es/jacara.htm/.

18. The Scarlatti fandango does not appear in his published works and was not discovered until 1984. It might represent an admirer's recollection of a fandango as played by Scarlatti, such as the keyboardist might have occasionally been asked to informally play after performing some of his sonatas. Questions have also been raised about the authenticity of Soler's fandango (dated ca. 1770). In any case, both works are typical eighteenth-century salon fandangos.

19. E.g., Paco de Lucía's "Aires choqueros" or Ramón Montoya's solo renditions of fandangos (cf. F. Núñez 2021, 348).

20. Berlanga (2021a) presents the most insightful summary of this development and is the main source for the information presented here.

21. "Un baile en Triana" ("A dance in Triana") and "Asamblea general . . ." Estébanez Calderón is somewhat vague as to whether he is describing an actual event, a composite account of a few events, or an imagined one, but the level of detail he provides strongly suggests the former.

22. See the interpretation of Álvarez Caballero 2003, 18–22.

23. During this period, rondeñas and malagueñas, in their guitar forms, were so similar that the names were often used interchangeably.

24. Important research by María Luisa Martínez on El Murciano is presented in, e.g., Martínez and Manuel 2015/2016.

Chapter 2. The Café Cantante Period: 1860–1920s

1. Thorough treatments include those of Castro Buendía (2014b, 18–39) and Campo and Cáceres (2013, 353–71).

2. This observation was made by Andalusian essayist Blas Infante ([1929–1933] 2010, 39–64), who came up with his own fanciful etymology, attributing the word to the Arabic *fellah mengu*, supposedly meaning "fugitive peasant." The first such documented

usage—albeit an ambiguous one—is in George Borrow's 1841 *The Zincali: An Account of the Gypsies of Spain.* He wrote (in English), "Gitanos, or Egyptians, is the name by which the Gypsies have been most generally known in Spain, . . . but various other names have been and still are applied to them; for example, New Castilians, Germans, and Flemings [in Spanish: *flamencos*]; the first of which titles probably originated after the name of Gitano had begun to be considered a term of reproach and infamy." At present, and in this book, the word "flamenco" can denote a "flamenco person"—that is, a performer or even a fan—and in Jerez and a few other places, it can also denote a Gitano, whether involved in flamenco or not.

3. The earliest usage of "flamenco" in relation to music discovered so far is a notice in the *Gacetilla de Madrid,* June 6, 1847, referring to "*un cantante flamenco,*" one Lázaro Quintano, a celebrated singer of the "*género gitano,*" who delighted the journalist with his "*canciones flamencas.*"

4. The nickname helps distinguish him from his father, anthropologist Antonio Machado y Núñez, and one of his sons, poet Antonio Machado y Ruiz.

5. On one occasion, Chacón, contracted to sing with a group at a juerga, invited Torre to perform with him. Although Torre was in a foul mood and sat glumly through the event without singing, Chacón, in charge of disbursing the fee at the end, paid Torre nevertheless. When the guitarists protested that his share should have been divided among them, he replied, "And what if he had sung?"

6. Donn Pohren (1992, 14) wrote of the 1930s–1940s: "Guitarists were few, such that most cantaores sang without accompaniment and as such had no conception of compás. Antonio Sánchez [1908–1994, father of Paco de Lucía] commented that it is surprising how many famous cantaores, even of recent years [the 1980s], sang out of compás. He mentioned a few well-known ones that were unaware that siguiriyas, for example, had a fixed compás. Previously, in singing without guitar, this wouldn't matter . . . but once the singing would be done with guitar, or dance, or both, maintaining the compás would be essential."

7. However, Marín's 1902 guitar manual notated tangos in standard duple meter.

8. Faustino Núñez (2021, 435–37), while acknowledging the transformations the tango underwent in Spain, insists on its Afro-Cuban origin and criticizes those who attempt to "hide" or deny it. I would respectfully argue that the transformations are so fundamental that it is misleading to regard the tango as coming from Cuba, which would be akin to saying that the Lamborghini came from the Mesopotamian oxcart. Meanwhile, the "habanera" beat ("ritmo de tango") is, one could say, compatible with the flamenco tangos and could even be rendered on palmas, but in other ways the tangos ostinato is quite distinct from any Cuban rhythm. Similarly, Núñez (2021, 474) points out the correspondence of the Cuban *clave* pattern with the cadential *cierre* in tangos, but the two-bar clave would be incompatible with the irregular phrasing that often occurs in tangos (see below, ch. 5). Castro Buendía (2014a, II:1458–66) argues that the flamenco tango derived from some primordial ternary-metered Afro-Cuban precedent. However, the contradanzas and habaneras that constituted models for the Spanish stage tangos were overwhelmingly in duple meter, and, for that matter, there is no shortage of West African music in duple meter.

9. For further discussion of this category, see Molina and Espín 1992.

10. See Manuel 2004 for further discussion of the varied forms of guajira circulating between Cuba and Spain. Also see F. Núñez 2021, ch. 13.

11. The most common among these involve the traditional lyric: "En la provincia de Cádiz ha nacido la Petenera, en un pueblo que le dicen Paterna de la Rivera" (The petenera was born in Cádiz province, in the village they call Paterna de la Rivera).

12. *Diario de la Habana*, October 30, 1844, cited by José Luis Ortiz Nuevo, in Castro Buendía 2014a, I:572.

13. See, e.g., Berlanga 2000, 117.

14. Thus, for example, Rafael Marín, in his 1902 guitar manual (p. 179)—prior to Chacón's invention—shows a very plain manner of accompanying "Granadina," writing, "I've shown the granadina as it is sung, and over this the beginner can use this base to accompany malagueñas, fandango, and jabera, because they all have the same style [*corte*]." Some believe that a florid version of a Granada fandango style by Frasquito Yerbabuena (or Yerbagüena, 1883–1944) was a source for Chacón's creation.

15. Washington Irving, writing in *Tales of the Alhambra* of his 1829 travels around Granada, was much charmed by the muleteers' songs.

16. Pedro Peña describes the informal domestic flamenco fiestas of his youth: "The absence of the guitar, I eventually realized, wasn't just a matter of tradition, but also had to do with the interruptive delays that would be involved in having to set the instrument to the different tonalities that people would sing in. It was felt, especially by elders, that guitar would diminish the purity and ancestral nature of the event" (2013, 22–23).

17. Sustained critiques can be found in Steingress 1991; Camacho Galindo 1977; and Campo and Cáceres 2013, 336–43.

18. Thus, for example, a recent publication asserts, "From the early 1800s to around 1860, jondo flamenco was at its peak" (Pardo Ballester 2017, 95). This sort of statement cannot be refuted, since no one has heard the music in question (if it existed at all).

19. Including Pedro Camacho Galindo (1977, 69).

20. An earlier relevant work, in some ways insightful but marred by a polemical antiflamenquismo, is Luis Lavaur's *Teoría romántica del cante flamenco* ([1968/1976] 1999).

21. When Steingress writes in this vein—"The Gitano in cante is basically a metaphor" (1998, 51)—or when an author like Mitchell (1994, 95) stresses how Gitanos, rather than being a strictly endogamous, distinct ethnic group, historically accommodated many assorted bohemians, there can be a danger of minimizing the Gitano contribution to flamenco.

Chapter 3. From Stagnation to Revival

1. This sort of antiflamenquismo finds a curious rearticulation in the sophisticated but polemical book of Timothy Mitchell, who links the art to an ethos of "self-pity, posturing machismo, hypersensitive adolescent egos, and a defensive flight to narcissistic ethnicity," grounded in a subculture centered on alcoholism (1994, 39, 137).

2. Baroja, in his 1904 novel, *La busca*, describes, with his characteristic sardonicism, a

performance in a seedy café cantante: "The cantaor started gurgling softly. . . . Then with his face inflamed, the veins in his neck tense and his eyes bulging out of their sockets, he let fly a guttural groan, doubtless of much difficulty, since his entire face, including his forehead, turned red" (2015, 82).

3. See Mitchell 1994, ch. 12. Among the amusements staged by notorious Jerez señorito José Domecq de la Riva ("El Pantera") in the mid-century decades was the staging of savage physical fights between women, with betting on the outcome. Mitchell regards the drunkenness and debauchery of such juergas as indicating that flamenco was fundamentally the music of a sociopathic "ethnic drinking subculture" (1994, 129). However, as noted earlier, firsthand accounts of juergas are far less uniformly negative, and as Loren Chuse astutely notes, "The juergas do not define flamenco" (2003, 294).

4. See, e.g., Juan Peña, "El Lebrijano" (1941–2016), in Espada and España 2022, 302.

5. For further discussion of this period see, e.g., Gamboa 2005, ch. 2; and Aix Gracía 2014, ch. 3.

6. Particularly important in the early period were Seville's El Guajiro (founded in 1952) and Madrid's La Zambra (1954), El Corral de la Morería (1956), and Las Brujas (1960) (Moore 2015, 171).

7. See Washabaugh (1996, ch. 9) for further discussion of the series.

8. For further discussion of Mairena and *mairenismo,* see, e.g., Quiñones 1989; Grimaldos 2010, 115–37; Mitchell 1994, 203–213, 217–18; Cenizo Jiménez 2011; Téllez 2003, 399–402; Gamboa 2005, ch. 2; and Aix Gracía 2014.

9. Ricardo Molina (2001, 431–35) asserts that a primary model and teacher for Mairena was local vocalist Savaorillo Hijo (1872–1955), whom Mairena opted not to publicly acknowledge, since he was not Gitano.

10. Aix Gracía (2014, 221–22) notes other ironies: while one of Mairena's goals was to liberate cante from accompanying dance, his many formative years spent singing for dancers shaped both his general style and his preference for the metered cantes used for dance, as opposed to, for example, the free-rhythmic fandango variants. Meanwhile, Mairena invoked a supposedly hoary tradition of Gitanos refusing to sing *alboreá* wedding songs in front of non-Gitanos but then proceeded to record these songs himself (246–47). Finally, his general project of rationally systematizing the cante and performing it didactically could be seen as a more stereotypically "payo" rather than Gitano approach (242).

11. Parallels to this sort of project can be found elsewhere during this approximate period, especially the efforts of V. N. Bhatkhande and Nur Ali Bourumand to compile, organize, and codify the repertoires of North Indian classical music and Persian court music, respectively.

12. A Spanish acquaintance wryly directed this epithet at me when I confessed that while I respect Pepe Marchena, I cannot stand listening to him.

13. For further discussion of guitar playing in this period, see Gamboa 2004, 121–41; Torres 2010, 59–74; and Álvarez Caballero 1981, 143–84.

14. For further information on Camarón, see Gamboa and Núñez 2003, and the video documentary *Camarón: Flamenco y revolución* (2018). Further literature on Paco de Lucía would include Téllez 2003; Sevilla 1995; Pohren 1992; and Torres 2010. The controversy regarding royalties is discussed in Manuel 2010.

15. On one occasion when Menese and his guitarist Manuel Molina were being arrested, Molina protested that he was merely Menese's accompanist, at which he was told, "Well, then you can accompany him to jail" (Gamboa 2004, 27–28).

16. See Manuel 1989a for further discussion of these developments.

Chapter 4. Structure

1. Enriqueta de la Santísima Trinidad Reyes Porras, 1937–1959.

2. A similar study is Lozano 2006, cataloguing the jaleo and tango estilos of Extremadura, again by means of vague verbal descriptions and discographic references to recordings, some of which are inaccessible and obscure. Even if most readers of such literature may not be able to read staff notation, without them such taxonomies and descriptions are of limited intelligibility and use. In recent years, younger scholars—especially Guillermo Castro Buendía and José Ortega—have included abundant notations in their publications.

3. An obvious example is the common estilo known as "Joaquín el de la Paula 2," which was notated fairly precisely by Eduardo Ocón in 1874, the year before de la Paula was born.

4. Bebeo (*babeo*) and other techniques are demonstrated in the YouTube series "Recursos vocales del flamenco con Alba Guerrero," at https://www.youtube.com/watch?v=_TFXJTb4_us&list=PLKYibIxbgRaxfpBtarNVGDAYdc2E5MSr4&index/.

5. "Te digo El Fillo que esa voz del broncano es crúa y no de recibo, y en cuanto al estilo ni es fino, ni de la tierra. Así te pido por favor . . . que no camines por sus aguas y te atengas a la pauta antigua y no salgas un sacramento del camino trillado" (and so I ask you, follow the old norms and don't depart from the acclaimed path).

6. By contrast, vocalist Fosforito popularized singing in a much more "squared off" maintenance of compás, disparaged by some as mechanical.

7. Some flamencologists, such as Hipólito Rossy (1966, 92) have described fandangos as "bimodal" in a different sense, in that the ritornello is in one modal tonicity and the coplas are in a different tonal key.

8. Zatania, in a perceptive article (2007b) on intonation, relates how near the end of a recording session, it was discovered that the cantaor had sung one item quite out of tune; the guitarist, eager to leave, exclaimed, "Let's just call it a 'caña of Jerez' and go home!"

9. This notation loosely resembles a falseta by Chicuelo (Juan Gómez).

10. Relevant literature includes Álvarez Caballero 1981; Wilkes 1990; Sevilla 1995; Manuel 2003; Pérez Custodio 2005; Bethencourt Llobet 2011; and Torres 2004, 2010.

11. Estela Zatania, p.c. At present, this falseta sequence can be found on YouTube under that name. Students of Diego del Gastor have referred to one angular bulerías falseta of his as "The Crab."

12. While innumerable examples of effective palmas can be found on YouTube, there may be no more brilliant and electrifying performance than a bulerías currently titled "Carmen Amaya y su troupe por bulerías—1961." This short clip, in which palmas repeatedly occupy the foreground, shows the kind of spontaneity, precision, and cohesion that can be achieved by a set of gifted artists who have been performing together for

months and are perfectly attuned to one another, to the inherent structure of bulerías, and especially to Amaya. Amaya herself leads the performance—singing, dancing, and at one point rapping her knuckles on a table.

13. On one occasion, attending a tablao in Seville in which only tourists were present, I was dismayed by the stony silence of the well-meaning but uninformed audience after one desplante, such that I took to vigorously shouting "Olé!" after subsequent ones, successfully inducing the rest of the spectators to clap. Then, when the dancer started doing palmas and audience members took it as a signal to applaud, I rose from my seat to shush them. I soon noticed that I had become the effective Director of Applause, as others in the room were looking at me for guidance.

Chapter 5. The Flamenco Repertoire

1. A particularly detailed chart designed by Faustino Núñez, on his informative site http://flamencopolis.com, involves color coding and hence would not reproduce well in a volume such as this one; he provides a more streamlined one in Núñez 2021, 314.

2. I notate and analyze the entire item in detail in Manuel 2006.

3. Flamencologist Brook Zern (in a now-defunct internet posting) described the bulerías compás in his characteristic witty manner: "Like the soleá, it can be heard as having accents on the third, sixth, tenth and twelfth beats; like nothing else, it can be heard (and clapped to) with beats on the first and second, fourth and fifth, seventh and eighth, and tenth and eleventh beats; it is often clapped with beats on one two three, seven eight, ten. Oh, and there's often an underlying emphasis on every other beat: two, four, six, eight, ten and twelve. Happy to have cleared that up for you."

4. Clear discussions of basic alegrías structure are found in Moore (n.d.), Fernández Marín (2005, 110–13), and Castro Buendía (2014a, II:1301–313).

5. Castro Buendía (2014a, II:1647–1701) presents a thorough study of such likely correlations.

6. "Gurugú" resembles various African-sounding nonsense words in negrista verse, whether from colonial Mexico or Andalusia. It can also reference a Gitano barrio by that name in Badajoz and Mount Gurugú in Morocco (the site of a disastrous defeat of the Spanish Army in 1921).

7. Like several flamencological works, López's book offers no transcriptions but refers the reader to recordings that may or may not be accessible. Eulalia Pablo Lozano (2006, 165–80) presents her own typology in similar fashion. The film *Latcho Drom* includes a lively song and dance session by Gitanos of Badajoz with collective singing. Audio excerpts of several tangos estilos are presented at Faustino Núñez's website, http://flamencopolis.com.

8. Audio examples of many fandango estilos are presented on the websites http://flamencopolis.com and http://cantandoporfandangos.blogspot.com.

9. The term *fandanguillo* may be used in Huelva to denote the "fandango de Huelva," but others may use the term in the opposite sense, to denote the free-rhythmic *fandango natural*. Given such inconsistency, the term is avoided in this book.

10. See Moore 2016 for one approach to contrasting the Marchena and Caracol styles.

11. While verdiales are regional fandangos, like the fandangos de Huelva, the two forms are not simply counterparts of each other. As Berlanga notes (2000, 194–96), their differences include the following: the fandango de Huelva, though numerous in its variants, is rooted in a very small area, whereas the verdiales-type abandolao fandangos were popular throughout the rest of Andalusia; their traditional accompanying ensembles are different; and, finally, the folk verdiales was cultivated in genuinely rural contexts, whereas the crucibles of fandangos de Huelva were towns (after which the names are named).

12. A YouTube or Google search for "malagueña" will reveal two non-flamenco items. One is the catchy light-classical piece by that name, by Cuban composer Ernesto Lecuona, who was inspired by the flamenco guitar palo, and uses the old-fashioned ostinato occasionally heard in verdiales and dance shows: E–G♯–B–E–G♯–B–A–C–B–A–G–F–E. The other "malagueña" is the popular Mexican *son huasteco*, which (unlike "La Petenera") bears no particular relation to its flamenco namesake.

13. Also cf. Diego Clavel's box set of discs, *31 Malagueñas* (Canoa Records, 1992). For insightful discussion and analysis of the malagueñas of Mellizo and Chacón, see Moore (2012) and Martín Salazar (1998).

14. Estela Zatania, p.c.

15. Useful studies of granaínas include Navarro García (1993); Martín Salazar (1998, 85–91); and sections of Martín Ballester et al. (2016).

16. Estela Zatania, p.c.

17. Cantaor Mariano Morcillo, being requested to sing a media granaína, sang three tercios of a granaína, stopped, and said, "There's your media granaína."

18. A similar transcription is presented in Fernández Marín 2011, 51.

19. For further analysis of these Levantine cantes, see Sánchez Garrido 2015; Herrero Rodes 2008; Ortega 2012; Riquelme and Ortega 2010; Castro Buendía 2015; and Martínez Delgado and Ortega 2010. Taranto can be sung in free rhythm, especially when not accompanying dance.

20. For further discussion of the complex historical relations between Cuban and Spanish guajira forms, see Manuel 2004.

Chapter 6. Flamenco Lyrics

1. Certainly he was not sympathetic to them; the story commences: "It seems that Gitanos were born into this world solely to steal: they are born to thieves, raised by thieves, trained by thieves, and grow up to be full-blown thieves."

2. These works include the aforementioned Don Preciso's *Colección de las mejores coplas de seguidillas, tiranas, y polos que se han compuesto para cantar a la guitarra* (1799) and Francisco Rodríguez Marín's *Cantos populares españoles* (1882–1883), containing over eight thousand verses.

3. Among the flamencologists who have argued this notion are Manuel Barrios (1989, 97–98) and Rafael Lafuente (1955, 99, 127–28).

4. Mairena and Molina (1963) 1979; Blanco Garza, Rodríguez Ojeda, and Robles Rodríguez 1999. Another study is Gutiérrez Carbajo 1990.

5. See also the thematic compilation in Soler Díaz 2020.

6. The best survey of these, from which some examples here are drawn, is Ortiz Nuevo's *Pensamiento político en al cante flamenco* (1985).

7. In 2014 a panel conference was held in Jaén on "El maltrato a la mujer en las letras del cante flamenco" (Mistreatment of women in flamenco lyrics). Newspaper critic Andrés Raya Saro and flamencologist Manuel Bohórquez are among those who have disparaged such feminist perspectives.

8. Estela Zatania, p.c.

Chapter 7. The Contemporary Scene

1. Interview, Revistalaflamenca.com, 30 December 2019.

2. Interview, Revistalaflamenca.com, 13 February 2017.

3. María José Pérez: "With this record I hope to call people's attention and show who I am," Deflamenco, 19 February 2018, https://www.deflamenco.com/revista/entrevistas/maria-jose-perez-with-this-record-i-hope-to-call-peoples-attention-and-show-who-i-am-1.html/.

4. See, e.g., Antonio Cortes Escobedo Flamenco, "Clases magistrales del Tío Chocolate . . ." 19 April 2020, https://www.youtube.com/watch?v=BWXmsVcAnlw/.

5. Estela Zatania, p.c.; see Calahorra Arjona 2018.

6. José Blas Vega (1995, 44) states that El Mochuelo recorded over thirty thousand cylinders. However, recording even ten items in a day into five devices would require six hundred day sessions to reach that number, which, though not inconceivable, seems hard to imagine. Blas Vega's essay is the primary source for data presented here on early flamenco recording history.

7. See Manuel 2010 for discussion of copyright in flamenco. Perhaps the most egregious abuses involved the practice (until 1995) of granting partial composition rights to individuals who merely transcribed songs and submitted them to SGAE (Sociedad General de Autores y Editores, the performing rights organization comparable to ASCAP and BMI in the United States). The most notorious instance of this exploitation involved José Torregrosa (d. 2005), a producer who, in notating and registering thirty-six compositions of Paco de Lucía, including four entire albums, evidently took advantage of the guitarist's trust to claim 50 percent of the copyright of these—royalties eventually worth millions of dollars that continued to be collected by his heirs. De Lucía was oblivious to this outrage, but his own heirs, learning of it, have since sued the Torregrosa estate (Berbell 2020).

In flamenco, as in various other genres, attempts to collect royalties for traditional material can naturally be misguided. Estela Zatania (2022) relates how, before a performance in the 1970s, an agent from the musicians' union appeared and instructed her to provide a list of the titles and composers of the songs to be performed, "even though I told him flamenco had no composers in the conventional sense. I remember first writing 'alegrías,' and the guy said to put the composer's full name and phone number, so I put 'Enrique Mellizo,' made up a phone number with a Cádiz area code and filled out the rest of the form with fanciful names and numbers."

8. Interview, Revistalaflamenca.com, 28 September 2017.

9. El Cabrero, interview, Revistalaflamenca.com, 7 July 2010.

10. Interview, Revistalaflamenca.com no. 12, September/October 2005. Rosalía's sonically elaborate blockbuster album *El mal querer* was recorded in the apartment of her collaborator El Guinche, using just a computer, a microphone, and a sound table.

11. E.g., Ricardo Pachón, interview, Revistalaflamenca.com, 11 November 2010.

12. At present these include expoflamenco.com, Deflamenco.com, jondoweb.com, Revistalaflamenca.com, and alaireycompas.com.

13. Review by Kiko Valle at expoflamenco.com, 20 February 2022.

14. These vicissitudes, and a prodigious wealth of detail, are covered in José Manuel Gamboa's four-volume 2016 opus on flamenco in the city, which, together with correspondence with Estela Zatania, is the main source for the information presented here.

Chapter 8. Perspectives on Flamenco Culture

1. An example of this sort of "confusing" production would be the rather simple music of popular German guitarist Ottmar Liebert, which he describes as "nouveau flamenco" (also the title of his 1990 hit album), despite its having nothing to do with that art.

2. In a similar vein, see "Editors" 2000.

3. For expansive discussion of the Rosalía polemic, see Manuel 2021b.

4. I explore this subject in more depth in Manuel 2021a.

5. Other insightful critiques of the theme can be found in Zatania 2014 and Soler Guevara and Soler Díaz (1992, 19).

6. However, this gingerly reticence continues, as in a recent biography of Antonio Mairena that conspicuously glosses over his sexual identity (Cenizo Jiménez 2011). By contrast, Mairena's antagonistic rival, Manolo Caracol, was openly derogatory ("In order to sing flamenco one must be very macho" [qtd. in Aix Gracia 2014, 203]).

Bibliography

Aix Gracia, Francisco. 2014. *Flamenco y poder: Un estudio desde la sociología del arte.* Madrid: Fundación Sociedad General de Autores y Editores.

Álvarez Caballero, Ángel. 1981. *Historia del cante flamenco*. Madrid: Alianza Editorial.

Álvarez Caballero, Ángel. 2003. *El toque flamenco*. Madrid: Alianza Editorial.

Amor, Carmen. n.d. "Del verso escrito al tercio cantado." https://www.jondoweb.com/contenido-del-verso-escrito-al-tercio-cantado-931.html/.

Anglés, Higinio. 1943–1964. *La música de las Cantigas de Santa María del Rey Alfonso el Sabio*. 3 vols. Barcelona: Diputación Provincial.

Aoyama, Yuko. 2007. "The Role of Consumption and Globalization in a Cultural Industry: The Case of Flamenco." *Geoforum* 38, no. 1, 103–113.

Aoyama, Yuko. 2009. "Artists, Tourists, and the State: Cultural Tourism and the Flamenco Industry in Andalusia, Spain." *International Journal of Urban and Regional Research* 33, no. 1, 80–104.

Arrebola, Alfredo. 1994. *Presencia de la mujer en el cante flamenco.* Málaga: Ediciones Edinford.

Baroja Pio. [1904] 2015. *La lucha por la vida: La trilogy: La busca, Mala hierba. Aurora roja*. N.p.: EriK Publications.

Barrios, Manuel. 1989. *Gitanos, moriscos y cante flamenco*. Seville: J. Rodríguez Castillejo.

Bécquer, Gustavo Adolfo. [1861] 1998. "Prólogo." In *La soledad: Colección de cantares populares y originales*, by Augusto Ferrán. Seville: Signatura Ediciones de Andalucía.

Berbell, Carlos. 2020. "Demanda millonaria contra los herederos del hombre que transcribió a partituras la música de Paco de Lucía, cobrando el 50% de sus derechos de autor." *Confilegal*. 9 August.

Berlanga Fernández, Miguel Ángel. 1998. "Los fandangos del Sur. Conceptualización, Estructuras Sonoras, Contextos Culturales." PhD diss., Biblioteca Universitaria, Granada.

Berlanga Fernández, Miguel Ángel. 2000. *Bailes de candil andaluces y fiesta de verdiales: Otra visión de los fandangos*. Málaga: Centro de Ediciones de la Diputación de Málaga.

Berlanga Fernández, Miguel Ángel. 2014. "La originalidad musical del flamenco: El compás." *Sinfonía virtual: Revista de música y reflexión musical* 26, January, 1–20.

Berlanga Fernández, Miguel Ángel. 2021a. "El baile flamenco: Antecedentes y primer desarrollo (1780–1890)." In *El Flamenco: Baile, música y lírica: Precedentes histórico-culturales y primer desarrollo (1780–1890)*, edited by Miguel Ángel Berlanga Fernández, 41–100. Granada: Editorial Universidad de Granada.

Berlanga Fernández, Miguel Ángel, ed. 2021b. *El Flamenco: Baile, música y lírica: Precedentes histórico-culturales y primer desarrollo (1780–1890)*. Granada: Editorial Universidad de Granada.

Bethencourt Llobet, Francisco Javier. 2011. "Rethinking Tradition: Towards an Ethnomusicology of Contemporary Flamenco Guitar." PhD diss., Newcastle University.

Beyhom, Amine. 2021. "Further Analyses from the VIAMAP." *Near Eastern Musicology Online* 6, no. 10, April (November) 2021, 5–36.

Beyhom, Amine, and Hamdi Makhlouf. 2021. "A VIAMAP Exploration of the Tunisian ṭubū." *CTUPM*: Tunisian Center of Musicological Publication.

Biddle, Ian. 2019. "Romance Cartographies: Flamenco Articulations of Queer Spaces in Urban Andalusia." *Radical Musicologies* 7.

Biddle, Ian. 2021. *The Flamenco Effect: Authenticity, Community, and Tradition in the South of Spain*. London: Routledge.

Binkley, Thomas, and Margit Frenk. 1995. *Spanish Romances of the Sixteenth Century*. Bloomington: Indiana University Press.

Blanco Garza, José Luis, José Luis Rodríguez Ojeda, and Francisco Robles Rodríguez. 1998. *Las letras del cante flamenco*. Seville: Signatura Ediciones.

Blas Vega, José. 1986. *Vida y cante de Don Antonio Chacón: La edad de oro del flamenco (1869–1929)*. Córdoba: Area de Cultura.

Blas Vega, José. 1995. "La discografía antigua del Flamenco (1890–1953)." In *Catálogo de discos de 78 y 80 rpm en el Centro de Documentación Musical de Andalusia*, 41–48. Granada: Consejería de Cultura, Junta de Andalucía.

Blas Vega, José. 2006. *El flamenco en Madrid*. Seville: Almuzara.

Bohórquez, Manuel. 2015. "¿Siguen teniendo sentido los concursos?" Expoflamenco.com. 17 August.

Bohórquez, Manuel. 2020. "Las fatigas del cantaor." *El Correo*. 5 March.

Borrow, George. [1841] 2015. *The Zincali: An Account of the Gypsies of Spain*. N.p.: Astounding Stories.

Brenan, Gerald. 1953. *The Literature of the Spanish People*. Cambridge, UK: Cambridge University Press.

Brenan, Gerald. 1957. *South from Granada: Seven Years in an Andalusian Village*. New York: Farrar, Straus, and Cudahy.

Caballero Bonald, José Manuel. 1988. *Luces y sombras del flamenco*. Seville: Algaida.

Calado Olivo, Silvia. 2007. *El negocio del flamenco*. Seville: Signatural Ediciones de Andalucía.

Calahorro Arjona, Manuel Ángel. 2018. "La metodología tradicional de enseñanza y aprendizaje de la guitarra flamenca: Un estudio diacrónico y sincrónico." PhD diss., Universidad de Granada.

Camacho Galindo, Pedro. 1977. *Los payos también cantan flamenco*. Madrid: Ediciones Demófilo.

Campo, Alberto del, and Rafael Cáceres. 2013. *Historia cultural del flamenco: El barbero y la guitarra*. Seville: Almuzara.

Canterla González, Juan Francisco. 2014. *El fandango de Huelva 1730–1944*. N.p.: Ediciones Consulcom.

Carrillo Alonso, Antonio. 1988. *La poesía tradicional en el cante andaluz*. Seville: Editorial Andaluzas Unidas.

Casa, José Ignacio de la. 1996. "Ayer se presentó en el Paraninfo un 'Manifiesto en defense del cante flamenco.'" *ABC Sevilla*, 5 December, 83.

Castro Buendía, Guillermo. 2010. "Los cantes sin guitarra en el flamenco: Antecedentes musicales y modalidades." *Revista de investigación sobre flamenco / La Madrugá* 2, 1–61.

Castro Buendía, Guillermo. 2011. "Los 'otros' fandangos: El cante de la madrugá y la taranta: Orígenes musicales del cante de las minas." *Revista de investigación sobre flamenco / La Madrugá* 4, 59–135.

Castro Buendía, Guillermo. 2014a. *Génesis musical del cante flamenco: De lo remoto a lo tangible en la música flamenca hasta la muerte de Silverio Franconetti*. 2 vols. Seville: Libros con Duende.

Castro Buendía, Guillermo. 2014b. "Música e historia del zapateado." *Revista del Centro de Investigación Flamenco Telethusa* 7, no. 8, 22–37.

Castro Buendía, Guillermo. 2015. "Identidad musical de los cantes mineros: Búsqueda y documentación." *Diagonal: An Ibero-American Music Review* 1, no. 1, 2–27.

Castro Buendía, Guillermo. 2018. "Del cómo, cuándo y por qué del toque del taranto." *Sinfonía virtual* 34, 1–58.

Cattaneo, Massimo. 2021. "'Clap Your Hands': Gender Role Distribution in Flamenco Guitar." *Ethnomusicology Ireland* 7, 61–81.

Cenizo Jiménez, José. 2011. *Antonio Mairena: La forja de un clásico del cante flamenco*. Seville: Almuzara.

Chaves Arcos, Rafael, and Norman Kliman. 2012. *Los cantes mineros a través de los registros de pizarra y cilindros*. Madrid: El Flamenco Vive.

Chinoy, Clara. 2022. "Flamenco *Is* Gitano: Reflections on the Expression of Gitano Identity in the Flamenco Fiesta." In *The Body Questions: Celebrating Flamenco's Tangled Roots*, edited by K. Meira Goldberg, 321–42. Cambridge, UK: Cambridge Scholars.

Chuse, Loren. 2003. *The Cantaoras: Music, Gender, and Identity in Flamenco Song*. New York: Routledge.

Cid Lucas, Fernando. 2019. "Americanismos en las guajiras flamencas: Arte entre dos continentes." *Revista de investigación sobre flamenco / La Madrugá* 16, 1–37.

Cordero Sánchez, Luis Pascual. 2014. "Viaje literario con José Manuel Caballero Bonald y Fernando Quiñones. Oriente-Andalucía-Occidente: Una ruta para reimaginar la Andalucía del tardofranquismo a la postnación." PhD diss., University of California, Berkeley.

Crivillé I Bargalló, Josep. 1983. *Historia de la música española 7: El folklore musical*. Madrid: Alianza Música.

Cruces Roldán, Cristina. 2003. *El flamenco y la música andalusí: Argumentos para un encuentro*. Barcelona: Ediciones Carena.
Cruces Roldán, Cristina. 2015. "El flamenco escénico y la división sexual del trabajo. Estudio estadístico de la bienal de flamenco de Sevilla, 2014." *Revista de investigación sobre flamenco / La Madrugá* 12, 1–33.
Curao, Manuel, ed. 2008. *Los flamencos hablan de sí mismos II*. Seville: Universidad Universal de Andalucía.
Curao, Manuel, ed. 2009. *Los flamencos hablan de sí mismos III*. Seville: Universidad Universal de Andalucía.
Curao, Manuel, ed. 2011. *Los flamencos hablan de sí mismos V*. Seville: Universidad Universal de Andalucía.
Dadson, Trevor. 2011. "The Assimilation of Spain's Moriscos: Fiction or Reality?" *Journal of Levantine Studies* 1, no. 2, 11–30.
Dembowski, Charles/Carlo. 1841. *Deux ans en Espagne et en Portugal, pendant la guerre civile, 1838–1840*. Paris: Librairie de Charles Gosselin.
Donnier, Philippe. 1996. "Flamenco: Relations temporelles et processus d'improvisation." PhD diss., University of Paris X.
Dumas, Anthony. 2012. "(Re)Locating Flamenco: Bohemian Cosmopolitanism in Northern California." PhD diss., University of California at Davis.
Durand-Viel, Ana María. 1983. *La sevillana: Datos sobre el folklore de la Baja Andalusia*. Seville: Biblioteca de Temas Sevillanos.
"Editors." 2000. "No tocarla más que así es la rosa." *Revista de flamencología* 12, no. 2, 3–4.
d'Erlanger, Rodolphe. 1949. *La Musique Arabe: Essai de Codification des Règles Usuelles de La Musique Arabe Moderne. Échelle Générale des Sons, Système Modal.* Vol. 5. Paris: Librairie Orientaliste Paul Geuthner.
Espada, Arcadi, and Antonio España. 2022. *Molde roto: Una conversación con flamencos*. Seville: Editorial Renacimiento.
Estébanez Calderón, Serafín. [1831] 1984. "Un baile en Triana." In *Dos escenas flamencas*, edited by Virgilio Márques, 11–30. Córdoba: Ediciones Demófilo.
Fernández Bañuls, Juan Alberto, and José María Pérez Orozco. 1983. *La poesía flamenca lírica en andaluz*. Seville: Consejería de Cultura, Junta de Andalucía.
Fernández Marín, Lola. 2005. *Flamenco Music Theory*. Madrid: Acordes Concert.
Fernández Marín, Lola. 2011. "La bimodalidad en las formas del fandango y en los cantes de Levante: Origen y evolución." *Revista de investigación sobre flamenco / La Madrugá* 5, 37–53.
Ferreira, Manuel Pedro. 2004. "Rondeau and Virelai: The music of Andalus and the Cantigas de Santa Maria." *Plainsong and Medieval Music* 13, no. 2, 127–40.
Ferreira, Manuel Pedro. 2016. "Emulation and Hybridisation in Iberia: A Medieval Background." *IEMS* 2, no. 2, 3–17.
Galán, Carlos. 2017. "La taranta, un ejemplo que desmonta los conceptos armónicos de consonancia." *Revista del Real Conservatorio Superior de Música de Madrid* 14.
Gálvez Jiménez, Marcelo. 2018. "La escuela jerezana de toque: Características técnico-musicales y desarrollo histórico." *Sinfonía virtual* 35, 1–124.

Gamboa, José Manuel. [2004] 2005. *Una historia del flamenco*. Madrid: Espasa Calpe.

Gamboa, José Manuel. 2016. *¡En er mundo! De cómo Nueva York le mangó a París la idea moderna de flamenco*. 4 vols. Seville: Athenaica.

Gamboa, José Manuel. 2018. "Manuel Torres: Del idolatrado . . . al despistado genio eterno." In *Manuel Torres*, by Carlos Martín Ballester et al., 387–412. Colección Carlos Martín Ballester.

Gamboa, José Manuel, and Faustino Núñez. 2003. *Camarón: Vida y obra*. Madrid: Sociedad General de Autores y Editores.

García Gómez, Génesis. 1993. *Cante flamenco, cante minero*. Murcia: Anthropos Editorial del Hombre.

Gelardo Navarro, José. 2014. *¡Viva la ópera flamenca! Flamenco y Andalucía en la prensa murciana (1900–1939)*. Murcia: Ediciones de la Universidad de Murcia.

Goldberg, K. Meira. 2019. *Sonidos Negros: On the Blackness of Flamenco*. New York: Oxford University Press.

Goldberg, K. Meira, and Antoni Pizá, eds. 2016. *The Global Reach of the Fandango in Music, Song, and Dance: Spaniards, Indians, Africans and Gypsies*. Cambridge, UK: Cambridge Scholars.

González Climent, Anselmo. [1955] 1989. *Flamencología: Toros, cante y baile*. Córdoba: Ayuntamiento de Córdoba.

González Climent, Anselmo. [1964] 1975. *Pepe Marchena y la ópera flamenca . . . y otros ensayos*. Madrid: Ediciones Demófilo.

Goodwin, Robert. 2015. *Spain: The Centre of the World 1519–1682*. New York: Bloomsbury.

Grande, Félix. 1979. *Memoria del flamenco*. Madrid: Punto de Lectura.

Grimaldos, Alfredo. 2010. *Historia Social del Flamenco*. Barcelona: Ediciones Península.

Gutiérrez Carbajo, Francisco. 1990. *La copla flamenca y la lírica de tipo popular*. Madrid: Editorial Cinterco.

Heffner Hayes, Michelle. 2009. *Flamenco: Conflicting Histories of the Dance*. Jefferson, NC: McFarland.

Hernández Jaramillo, José Miguel. 2009. "La petenera preflamenca como forma musical: Naturaleza genérica y rasgos estilísticos (1825–1910)." PhD diss., Universidad de Sevilla.

Herrero Rodes, Sixto Manuel. 2008. "La murciana: Dos versiones para un cante minero." *Anuario Musical* 63, 231–66.

Hoces Ortega, Rafael. 2012. "La transcripción musical para guitarra flamenco." *Revista de investigación sobre flamenco / La Madrugá 6.*

Holguín, Sandie. 2019. *Flamenco Nation: The Construction of Spanish National Identity*. Madison: University of Wisconsin Press.

Howson, Gerald. 1993. *The Flamencos of Cádiz Bay*. Westport, CT: The Bold Strummer.

Hudson, Richard. 1970. "The *Zarabanda* and *Zarabanda Francesa* in Italian Guitar Music of the Early 17th Century." *Musica Disciplina*, 125–49.

Infante, Blas. [1929–1933] 2010. *Orígenes de lo flamenco y secreto del cante jondo*. Seville: Junta de Andalucía.

Ivanova, Anna. 1970. *The Dance in Spain: A History*. New York: Praeger.
Jairazbhoy, N. A. 1971. *The Rags of North Indian Music: Their Structure and Evolution*. Middletown, CT: Wesleyan University Press.
Jiménez de Cisneros Puig, Bernat. 2015. *Ritmo y compás: Estructura métrica y articulación rítmico-armónica de los géneros flamencos acompasados* (PDF audiobook). http://atrilflamenco.com/ritmo-y-compas/.
Jiménez de Cisneros Puig, Bernat. 2019. "Aproximación musicological a las palmas flamencas a través de la fonografía y la praxis contemporánea." PhD diss., Universitat Autónoma de Barcelona.
Junta de Andalucía. 2004. *La demanda de turismo de flamenco en Andalusia*. Seville: Consejería de Turismo, Comercio y Deporte.
Klostermann, Vittoria. 1976. "The Origins of the Saeta." *Romanische Forschungen* 88, 383–94.
Kramer, Corinna, and Leo Plenckers. 1998. "The Structure of the Saeta Flamenca: An Analytical Study." *Yearbook for Traditional Music* 30, 102–132.
Lafuente, Rafael. 1955. *Los gitanos, el flamenco y los flamencos*. Barcelona: Editorial Barna.
Lavaur, Luis. [1968/1976] 1999. *Teoría romántica del cante flamenco: Raices flamencas en la coreografía romántica europea*. Seville: Signatura de Flamenco.
Leblon, Bernard. 1995. "Algunas reflexiones sobre la evolución actual del flamenco." *Revista de flamencología* 1, no. 1, 93–94.
Leblon, Bernard. [1994] 2003. *Gypsies and Flamenco*. Hatfield, GB: University of Hertfordshire Press.
Leblon, Bernard. 2018. *Los gitanos de España*. Barcelona: Editorial Geblisa.
Lefranc, Pierre. 2000. *El cante jondo de territorio a los repertorios: Tonás, siguiriyas, soleares*. Seville: Universidad de Sevilla.
Lefranc, Pierre. n.d. "La génesis del martinete." Jondoweb.com/.
Livermore, Ann. 1972. *A Short History of Spanish Music*. New York: Vienna House.
Llano, Samuel. 2017. "Public Enemy or National Hero? The Spanish Gypsy and the Rise of *Flamenquismo*, 1898–1922." *Bulletin of Spanish Studies* 94, no. 6, 1–28.
Llano, Samuel. 2018. *Discordant Notes: Marginality and Social Control in Madrid, 1850–1930*. New York: Oxford University Press.
López Castro, Miguel. 2007. "La imagen de las mujeres en las coplas flamencas: Análisis y propuestas didácticas." PhD diss., Universidad de Málaga.
López Godoy, Juan Pedro. 2008. *Tangos extremeños*. Badajoz: Peña "Amigos del Flamenco" de Extremadura.
López López, Juan de Dios. 2015. "Más allá de la piel y la máscara: Turismo, autenticidad y prácticas expositivas en el Sacromonte." *Revista de Dialectología y Tradiciones Populares* 70, no. 2, 527–46.
López Rodríguez, Fernando. 2017. *De puertas para adentro: Disidencia sexual y discomformidad de género en la tradición flamenca*. Madrid: Egales.
López Rodríguez, Fernando. 2020. *Historia Queer del Flamenco: Desvíos, Transiciones y Retornos en el Baile Flamenco*. Madrid: Egales.
Lozano, Eulalia Pablo. 2006. *Jaleos y tangos: Vengo de mi Extremadura*. Seville: Almuzara.

Machado y Álvarez, Antonio ("Demófilo"). [1881] 1975. *Colección de cantes flamencos.* Madrid: Ediciones Demófilo.

Machin-Autenrieth, Matthew. 2016a. *Flamenco, Regionalism, and Musical Heritage in Southern Spain.* London: Routledge.

Machin-Autenrieth, Matthew. 2016b. "The Zambra, Tourism, and Discourses of Authenticity in Granada's Flamenco Scene." *MUSICultures* 43, no. 2, 157–79.

Mairena, Antonio. 1976. *Las confesiones de Antonio Mairena.* Seville: Universidad de Sevilla.

Mairena, Antonio, and Ricardo Molina. [1963] 1979. *Mundo y formas del cante flamenco.* Seville: Librería al-Andalus.

Manuel, Peter. 1989a. "Andalusian, Gypsy, and Class Identity in the Contemporary Flamenco Complex." *Ethnomusicology* 33, no. 1, 47–66.

Manuel, Peter. 1989b. "Modal Harmony in Andalusian, Eastern European, and Turkish Syncretic Musics." *Yearbook for Traditional Musics* 21, 70–94.

Manuel, Peter. 2002. "From Scarlatti to 'Guantanamera': Dual Tonicity in Spanish and Latin American Musics." *Journal of the American Musicological Society* 55, no. 2, 313–38.

Manuel, Peter. 2003. "Flamenco Guitar: History, Style, and Context." In *The Cambridge Companion to the Guitar,* by Victor Coelho, 13–32. Cambridge, UK: Cambridge University Press.

Manuel, Peter. 2004. "The Guajira between Cuba and Spain: A Study in Continuity and Change." *Latin American Music Review* 25, no. 2, 137–62.

Manuel, Peter. 2006. "Flamenco in Focus: An Analysis of a Performance of Soleares." In *Analytical Studies in World Music,* edited by Michael Tenzer, 92–119. New York: Oxford University Press.

Manuel, Peter. 2010. "Composition, Authorship, and Ownership in Flamenco, Past and Present." *Ethnomusicology* 54, no. 1, 106–135.

Manuel, Peter. 2016. "Flamenco Jazz: an Analytical Study." *Journal of Jazz Studies* 11(2), 29–77.

Manuel, Peter. 2017. "World Music and Activism since the End of History." *Music and Politics* 11, no. 1, 1–16.

Manuel, Peter. 2021a. "Authenticity, Universality, and Expression in Song: The Case of Flamenco." *Contemporary Aesthetics* 19, no. 21.

Manuel, Peter. 2021b. "The Rosalía Polemic: Defining Genre Boundaries and Legitimacy in Flamenco." *Ethnomusicology* 65, no. 1, 32–61.

Marín, Rafael. [1902] 1995. *Método de guitarra: Por música y cifra: Aires andaluces.* Córdoba: Ediciones de la Posada.

Martín Ballester, Carlos, and Ramón Soler Díaz, Guillermo Castro Buendía, and José Manuel Gamboa. 2016. *Don Antonio Chacón.* Colección Carlos Martín Ballester.

Martín Ballester, and Ramón Soler Díaz, Norberto Torres Cortés, and José Manuel Gamboa. 2018. *Manuel Torres.* Colección Carlos Martín Ballester.

Martín Cabeza, Juan Diego. 2016. "La obra literaria y pictórica de Francisco Moreno Galván: Estética, compromiso y cultura popular." PhD diss., Universidad de Sevilla.

Martín-Casares, Aurelia, and Marga Barranco. 2009. "The Musical Legacy of Black Africans in Spain: A Review of our Sources." *Anthropological Notebooks* 15, no. 2, 51–60.

Martín Corrales, Eloy. 2000. "Los sones negros del flamenco: Sus orígenes africanos." *La factoría*. 8 July.

Martín Salazar, José. 1998. *Las malagueñas y los cantes de su entorno*. Motril, Spain: Guadalfeo.

Martínez, María Luisa, and Peter Manuel. 2015. "El Murciano's 'Rondeña' and Early Flamenco Guitar Music: New Findings and Perspectives." In *Música Oral del Sur: Revista Internacional* 12.

Martínez, María Luisa, and Peter Manuel. 2016. "El Murciano's 'Rondeña' and Early Flamenco Guitar Music: New Findings and Perspectives." In *The Global Reach of the Fandango in Music, Song, and Dance: Spaniards, Indians, Africans and Gypsies*, edited by K. Meira Goldberg and Antoni Pizá, 153–81. Cambridge, UK: Cambridge Scholars Publishing.

Martínez Delgado, María Eugenia, and José Ortega. 2010. "Una aproximación didáctica a los cantes de las minas." *Revista de investigación sobre flamenco / La madrugá*, 1–26.

Mercado, José. 1982. *La seguidilla gitana*. Madrid: Taurus Ediciones.

Mitchell, Timothy. 1994. *Flamenco Deep Song*. New Haven, CT: Yale University Press.

Molina, Ricardo. 2001. "Apéndice." In *Recuerdos y confesiones del cantaor Rafael Pareja*, by Juan Rondón Rodríguez, 409–41. Córdoba: Arte Flamenco.

Molina, Romualdo. 1998. "La bibliografía flamenca, a debate." Jerez de la Frontera, Spain: Centro Andaluz de Flamenco. Dep. Legal SE-1.320-98.

Molina, Romualdo, and Miguel Espín. 1992. *Flamenco de ida y vuelta*. Seville: Guadalquivir S. I. Ediciones.

Moore, John. n.d. "*Alegrías* and *Cantiñas*—Major Key *Cantes*." http://idiom.ucsd.edu/~moore/cantinas.pdf/.

Moore, John. 2012. "Carnival and Flamenco." PubWages.com. https://www.pubwages.com/06/carnival-and-flamenco.

Moore, John. 2015. "Purity and Commercialization: The View from Two Working Artists, Pericón de Cádiz and Chato de la Isla." In *Flamenco on the Global Stage: Historical, Critical, and Theoretical Perspectives*, edited by K. Meira Goldberg et al., 166–77. Jefferson, NC: McFarland.

Moore, John. 2016. "Cante Libre Is Not Free—Contrasting Approaches to *Fandangos personales*." In *The Global Reach of the Fandango in Music, Song, and Dance: Spaniards, Indians, Africans, and Gypsies*, edited by K. Meira Goldberg and Antoni Pizá, 28–44. Cambridge, UK: Cambridge Scholars.

Moore, John. 2019. "Malagueñas de Mellizo and Chacón: The racialization of *cante andaluz*." In *Transatlantic Malagueñas and Zapateados in Music, Song, and Dance*, edited by K. Meira Goldberg, Walter Aaron Clark, and Antoni Pizá, 307–322. Cambridge, UK: Cambridge Scholars.

Múgica, Paco Sánchez. 2020. "Mateo Soleá [interview]: 'Antes tenías que cantar a un señorito por fuerza; hoy no pasa fatigas nadie.'" *Lavozdelsure.es*, 3 March.

Murillo Saborido, Eduardo. 2017. "Los tablaos flamencos en Madrid entre 1954–1973:

Una aproximación académica a su escena musical." PhD diss., Universidad Complutense de Madrid.

Navarro García, José Luis. 1993. *Cantes y bailes de Granada*. Málaga: Editorial Arguval.

Navarro García, José Luis. 1998. *Semillas de ébano: El elemento negro y afroamericano en el baile flamenco*. Seville: Portada Editorial, S.L.

Núñez, Faustino. 2021. *América en el flamenco*. N.p.: Ediciones Flamencópolis.

Núñez de Prado, Guillermo. [1904] 1986. *Cantaores Andaluces*. Seville: Biblioteca de la Cultura Andaluza.

Ocón y Rivas, Eduardo. 1874. *Cantos Españoles: Colección de aires nacionales y populares*. Leipzig: Breitkopf and Härtel.

Ortega, José F. 2011. "Las tarantas primitivas." *Revista de investigación sobre flamenco / La Madrugá*, 55–75.

Ortega, José F. 2012. "Formas flamencas de la región de Murcia: Rasgos musicales." *Revista de investigación sobre flamenco / La Madrugá*, 101–136.

Ortega, José F., Luis Soler Guevara, Rafael Ruiz García, and Antonio Gómez Alarcón. 2019. *Malagueñas: Creadores y estilos*. Málaga: Editum/Universidad de Málaga.

Ortiz Nuevo, José Luis. 1985. *Pensamiento político en el cante flamenco*. Seville: Biblioteca de la Cultura Andaluza.

Ortiz Nuevo, José Luis. 2010 [expanded version of 1996]. *Alegato contra la pureza*. La Puebla de Cazalla, Spain: Ediciones Barataria.

Ortiz Nuevo, José Luis. 2012. *A Thousand and One Stories of Pericón de Cádiz*. Translated by John Moore. Licking, MO: Inverted-A Press.

Pablo, Eulalia, and José Luis Navarro. 2007. *Figuras, pasos y mudanzas: Claves para conocer el baile flamenco*. Seville: Almuzara.

Pacholczyk, Josef. 1983. "The Relationship between the Nawba of Morocco and the Music of the Troubadours and Trouvères." *World of Music* 25, no. 2, 5–16.

Pardo Ballester, Trinidad. 2017. *Flamenco: Orientalismo, exotismo y la identidad nacional española*. Granada: Editorial Universidad de Granada.

Pedrell, Felipe. [1900] 1958. *Cancionero musical popular español*. Vol. 1. Barcelona: Boileau Casa Editorial de Música.

Peña Fernández, Pedro. 2013. *Los gitanos flamencos*. Seville: Almuzara.

Pérez Custodio, Diana. 2005. *Paco de Lucía: La evolución del flamenco a través de sus rumbas*. Cádiz: Universidad de Cádiz.

Pérez Paíz, Julián. 2018. "Enrique Morente: De la revaloración del cante (1963–1970) a la renovación del flamenco (1970–2010). Actitud y procesos de un flamenco contemporáneo." *Sinfonía virtual* 34, 1–118.

Phillips, Miriam. 2013. "Becoming the Floor / Breaking the Floor: Experiencing the Kathak-Flamenco Connection." *Ethnomusicology* 57, no. 3, 396–427.

Pichardo y Tapia, Esteban. 1836. *Diccionario provincial de voces cubanas*. Matanzas: Imp. de la Real Marina.

Poché, Christian. 1995. *La musique arabo-andalouse*. Arles, France: Cité de la musique: Actes Sud.

Pohren, Donn. 1962. *The Art of Flamenco*. Shaftesbury, England: Musical New Services.

Pohren, Donn. 1980. *A Way of Life*. Madrid: Society of Spanish Studies.

Pohren, Donn. 1988. *Lives and Legends of Flamenco: A Biographical History*. Madrid: Society of Spanish Studies.

Pohren, Donn. 1992. *Paco de Lucía y familia: El plan maestro*. Madrid: Sociedad de Estudios Españoles.

Pourjavady, Amir Hosein. 2019. "Music Making in Iran: Developments between the Fifteenth and Early Twentieth Centuries." PhD diss., Graduate Center of the City University of New York.

Preciso, Don [Juan Antonio de Iza Zamácola]. 1799, 1816. *Colección de las mejores coplas de seguidillas, tiranas y polos que se han compuesto para cantar a la guitarra*. Vol. 1. Madrid: Imprenta de Villalpando, 1799. Vol. 2. Madrid: Imprenta de Repullés, 1816.

Quiñones, Fernando. 1989. *Antonio Mairena: Su obra, su significado*. Madrid: Cinterco.

Ray, John. 2014. *La escuela granadina de guitarreros / The Granada School of Guitar-Makers*. Granada: Diputación de Granada.

Reynolds, Dwight. 2005. "La música andalusí como patrimonio circum-Mediterráneo." *Patrimonio inmaterial y la gestión de la diversidad: PH Cuadernos*. Seville: Junta de Andalucía, Consejería de Cultura, 129–41.

Reynolds, Dwight. 2021. *The Musical Heritage of al-Andalus*. London: Routledge.

Ribera y Tarragó, Julián. [1927] 2000. *La música árabe y su influencia en la española*. Valencia: Pre-Textos.

Rioja, Eusebio. 2008. "El guitarrista Julián Arcas y al flamenco: El flamenco en la cultura andaluza a través de un guitarrista decimonónico." www.jondoweb.com/.

Riquelme, Pedro Fernández, and José Ortega. 2010. "El cante por cartageneras: un acercamiento a través de los textos y sus melodías características." *Revista de investigación sobre flamenco / La Madrugá*, 1–58.

Rodríguez Gómez, Fernando (Fernando el de Triana). 1935. *Arte y Artistas Flamencos*. Madrid: Imprenta Helenica.

Rodríguez Marín, Francisco. 1882–1883. *Cantos populares españoles*. Sevilla: Francisco Álvarez.

Rojo Guerrero, Gonzalo. 2015. *Juan Breva: Vida y obra*. Seville: Servicio de Publicaciones Fundación Unicaja.

Rossy, Hipólito. 1966. *Teoría del cante jondo*. Barcelona: Credsa.

Ruiz, J., and A. Pérez. 2011. *Estudio económico sobre la importancia del flamenco en las industrias culturales de Andalucía*. Seville: Instituto Andaluz del Flamenco, Consejería de Cultura.

Ruiz Mayordomo, María José. 2003. "Jácara y zarabanda son una mesma cosa." *Edad de Oro* 22, 283–307.

Sánchez Garrido, Doña María José. 2015. "Estudio melódico de la taranta minera." PhD diss., Universidad de Sevilla.

Schreiner, Claus, ed. 1985. *Flamenco: Gypsy Dance and Music from Andalusia*. Portland, OR: Amadeus Press.

Schuchardt, Hugo. 1990. *Los cantes flamencos (Die cantes flamencos*, 1881). Edited, translated, and commentary by Gerhard Steingress, Eva Feenstra, Michaela Wolf. Seville: Fundación Machado.

Sevilla, Paco. 1995. *Paco de Lucía: A New Tradition for the Flamenco Guitar*. San Diego, CA: Sevilla Press.

Soler Díaz, Ramón. 2016. "The Fandango in Málaga: From a Dance to a Rending Song." In *The Global Reach of the Fandango in Music, Song, and Dance: Spaniards, Indians, Africans, and Gypsies*, edited by K. Meira Goldberg and Antoni Pizá, 45–68. Cambridge, UK: Cambridge Scholars.

Soler Díaz, Ramón. 2020. "Los inicios de la lírica flamenca: El Cancionero de Abraham Israel (1761–1770)." In *El Flamenco: Baile, música y lírica: Precedentes histórico-culturales y primer desarrollo (1780–1890)*, edited by Miguel Ángel Berlanga Fernández, 217–348. Granada: Editorial Universidad de Granada.

Soler Díaz, Ramón, and Norberto Torres Cortés. 2018. "Análisis del cante y de la guitarra." In *Manuel Torres*, by Carlos Martín Ballester, Ramón Soler Díaz, Norberto Torres Cortés, and José Manuel Gamboa, 223–386. Colección Carlos Martín Ballester.

Soler Guevara, Luís, and Ramón Soler Díaz. 1992. *Antonio Mairena en el mundo de la siguiriya y la soleá*. Málaga: Fundación Antonio Mairena.

Steingress, Gerhard. 1991. *Sociología del cante flamenco*. Seville: Signatura Ediciones de Andalucía.

Steingress, Gerhard. 1998. *Sobre flamenco y flamencología*. Seville: Signatura Ediciones.

Stevenson, Robert. 1962. "The Sarabande: A Dance of American Descent." *Inter-American Music Bulletin* 30, 1–14.

Stevenson, Robert. 1968. "The Afro-American Musical Legacy to 1800." *Musical Quarterly* 54, 475–502.

Suárez Ávila, L. 1989. "El romancero de los gitanos bajoandaluces: Del romancero a las tonás." In *Actas de la Conferencia Internacional Dos Siglos de Flamenco*. Jerez de la Frontera: Fundación Andaluza de Flamenco, 143–45.

Suárez Ávila, L. 2010. "La memoria viva, el olvido y el fragmentismo, poderosos agentes fundacionales del flamenco." *Boletín de la Real Academia Sevillana de Buenas Letras: Minervae Baeticae* 38, 289–314.

Téllez, Juan José. 2003. *Paco de Lucía en Vivo*. Madrid: Plaza Abierta.

Téllez, Juan José. 2007. "El flamenco, una polémica exclusiva." *La Nueva Alboreá* 1 (January/March), 44–47. Instituto Andaluz del Flamenco.

Torres Cortés, Norberto. 2004. *Guitarra flamenca*: Vol. 1: *Lo Clásico*. Seville: Signatura Ediciones de Andalucía.

Torres Cortés, Norberto. 2010. *Historia de la guitarra flamenca*. Seville: Almuzara.

Torres Cortés, Norberto. 2018. "Consideraciones generales en torno a la guitarra." In *Manuel Torres*, by Carlos Martín Ballester, Ramón Soler Díaz, Norberto Torres Cortés, and José Manuel Gamboa. Colección Carlos Martín Ballester, 197–221.

Totton, Robin. 2003. *Song of the Outcasts: An Introduction to Flamenco*. Portland, OR: Amadeus Press.

Troncoso, J. 2011. "El piano flamenco: génesis, recorrido diacrónico y análisis musicológico." PhD diss., Universidad de Sevilla.

Valenzuela Lavado, Salvador. 2016a. "Armonía modal: Modo de mi y flamenco: Aproximación al 'modo de Mi armónico' como sistema musical de tradición hispánica." PhD diss., Universidad de Granada.

Valenzuela Lavado, Salvador. 2016b. "Modo de mí flamenco: A propósito de la bimodalidad." *Sinfonía virtual* 31, 1–19.
Washabaugh, William. 1996. *Flamenco: Passion, Politics and Popular Culture.* Oxford: Berg.
Washabaugh, William. 2012. *Flamenco Music and National Identity in Spain.* Burlington, VT: Ashgate.
Weich-Shahak, Susana. 1992. "A Musical Approach to Flamenco Dance Steps." *Anuario Musical* 47, 1–25.
Wilkes, Humberto. 1990. *Niño Ricardo: "Rostro de un maestro."* N.p.: Bienal Arte Flamenco.
Woodall, James. 1992. *In Search of the Firedance: Spain through Flamenco.* London: Sinclair-Stevenson.
Wright, Owen. 1978. *The Modal System of Arab and Persian Art Music A.D. 1250–1300.* London: School of Oriental and African Studies.
Wright, Owen. 1992. "Music in Muslim Spain." In *The Legacy of Muslim Spain*, edited by Salma Khadra Jayyusi, 555–79. Leiden: E. J. Brill.
Ybarra Ramírez, Luis. 2021. "El laborioso trabajo de grabar un disco de cante flamenco." *ABC.* 5 February.
Zatania, Estela. 2007a. *Flamencos de Gañanía: "Una mirada al flamenco en los cortijos históricos del bajo Guadalquivir."* Seville: Ediciones Giralda.
Zatania, Estela. 2007b. "Mundo y formas de la desafinación." *Sevilla Flamenca.* May.
Zatania, Estela. 2014. "El flamenco, las panderetas y el bon sauvage: Meditaciones sobre el flamenco festero." *Sinfonía virtual.* January-May.
Zatania, Estela. 2018. "El elemento canastero en el cante." Expoflamenco.com. 18 August.
Zatania, Estela. 2019. "So You Want to Learn to Sing Flamenco." Expoflamenco.com. 11 April.
Zatania, Estela. 2021. "What Ever Became of Tientos?" Expoflamenco.com. 10 April.
Zatania, Estela. 2022. "Feathers, 'Vedettes,' and Flamenco. Expoflamenco.com. 11 January.

Index

Performers' names are alphabetized according to their most familiar forms. Hence: "Camarón de la Isla (José Monje Cruz)," not "Monje Cruz, José" (nor "Isla, Camarón de la").

PETER MANUEL is a professor emeritus of ethnomusicology at the John Jay College of Criminal Justice and the autthor of eight books, including *Tales, Tunes, and Tassa Drums: Retention and Invention in Indo-Caribbean Music.*

The University of Illinois Press
is a founding member of the
Association of University Presses.

University of Illinois Press
1325 South Oak Street
Champaign, IL 61820-6903
www.press.uillinois.edu